A Gulf So Deeply Cut

A Gulf
So Deeply Cut

American Women Poets
and the Second World War

SUSAN SCHWEIK

The University of Wisconsin Press

Susan Schweik

The University of Wisconsin Press
114 North Murray Street
Madison, Wisconsin 53715

3 Henrietta Street
London WC2E 8LU, England

Library of Congress Cataloging-in-Publication Data

Schweik, Susan M. (Susan Marie), 1956–
    A gulf so deeply cut: American women poets and the Second World
War / Susan Schweik.
        398 pp.   cm.
    Includes bibliographical references and index.
    ISBN 0-299-13040-1   ISBN 0-299-13044-4
    1. American poetry—20th century—History and criticism. 2. World
War, 1939-1945—Literature and the war. 3. Women and literature—
United States—History—20th century. 4. American poetry—Women
authors—History and criticism. 5. War poetry, American—History
and criticism. I. Title.
PS310.W68S39   1991
811'.5209358'082—dc20   91-6577

for my parents
Joanne Lovell Schweik and Robert C. Schweik

and for this book's other nurturers
Jane Cooper and Rodney McElroy

Contents

Preface

Jane Cooper began this book, by introducing me to H.D.'s *Trilogy* and to questions about women's war poetry in a seminar at Sarah Lawrence College in 1978. To her go my first thanks. I am deeply grateful for her example and her inspiration.

I'm grateful, too, to my teachers at Yale, where this project took its first shape as a dissertation. Richard Brodhead gave me crucial early encouragement. Louis Martz, Patricia Spacks, and Harriet Chessman generously offered advice in the later stages of my thesis. To my thesis advisors Margaret Ferguson and R. W. B. Lewis I give special thanks for their critical support.

The National Endowment for Humanities Summer Stipend program and the Mrs. Giles G. Whiting Fellowship program at Yale University gave grants which helped support this project. I am very grateful to Barbara Hanrahan for shepherding this book through its initial steps at the University of Wisconsin Press, and to Lydia Howarth for her careful and painless copy-editing.

My special thanks for the advice of several scholars who read part or all of this book while it was in progress: Susan Stanford Friedman, Robert von Hallberg, Susan Gubar, Cheryl Walker, and Susan Squier.

I scarcely know where to begin or end my thanks to my community at the University of California, Berkeley. Among the many friends in the English department who have sustained and changed this book in one way or another, I want especially to thank Carolyn Dinshaw, for the loving scope and depth of her involvement with this project, help I couldn't have done without; James E. B. Breslin, Carolyn Porter, and Alex Zwerdling, for their detailed readings of the entire manuscript, their good counsel, and their consistent easygoing mentoring as well as their friendship; Mitchell Breitweiser, Jennifer Clarvoe, Catherine Gallagher, Paul Alpers, Helen Emmitt, and Steven Goldsmith for their perceptive readings of drafts of this book in part or whole; Vicki Graham, Jeredith Merrin, Jeff Peterson, and JoEllen Green for the direct inspiration of their work on modern poetry; Elizabeth Abel and Janet Adelman for the stimulus of many conversations and their feminist companionship; and Carol Christ and Anne Middleton for their administrative and intellectual support in the book's later stages. One key way in which the University of California at Berkeley has enabled the writing of this book is through the funding of research assistants. My thanks especially to Julie Chang, Jane Morrison, Rob Kaufman, Judy Berman, Bev Chandler, and Elizabeth Young; their research help was invaluable. Thanks, too, to all those who administered the undergraduate research programs sponsored by Peace and Conflict Studies and by the Berkeley Women's Center. Most of all, I thank my students at Berkeley for insights and influences far too numerous to tabulate or cite. I am especially indebted to the participants in my Spring 1988 graduate seminar on gender and war, who helped to hone and focus my arguments here and throughout.

At various stages of the writing of this book three writing groups have provided me with firm deadlines, sage advice, and sustaining friendship. My thanks to all the women who gave me so much in (and outside of) these group contexts: Deborah Clarke, Wendy Moffat, and Madeleine Bergman; Ramsay Bell Breslin, Kitty Hughes, and Susan Harris; and Valerie Miner, Madelon Sprengnether, and Kalima Rose. I am grateful, too, to those of my other friends who went out of their way to befriend this book as well. Wendy Owen, Clement Hawes, and Susan Meyer inspired me early on; their critical readings of the dissertation laid the groundwork for much of the book. Stan Yogi gave vital, expert help with the chapters on Japanese American literature. Gloria Bowles's friendship has done much to make the writing of this book a pleasure. She has unstintingly shared ideas and resources and provided me with a role model for feminist work. My conversations on gender and war with Susan Grayzel have been crucial for the development of my thinking. During the intensive period of writing while I was on sabbatical in England, Eileen Daffern, Fiona Forsyth, and Rachel Bowlby welcomed me warmly and encouraged this project. The book benefited greatly, too, from conversations that year with Alan Sinfield, Cora Kaplan, and Jacqueline Rose. Pat and Hilary Hickman helped me through the book's nearly final stages in countless daily ways. Betty Westman and Charles Schweik gave practical help and encouragement. And Blakey Westman offered the most important thing of all—marvelous distractions.

I thank my mother, Joanne Schweik, in the words of Olive Schreiner: "And yet, if the truth be told, it is not ultimately on these grounds that many of us base our hope and our certitude with regard to the future of woman. Our conviction as to the plenitude of her powers . . . springs not at all from a categorical enumeration of the attainments or performances of individual women or bodies of women in the past or present; it has another source. . . . There is one woman known to many of us, as each human creature knows but one on earth, and it is upon our knowledge of that woman that we base our certitude."

I thank my father, Robert Schweik, for his enthusiasm, his encouragement, his good advice and technical help, and most of all for the example he has always provided me as a teacher and a scholar.

There isn't an aspect of the writing of this book — intellectual, political, emotional, practical — that Rod McElroy hasn't helped me with, day by day over the long haul. For that, and much more, I thank him with all my heart.

A Gulf So Deeply Cut

Introduction

"THE reason may or may not be the war," wrote Louise Bogan in a 1944 review of poetry for the *New Yorker;* "the fact is," she continued, "an unusually large number of books written by women have appeared at the beginning of this fall season. I do not believe that women should be dealt with critically in isolation in any department of art, but the appearance in quantity, just now, of poetry by women brings one or two general observations to mind."[1] *A Gulf So Deeply Cut* is about the appearance in quantity, just then — in the years of declared war for the United States, 1941 to 1945 — of poetry (and in particular of war poetry) by American women. It is also about the "general observations" about gender, war, representation, and rhetoric which have been brought to bear upon those poems, both at the time and later.

Wars have a way of revealing with special clarity how men as well as women are both intensely and uneasily gendered. For this reason, and because the meanings attached to femininity in war are always opposed to those attached to masculinity (though both unsettle in historical crisis), this book includes discussions of male-authored texts. It surveys a range of arenas for literary production and reception by both women and men on the home front (modernist and middlebrow journals and anthologies, ethnic presses, government-sponsored overt propaganda, private notebooks). But it focuses in especially close detail on a group of poems written by women. I read these poems in their relation to the social practices of war-making (and of "gender-making") at the time, analyzing both how they reproduce dominant constructions of war and gender and how they contest them.

Some of these texts are long poems or poetic series, some clusters of lyrics. Some are by well-known authors whose work shows up relatively frequently in general academic histories of American poetry, some by poets less familar in those circles. My aim has been to give a fuller account than is usual of the production of American poems, within a very specific historical context. I have tried to think — even in the context of a period of intense nationalism and strenuous state intervention — in terms of American cultures rather than of American culture.

Cries of "Where are the war poets?" in the popular American press immediately after Pearl Harbor soon gave way to publication of a flood of war poems, as well as to passionate arguments about poetry's responsibility to history. In the thirties, a number of left-wing American literary subcultures had demanded and produced overtly didactic, topical, and political poems. Now such texts, in the particular form of the "war poem" (each with its own relations, sometimes directly oppositional, often complicated and vexed, to previous models of "political commitment" in literature, to the aesthetics of modernism, to the developing strictures of New Criticism, and to the state-sponsored cultural arena) moved even more noticeably to the center of the forming contemporary canons. A large number of these war poems, as Bogan's review suggests, were written by women.

Surprisingly large, since like the military itself, traditionally the most overtly male of preserves, the war poetry presented in recent bibliographies and anthologies is especially and intensely androcentric. In the modern war poem as it is usually defined, the experience of the masculine soldier and the voice of the masculine author predominate. In 1941, when American editors and critics sought to answer that urgent and irritating question — "Where are the war poets?" — they expected, and were expected, to seek out military men, men whose poems could engage the war with the effect of authenticity, of earned outrage and courage, which the poems of the famous Great War soldier poets, then again widely in circulation, possessed.

But such a model of the war poet had always been partially misleading, and was increasingly inappropriate. The total war was being fought, as the Great War had already to a lesser extent been fought, not by armies but by populations. By the end of the Second World War, the carpet bombing which culminated at Hiroshima and Nagasaki, and the mass killing which in its most extreme form we call the Holocaust, had in one sense rendered meaningless the abstract concept of the "front line." Women had always played actual roles in warfare and militarized cultures, and those roles were acutely and systematically obvious in the forties. In the context of the mass influx of women into new war jobs and a major short-term upheaval of gender roles and relations within American culture, a newly respected figure, the war poet as woman, took her place next to the soldier in the photographic frontispieces and the tables of contents of war poetry collections. There she revealed what later critics and anthologists of war literature have, with a few important and recent exceptions, tended to ignore: the active presence of women *as subjects* in the action and the discourse of the war.

My aim in this book is more than to recover a female-authored or a "feminine" body of work. A revised version of that plea from the forties — "Where are the *women* war poets?" — cannot be by itself a sufficient question. I am interested less in supplementing literary histories of the male-authored canon of war poetry with a distaff wing than in analyzing what the war poems that I discuss inscribe forcefully: the dynamics of gender in the politics of war and of war poetry.

The events and structures of the war had, to a significant extent, broken down distinctions between front and home and between combatants and noncombatants. But the gender ideology in which men are called upon to "protect" and women and children to "be protected" still, nonetheless, held sway, particularly in the relatively sheltered continent of North America. Jane Cooper has written an eloquent account of the effects on American women writers of these wartime constructions of gender. Bogan seems to imply, in the review I quoted above, that the war inspired or enabled women poets ("the reason may or may not be the war"). Cooper, by the end of her argument, implies exactly the reverse. Her analysis of her war and immediate postwar years begins with a strong claim for the war as "peculiarly a civilian's war,"

the war of bombed-out cities and of ruined, isolated country houses in northern France. Even now, two years later, the dark bread, made of potatoes or sometimes even sawdust, flattened almost to the tabletop when you pressed it with a sharp knife. . . . I thought, at the same time, that all wars are probably total for the people living through them: the Hundred Years' War must have been a total civilians' war. For civilians, read women — women-and-children, women-and-the-sick-and-the-old. Yet of course, women had not just been civilians during World War II, not just the passive receivers of suffering.[2]

At the end of this passage, however, a less empowering and self-respectful narrative of American war and gender begins to assert itself:

I hated the very idea of war, all its details, yet obviously, I was excited and absorbed by it, and also I felt guilty because I had not participated in any direct way, only through association. And how could you write except from experience?

Perhaps, as Grace Paley has suggested, this was one of the true problems of women writers at that time. The men's lives seemed more central than ours, almost more truthful. They had been shot down, or squirmed up the beaches. We had waited for their letters. (23–24)

How could you write except from experience? A generation earlier, one highly influential tradition of Great War literature, the British protest literature of combatants such as Owen, Sassoon, and Graves, had sternly insisted upon "the authority of experience" as an absolute prerequisite for

war writing, and had memorably indicted women for their naive, invari-
ably war-mongering lack of that authority. Cooper here both speaks their
script and protests its silencing effects upon her. My argument is concerned
in part with exploring and questioning "experience of war" as an ideologi-
cal construct, with tracing its conceptual links to masculinity, and with
considering its implications for writers and for readers of both sexes —
projects undertaken in many of the women's poems themselves in the
pages which follow. Describing the Second World War's difference from
the First, inscribing its historicity, was these women poets' task, and mine
too. But my repeated references throughout this book to an anachronistic
set of Great War models — and especially to the work of that dead young
officer Wilfred Owen, established in the Second World War as *the* war
poet — reflect both the stubborn persistence of those paradigms and the
new readiness of women, a generation later, to talk back to them.[3]

The model which granted "experience" to men alone, and which posited
a necessary but problematic gap between men "at war" and women "back
home," was not, of course, only literary, and in the Second World War
period in the United States it regained a contemporary currency. "In war-
time men and women get out of step and begin to wonder about each
other."[4] So began an essay written in 1946 by Margaret Mead, who had
been commissioned to give returning veterans the real story about what
American women did for the duration. Mead's article ended with this for-
mulation of sexual difference: "Just as the man in the cartoon is pictured
as looking at his rifle and saying 'I've given you the best years of my life,'
so the women of the 1940s realize the years which have been dedicated
to absence . . . and to a break in experience" (289). The story Mead tells
here is broad and familiar, a version of the stock ahistorical plot Roland
Barthes has described: "Woman is faithful (she waits). . . . It is woman
who gives shape to absence, elaborates its fiction, for she has time to do
so."[5] An old story, then; but this was a new crisis. Mead's reference has
sharp and immediate topical reverberations, to the well-known half-ironic,
half-elegiac "best years of my life" cartoon by GI cartoonist Bill Mauldin,
and to that famous filmic representation of postwar difficulties, *The Best
Years of Our Lives*, then only recently released. My claim is that heterosex-
ual gender relations in the United States in the early and mid-forties were
characterized by an especially intense cultural anxiety, a sense of an often
uncrossable gap between the male soldier who was understood to have
experienced too much and the woman left behind who was understood
to have experienced nothing at all.

The ideological pressures of morale, of the constructed "united war
effort," required that the gap be sealed. At the same time, the material

pressures of history, of everyday home-front life, called into question formulations of a feminine identity dedicated only to absence and a woman's war constituted solely as a break in experience. But much war poetry of the period organizes itself somehow around that gulf nonetheless, in acquiescence or in opposition. It is the gulf between sexes, but also between home front and overseas, between combatant and noncombatant, between the dead and the survivor, between literal and figurative, between bodily experience and record; as the binary "gulf between" it works to conceal other gulfs and fissures *within* these categories, though those gaps too show up within the poems. The "gulf so deeply cut" of my title is taken from Virginia Woolf's Second World War text *Three Guineas*, in which a woman answering a man who has written asking for her aid in preventing war and stopping fascism writes an ellipsis, and then continues: "those three dots mark a precipice, a gulf so deeply cut between us that for three years and more I have been sitting on my side of it wondering whether it is any use to try to speak across it."[6] How American poets in the forties, especially the women, wrote that gulf, and wrote across it, is my main subject here.

One poem will serve as an entranceway into this book, first because it stands as representative (the questions it raises about gender and authority in war literature will be crucial here throughout), but second because it differs in significant ways from the other texts which follow. Louise Bogan's "To My Brother Killed: Haumont Wood: October, 1918," published in 1937, is in one sense a quintessential Second World War poem, for it locates its voice in the aftermath of one historical catastrophe and in the apprehension of another, and it takes as its subject the unceasing recurrence of violence.

> O you so long dead,
> You masked and obscure,
> I can tell you, all things endure:
> The wine and the bread;
>
> The marble quarried for the arch;
> The iron become steel;
> The spoke broken from the wheel;
> The sweat of the long march;
>
> The hay-stacks cut through like loaves
> And the hundred flowers from the seed;
> All things indeed
> Though struck by the hooves

O disaster, of time due,
Of fell loss and gain,
All things remain,
I can tell you, this is true.

Though burned down to stone
Though lost from the eye,
I can tell you, and not lie,—
Save of peace alone.[7]

Sexual difference does not seem to exist in "To My Brother Killed." By the poem's account, all differences have — difference itself has — been eradicated, as the repeated line, "All things . . . All things," insists. "War," write the editors of a recent feminist anthology on the subject, "must be understood as a *gendering* activity, one that ritually marks the genders of all members of a society," but this war poem does not appear to know it.[8] All traces of the ritual marks of gender appear to have been removed in the process of general annihilation, "burned down to stone" and "lost to the eye."

In the wake of difference, the poem enacts metaphorically the very reductions it mourns: first the militarization of objects and bodies; then their destruction. No sign stands outside the catastrophic system represented here. By the end of "To My Brother Killed," even the "wine and the bread," for all their initial redemptive force, are shown to be nothing but props in a ceaseless sacrificial ceremony.

Bogan uses in this poem a device she employed elsewhere, a figurative landscape in which the body and all that belongs to the body—desire, labor, death—are connected metaphorically to land or to a rural and agricultural scene. She often used such poems to explore the representation of the female body in Western history. Frequently, for instance, her poems take up the ancient "woman as furrow" metaphor described by classicist Page duBois: "the metaphorical complex that associated earth and the female body while, at the same time, stressing *plowing* the body," giving it over to the male who must break it open and cultivate it.[9] Bogan's "Chanson Un Peu Naive" begins with the riddle of the female body: "What body can be ploughed, / Sown, and broken yearly?" (23). In her "Cassandra," a poem whose title declares its ties to some of the most influential of Western representations of war, the supernatural voice of the speaking prophetess who bares the truth of violence is contrasted with the mute, natural body of the mother who bears the brunt of violence: "I am the chosen no hand saves: / The shrieking heaven lifted over men, / Not the dumb earth, wherein they set their graves" (33).

In "To My Brother" the body-landscape is not feminine, not furrowed, but an open, everywhere trampled field. Its gouges seem ungendered, the marks of an abstract violence to which everyone is equally subjected and within which universal subjects live and die. Or if they refer to a specific body, it is the body of the brother, the soldier: his sweat, for instance, in the long enforced march of military advance or retreat or capture. "The marble quarried for the arch" suggests first of all the Arc de Triomphe and other military monuments, but it might suggest as well a breaking and appropriation of a body, "mined," as Page duBois puts it in her discussion of Greek uses of stone metaphors for women's bodies, "taken out of its interiority, forced into service" (86). Here, though, the violated body is not marked female; it refers to any body, or, as the elegiac force of this text's title reminds us, to one man's body.

It also refers glancingly to the body of the poem, since the arch – classic, crafted, reaching – stands for art and for sheer form in much of Bogan's work. In this way poetic form is implicated, too, in the enforcement of war, and represented as pressed into war's service. Ezra Pound, in his 1919 "Envoi," part of the Great War "Hugh Selwyn Mauberley" sequence, had praised the power of poetry to memorialize a female muse, to transcend historical crisis, and to endure "Till change had broken down / All things save Beauty alone."[10] In Bogan's elegy, what lasts is devastation alone, not Beauty; no female muse appears to be celebrated and consoled; and the poem represents itself as holding no power to preserve the man to whom it is dedicated. "All things remain" means *nothing* remains.

Two aspects of the poem suggest that gender differences remain as well, even as the emphasis on "all, all things" denies them. Traces of the traditional gendering of landscape do in fact suggest themselves here. The second stanza's images of rock-hard labor – steel, spoke, triumphal arch – might be read as cultural signs of masculine making; the third stanza's more earthy imagery of domestic agriculture – trampled hay, loaves, and flowers – might in turn be read as cultural signs of the feminine *unmade*.[11] In the end these images are linked and undifferentiated. But in the clean division between the two distinctive stanzas, a gender gap, and an implicit feminist analysis of war's constructing and destroying systems, might be inferred.

At the same time, the title and the poem's female signature inscribe gender difference, but in a way that works against any argument for women's primary victimization in war. They mark the poem as in one sense a classic *woman's* war poem, in the form of the sororal elegy. In 1944, when Bogan met Marianne Moore, Moore greeted her warmly, "and kept remarking," Bogan wrote, "that I had done her a great service in writing that poem to my brother. (I never quite understood this)." "Apparently," Bogan's biographer Elizabeth Frank glosses this exchange, "she did not know that Moore's brother had served in World War II as fleet captain on Admiral Nimitz's flagship in the Pacific."[12] Several of the other poets whose work I will consider in this book wrote war poems under the shadow of mourning or worry for actual brothers: H.D., whose brother had died like Bogan's in the Great War; Gwendolyn Brooks, who dedicated poems to her brother overseas; Hisaye Yamamoto, whose brother died in combat in Italy. More generally, beyond biography, the brother, like Woolf's "private brother" in *Three Guineas* (105), comes to stand in American women's war poetry for the man not yet militarized and the man loved intimately. Because the brother in Bogan's poem is "my brother," killed in a particular place at a particular time, the poem speaks in two voices, the immemorial but also the memorial, the universal but also the familial, the indifferent but also the affectional, the oracular calm of Ecclesiastes but also the grief and rage of tragedy.

"One of the most powerful challenges to the earth/body metaphor," writes duBois, "comes through tragedy, itself a product and producer of democracy. If the woman's body is like the earth . . . then how can she speak?" (69). In "To My Brother Killed," a text in which all bodies in the end are like earth and in which the only democracy the world has been made safe for is a democracy of destruction, ability to speak is a crucial issue. "I can tell you" is its recurring refrain.

This line bears, very starkly, the weight of the poem's central irony. The reassurance to the dead—"I can truthfully tell you, what you died for lives on"—turns out to mean solely "what lives on, what you died violently for, is violence and death." At the same time, very subtly, "I can tell you" suggests something else as well. "*I* can tell you": it is a weary moment of self-assertion. It says: I, the sister, am also part of this landscape (which is universal, not only fraternal like the imaginary terrain of so much war discourse); I can speak; I have something to say in this torn, exposed field.[13]

To read "To My Brother" as an allegory of the woman poet's claim to authority in the field of the modern war poem would be to read it in a way that the poem itself would judge naive and obscene. But finding a way to say "I can tell you" to the eloquent, "masked and obscure" Great War soldier-poet precursors, or to the private brother, and to "say" it without obscenity or naivety, was one of the major tasks which confronted the American women writers whose poems I examine here.

At the same time, however, Louise Bogan cannot simply represent the generic "American woman writer." In fact, she provides a cautionary as much as an exemplary starting place for a book on war poetry by women, since she resisted both the category "woman poet" and the category "war poetry" (resisted, that is, at the very least, her own relation to them). In her 1944 *New Yorker* review surveying recent women's verse, she implied that the intertwining of the two categories brought out the worst in both:

Even granted that no more critical blame should be attached to bad women poets than to bad men poets, the overtones and implications of second-rate feminine verse are somehow particularly pervasive. The sentiment of a given period is nowhere so well distilled as in the contemporary verse written by women. . . . The fashionable attitude, the decorative emotion, the sweeping empty enthusiasm, the sigh that is not yet a tear come through in the works of female versifiers so vividly that we are at once carried off into a "period" mood of one kind or another. . . . The lesson in all this is that women poets must be . . . able to see around their situation on all sides, and to rise above their time, if their work is not to resemble, after twenty years or so, the dated illustrations in a household magazine. (91)

Too domestically dedicated to absence and at the same time too impressed by the banalities of history, too little an author of her time and too much of her "period," the versifier stands here as a premonitory figure for the would-be woman poet in a time of historical crisis.

"To My Brother Killed" seems in every way calculated to circumvent the charges leveled against this feminine versifier. Its refusal to be "dated" extends even to its manuscript history. Although at its publication, in 1937, it had, as I have said, an obvious topical force, the occasion of its composition is elusive. Bogan wrote it, according to Elizabeth Frank, sometime in the twenties. She sent it to a friend; when he returned it to her in 1935, she "could not even remember when she had written it" (256). This memory lapse seems entirely in keeping with the poem's own repression of historical specificity. Seemingly aloof not only from modernity but also from any temporality, it represents itself as (almost) beyond sentiment, (almost) beyond period, and (almost) entirely stripped of reference to gender.

Unlike Bogan's, most of the women's war poems I examine in this book present themselves in some way or at some point as explicitly, deliberately "dated." They refer, at moments, specifically to their immediate period. If they "rise above their time" it is only after locating themselves emphatically within it. Falling into history, into politics, into occasion, they fall also into gender; the differences Bogan's poem renders impertinent—the "ritual markings" of man/woman, civilian/combatant, front/home, all culture/this culture—become live issues, make their presence known. Finding a way, in the shadow of the versifier, not only to write topically but to admit gender *as topic* into their war poems: this was another crucial task confronted by the women poets I consider here.

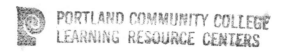

Some braved the label "versifier"; some intricately evaded it; some stopped writing or publishing in the face of it. Bogan herself is part of this last group. In her 1944 *New Yorker* review she suggested that the war had sparked women's poetic productivity; but she herself — despite or perhaps because of this supposed boom — wrote no poems between 1941 and 1948. The reason, to paraphrase her own words, may or may not have been the war. But the dates are suggestive. Bogan's standards of literary decorum were extraordinarily stern and finely tuned. In a period difficult, almost impossible, to "rise above," she chose or endured an austere poetic silence.

Bogan's rejection of "second-rate feminine verse" raises an issue important to address here at the outset: the "question of bad poetry," as Jan Montefiore puts it in her *Feminism and Poetry* (1987). In the section of her book under that subtitle, Montefiore reviews Catherine Reilly's recent, groundbreaking anthology of women's (mostly British women's) Great War poetry, in order to warn pointedly against feminist overvaluation of "second-rate" work by women:

There is . . . a genuine problem in "placing" bad or mediocre poetry by women (which certainly exists) in the context of a woman's tradition . . . it has to be admitted that sometimes the "buried treasure" does turn out to be just old iron. . . . However grateful we are to the editor for disinterring these poems (which are full of interest to the social historian of ideologies), it cannot be pretended that many of them are good. . . . the general effect is conventional, sincere, and amateurish. . . . most of the women poets of *Scars Upon My Heart* demonstrably failed to transcend the chauvinist ideologies and literary clichés of their time. . . . [14]

Does my own book, also a presentation of a set of women's war poems, concern mostly "buried treasure" or "old iron"? Answering that question is not my purpose here. I want, rather, to investigate its terms, to take up the *question* of the question, and to suggest some reasons why for me, in this case, "the question of bad poetry" is (productively) unanswerable.

It is not surprising that the example of bad poetry which emerged for Montefiore was a collection of war poems. Distinguishing itself by definition from the treasure-trove of "pure poetry," the "war poem" categorically admits at least traces of the impurities of ideology and of history.[15] It admits these impurities in two senses. It embraces them; it confesses to them. Consider the properties of Montefiore's metaphorical iron. It is matériel, something of practical and current use, not ideal, not precious, and not an object for display. Poems which signal their relation to what H.D. called the "iron-ring" of war necessarily take on those properties — if only to attempt to shake them off.[16] Modern war poetry, especially that written during wars, might be said to specialize in demonstrably succeeding at failing to entirely transcend its time.

The poems in the pages that follow are full of interest to the social historian of ideologies. I have proceeded here as that historian. I do not think it is desirable or possible to refuse the task of aesthetic assessment categorically, under any circumstances. But I am not generally concerned, *for the duration of this project*, with showing how "the poetic" differs from, or stays aloof from any taint of, Bogan's "dated illustrations in household magazines." Maureen Honey and other feminist scholars have demonstrated the importance of studying the illustrations in those magazines for what they tell us about the changing frameworks of gender ideology within which American women lived out their war years.[17] I intend this book as a supplement to such feminist work, not its polar opposite, and I am more interested here in tracing connections than in making distinctions between the production of images in magazines and the production of images in women's poems.

This is, then, an analysis of the ideological constitution of poetry. As such, it pays extended attention to conditions of authorship and readership on the home front and to the political content of poems. Poetic content, of course, never comes unmediated by poetic form. As I focus on Muriel Rukeyser's use of the sestina, or Gwendolyn Brooks's manipulations of the sonnet, or Elizabeth Bishop's similes, I am interested equally in poetics and politics, and in the dynamic interaction between them. But the kinds of debate over the politics of gender and war which I examine here are not contained by poetic forms, any more than they are filtered out by those forms. They refer to, and are intertextually related to, a wide range of other wartime discursive and signifying practices.

Still, the question of bad poetry, in particular, is in one sense very much my subject, insofar as that question is posed historically.[18] This book presents a case study of conflicts in poetic evaluation in and around the years from 1941 to 1945 in the United States. I explore conflicts within the writing practices of individual poets, as those writers judged and rejudged the worth and function of their own work.[19] I examine conflicts, also, within individual readers struggling with their attraction to opposing standards. And I describe conflicts between groups of writers and readers, groups with opposed agendas or differing political/aesthetic criteria, over what the phrase "good poem" meant in the midst of a hot war. My aim is to trace the social processes of valuation at the time when and the sites where these poems were first produced and read. I have tried to show the historical specificity of those processes — their historical *otherness* — as well as their structural links to modes of literary evaluation in later periods up to and including my own.

Jan Montefiore remarks at one point in her discussion of the low quality of most works in Catherine Reilly's Great War anthology that the poems in Reilly's later collection of women's writing during World War II are, in general, better than those that Reilly culled out of World War I.[20] This analysis, with its easy and categorical distinction between the worse and the better, depends, as Tony Bennett puts it, upon the "discursive construction of the category of a universal valuing subject."[21] I have attempted to conceive the problem of value differently, taking into account the historicity of evaluative strategies and contestations in American culture. It is no surprise, I would argue, that the poems in Reilly's Second War volume satisfy Montefiore more readily than those in the First War volume do. After all, the criteria for assessment she uses — and their theoretical underpinning, the notion of constant, immanent value — were being refined and vigorously promulgated during the 1940s by the New Critics, out of modernism, and in the increasingly influential postwar English departments.[22]

I see my task in relation to the question of value as threefold. First, I have tried to understand the historical contingency of dominant current theories of literary value; that means in part recognizing their roots in the forties. Second, I have tried to understand the historical contingency of Second World War theories of literary value as they competed with each other; that means in part understanding their difference from the present. Finally, and most important, I have tried to show how historically specific assumptions about gender have shaped assessments of value when women's war poems were appraised.

I do not mean, however, to settle the problem of value by referring it back to the "facts" of a positivized history. The question of bad poetry is a question of politics; the war poem is still the locus of politicized contention. To write about war poetry I have had to locate myself as well as the women whose work I analyze on the very ground from which many models of women's relation to war would most exclude us — a political arena. That site is *unsettled*, in the sense that it offers no stability, but not in the sense that it is free and unmarked terrain.

There are a variety of charged and sometimes contradictory models which I (and readers like me) bring to historical appraisal of these texts. I read forward, for instance, toward the Second World War through the strong tradition of mistrust of rhetoric and propaganda which World War I engendered. I read backward through the Vietnam War, which for many poets, as Cary Nelson has shown, called the myth of redemptive American democracy, and indeed all American language, into question.[23] (For some poets, of course — Gwendolyn Brooks and other Black poets, for instance—that myth had long been under suspicion.) On the one hand, I read with the sense that I grew up with: that the Second World War, interpreted as a fight against fascism, constituted "a notably moral common cause," that it was a "war against palpable evil."[24] On the other, I read with an understanding derived from Jarrell, Heller, and Pynchon that war-making is murder and "passive misery." And I read as an inheritor of and participant in a modern academic tradition which judges literature not by its content but by its demonstration of self-referential artifice.[25] All of these teachings and more inform my approach and render it difficult; ethnic and cultural differences as they bear on the politics of evaluation make it even more intricate.

Another factor complicates this list still further: the difficulty of sexual difference. Recent aesthetic and political assessments of past war poetry are often implicitly or explicitly gendered. Conventional narratives about gender and war exert strong pressure on the terms by which modern war poems are judged today. Take, for instance, an account by James Longenbach in his very useful book on Pound, Yeats, and modernism, *Stone Cottage*, of the November 1914 "war verse" number of *Poetry*. That issue published the results of a prize competition for the best war or peace poem "based on the present European situation." Longenbach describes how the then-unknown Wallace Stevens sent his sequence "Phases" to Harriet Monroe, too late to win the prize, though she published sections from it in the war collection. Characterizing this early sequence by Stevens as "cast in a rhetoric borrowed from Kipling and Housman," Longenbach adds: "Stevens's poems were among the best in a jingoist collection filled with Kipling's imperialism and Housman's soldiers dying young. The prize for the best poem was awarded to Louise Driscoll's 'The Metal Checks'—causing Pound to refer to the whole incident as 'the war-poetry scandal.'"[26]

What, exactly, was the scandal in the war poetry? Longenbach goes on to outline, meticulously, Pound's objections to a poetry of occasion, his worries about a glib and opportune poetic representation of violence, and his concerns about the constrictions of poetic scope which the phrase "war-poem" implied. But the brief reference, not pursued, to Louise Driscoll suggests that the scandal lies most of all in the woman poet and her poem, and presumably in that poem's jingoism and sentimentality, its parroting of "Kipling's imperialism," of "Housman's soldiers dying young." Other critical accounts of the war verse issue, usually offered as background to a discussion of Stevens's poetic development, suggest the same thing, and one of the implications of that suggestion is that "jingoism" and "sentimentality" are poetic traits associated particularly with the feminine.[27] A long tradition — stemming in part, as I will show, from the damning representation of the patriotic poetess in Great War works like Wilfred Owen's "Dulce et Decorum Est" — lies behind this assumption, one which Longenbach himself in other work has done a great deal to counteract.

A look back to Driscoll's poem in the context of the war verse number as a whole suggests a different story. It is startling, first of all, to notice how much of the work which appears in the pages of this issue is authored by women; at this very early moment in the history of modern American poetry's construction of the subgenre "war poem," in this female-edited journal, women writers played a noticeable and integral part. Startling, too, to read Louise Driscoll's winning entry. "The Metal Checks" is a verse play. Its two characters, "The Counter, who is Death," and "The Bearer," who is "the World, that bears the burden of war," tally and dispose of "the little metal disks that have been used for the identification of the slain common soldiers."[28] In the service of an American anti-interventionist (and a feminist) pacifism, this allegory emphasized the enormity of the death toll, the meaninglessness of the conflict, and the impersonality of a war machine which turns men (particularly working-class men) into its counters.

"The Metal Checks" could be faulted on a number of technical grounds; undoubtedly for Pound its "scandal" lay in part in its cumbersome verse. It could also be faulted on ideological grounds, one of which might be the way in which its figure of man as metal counter reinforced the very objectification it purported to critique. But one thing is clear. The poem's impulse was decidedly not jingoistic, its representation of the dead male body emphatically not like Housman's. At one point, Driscoll's Bearer imagines a lake of blood, consigning men like Kipling's and Housman's to Hades, and refuting in strong terms the roles of welcomer, cheerleader, and mourner traditionally assigned to women in war:

> Perhaps in Hell
> There's some such lake for men who rush to war
> Prating of glory, and upon the shore
> Will stand the wives and children and old men
> Bereft, to drive them back again
> When they seek haven.
>
> (52)

Surely it was precisely the political functions of the poem — its anti-imperialism, its antisentimentalism, and its pacifist feminism — that prompted the judges of the *Poetry* war verse contest to award Driscoll first place. In a later critical tradition which has tended to disparage historical topicality, to privilege modernism, and to valorize pacifism only by granting it to the "experienced" male, those functions are often unreadable. But there are other standpoints from which to view this case. From the perspective of the 1914 contest judges, there was, it is worth recalling, no war poetry scandal. From my perspective now, the scandal is the scandal of gender.

Remembering the differences of opinion between Ezra Pound and Harriet Monroe's committee of judges not only over what constituted a prize poem but also over what constituted a valid contest, I have proceeded here — and in this I follow Barbara Herrnstein Smith, Terry Eagleton, Anne McClintock, and others — with the understanding that value is never immanent but rather "contingent" and "transitive," historically and culturally determined.[29] For this book, the question of bad poetry means always the question of bad (or good) poetry *for whom*?[30] To the statement in the introduction of the recent book on women and the World Wars, *Behind the Lines*, "The most powerful of women's writings about war rely on indirection, on writing 'slant,'" my response is, "Powerful on whose terms? What kind of power? And whose power?"[31] Of the poems I address in this book, the one least likely to be designated "powerful" in a literary critic's assessment today (and in many critics' judgments at the time) is the one most likely to have made something happen in 1942: Edna St. Vincent Millay's "The Murder of Lidice," written at the request of the Writer's War Board and part of an influential — and powerful, and in no way oblique — government campaign to increase American antagonism to Nazism.

One poem more than any other I encountered while researching this book raises for me the problem of the question of bad poetry, or of poetry and its contingencies. Its clumsiness is undeniable, but its history of reception complicates the reading of that clumsiness. Two of its reviews in the forties provide an especially eloquent challenge to formalist evaluations of political poetry. These reviews do not, and cannot, conclusively rebut the case for calling some poems bad on technical grounds; but in their historical context they resonantly make the case for other, vital standards of assessment.

The poem, a slim book-length sequence, is called *Behold the Jew*. Its author is an English Christian, Ada Jackson. It came out first in England in 1943; Macmillan published its American edition in 1944. Here is its first stanza, which begins the poem, as Bogan's "To My Brother Killed" begins, with an invocation of "all, all things," but for very different reasons:

Jew, I say—and in my heart
it rhymes with all the hunted things
that cower in brakes or die in reeds
of shattered breasts and broken wings,
so that upon the selfsame breath
I pray for Jews and driven birds
and badgers baited to their deaths,
and bulls that, with nor wit nor words,
must bleed for strutting matadors—
beseeching God for such as press
all night against the trap's steel teeth,
for otters slain for wantonness,
for foxes and for hunted deer
and all the creatures man pursues,
the blinded and the lamed, the scourged
and prison-fast—but most for Jews.[32]

Ada Jackson goes virtually unread today. No history of women's poetry
that I know of mentions her; it's not hard to see why. The kind of techni-
cal analysis literary critics learn to do reveals obvious weaknesses here:
verbal awkwardnesses; jangling, unvaried meter; redundancy and overstate-
ment. Jackson seems a clear-cut case of "old iron," her poem exactly the
kind of weepy, mediocre period piece Bogan deplored.

At one time, despite these flaws, Jackson had a substantial following
on both sides of the Atlantic. Her depression-era pacifist poem "Two Headed
Penny" (sometimes titled "Thirty Years After") was broadcast over British
radio, praised in a column devoted to it by Eleanor Roosevelt, and, in the
words of a publicity blurb for *Behold the Jew,*

posted up in prominent places all over the United States, in picture houses, schools
and churches. Saint Louis, Missouri, American Legion sent the author a resolution
expressing their thanks. The Library of Congress, Washington, asked for a MS. of
the poem, which is now in their care, and Lockwood Memorial Library, University
of Buffalo, have asked for methods of working and notebooks which they now use
in their English course.[33]

By the time "Two Headed Penny" was published in a verse collection, Jack-
son's 1940 *Against the Sun,* it was followed by a poem called "Pacifist 1939"
which rejected the author's earlier antimilitarism. The book staged itself,
therefore, as the drama of a thirties pacifist's reluctant and inevitable coming
to war, and that narrative had, apparently, considerable popular appeal.

Three years later, Jackson's *Behold the Jew* was awarded the British
Poetry Society's Greenwood Prize. It was widely distributed, and one of
its sections in particular was frequently quoted. The section begins,

> If I keep silence all these things
> are done of me and in my name,
> and mine the guilt of bludgeonings
> and massacres —
>   If I speak not —
> if I forbear — I am as one
> turned murderer. It is as tho'
> my own hands bore the knife, the gun.
>
>   (21)

Asserting that she would "sooner die in Dachau's camp / . . . than be but for a second's space / of those who ride to trample you," the speaker pledges to "the Jew" the "one talent I call mine," her words: "I will lift up my hand for you / in all men's sight, where all men meet / . . . speaking your wrongs while daylight lasts . . . " (21, 22). Then, after a sharp break, the poem starts again with a single, disjunctive line: "While you read they die" (22). I have added the period there; the line stands squarely in the middle of the page, and part of its startling effect derives from its lack of final punctuation.

Jackson's American admirers included Marianne Moore, who worked hard to get *Behold the Jew* published in the United States, and arranged to review it for the *New Republic* in an effort to increase its distribution. Moore's review did not ignore the question of aesthetic judgment. She noted that "as poetry" one section of *Behold the Jew* "perhaps has an effect of over-tragic imbalance" and that in another — her tactfulness shows here — "one would prefer a neater wording." At the same time she praised the poem's "eloquent reiteration" and "expert allusiveness." (Jackson's poem is long, and it shifts tone at many points; readers curious about the disjunction between the lines from Jackson I have quoted and Moore's assessment of the poem might find it worthwhile to look at the entire text.) But in the end Moore chose to champion *Behold the Jew* for reasons other than artistic ones. The review concludes: "And 'while you read they die, they died'; they, by way of whom all our moral advantages have come. If we yet rescue them — those who are alive to be rescued — we are still in debt and need to ask ourselves who would have rescued whom."[34]

Here Moore exemplifies a reading practice in which moral and political considerations take primacy over aesthetic ones. That practice is shared by the famous modernist Yiddish poet Jacob (Yankev) Glatshteyn, writing in New York for a Yiddish-speaking audience between 1945 and 1947. In a dazzling review of Moore, Glatshteyn analyzed her poetic technique with the keen eye of a fellow modernist craftsman; but he also emphasized her old-fashioned spiritual and timely political integrity, an honesty he illustrated in part through references to her promotion of *Behold the Jew*. In another review — the one which most interests me here — he turned to a reading of *Behold the Jew* itself.

I first discovered the Glatshteyn review of Jackson in a brief reference in Benjamin and Barbara Harshav's anthology of American Yiddish poetry, which includes translations.[35] Tracking it down, I found it existed only in Yiddish (a language I don't speak and can't read), and during the period in which I waited for its translation I had ample time to speculate about what he would have to say. I knew, on the one hand, something about Glatshteyn's virtuoso modernism, his "If Joyce Had Written in Yiddish," and his avant-garde *Yiddishtaytshn* (recently translated as *Exegyddish*).[36] I knew, on the other, my own reaction from my vantage point in the eighties to Jackson's poem, which I found embarrassingly turgid and unconsciously anti-Semitic in its patronization of Jews and its "Gentile gaze." I assumed — the kind of historicizing approach I am trying to practice here does not come effortlessly — that Glatshteyn would share my response. The review, when it arrived, was a surprise.

Glatshteyn's discussion of Ada Jackson began by addressing squarely the question of bad poetry, only in order to dismiss it: "Is *Behold the Jew* an artistic achievement? As one reads the poem, one completely forgets to ask this question."[37] Art, Glatshteyn went on, is "measure, cadence, the elimination of the unnecessary," a kind of productive "stinginess." But art is also, he argued, a kind of "self-inflation" and a sign of self-absorption, "a play for immortality." "Should an individual," he asked, "want his word to live at the expense of so many dead?"

Describing Thomas Mann's response to I. I. Singer's request that Mann write a manifesto against Hitler for the Peretz Writer's Union a few years earlier, Glatshteyn bitterly indicted the artist's urge to write "slant" and to rise above his time. When Mann sent his piece, Glatshteyn writes, "we all turned cold." For "he sent us a piece of literature. He put on his artist dress clothes and didn't mention Hitler at all. Nor did he mention the Jews. He wrote his outcry for Eternity. He did not forget for a minute that he was an artist, and that the suffering of the Jews is a transitory phenomenon. Of course nothing came of the whole project." Over and against Mann's "manifesto," Glatshteyn privileged Jackson's *Behold the Jew*. He praised its sincerity ("one feels that the poet isn't exploiting our infirmity and enslavement"), its humility, and its refusal of an aesthetic of timelessness. The poem, he wrote, performed an urgent mission, "without flirting with classical immortality."

Above all, Glatshteyn valued Jackson's attempt at political intervention. He emphasized the demands *Behold the Jew* placed on American and British readers of poetry in 1943 and 1944: "Until Ada Jackson those who did not participate in pogroms could go around with heads held high, and innocent faces, but the poet shows that passivity is also an active role in the extermination of the Jewish people. . . . There isn't any middle way." He concluded, "Either become a murderer or cry out and put oneself in danger of being a victim." Jackson, he argued, both comprehended and conclusively exposed the demands of this situation.

On the one hand, Glatshteyn's review of Jackson declared the impossibility of any project of literary valuation. To the question of bad poetry he answered: "What is this kind of poetry? In the face of total annihilation of a people, of the methodically cold preparation of lime ovens and gas chambers, of turning whole Jewish families to ashes, of wiping out whole Jewish genealogies, whole family chronicles, what is this kind of literature? . . . Who can evaluate literature now?" But on the other hand, Glatshteyn reclaimed value and redefined it, systematically overturning categories and hierarchies of assessment to which the modernist reviewer had himself at one time subscribed. Accepting the question of bad and good poetry, he responded to it differently: "May Jews especially designate the name of the poet Ada Jackson for immortality, who in 1943 in England cried out to her readers, in the simple words: *While you read they die.* If a singer would simply go from courtyard to courtyard crying out a call of warning — that line would be the greatest poem. . . . " Contrasting *Behold the Jew* with "carefully crafted sonnet crowns, which beautifully lull our pain into frozen silence," Glatshteyn argued that parts of Jackson's poem were indeed "good poetry about an abstract Jewish tragedy. Such poetry has the sound of ancient Hebrew melodies." But those parts, he claimed, were precisely the *weak* points of the poem; what he valued were the moments in *Behold the Jew* in which poetry "breaks off . . . with a scream, and you fall back into your narrow corner, where you sit in mourning."

Behold the Jew as Glatshteyn understood it earned its literary value paradoxically, by defying literary value. The poem moved outside the margins of literature; therefore, he argued, it came to take its rightful place as literature. Or else the margins themselves became a rightful place, the site of works which are more than rather than less than literature, for the canon in which he situated *Behold the Jew* was, in the end, *the* canon beyond the mere literary — the Holy Scriptures themselves:

You can't pass by and pretend not to know and not to see. Behold the Jew — and don't say you are too weak. . . . This clear emphasis on the responsibility of the Christian world elevates the poem above literature. There was a time when we would have brushed off such a classification as "beyond literature," equating it with "beneath literature." But now we know that such a poem is a true continuation of holy writings.

Value for whom, and for what? Glatshteyn's answer was unequivocal: for the survival of the Jewish people. Set his review next to Bogan's indictment of the "period moods" of female versifiers, and Ada Jackson, who as early as 1943 was writing the word Dachau for an Allied audience and writing it with a clear sense of what was at stake, begins to trouble distinctions between buried treasure and old iron. On the question of the worth of Jackson's poem Glatshteyn was militant. We need to hear that militance, in its opposition to the now familiarly compelling kind of formalist argument that Bogan made, in order, I think, to begin to understand sufficiently the situation of poets and of poetry in U.S. culture during the Second World War. This is, in Barbara Herrnstein Smith's words, "what genuine evaluative conflict sounds like," and what it sounded like.[38]

The line of Jackson's which both Glatshteyn and Moore singled out repeatedly for special quotation — "While you read they die" — is, however, particularly amenable to praise on conventional New Critical aesthetic grounds. Its artfully disjointed plainspokenness and textual self-consciousness conform to formalist criteria as much as they undo them. Glatshteyn praised it on the grounds that it went *further* than poetry, "broke off" into pure lament or scream; but of course one could also argue that here poetry *peaks*, staging its own furthest reach. Glatshteyn's emphasis on this line suggests a hidden contradiction in his own reading. He was militant, yes; but on the subject of abstract value he was also ambivalent. The conflict over value in his review was private as much as public, internal as much as external. It was within Glatshteyn the modernist, as he called into question his own previous aesthetics, as much as between Glatshteyn and the more insular modernism he illustrated with Thomas Mann. And Glatshteyn himself, it is important to note, went on to write Holocaust poems which, in their verbal intensity and virtuosity, sound nothing like Ada Jackson's. Glatshteyn's review does not and cannot resolve the question of bad poetry. But its contradictions illustrate clearly some of the terms in which, in this book, that question needs to stay uncomfortably unresolved.

To the question, *Value at all?*, Glatshteyn's answer was equivocal. If Ada Jackson's poem, like the events it represents, exemplified for Glatshteyn the undoing of all literary value, it also — in its opposition to what it represents — tempted him to invoke the most exalted terms of value at his disposal, to nominate the poem as sacred text. Rejection of the canon and the refusal of all aesthetic standards went hand in hand in his review with canon formation and the formulation of new political standards. I recognize this ambivalence, for in different form it also attends my own reading and writing position, and it shapes the project of this book, as it shapes any feminist revisionary project.

It would, of course, be ingenuous for me to imply that no evaluative strategies have gone into the making of *A Gulf So Deeply Cut*. My selection of some texts rather than others for lengthy discussion, or for mention at all, is an evaluative act (though there are many more that space – and time – alone prevent me from including: the war poems of Jane Cooper, for example, and Kadia Molodowsky, and Kay Boyle; wartime writing within Latina, Native American, Chinese American, Filipina, Italian American, and German American communities; and many male-authored war poems, particularly the influential Auden's and examples of men's Second War pacifist poetry such as Lowell's or Everson's). My detailed readings of some of the texts I have chosen imply that I think them worthy of attention (though I offer those readings in the spirit of demystification as much as celebration).

I read here as a feminist with a special interest in war and in women's poetry. I have, therefore, selected those poems which seem to me to illustrate with special clarity and sufficient variety what American women's poetry *made* of gender and war during the war years – "*made*" both in the sense of "thought" or "theorized" and in the sense of "constructed."

I owe a great deal to two overlapping strands of prior feminist work. My hope is that this book will extend even as it responds to both. My first debt is to feminists who have analyzed women's poems (and, more broadly, gender and poetry), from the pioneering literary histories by Emily Stipes Watts, Suzanne Juhasz, Cheryl Walker, Cora Kaplan, and more recently Alicia Ostriker and Jan Montefiore to the increasing number of book-length studies of some of the individual authors whom I discuss.[39] I am equally indebted to feminists who have theorized about gender and war or specifically, about gender and the Second World War – Cynthia Enloe, for instance, and Susan Hartmann – and most especially to those who, during the years I have been at work on this project, have considered the issue specifically in relation to literary representation: Sandra Gilbert and Susan Gubar, Jane Marcus, and the editors of and contributors to the recent anthologies *Behind the Lines* and *Arms and the Woman* among many others.[40] What I have taken from these two intersecting traditions of feminist work will, I think, be obvious; for now let me spell out some of what I hope to give to them in turn.

Feminist histories of modern American women's poetry often include a brief afterthought or aside which recognizes the presence of a tradition generally excluded from the bounds of their surveys: those poems placed under the heading of the overtly "political."[41] Accounts of some contemporary women writers (Rich or Lorde or Grahn or Levertov) have, certainly, centered emphatically on "socially conscious" poetry. But most overviews of earlier, "modern" women's poems have focused primarily on women's responses to the tradition of the private lyric, or on gender and the language of modernism; they have concentrated, in short, on poetry and *sexual* politics. These studies have devoted correspondingly less attention to the many poems which are political not in the slant and broadly revisionary but in the most explicit and narrowly conventional sense.

Alicia Ostriker suggests in a brief note toward the end of her general survey that such "socially conscious" poems comprise an additional "third style" of twentieth-century women's poetry (the other, predominant two are those of the "lyricist" and the "modernist innovator").[42] This book puts that third style first. Lyric and modernist innovation will both be my subjects, but only in their relation to the overtly topical, directly political, stubbornly public poems that the age and the war culture demanded. (Where there have been two long war poems by one woman poet, one written in the heat of response to wartime conditions and one written in their aftermath, I have, therefore, chosen to concentrate on the former: Brooks's "Gay Chaps at the Bar" rather than her "Anniad," H.D.'s *Trilogy* rather than her *Helen in Egypt*.) Close up, the "third style" will reveal itself in turn as many styles. "Social consciousness" varies significantly in poets; social situation varies drastically for poets; part of my project here has been to show how.

This book is narrower in scope, and consequently more variegated in detail, than most other studies of writing on war by modern American women. Looking closely at versions of a single literary genre written or published during a short span of time, I have tried to uncover ideological contradictions within the female-authored texts I analyze at length, as well as differences between those texts; to locate intertextual links and political alliances between the women's poems and male-authored war poetry, as well as breaks between feminine and masculine traditions; and, most importantly, to explore the specific subcultural contexts in which each of those texts was produced, received, and defined.

Chapters 1 and 2 of this book trace the vexed wartime cultural practices and home-front critical reception of two then famous women poets: Marianne Moore and Edna St. Vincent Millay. Millay's antagonistic, antifascist poetry, some of it written on demand for the Writer's War Board, was lauded by some and greeted by others with an especially virulent critical backlash; Moore's agonistic war poem "In Distrust of Merits," received far more warmly in literary circles, is a no less defensive and troubled text. Though each of these chapters focuses primarily on a woman poet, each also pays significant attention to the related work of a man. Pairing Moore with Randall Jarrell, Millay with Archibald MacLeish, I propose to show

how not only women but also men contested dominant gender ideologies in their war poems – and, at the same time, how not only men but also women recuperated those ideologies in their war poems. I argue, too, that in these cases the male-authored and the female-authored texts carry out these tasks in different ways. Since this book analyzes the construction of gender, poems authored by men will be pertinent throughout; since its primary commitment is to the study of women's writing, poems authored by women will be placed in the foreground, except in chapter 3.

The next three chapters rehearse the history of one peculiar type of modern war poem, the poem as a soldier's letter from the front to a woman waiting back home. Chapter 3 focuses on constructions of gender and politics in examples of this epistolary subgenre written by male poets across the two World Wars. Here the male-authored tradition of war poetry comes under closest scrutiny. My concern is with distinctions between men – generational (Great War versus Second War) and situational (civilian versus soldier poets) as well as political. But I have also explored the ways in which these very different poems all work to reinforce masculine control over and masculinist conceptions of the discourse of war-making or war protest.

Chapters 4 and 5 show how two women's poems answer back to that convention of the male soldier poet's letter. Gwendolyn Brooks responds by replicating the form and making it Black; Muriel Rukeyser, by reversing it. These two women wrote within two hotly politicized discursive settings I have delineated at length: Brooks in the context of the Second World War Black press, Rukeyser in the context of left writing and the Popular Front. The struggle around epistolary form in the forties war poem reveals the gendered "gulf so deeply cut" in its crudest outlines; these chapters map out two different cultural arenas in which those outlines were felt and were challenged by women.

Two more chapters center on a very literally delimited arena of war, the internment camp, and on the poems of internment and relocation written by Japanese American (specifically Nisei) women – poems which represent a civilian war experience as direct and scarring as any soldier's. Chapter 6 sketches in a general account of the conditions for writing these women faced in the war years, and then focuses on one poet writing in the Topaz camp, Toyo Suyemoto, who like Rukeyser – though by necessity in far more coded ways – transformed the private "woman's lyric" into protest. Chapter 7 examines other, more open poetic representations of identity by Japanese American women within a national culture which both ignored and threatened their self-constructions. It considers political poems by Chiye Mori, Hisaye Yamamoto, and Mitsuye Yamada, some writ-

ten in the years leading to Pearl Harbor and some published long
after. The poems in these two chapters differ substantially from the other
texts I read in this book; not despite this but because of it, they are crucial
for an understanding of what "war poetry" is when meaningful distinc-
tions between war front and home front do not apply.

The last two chapters also call the category "war poem" into question,
but from a very different perspective. Chapters 8 and 9 treat high lyricism
and modernism, querying their relation to the "socially conscious" poems
I have been following throughout. The first focuses on the war-related
lyrics of Elizabeth Bishop's *North and South*, the second on H.D.'s *Trilogy*,
written in London where the home front was also a war zone. In earlier
chapters cultural conflicts over war and gender are shown to be worked
out across the image of the common soldier's letter. In these chapters I
situate H.D.'s and Bishop's work in the context of Second War poems
that, for similar ends, invoke an equally popular but "higher" discourse:
Christian scripture.

H.D. once said, in dismissive response to Muriel Rukeyser's political
poems, that "it was difficult to concentrate on the trial of the Scottsboro
boys during a Mozart ballet."[43] Rukeyser, Brooks, Yamada, and Millay,
perhaps even Moore at points during the forties, might have responded
that it was also difficult to concentrate on a ballet during the trial of the
Scottsboro boys — though few of them, perhaps not even Moore, would
have finally accepted the distinction between the ballet and the trial, in-
sofar as it applied to poems. In one sense, these last two chapters might
be read as a turn from the combative activism Scottsboro represents to
the unswerving formalism Mozart represents, a turn which in my view
needs to be read not as progress but simply as difference. But conflict
infiltrates Bishop's and H.D.'s ballets; these elegant poems are also at war.
Intricately, obliquely, they too challenge the compelling distinctions be-
tween front and home, spectacle and spectator, center and margin, pri-
vate and public, and masculine and feminine which underlay American
conceptions of the Second World War and the Second World War poem.

In W. H. Auden's "The Shield of Achilles" (1952), "Thetis of the shining
breasts" cries out in dismay when she sees that the shield Hephaestos has
fashioned for her son reveals not the graceful scenes she has expected but
a prophetic "weed-choked field."[44] It is a later version of the landscape
Bogan mapped in "To My Brother Killed": the world of crucifixion and
torture, mass armed conflict and the concentration camp. Auden's poem
constructs itself around sites of contestation we will revisit repeatedly in
this book: the politics of the female gaze at and the female voice in military

conflict; women's connection to martial and apocalyptic prophecy; the place and function of the mother in systems of militarism; wartime art and women's relation to it. But the women poets I turn to now wrote this scene differently, whether they deployed or rejected Thetis's maternal cry. They inscribed themselves as implicated makers, not only viewers, of the inadequate "shields" of war art.

This holds true for women's war poems in the United States across the twentieth century, but the Second World War years provide, I think, an especially fruitful period to study, for three reasons. First, because American women poets in the forties wrote with powerful and extensive traditions of antiwar discourse already behind them, some of them developed by male precursors (as in the case of the Great War combatant protest writers) and some by female (as in the case of pre- and post–Great War feminist pacifism). Unlike Auden's Thetis, they could claim little ignorance. Second, because within broad U.S. culture the Second World War has been and is still the modern war least susceptible to pacifist protest, the one most likely to be understood as just. The questions of distinctive female peacefulness and of the politics of literary pacifism are thus intensified and problematized here, in ways still pertinent today for thinking about the meaning and the politics of Thetis's cry. Third, because feminism had exerted such a strong influence in the first three decades of the century before the U.S. war — groundwork extended further and in unexpected ways by the unprecedented alterations of gender arrangements in the war economy.

Praising Ezra Pound in reviews in the thirties for seeing "a connection sometimes where others do not: between books and war, for instance," Marianne Moore added a rebuke: "is not the view of women expressed by the Cantos older-fashioned than that of Siam and Abyssinia?"[45] Seeing the connection between books and war, American women poets of the forties also saw the connection of both to constructions of gender. Chapter 1, on Moore, will begin to show how they represented those connections, charting the links and gulfs within the war system in which they lived and wrote.

Part One

Gender and Authority in Second World War Poetry

1

Writing War Poetry "Like a Woman"
Moore (and Jarrell)

I

A reader today of didactic discussions of war poetry written during the Second World War might be surprised at the frequency with which American literary critics held up a text written by a woman as the single exemplary war poem: Marianne Moore's "In Distrust of Merits." W. H. Auden, for instance, called "In Distrust" "the best of . . . all" war poems of World War II.[1] Moore was so lionized on the American home front, her poem so praised, that Randall Jarrell began his famous answer to "In Distrust" with a mock-apologetic "Miss Moore is reviewed not as a poet but as an institution," going on to cite, acerbically, a reviewer who had called Moore "the greatest living poet" and then demanded that she be "placed in Fort Knox for the duration."[2]

The uses of Moore as institution, for the duration, deserve closer study than Jarrell's ironies might suggest; they shed light on assumptions prevalent in both the 1940s and the 1980s about what "war" means, what "war poetry" means, and where "woman" stands in relation to both. In the following pages, I am concerned specifically with how Moore's work invokes and attempts to revoke traditional formulations of sexual difference in wartime, and with how Jarrell's responses undertake a related task. I am also concerned, more broadly, with constructions of gender in the early forties theoretical controversies over the criteria by which war poetry should be judged, particularly over standards of authorial credibility. These arguments matter because they set terms which still tend to define the parameters of current aesthetic and political evaluations of the war poem—values shared by texts as magisterial as the recent *Oxford Book of War Poetry* and as adversarial as collections of poems by Vietnam War protesters or veterans. But a look back to the volatile home-front debates about the decorum of the growing subgenre of war poetry reveals the extent of women's participation in the making of the forties "war poem" — participation today's anthologists and theorists of war literature often tend to minimize or forget.

In the forties, many critics seized on "In Distrust of Merits" as a way of reforming the canon of war poetry, a canon till then largely shaped by the masculine "soldier poems" of British Great War poets such as Wilfred Owen and Siegfried Sassoon. First World War soldier poetry had, of course, never been a stable commodity; it could never be guaranteed to be written by a genuine soldier from a genuine trench, as Robert Graves' pointed summary of the tradition, written in 1948, makes clear:

> When war poetry became a fashion in 1915, a good deal of it was written imitatively by civilians who regretted that age or unfitness prevented them from also 'making the supreme sacrifice. ' . . . Also, many soldiers wrote as though they had seen more of the war than they really had. Robert Nichols, for instance, whose brief service in France . . . was ended by sickness . . . scored a great success . . . as a crippled warrior, reading . . . to University and women's club audiences.[3]

These falsehoods only go to prove, rather than render suspicious, the power of the standards for war poems which became normative in the university and the women's club during and after the Great War. Within the developing tradition of war poetry, those poems were privileged which were, or seemed to be, rooted in the original ground of men's literal combat experience. War poems should be backed, as Sassoon described Owen's work, by the authority of experience of the infantry soldier.[4]

In the Second World War, however, that lonely masculine authority of experience — the bitter authority derived from direct exposure to violence and mechanized terror — was rapidly dispersing among general populations. Graves noted that the Second World War soldier "cannot even feel that his rendezvous with death is more certain than that of his Aunt Fanny, the firewatcher."[5] American culture was, obviously, characterized by far greater disjunctions between male and female "experience" of war than the British blitz society Graves described, and the modern tradition of soldier poetry, with its ironic emphasis on unmendable gaps between the soldier author and the civilian reader, retained its strong influence. Still, public discussions of war and literature in the United States dwelt frequently on the new conjunctions between civilians and soldiers, front and home front, and men and women, focusing on their shared morale or effort as well as on their common deprivation and vulnerability.

In a war newly perceived as "total," Moore's work could exemplify the power of a representative civilian voice. It could also represent modernism provisionally embracing realist and didactic functions, coming round to correcting earlier trends toward self-referentiality. Thus Richard Eberhart, arguing in his introduction to a well-known anthology of war poetry that "the spectator, the contemplator, the opposer of war have their hours with the enemy no less than uniformed combatants," praises Moore for abandoning the "complacencies of the peignoir" to write "In Distrust of Merits."[6] His phrasing links Moore with another civilian war poet, Wallace Stevens. Placing Moore inside the scene of Stevens' "Sunday Morning" in order to show her departing from it, Eberhart suggests that she has abandoned leisurely philosophizing for the new rigors of historical engagement. And dressing her in Stevens' peignoir in order to show her doffing it, he represents her as a formerly feminine object of desire who has emerged from the coquetries of her sex into a new, superior, gender-free authority.[7] Now, Eberhart argues, "the bloodshed of which she writes has caused her to break through the decorative surface of her verse" to a "different kind of utterance."[8] For Eberhart, the poem's value lies in its violation of Moore's usual mannered aestheticism. She "breaks through" a feminine surface, as if puncturing skin, but the result is not a wound but a mouth: a "different kind of utterance," in which "the meaning has dictated the sincerity" (xiii).

Oscar Williams, in the preface to a comparable anthology, also reads the poem as a model of transparent earnestness, offering it as a solution to the problem of Edna St. Vincent Millay, the "bad" woman war poet who is excoriated in these discussions as often as Moore is extolled. Describing one of Millay's war poems as "a sentimental piece of verse written by an American civilian, designed to be read by . . . people themselves out of danger because they are protected by a wall of living young flesh, much of which will be mangled," Williams contrasts Moore's "In Distrust of Merits":

But with true poets the poetry is in the pity. . . . I ask the reader to study closely a war poem peculiarly fitted to illustrate my present thesis. It is also written by a woman, a civilian. "In Distrust of Merits," by Marianne Moore, is the direct communication of honest feeling by one ready to search her own heart to discover the causes of war and accept her full share of responsibility for its effects.[9]

Moore's poem was indeed "peculiarly fitted to illustrate" Williams's anxious argument for a civilian war poetry, a pure "heart" which could express the "pity" of war—Owen's famous dictum—with no more false sentiment and no more indirection than a soldier poet would bring to the subject.

As peculiarly fitted for illustration as the poem was, however, it could not transcend the intensities of the debates in which it was held up as an example, and it could not render the disputations over literary representation of war any less likely or necessary. "In Distrust of Merits" is no less didactic, no less overtly ideological, and no less a marked product of its own time than the patriotic poetry Millay wrote under the guidance of the Writer's War Board. Later readers, in fact, may well be more struck by what Moore's and Millay's war poems have in common than by the ways in which they diverge. Contemporary critics of Moore's work tend to dismiss "In Distrust" if they do not ignore it entirely; one of Moore's most sympathetic readers, Bonnie Costello, expresses her distaste in terms which might be used to define Millay's war work: the poem's conventional pronouncements "show too much the pressure of news."[10] This "too much," the offhand signal of shared evaluative norms, adumbrates for Costello's contemporary audience—one composed, presumably, largely of literary critics—a familiar set of postwar aesthetic values. A good poem—that is, a poem unpressured, or pressured just enough—will be cleanly universal and timeless, where "In Distrust" bears too obviously the imprints of an immediate historical and cultural context; it will be neutral, where "In Distrust" is polemical; it will enact poetically, where "In Distrust" spouts off oratorically; it will address an elite readership, where "In Distrust" invites the same kind of attention as the *Saturday Evening Post*.

But in another context—that, for instance, of forums organized during the Second World War to express and to prove American high culture's commitment to the war effort—a poem may be more likely to be judged uncompelling if it lacks ideological commitment and fails to appeal to a mass audience, if it shows too little "the pressure of news."[11] We can sense the force of the strong demand during the war years for a literature which was overtly topical and politically engaged in Elizabeth Bishop's anxious words to the publisher of her first book of poems in 1945: "The fact that none of these poems deal directly with the war . . . will, I am afraid, leave me open to reproach."[12] Open to reproach then and now, either for its overt political commitment or for its lack of it, an obvious reminder of shifting standards of literary value and the ideological construction of poetry, the war poem of the forties often proves embarrassing. It is no surprise that Moore herself, in 1961, dismissed "In Distrust of Merits": "It is sincere but I wouldn't call it a poem. . . . As form, what has it? It is just a protest."[13]

During the forties, critics and anthologists like Williams and Eberhart encouraged their readers to understand Moore's poem as a firm resolution of wartime aesthetic crises. But we need not look later than the war period itself for evidence of "pressure" on and in the poem. Moore's private work-sheets point to her own engagement with "In Distrust" as a field of dynamic and unresolved tensions, not to the poem's status as the one calm eye at the core of a storm. And Randall Jarrell's public critique of "In Distrust of Merits" declares a crisis of representation which, Jarrell argues, Moore's poem not only fails to assuage but also exacerbates. For both Moore and Jarrell, the conflicts of writing and reading about war provoked by "In Distrust" arise, particularly, around notions of sexual difference; for both of them, not least of the pressures the poem showed too much was the pressure of gender.

II

By Moore's own account, "In Distrust" did indeed originate out of the "pressure of the news": she once said that her incentive for writing the poem was a newspaper photograph of a dead soldier.[14] That image remains in the finished poem, flickering at its center: "O / quiet form upon the dust, I cannot / look and yet I must."[15] Like another battlefield image in another Moore war poem, "Keeping Their World Large"—"That forest of white crosses! My eyes won't close to it"—the scene of the dead soldier both repels and compels attention (*CP* 145). These images draw the eye with hypnotic, irrational power and hold it there, trapped in its helpless, frightened gaze at the nightmare facts the pictures represent. Unlike other cultural artifacts represented in dozens of other Moore poems, these printed battle scenes elicit a strong resistance or an inability to attend to them carefully; the eyes try unsuccessfully to close, the face to swerve away.[16] In general, as Costello notes, Moore "is always observing while she is making observations."[17] But this poem seems to represent the process by which its author works as a constant struggle against evasion: here, it suggests, I am always fighting against the desire *not* to observe while I make measured assertions about the meaning of warfare.

Moore's letters and workbooks in the years preceding the publication of "In Distrust of Merits" reveal the force of that struggle.[18] Several developing ideas about war laid the groundwork for the poem's arguments. In 1939, Moore wrote to her brother, who was a naval chaplain on a ship in the Atlantic, that in the process of reading Reinhold Niebuhr she had come to the conclusion that "intolerance is at work in us all *in all* countries,— that we ourselves 'persecute' Jews and Negroes & submit to wrongful tyranny. Or at least feel 'superior' in sundry ways."[19] Earlier, in her conversation notebook in June of 1938, Moore had observed: "In ancient times, people (barbarous) razed cities and murdered the innocent. One is faint before it and these people are with us now. One does not feel detached by one's horror — even if they are not of our country. They are *we*. They are of our kind."[20] This sense of war as a self-reflexive fight against personal intolerance shows up in the ending, borrowed from a sermon, of an earlier poem, "The Labors of Hercules," in which one of the almost impossible labors is "to convince snake-charming controversialists / that one keeps on knowing . . . that the German is not a Hun" (*CP*, 53). It appears, too, in the "promise we make to the fighting" in "In Distrust of Merits": "We'll / never hate black, white, red, yellow, Jew, / Gentile, Untouchable."

We can trace in the notebooks the ongoing development of an idea of "inwardness" which becomes the central principle of "In Distrust"; much of this idea, as Laurence Stapleton has determined, derives from and re-vises conversations Moore had with her mother. On 23 July 1942, she notes down in her poetry notebook the crucial phrase, "There never was a war that was not inward"; in the same entry, the climactic end of the poem is worked out: "I inwardly did nothing. / O Iscariot-like crime! / Beauty is everlast-ing / and dust is for a time"; and an entry on 22 March 1943 explains the crime more explicitly than it is defined in the published version of the poem: "Black white red yellow mixed Jew gentile and untouchable — they're begging and I inwardly did nothing. . . . " On a later page, in an undated entry, Moore further explores the value of inward action and inwardness, setting down the following: "Outstanding. Futile word. No indwelling."[21] This comment may be read as a partial gloss on the title of the poem: "merits," which are to be distrusted, are external, static signs of what a culture determines to be "outstanding"; successful "indwelling" struggle, in contrast, secret, dynamic, and uncategorizable, cannot be signified in fixed medals or badges. Outward wars, in which men urged to be outstand-ing try to outstand each other, are caused, so the major argument of "In Distrust" goes, by a failure of each of us to exercise a continual inward struggle against the imperious and aggressive aspects of our own selves. Only by vigilantly practicing a form of inward warfare can we avoid ex-ternal catastrophe.[22] "It is a violence from within that protects us from a violence without": Moore quotes Stevens approvingly in a wartime review of his work she entitled "There Is a War That Never Ends," adding that Stevens "and the soldier are one."[23] If Stevens was a soldier poet, associated not with the "peignoir" but with combat gear, Moore might be one too, fighting in an ongoing conflict which was no less vital for being intellectual, spiritual, and figurative rather than bodily and literal.

Steven's concept of inward wars offers the imagination and its supreme fictions alone as a way of understanding and solving world conflict. Moore's offers more orthodox Christian consolations as well, incorporating ideas of Christian spiritual warfare, as expressed in such conversation notes as the following: "It is not that we fear to have the body struck down from the soul that we hate war, but because man is not complete unless he has the power of peace in his soul" (14 August 1937); "The one good of war is that it brings people in their helplessness to pray. It keeps people from being satisfied with an indolent peace . . . " (2 November 1935).[24] In "In Distrust," Moore will develop this idea of inward spiritual warfare in language which openly declares its ties to the authoritative rhetoric of Scripture ("O / Star of David, star of Bethlehem,").

But for every self-confident aphorism which generates a legitimate meaning for the war or imposes some kind of order upon it, we can locate others in the notebooks which demonstrate Moore's hesitation and anxiety.[25] Moore can speak emphatically about the symbolic war within, but when she turns to the particular manifestations of the war without — its battles and body counts, the daily events which filled the pages of the newspapers — her voice assumes a deferent and nervous tone. "I:?" reads a mysterious note in the conversation diary for August 1937, continuing, "was the nobly fought for nothing. If they aren't killed they come back maimed or ["considerably weakened" is crossed out here] and disabled prospectively." In September 1940, "May those who fight in squadrons have a vision. We are sending them to their death." In the spring of 1943, amid several pages of scattered notes for the poem, the war within is first figured positively — "how does one resist invasion / but by resistance inwardly?" — but then loses its power, becoming a trap or a cage: "Prisoner of inwardness."[26]

A nearby passage exemplifies the difficulty of Moore's struggle to authorize her own voice as representative and universal: "(may humbly but with — confidence (may as one.) Say OUR."[27] Moore, I believe, is exploring here, amid considerable self-doubt, the possibility of assuming the voice of a collective "we," a pronoun which would function, as John Ellis has suggested it does in wartime film documentaries, to articulate a nation, or the whole world, "as both actor and observer, enunciator and addressee."[28] "Say OUR," she orders herself — or recalls someone else's order — after speaking in muted parentheses. But for Moore, who is well aware of distinctions which cannot be entirely erased between herself as American civilian and the young male soldiers whose anonymous forms filled news photographs, the urge to "say our" may be a difficult, dangerous, and even reprehensible ambition. The line which begins, in a preliminary version of "In Distrust of Merits," "*we* are fighting fighting fighting" becomes, in the chastened final version, "they are fighting fighting fighting."[29] "All too literally," goes the epigraph of her "Keeping Their World Large," "their flesh and their spirit are our shield" (*CP,* 145). The "our" here is limited, indebted pronoun. The poet who is a civilian and a woman can write of figurative war with aplomb, but of all too literal warfare she is wary and unsure, and she feels herself all too literally to be speaking passively, helplessly. In the context of the war, can a protected American woman "say our"?

"The difficulty is one of language," Moore wrote in one of her reading notebooks, copying a passage from Alexander G. Clifford's *Conquest of North Africa, 1940–1943*. "The facts of modern warfare are outside normal human experience and strictly speaking only the facts of normal human experience are reproductive in words." She went on to write out sections of a review of the book by Colonel Joseph I. Greene: "He shows the highly observant [sic] details that have a special meaning in war: Few things have a smaller comparative secondhand value than battle."[30] These passages, taken together, allow us to differentiate between two kinds of difficulty which, Moore felt, complicated and troubled the representations of war in her poems. One is a universal difficulty inherent in all language, which shapes its vocabulary, according to Clifford's argument, out of an everyday human consensus; it therefore can never "reproduce" modern warfare because modern warfare, by definition, renders the "known" world abnormal and unknowable, completely resistant to mimesis. The other is a difficulty specific to the protected American, who can bring to her war poem no telling details derived from her own experience and who can only describe battle "secondhand," in inadequate comparisons. If the difficulty is one of language, it is also one of gender, of age, of all other specific cultural, psychological, and biographical contexts which determine the exact place of a civilian woman writer.

Women, of course, acted and suffered in the most direct ways in the war of 1939–1945, many American women among them. At the same time, many American men, even many American soldiers, experienced the war no more directly than their average female counterparts.[31] Several well-known soldier poets of the Second World War – Randall Jarrell and Richard Eberhart, for instance – did not actively participate in combat. In the end, though, Jarrell's actual distance from the "front lines" matters very little, while Moore's matters very much. Jarrell and Eberhart were "men as men," speaking for men, and therefore had imaginative right to the voice of the soldier, the terrain of the "front." Cynthia Enloe has described how "society's bastion of male identity," the military, "believes it must categorize women as peripheral, as serving safely at the 'rear' on the 'home front.' Women *as women* must be denied access to 'the front,' to combat. . . . The military has to constantly redefine 'the front' and 'combat' as wherever 'women' are not."[32] Marianne Moore, writing from where women were, wrote inevitably about war within a situation of lack and absence, within a sense of herself as peripheral rather than central. Williams, Eberhart, and Auden might tout "In Distrust" as a universal war poem, but it, and all Moore's writing on war, show marked evidence of the specific stresses which result when an American woman writes a Second World War poem *as a woman*. I want to look closely at the poem, not in order to defend its "merits" but to proceed in affectionate distrust, examining the ideological forces which buffetted it from outside and shaped it from within.

III

In "In Distrust of Merits," the tension between moral self-confidence on the one hand and felt or feared inadequacy on the other is pronounced and strenuous. Suspicious of herself but awed and moved by Allied soldiers, speaking in a voice half subdued and half, like the gyroscope's fall in another Moore poem, "trued by regnant certainty" (*CP*, 134), Moore engages in what Geoffrey Hartman has called her "dialogue of one, an ironic crossfire of statement that continually denies and reasserts the possibility of a selfless assertion of the self":[33]

> Strengthened to live, strengthened to die for
>   medals and positioned victories?
> They're fighting, fighting, fighting the blind
>   man who thinks he sees —
> who cannot see that the enslaver is
> enslaved; the hater, harmed. O shining O
>   firm star, O tumultuous
>   ocean lashed till small things go
>   as they will, the mountainous
>   wave makes us who look, know
>
> depth. Lost at sea before they fought! O
>   star of David, star of Bethlehem,
> O black imperial lion
>   of the Lord — emblem
> of a risen world — be joined at last, be
> joined. There is hate's crown beneath which all is
>   death; there's love's without which none
>   is king; the blessed deeds bless
>   the halo. As contagion
>   of sickness makes sickness,

> contagion of trust can make trust. They're
>   fighting in the deserts and caves, one by
> one, in battalions and squadrons;
>   they're fighting that I
> may yet recover from the disease, My
> Self; some have it lightly; some will die. "Man's
>   wolf to man" and we devour
>   ourselves. The enemy could not
>   have made a greater breach in our
>   defenses. . . .

Who is the subject of the first two lines of the poem? An "I"? A "she" or a "he"? An "us"? ("Say our.") Only after some uncertainty are we brought to a decisive distance from the active third-person subjects of the poem. The strengthened ones turn out to be "they" alone, the "they" of the professional army in distant places, surveyed as if by telescopic lens, "lost at sea before they fought," or "fighting in deserts and caves, one by / one, in battalions and squadrons," "Some / in snow, some on crags, some in quicksands."

These stylized summations of the various landscapes of combat are the poem's most "literal" moments. Moore strives here to represent the actual conditions of warfare in the Second World War but does so in the language of the newsreel. More often, however, the war represented in "In Distrust" is entirely disengaged from history, becoming a figurative or archetypal war of wars rather than a specific historical event labeled "Second" and "World." The enemy has both a relatively literal status and a more predominantly allegorical one within this poem. For instance, the "blind / man who thinks he sees — / who cannot see that the enslaver is / enslaved" and who later is described as "small dust of the earth / that walks so arrogantly" may refer to Hitler or Mussolini or Hirohito, or to any men who live in and fight for a nation-state whose dominant ideologies are "fascist" or "militarist," but he also stands for an archetypal Everyman and Everywoman. Very much like Orgoglio or Archimago in *The Faerie Queene*, he represents an interior spiritual danger, Blindness and Aggression and Pride, while the speaking "I" and the "we" that the "I" addresses stand, like Spenserian allegorical heroes, for the self which must struggle with its own inward enemies in order to achieve and maintain a patient self-knowledge. Moore's narrative of spiritual trial recounts an essential, universal struggle within all selves for perfection of the soul, and it accounts for warfare as both a part of that struggle and the result of its lapses: "I must / fight till I have conquered in myself what / causes war." The poem's world is a world of inward emblems in which all selves have the opportunity to choose, and continually work toward, the archetypal qualities they wish to incorporate and embody: "There is hate's crown beneath which all is / death; there's love's without which none / is king; the blessed deeds bless / the halo."

At several crucial points in "In Distrust of Merits," however, the speaker's certainty dissolves, and the voice becomes mistrustful of itself and its surroundings. The formless force of the tidal wave which, apparently, has sunk a military ship near the start of the poem "makes us who look, know / depth," Moore writes—but whether the depth "we" discover is a new spiritual dimension of ourselves or simply the terrifying flux of an uncontrolled and uncontrollable world ("O tumultuous / ocean lashed till small things go / as they will") we cannot be sure. At other moments, the speaker's voice more openly undermines itself. Earlier I quoted one of the poem's most determined liberal morals: "We'll / never hate black, white, red, yellow, Jew / Gentile, Untouchable." In context, this message, set off by quotation marks, retains its power, but the speaker severely undercuts her own authority:

> We
> vow, we make this promise
> to the fighting—it's a promise—"We'll
>   never hate black, white, red, yellow, Jew,
> Gentile, Untouchable." We are
>   not competent to
> make our vows. With set jaw they are fighting,
> fighting, fighting . . .

Here the promise is first subtly questioned in Moore's use of the pat phrase, "it's a promise," a colloquial form of emphasis which, like "without a doubt" or "really," subverts its own assurances by being overly reassuring. A more open interrogation follows, as the speaker's voice entirely discredits itself and its collective audience: "we are not competent." Inability to vow, in a world which demands strong action and speech, constitutes a desperate handicap; moreover, this vision of the self as unstable and ineffective is inimical to the vision of the ultimately capable self which must be implicit in the "spiritual warfare" narrative in other parts of "In Distrust of Merits." Although the self in any "inward warfare" plot must have serious weaknesses to combat, it must as well have access to competence— an access in serious question here.

Other moments of high moral certitude in the poem are followed by other instances of equally radical self-distrust. The assertion that "there never was a war that was / not inward" ends "I must / fight till I have conquered in myself what / causes war, *but I would not believe it*" (my italics). Moore asserts her moral and then withdraws, anxiously, painfully. The next lines — "I inwardly did nothing. / O Iscariot-like crime!" — suggest a reading which aligns itself with the tradition of spiritual warfare narrative: "I would not believe it," in the past imperfect tense, can be read as a statement of self-castigation following a confession of a crime which can only now be atoned for ("I would not believe it then"). But it can also be interpreted as "I refuse to believe it now — I continue to be recalcitrant"; here, again, doubt and resistance threaten to replace confidence and preclude continuation of the redemptive spiritual warfare plot. "They are fighting," Moore writes in stanza five, " . . . that / hearts may feel and not be numb. / It cures me; or am I what / I can't believe in?" The extremity of personal doubt here, which goes beyond the requisite moral self-suspicion of the spiritual warrior, calls into question the veracity and validity of the war poem which interrupts.

Or am I what I can't believe in? This kind of self-questioning may certainly be an attempt to put into literary practice the kind of humility Moore advocates in "In Distrust of Merits." But it also seems to be a response to her distance from the violence of which she is attempting to make sense. She writes,

> If these great patient
> dyings — all these agonies
>   and wound-bearings and bloodshed —
> can teach us how to live, these
>   dyings were not wasted.

If they can teach us, she says, not "they can teach us." The affirmations of meaning and purgations of suffering here are conditional, fragile, subject to denial from within the poem itself — a poem with "distrust" in its very title. We can feel the language straining in this passage, with its overblown "wound-bearings," an abstract euphemism atypical of Moore's style. When Americans safe on our own continent attempt to write about war, Cary Nelson has argued, "our own physical security makes the language flat and unconvincing. We have no historical ground for sympathetic identification; such words will not come to us."[34] In "In Distrust of Merits," Moore calls for such words to come to her, but she also, at key points, dramatizes her own failure to find them.

The poem is interspersed throughout with ringing assertions of piety, such as its ending: "Beauty is everlasting / and dust is for a time." But this confident declaration is prefaced immediately by three notably self-suspicious lines: "I would not believe it. / I inwardly did nothing, / O

Iscariot-like crime!" Even this last apostrophe, the figure Jonathan Culler calls the most "pretentious and mystificatory in the lyric," cannot entirely dispel the demystifying force of the comparison of the self to Judas.[35] Before simply dismissing as sentimental the final couplet, which reverts suddenly to traditional accentual meter instead of the pure syllabic verse Moore usually preferred, we would do well to remember Jane Tompkins' warnings about the politics of those labels when they are applied to nineteenth-century popular novels, works whose function is "heuristic and didactic rather than mimetic" and which "do not attempt to transcribe in detail a parabola of events as they 'actually happen' in society": "What the word *sentimental* really means in this context is that the arena of human action . . . has been defined not as the world, but as the human soul. [Such works develop] a theory of power that stipulates that all true action is not material, but spiritual."[36] In "In Distrust," however, the spiritual cannot, except momentarily, supersede other theories of power; definitions of "the arena of human action" waver. In a variety of ways familiar to readers of modern poetry, the poem undercuts its own apparent anti-ironic commitment to the war well fought. Part of its force for its contemporary audience surely lay in its expression and partial resolution of conflicts between Christian typology and modernist suspicion.

The poem's shaky mixture of tempered heroic assertion and strong ironic contradiction guaranteed its great appeal for forties critics and anthologists, who, with the harsh memory inscribed in the antiwar soldier poetry of the last war behind them, faced the difficult task of reshaping a canon which could at once convey the war's brutality and represent its necessity, recognize both its justice and its meaninglessness. "In Distrust," which could be read as either an inconclusive or a conclusive "just war" plot, as patriotic or antipatriotic, satisfied their needs precisely.[37] But Moore's most appreciative respondents tended to mute the conflicts in the poem in their public reviews, subsuming its self-fragmentations into a clear, single, reassuring spiritual quest narrative. Her own later description of the writing of the poem shares these critics' emphasis on authenticity of feeling—"It is sincere. . . . Emotion overpowered me"—but her account emphasizes, much more than theirs, the presence of contradictory drives and inward disjunctions: "Haphazard; as form, what has it? It is just a protest—disjointed, exclamatory. Emotion overpowered me. First this thought and then that."[38] For Moore, as she looks back on "In Distrust," the major effect of the poem is that of breaks and outbreaks, a sense of unresolvable conflict.

IV

In a 1945 issue of *Partisan Review,* shortly after "In Distrust" was published in the volume *Nevertheless* to wide acclaim, Randall Jarrell undertook a dissenting opinion. His review's opening lines manage at once to acknowledge and gently mock Moore's privileged position in the new canon of war poetry. Its closing lines, too, bow to Moore with respect and a trace of condescension. In between, Jarrell constructs an impassioned argument, one which forces its readers to grapple with some of the most powerful and intractable cruxes in the interpretation of modern war literature. At the same time, like the male reviewers with whom he argues over Marianne Moore, he systematically misreads her war poems, ignoring their dynamic processes, overemphasizing the static quality of images within them, and presenting Moore as exaggeratedly stolid and simpleminded.

From the start, his review of "In Distrust' introduces Moore's entire poetic project as a fussy exercise in formal tedium. Moore operates with "static particulars . . . at the farthest level of abstraction from the automatically dynamic generalizations of the child or animal"; her lines merely fix "specimens on their slides"; her rhymes produce the opposite of the kinesthesia of common English rhyme; "everything combines to make the poem's structure . . . a state rather than a process" ("PWP," 127–28). Jarrell's emphasis, however disapproving, on the visual aspects of Moore's poetics, on the defamiliarizing textuality of her poetry, provides a useful corrective to readings such as Williams' or Eberhart's which treat the war poems as direct utterances from the heart. But his insistence on the sterile calm of the poems precludes assessment of the kind of tension I have been describing in "In Distrust."

This initial suppression of the agonistic elements in Moore's entire body of work prepares Jarrell for a more particular erasure of struggle in her war poems. With a fierce wit which suggests that there is a great deal at stake for him in this argument, Jarrell objects to Moore's *Nevertheless* on several grounds. She writes too much about inanimate or nonhuman characters (referring to the poem "Nevertheless," a parable which involves a regenerating strawberry, he asks dryly, "how can anything bad happen to a plant?" ["PWP," 128]). Her fables concerning things and animals evade the complexities of the human, of consciousness, and they evade hard facts of social and political relationship; what's more, they evade the presence of inexplicable violence in the world, as Jarrell illustrates with a fable of his own:

The way of the little jerboa on the sands — at once True, Beautiful, and Good — she understands; but . . . the little larvae feeding on the still-living caterpillar their mother has paralyzed for them? We are surprised to find Nature, in Miss Moore's poll of it, so strongly in favor of Morality. . . . To us, as we look skyward to the bombers, . . . [she] calls *Culture and morals and Nature still have truth, seek shelter there,* and this true; but we forget it beside the cultured, moral, and natural corpse. . . . At Maidanek the mice had holes, but a million and half people had none. ("PWP," 128)

It is worth noting the obvious, in the face of Jarrell's impressive appeal to the hard facts about real nature (as opposed to what he defines as Moore's weak, selective version): this is an unresolvable ideological quarrel. The slim grape tendril in Moore's "Nevertheless," which represents how "the weak overcomes its / menace" (*CP,* 126), bears no less and no more essential and immediate a relation to human experience than Jarrell's caterpillar unable to escape from the sinister larvae-mother, or than the mice at Maidanek who, serving a different rhetorical purpose, *can* escape into a hole. Whether or not a reader can return to "Nevertheless" after hearing Jarrell's case out and find the poem of equal value will depend on — among other things — the reader's assumptions about the efficacy or the futility of individual human action, beliefs about what constitutes the self, and, not least, predilections for or aversions to traditional forms of Christian verse such as allegory or parable.

For at issue here are hard questions not only about what human nature "is," but also about how it should be represented. Should war and can war be depicted by emblems, fables, moral allegories? Or is it incomparable, unrepeatable, irreducible, like each individual person lost to torture, or to genocide, or to battle, or lost for no reason those who survive will ever know? Should this war, and can it, be depicted at all, or does Maidanek, as Elie Wiesel has argued, negate "all literature as it negates all theories and doctrines?"[39]

In the presence of the silent object of the corpse, Jarrell argues, linguistic and symbolic orders collapse; the adjectives "cultured" and "moral" cannot adhere in any meaningful way to a dead and tortured body that remains "natural" only in the most literal sense we have for that word. Moore has made a similar point, in her reading notes: "The difficulty is one of language." Yet Jarrell's corpse, whose presence temporarily erases the memory of all reassuring symbolic order, is itself a symbolic construction, placed "beside" us through a linguistic act, within a cultural artifact which is also a moral argument about the truth of nature. Jarrell does not elaborate on Maidanek's possible undoing of all poetry, his own as well as Moore's. He seeks, provisionally, to affirm a notion of aesthetic decorum: that the war demands literary treatment which, though always overtly acknowledging language's difficulties, still represents itself as relatively literal, relatively rooted in the external world of actual Second World War experience, in contrast to Moore's obviously stylized and overtly figurative fables of inward warfare.

Underlying this aesthetic dictum is an implicit political aim. War is, in a word which crops up repeatedly in Jarrell's reviews of this period, "incommensurable"; its dark realities resist easy simile or analogy; to openly imagine metaphors for what happens to people in war — unless those metaphors refer eventually, emphatically, back to the suffering body — is, therefore, to participate directly in war's perpetuation by falsifying the truth. Jarrell implies that traditional literary techniques such as allegory or fable, which fail to satisfy strict standards of verisimilitude in their depiction of human pain and violence, carry with them a proclivity for, if not a necessary relationship to, warmongering, since they do not show sufficiently the pressure of the literal. For Moore, as for Jarrell, a good war poem is an antiwar poem, but Moore assumes, with a strong tradition of Christian rhetoric and ethics behind her, that parables have special power, not only to comfort sufferers but to change behavior. Writing, however ironically, within that tradition, she is primarily interested in war's relation to the states of the cultured, moral, and supernatural *soul*. And indeed there is no clear evidence that Moore's work impressed her wide audience with the wrongness of war any less or any more than Jarrell's, or that the difficulty which was one of language was any less or more apparent to her readers.

Although gender seems to be of no concern in this discussion of the relation between literary technique and political values, Jarrell makes use of conventional formulations of sexual difference throughout as he shapes his terms and rhetorical strategies. He employs, for instance, an underlying image of an oblivious woman, "timid" and "private spirited" in her patterned garden while war rages around her, a figure whose presence pervades literature about women's roles in wartime.[40] In order to carry off this reading of Moore, which demands that she be inert and impervious, Jarrell ignores moments in the war poems, such as those I have traced in "In Distrust," which suggest a troubled, conscious relation to her distance from direct conflict and suffering. In "In Distrust of Merits," for instance, he ignores most notably the moment of resistance to looking at the photograph of the dead soldier ("I cannot / look and yet I must"), a point at which Moore's poem itself enacts the fear which precedes the moment of forgetting all ethical consolations "beside the cultured, moral, and natural corpse."[41] Moore seems to demonstrate here, in fact, the very qualities Jarrell praises in Ernie Pyle, the legendary Second World War correspondent, who, Jarrell says, "knew to what degree experience . . . is 'seeing only faintly and not wanting to see at all.'"[42]

What distinguishes Pyle's sight and aversion to sight from Moore's is, of course, his eyewitness status; he, unlike Moore, has the right to claim the words from Whitman which Jarrell cites often: "I was the man, I suffered, I was there."[43] Jarrell's eulogy for Pyle, written a few months before his review of *Nevertheless*, provides an instructive contrast to his treatment of Moore's war poetry. Paradoxically, Pyle's open recognition of his inability to "see" or know war in some primary, unmediated way functions, for Jarrell, only to reconfirm the credibility of his testimony, to further authenticate his eye. In the Pyle piece, Jarrell shifts repeatedly, sometimes even instantaneously, between tributes to two contradictory principles, both part of the aesthetic which Second World War poets inherit from modernism: that authentic experience, felt beyond cliché, is vital ground for the work of art, and yet that all language is nonreferential and all experience is inseparable from already determined cultural and linguistic systems.[44] Or as Gertrude Stein writes in her *Wars I have Seen*, a predictably playful critique of referentiality in war literature, "However near a war is it is not very near. Perhaps if one were a boy it would be different, but I do not think so."[45] Praising Ernie Pyle, Jarrell negotiates with great care between mythologizing and demythologizing the idea of transparent representation of direct experience. He begins a statement about Pyle, "What he cared about was the facts," but then adds "But facts are only facts as we see them, as we feel them"; he places "real and imaginary" in close proximity, following his phrase "the real war" with "that is, the people in it, all those private wars the imaginary sum of which is the public war" ("EP," 112). Still, despite the repeated, cautious moments in Jarrell's treatment of Pyle which emphasize the mediated and mediating aspects of Pyle's writing, it is Pyle's *nearness* to war — the nearness of what Stein calls "boys," a close masculine contact with literal combat — which finally, for Jarrell, renders his work of value.[46]

When Jarrell turns in his review of Moore to an angry, eloquent reading of "In Distrust of Merits," he once again identifies his own stance, with some careful qualification, as less mediated in relation to the real war than Moore's. Here again he partially misreads Moore, and does so eloquently, imaginatively, in the service of a landmark modern protest against war. Objecting to Moore's representation of warfare as heroic ("fighting," he writes, "is the major theme of the poem"), he chides her for her failure to understand and remember that [soldiers] are heroes in the sense that the chimney sweeps, the factory children in the blue books, were heroes: routine loss in the routine business of the world . . . that most of the people in a war never fight for even a minute—though they bear for years and die forever. They do not fight, but only starve, only suffer, only die: the sum of all this passive misery is the great activity, War. . . . Who is "taught to live" by cruelty, suffering, stupidity, and that occupational disease of soldiers, death? The moral equivalent of war! Peace, our peace, is the moral equivalent of war. ("PWP," 129)

The sudden interpolation of the famous title phrase of William James's "Moral Equivalent of War" points to implicit concerns which are at the heart of Jarrell's argument with "In Distrust of Merits." Jarrell rightly finds traces of James's influence on Moore's representations of war. Those echoes are complex enough to merit a detailed study in themselves, but what matter here are simpler questions: How does Jarrell read James's essay, and why does he cite it with such sardonic emphasis here?

James functions as a representative of several political and aesthetic evils with which Jarrell wishes to connect Moore's war work and from which he wishes to strongly differentiate his own. He objects, as I have said, to any process of image making which attempts to find overt "equivalences" for war. He objects as strenuously to an idea of human nature which emphasizes what James calls "energies and hardihoods," or human intentionality, at the expense of ignoring or minimizing human dependence, powerlessness, and suffering. James proposes systems for developing, as a substitute for war, "toughness without callousness, authority with as little criminal cruelty as possible";[47] Jarrell would argue that there is no toughness without callousness, no authority without cruelty, and that most people are the subservient victims of both. Finally, and most radically, Jarrell objects to James's and Moore's constructions of the idea of masculinity in their arguments for positive and peaceful modes of combat. James's main argument—that military conflict will persist until antimilitarists find an adequate substitute (the "moral equivalent") for the central function of war, "preserving manliness of type"—is energized by a pervasive anxiety about constitutions of masculinity, a fear that martial experience alone can make a man.[48] Linking Moore's images of inward war to James's manly equivalents, Jarrell articulates his difference from both writers: where they see only the exemplary heroism of stalwart foot soldiers, he sees pernicious myths of manhood, and his critique of "In Distrust" gathers force and turns to outrage as he seeks to undo what he perceives as deadly codes of masculine style.

Jarrell's challenge to social constructions of masculinity points to a paradox. Bonnie Costello describes his review as upholding "in clear sexual categories" a brutal "male vision of amoral nature"; but Sara Ruddick, the feminist pacifist, has cited Jarrell as a "'maternal' man" whose war work exemplifies the kind of "preservative love" generally taught to and practiced by women.[49] What aspects of Jarrell's work allow these two widely divergent interpretations? Why does Jarrell simultaneously *refer* to rigid distinctions of sexual difference, in his reading of Moore as a woman in a garden and in his own claim to the authority of a soldier, and *refuse* to accept conventional scripts for masculine soldierly behavior? How can he write at once like a man and like a woman, and at the same time criticize Moore both for writing like a woman (timidly, privately, obliviously) and writing like a man (glorifying intention, and Truth, and cause, and war)?

Ways of "writing like a woman" or "writing like a man," as J. Hillis Miller has suggested, often "tend to change places or values in the moment of being defined and enacted": "The male thinks he is writing constatively, but in fact his affirmations are groundless performatives. The woman writer knows there is no truth, no rhythm but the drumbeat of death, but this means that her broken, hesitant rhythms are in resonance with the truth that there is no truth."[50] In Jarrell's argument with Moore, it is the woman poet who is placed in the position of the "constative," "masculine" writer who actually produces "groundless performatives," and it is the male critic who places himself in the role of the feminine writer who knows no rhythm but the drumbeat of death. But if Moore and Jarrell do exchange "places and values" of masculinity and femininity, they do not do so randomly or idiosyncratically. Their shifting reenactments and redefinitions of selfhood have strong political motives and implications within the specific social context of the American Second World War home front.

"Dividing the protector from the protected, defender from defended, is the linchpin of masculinist as well as military ideology," Ruddick writes.[51] Both Moore's distrustful text and Jarrell's even more distrustful review of that text seem to circle around the same linchpin, at once overdetermined by structures of sexual difference in wartime and evasive of those structures. Evasive and exaggerated in opposite directions: where Moore, the female civilian, attempts to imagine a world where everyone could be a soldier, Jarrell, the male soldier, attempts to imagine a world where everyone could be an innocent.[52] We might say that Moore writes "In Distrust of Merits" as if to argue that everyone can act "like a man," and Jarrell his review as if to argue that everyone is passive "as a woman."

The tradition of ironic soldier poetry which has dominated critical discussion of war poems for most of this century encourages sensitive readings of Jarrell's project but not of Moore's. Another look at Jarrell's critique of Moore's images of war may help to explain this situation. "Most of the people in a war," Jarrell writes, "never fight for even a minute — though they bear for years and die forever" ("PWP," 129). "Bear for years" is a peculiar phrase — oddly abstract in the midst of a relatively concretizing series of passive verbs — and an apt one. The word "bear," though it does not necessarily signify a feminine condition (people of both genders bear burdens and bear pain), carries nonetheless a strong association with the female body. In our culture generally, as Margaret Homans has argued in her *Bearing the Word*, "the literal is associated with the feminine, the more highly valued figurative . . . with the masculine," and this "complex and troubling tradition" originates in a simple actuality: "that women bear children and men do not."[53] Jarrell's "bear" invokes an image of childbirth to redescribe war not just because childbearing is linked to pain or because it is associated with submission to the brunt of things, but because it represents a prolonged encounter with unmitigated, unmediated fact. Childbirth, in Homans' words, is inherently a structure of literalization, in which "something becomes real that did not exist before — or that existed as a word, a theory, or a 'conception'" and by which "the relatively figurative becomes the relatively literal."[54] Throughout his career, but particularly in the early forties, Jarrell strove to define a poetics of war which could adequately recognize that warfare itself is a "structure of literalization": "what in peace struggles below consciousness in the mind of an economist," he writes, "in war wipes out a division" ("EP," 113).

Valuing a war poetry which is rooted, as nearly as possible, in the concrete, the material, the "borne," Jarrell writes within a strong tradition of masculine antiwar protest in which the soldier becomes responsible for transcribing the literal. The more "literal" the representation of men's experience within this tradition of soldier poetry, the more feminized those men will appear, as their function shifts from "fighting" to "bearing." Thus, in Owen's classic, inaugural war poem "Dulce et Decorum Est," the depiction of gas warfare, which represents itself as starkly realistic in opposition to earlier clichés, begins with a description of the men as bent "like hags."[55] "Dulce" was originally titled "To A Certain Poetess" and written in angry response to Jessie Pope's metaphors of war as, among other things, football. In the tradition of soldier poetry established by twentieth-century literary criticism, men come to occupy the place of the literal *as well as women*, or to displace women entirely; the figurative, in turn, is associated especially with the feminine, with the abstract allegories and stylized banalities of "certain poetesses." And in this case, the text's commitment to "literal" representation, its firm alliance with an authority of male experience, makes it *especially* highly valued and qualifies it for inclusion in the ranks of canonical war poetry.[56]

I do not want to deny the importance, the potential efficacy, or the polemical brilliance of the appeal to literal experience in the modern tradition of war literature.[57] Nor do I want to celebrate allegory per se. What I wish to emphasize is this: when experience is privileged or even required as an aesthetic, political, and moral criterion for the proper war poem, the attendant dangers are several. Overvaluation of the concrete and particular may prevent recognition of war poems which have overtly given expression to significant ideological principles and conflicts — even when those poems, like Moore's "In Distrust," clearly speak in abstract terms which large audiences of contemporaries found compelling.[58] Where obviously stylized and didactic literary techniques such as Moore's allegory signal from the start both their literariness and their political and philosophical stakes, a more narrative war poem which refers more openly to real experience may not recognize the limits of what constitutes the "real" within it.[59] In American forties war poetry, for instance, "experience of war" was generally taken to comprehend the experience of the soldier but not generally, during the war itself, the experience of the Holocaust victim, the Japanese American in an internment camp, or a woman working in a defense plant. Finally, reading war poetry as we have so often been taught to read it — as a register of difference between and within men over the affairs of manhood, in which, say, the euphemisms of generals are broken open by the literalizing story of the soldier — we may once again be complicit in rendering women (who have also, always, had our say about war) silent and invisible and static, suppressing our own dynamic and complex relations to systems of war making. Rereading "In Distrust" in the context of a different set of texts — the body of highly abstract works by women which enact inward wars rooted in spiritual traditions, from Emily Dickinson's Civil War meditations to two of the most influential poems of the Second World War, Edith Sitwell's "Still Falls the Rain" and H.D.'s *Trilogy* — we may begin to understand not only the potential power of figurative models of representation and protest in war literature, but also how thoroughly and insistently Moore writes her war poems "like a woman."

V

In his *Complete Poems*, Jarrell's "Eighth Air Force" appears as the first poem of a section called "Bombers," a classic collection of soldier poems of the modern ironic type. Beginning with a representation of a tangible scene of a soldier's encampment—what tune the drunk sergeant whistles, what ordinary card games three soldiers play between missions—"Eighth Air Force" shifts quickly back and forth from literal narrative to meditation, till its representational mode is replaced entirely by a lyric soliloquy spoken by Pilate at Christ's trial, or, more accurately, by a voice which sounds partly Pilate-like.

The poem is almost obsessively concerned not just with humanity but with masculinity—the speaker explicitly identifies himself as "a man, I," and the word "man" occurs, with heavy stress, at the end of over a third of the poem's lines and repeatedly within them. It therefore seems a culmination of and a self-reflexive commentary on the androcentric traditions of war poetry and war making. "Eighth Air Force" is, we might say, a poem about how a man looks at other men, and how he struggles to come to terms with what "manhood" means for himself in a culture at war. Yet the poem's first turn away from literal description and toward the abstract question of manhood, accomplished through an allusion to Plautus, suggests a more pressing intertextual relation to an influential contemporary text by a woman. "'Man's wolf to man,'" Moore quotes Plautus's words in "In Distrust", "and we devour / ourselves." Jarrell writes: "shall I say that man / Is not as men have said: a wolf to man?"[60]

Other connections between the two texts suggest that despite Jarrell's distaste for "In Distrust" in his review, the power of the poem was not so easily dismissed.[61] The struggle with the meaning of manhood in "Eighth Air Force" may be read as energized not by the fellow soldier's sight of real men but by the fellow poet's reading of a civilian woman's work. Jarrell's poem, in a number of ways, deliberately retraverses Moore's terrain. Both poets, for instance, employ the device of representing the soldier as Christ (a strategy used by patriotic and antiwar poets alike throughout this century); both poems focus inward, on the dilemma of the observer of the crucifixion. When placed within the context of the American literary culture which lauded Moore's Second World War poetry, Jarrell's portrayal of the Pilate-like observer, which might otherwise seem a meditation on enduring, universal questions about guilt, justice, and forgiveness, can now be understood as a specific, topical revision of Moore's influential representation of the self as Iscariot-like.[62] His soldiers, half innocents and half murderers, bear, too, a direct revisionary relation to Moore's heroic, patient fighters.

Although Moore's uses of Plautus and New Testament narrative appear at first to be far more dogmatic than Jarrell's, in the context of "In Distrust" they are undercut as dramatically. It seems to me likely that whether Jarrell consciously recognized it or not, he found a model for the self-questioning, "disjointed, exclamatory" voice of "Eighth Air Force," one of the most significant "soldier poems" to come out of the Second World War, in the searching voice of "In Distrust of Merits." Jarrell comes to sound most like Moore in a poem which, more than any other of his war works, acknowledges that no poetic text can say with unequivocal, literal meaning, "I was the man, I suffered, I was there," and that all poetic representation must also take place, in part, from the position of Pilate, the implicated observer who says, "Behold the man!" If we are to better understand the relation of suffering to observing, "there" to "not there," front to sidelines in twentieth-century war and twentieth-century war poetry, present-day critics and anthologists must recognize that the discourse of war consists not just of "what men have said" but also of what women like Marianne Moore have written.

Coda: It Must Be the Hand of a Man

"Bad, already existing, stories are a waste of time even for polemical purposes," David Bromwich has written in a response to a version of this account of Moore and Jarrell.

I am not familiar with the critics who classified Wilfred Owen as a "masculine" poet . . . but they were obviously poor readers and poor observers of character. A better-informed cliché about Owen used to say that of all the World War I poets, he was possessed of the most "feminine" sensibility: this gave a depth to his sympathies, though it had earlier been a vice to be reformed. Neither of these judgments comes close to a truth about his poetry. . . . Randall Jarrell was a fine appreciator of Marianne Moore's poetry. But as a reviewer of "In Distrust of Merits," he appears to have suffered a rare lapse into commonplace, and he invoked versions of both war-poet clichés: male-particular-actual suffering versus female-general-abstract sympathy. These pairs, which can be altered at pleasure depending on the culprit, have never helped anyone to read a poem.[63]

These comments have prompted me to clarify the assumptions on which my work is based; I want to pause for a moment here to specify them further.

The first is that sometimes bad stories are worth the telling. Some of the baddest, meanest stories in town are stories of gender, and particularly stories of gender and war; men and women can die for them. We might say that gender itself *is* bad story. Around us an ever-present narrative of sexual difference tells our stories for us; when we stop to examine them, they inevitably seem too limited, too obvious, too boring, too banal. Jarrell's uneasy slip into such a mean story may be for him a rare lapse, but the "commonplace" into which he falls is common indeed in his American culture and in mine. What Bromwich defines as Jarrell nodding, I prefer to analyze as ideology speaking, and I consider that ideology—for its scope and its force—worth studying.

"These pairs," the inevitable couples of gender dualism, "never," Bromwich argues, "have helped anyone to read a poem." It is my starting contention that they have hindered some women from writing poems, and that they have constrained and shaped some of the war poems women like Moore have written. It is also my contention that those pairs have in fact very often "helped" modern readers read American war poems, determining some of—and sometimes, as in certain moments on the forties home front, a great deal of—their (or our) terms of response.

"Poetry" and "identity" have a way of exceeding and transgressing the commonplaces of gender. Take, for example, the case of Wilfred Owen, who as the classic, founding modern "antiwar" poet appears at several points in the chapters following. Aspects of Owen's poems and of Owen's posthumously constructed authorial persona may be associated with the feminine or the masculine. The poems, or the rehearsal of Owen's biography, can admit both gendering readings. Both, I would argue, are "true," and neither "poor," in this sense: both have been put forward and have carried cultural weight, as "Owen" the phenomenon has been constituted and reconstituted in the arenas of contention where war poetry has been and continues to be defined. In readings of Owen's work, the pair "masculine/feminine" wavers and alters, but rarely, if ever, "at pleasure"; there are, for instance, political stakes in emphasizing his sensitivity over his valor, or vice versa.

Tracking something like the feminine in Owen's writing, we might look toward his deployment of and association with terms like "passivity" and "pity"; or toward his passionate interest in a female precursor, Elizabeth Barrett Browning, whose late antiwar poems may have influenced his own; or to the moments in which voice in his poems opposes itself to patriarchs.[64] My argument in this book pays some but relatively little attention to such feminizing readings of Owen and the other male writers considered here. It does so for this reason: I want to highlight an equally salient and, in the period I am primarily studying, more frequent account of the poet, the version which stresses his authority as a male combatant, a man among men. Reading, for instance, the following summary from Seamus Heaney's recent review of a new Owen biography, I am struck especially by the way in which the issue of effeminacy is subsumed under, and Owen recuperated by, a rhetoric of masculinity. Heaney describes Owen as "a man who not only survived shell-shock," and (it now appears more emphatically) the experience of his own "cowardice" in the trenches, but who then returned to the Front in 1918 without illusions and with a steady nerve. It is not, after all, our tested admiration of Owen's art that makes us wince at Yeats's reference to "sucked sugar stick" or Siegfried Sassoon's initial patronizing remarks about "little Owen." What is slighted by these characterizations is our respect for a man honourably and extremely involved in the Keatsian process of developing from an intelligence into a soul.[65]

The gendered valences here are complex to the end; Keatsian sensitivity is not necessarily proof of "manhood." But the honor and extremity granted to Wilfred Owen suggest a tested potency. Later in the review, Heaney stresses that Owen's gradual understanding of his sexuality allowed him to "draw a parallel between the initiated, outsiderish condition of . . . [homosexual men] and the plight of frontline soldiers"; the consequence of this realization, Heaney suggests, is a new poetic tone, "saddened, resolute and authoritative" (382). These adjectives gesture implicitly toward the conventionally manly. "Sucked sugar stick" gives way to (albeit mournful) phallic power.

Modern war poems, as Jarrell has shown, often offer moments which undermine notions of unified masculinity. In them we can read inscriptions of male anxiety, of men's protests against militarized manhood, of men's doubts and incapabilities, of erotic bonds between men which exceed the permissible fraternal connections, of differences between classes of men, ranks of men, nations of men. The problem for feminists thinking about gender and the war poem, as I see it, is how to recognize these dynamics without minimizing the modern "war poetry" canon's function as a stronghold without and against women.

There is a poem by Wallace Stevens which seems to me a quintessential product of and comment upon that stronghold. Its title is "Life on a Battleship." The battleship is named *The Masculine*; on its deck a captain meditates upon questions of power and interpretation pertinent to men. On the one hand the poem represents *The Masculine* as the site of schemes of violent, total domination. On the other hand it replaces the grand Masculine, "much magnified," with a more mocking, lyric, and nuanced image of the phallogocentric:

> But if
> It is the absolute why must it be
> This immemorial grandiose, why not
> A cockle-shell, a trivial emblem great
> With its final force, a thing invincible
> In more than phrase? There's the true masculine,
> The spirit's ring and seal, the naked heart.[66]

Cockiness gives way here to the echoing spell of the cockleshell, a different way of writing the male body in the world.[67] If this image is an emblem of desire for a "true" masculine, it is also the sign of a fault and a falseness in the very law of gender itself: "It implies a flaw in the battleship, a defeat / As of a make-believe."

These competing notions of The Masculine and the masculine, of gender excessive or gender collapsing, are both satirized in the poem. Stevens speaks them through the captain, who is explicitly identified early in the poem with a bad Marxism, and he disqualifies them further by representing a "splurging" natural world which resists in its multiplicity of parts the dominion of the battleship imagination. But by the end of the poem they seem as well to be synthesized, and the M/masculine is recuperated; all hands are subsumed under one which produces "rhapsodic strophes": "Our fate is our own. The hand, / It must be the hand of one, it must be the hand / Of a man."

The conventional modern canon of war poetry, the one put forward in anthologies, seems to me much like Stevens's battleship. It is rife with class conflict, and conflict *about* class conflict; its crew debates its situation with great complexity, generating alternative images of masculinity; but still it invests special meaning, and meaning-making power, in the male. More often than not, it declares or implies that the hand which steers its strophes must be the hand of a man.

Take, for instance, a moment at the founding of the modern "war poem." This bad story starts in 1919. The first published gathering of Owen's work was the group of seven poems printed in the fourth cycle of Edith Sitwell's magazine *Wheels* in November of that year, a year after his death.[68] Sitwell was part of the burgeoning experimental movement in modern poetry, a movement which included women; it was this period which saw the beginning of the development of a body of women's modernist poetry. Marianne Moore, H.D., Mina Loy, and Gertrude Stein were all engaged in writing the early works which laid the cornerstones for their careers. At the same time, the new concept of war poetry was coming into existence, and Sitwell was determined to be part of its definition. Because she had known Owen slightly through her brother Osbert, she was given initial control over the poems by Susan Owen, Wilfred Owen's mother, and authorized to edit and introduce the first collected works.

In June of the same year Sitwell wrote to Susan Owen that she had an offer by a man named Henderson to publish the volume: "He is a good publisher, but if the poems went to him, it would be necessary to get a man (say Siegfried Sassoon) to see to the business . . . as he needs a firm hand."[69] (It must be the hand of a man.) Sitwell then wrote to the famous soldier poet Sassoon, who arrived on her doorstep insisting that it would have been Owen's wish that he have total editorial control over the edition. In an apologetic letter to Mrs. Owen, Sitwell explained her decision to give the Owen manuscripts to Sassoon, a self-defeat she herself had initiated by her dependence on a man's firm hand: "In those circumstances I could do nothing but hand them over to him; though it has cost me more to relinquish them than I can tell you."[70] By 1937, in her lecture series on modern poetry at the University of London, Sitwell was presenting a slightly different story of the origin of the Owen edition, obscuring the power struggle between her and Sassoon while insisting on the credit due to her for the initial preservation and editing of the poems: "The poems were left in my care by my friend Mr. Siegfried Sassoon, who had to go to America and who eventually edited them, and it was I who disentangled from the highly complicated drafts, the words which I believed Owen wanted used."[71]

Sassoon's acknowledgement of Sitwell in his first edition of Owen's work confirms her account of her importance in the early editing process, but many later editions omit or bury mention of her connection to the poems. Credit to Sassoon as the preserver of the manuscripts is prominent in all later editions; Blunden, for example, writes in his 1931 preface that Owen's "friend Siegfried Sassoon revealed to lovers of poetry and the humanities how great a glory had departed" when Owen died, words which define Sassoon as a prophet or privileged apostle.[72]

My point is not to disparage Sassoon's competent and sensitive editorial project, nor to question the depth of his friendship with Owen or even the rightness of his sense of what Owen would have wanted done and by whom (though this remains uncertain; *Wheels* and Sitwell offered a modernist affiliation to which we know Owen was attracted in his final months).[73] What matters is that the critical apparatus of the Sassoon edition and its descendants reinforced and exaggerated the myths of male camaraderie in the poems themselves. Based on the premise that only soldiers can interpret for soldiers, the early Owen editions had strong influence on ideas in the Second World War period about what war was and who could write and respond best to it. The moment at which Sitwell "handed them over" to Sassoon is emblematic; we can locate in it the moment of exclusion of women from serious reading of the modern war poem, which meant, in turn, even more rigid exclusion from the ongoing process of answering and reinterpreting Owen's vision of war and writing.

This particular "bad story," this account of snatched (or, more accurately, relinquished) editorship fails to represent, of course, the full complexities of the situation of woman poets in the *forties*. Like Marianne

Moore, Sitwell was held up during the later war as a model war poet. Her passional meditation on the London air raids in 1940, "Still Falls the Rain," crops up in Second War discussions of war poetry with a frequency that rivals citations to Owen. Cecil Bowra was not expressing a singular opinion when he wrote that upon reading Sitwell's Second World War poems "even the old-fashioned must feel that she has now joined the great tradition of English poetry."[74] Here is an exact reversal of the story of Sitwell and Owen's manuscripts. The illegitimate Great War editor regains her legitimacy as Second War author and joins the canon of war literature, taking her place, at once compatriot and opposite to the figure of the soldier poet, among its numbers.

Unlike Moore, however, Sitwell "experienced war directly," in the form of the bombing of London. She was, therefore, an especially authoritative civilian writer, and somewhat more than civilian: more threatened, more proven. Sitwell's great iconic moment as aged civilian came when, as she read her poetry aloud to an audience in the Allied Forces' Churchill Club, the city around her was bombed. Moore had an equivalent moment, at a conference held in New Hampshire in 1943, but there the planes flying overhead which drowned out her lecture were American planes on drill.[75] There is both no difference and a very large difference between these two narratives of a woman's voice refusing to be silenced by the machines of total war.

Moore recognized that fact, and struggled with it in "In Distrust of Merits." Her poem might be read as a meditation on the imaginary American "battleship," on its guilt and on its power, and on why and how all hands on its deck must not be men's. Edna St. Vincent Millay, whose war work I turn to now, engaged in a less ruminative and more topical version of the same project; her Second World War poems are even more troubled by gender's worst stories.

2

Writing Propaganda "Like a Man"
Millay (and MacLeish)

I had been astonished and worried by the poetry she had been publishing during
the war, on a level of wartime journalism of which I had not imagined her capable.
I tried to explain it as partly due to the natural anxieties of Eugen [Millay's hus-
band, who was Dutch] when Holland was seized by Hitler, and I remembered
Henry James' description . . . of Mrs. Browning's "feverish obsession" with the
Italian Risorgimento. . . . I concluded that when women of genius got carried
away by a cause, this was the kind of thing that deplorably sometimes happened.
Edmund Wilson, on Edna St. Vincent Millay, 1952[1]

I

The kind of thing that sometimes happens happened often in forties
home-front culture. Even the measured Moore, as we have seen, found
herself "carried away" in the protests of "In Distrust"; but the bookstores
and airwaves were filled with women's poetic voices even more feverishly
caught up in, or firmly committed to, particular wartime causes. Some
readers deplored the phenomenon; others admired and encouraged it.
Alice Duer Miller's famous call for England's defense *The White Cliffs*
(1940), Ada Jackson's *Behold the Jew* (1943), Muriel Rukeyser's pamphlet
on the Pacific war *Wake Island* (1942), Kay Boyle's antifascist tribute to
her enlisted husband *American Citizen* (1944): each of these long poems
gained considerable popular approval.[2]

Women's openly propagandist poems gave voice to a political ardor less
personal, of course, than institutional. They came out of and fed into the
developing mechanisms for distribution and consumption of literature in
the name of the U.S. and Allied war effort, and their fevers can only be
charted in that context. But those charts cannot be simple. Home-front
networks of reception and of propaganda production were stubbornly com-
plex, as those who tried to monitor or coordinate them knew well. In

many literary circles, often in conflicted relation to the semiofficial (and themselves internally conflicted) "war book" industries, texts like the poems listed above met with disdain — sometimes with outrage — often expressed in intensely misogynist terms. None generated greater furor than Edna St. Vincent Millay's poems on the Nazi threat, especially her widely publicized verse radio drama written at the request of the Writer's War Board, *The Murder of Lidice.*

Millay was damned as war poet where, and almost to the exact extent that, Moore was lauded. Not everywhere, it should be noted first; *The Murder of Lidice* had its share of praise, and reached an audience undoubtedly broader than any readership of Moore's. But in epideictic literary discourse during the war the two women were frequently set up in polar opposition to each other in order to privilege Moore: Moore's agonistic meditation versus Millay's open antagonisms, Moore's effect of searching inwardness versus Millay's representation of Nazi danger from outside, Moore's impulses toward integration versus Millay's toward agitation, Moore's modern poem versus Millay's propaganda.[3] A version of this opposition still applies in literary discourse now. At present Moore's once famed "In Distrust" is seldom read; but Millay's equally famous memorial to Lidice, now almost never mentioned, is generally treated as if unreadable.

I aim to read it, not in order to prove its literary worth but in order to analyze the politics of gender in the verse play's reception and production. Broad ideological conflicts in home-front literary culture were fought out vehemently over *The Murder of Lidice* and Millay's earlier topical Second World War poems — battles over isolationism and intervention, the relation of poetry to propaganda, and, not least, the political implications of centering the war poem either in representation of civilians or in representation of combatants. In part, this chapter traces those debates, which in their moments of bald misogyny reveal much about the situation of any woman poet living in the United States, however different from Millay in style or stance, who sought to write about the war.

In larger part my analysis is not only contextual but more specifically (inter)textual, focusing on a struggle over gender "close to home" which accompanies *The Murder of Lidice*'s "public," international, conventionally political concerns. Female voice as it is figured in *The Murder of Lidice*, I argue, speaks three ways: to arouse the general American public; to appease the discrediting (self) critic; and also to bespeak its difference from the versions of civilian prophecy and admonitory or violated femininity put forward in earlier Second World War poetic propaganda, particularly in verse radio plays written by Millay's precursor Archibald MacLeish. In the end, the limits as well as the powers of that voice as

Millay constructed it are my subject here. Millay, I argue, authorizes her verse play finally by de-authorizing herself — that is, by defeminizing herself and appealing to a political authority implicitly defined as male.

II

Four months before the first production of Millay's dramatic poem, a Nazi radio broadcast had announced to the world the destruction of the Czech town of Lidice:

Since the inhabitants of this village have in the most uncompromising manner opposed the written laws through their activity, and have given support to the murderers of SS-Obergruppenführer Heydrich, the male adults have been shot, the women sent to a concentration camp, and the children placed in suitable educational institutions. The buildings have been razed to the ground and the name of the place has been erased from the records.[4]

In retaliation for the village's suspected shelter of underground leaders who had assassinated Reinhard Heydrich, 173 men and boys, we know now, were shot to death; 81 out of 104 children were gassed in Chelmno, Poland, and the few remaining children dispersed into German families or orphanages; 203 women were deported to the Ravensbruck concentration camp; 143 of those women survived to return to Lidice in 1945, for the first time hearing what had happened to the men and the children. The Nazis themselves carefully documented Lidice's eradication. Documentary footage of the town's destruction, filed under the heading "Instructive and Cultural Films," was intended to teach Nazi soldiers how to raze a village.[5] Except for this use, the town of Lidice was meant by the German government, as the Writer's War Board's foreword to the published version of Millay's play put it, to be "forever erased from the map and memory of the world."[6]

The Murder of Lidice is one of many urgent forms of cultural intervention through which people around the Allied and neutral world sought in the immediate aftermath of the Nazi radio announcement to reconstruct Lidice on the map and in the memory. Some were written texts (poems, editorials), some visual representations (such as Hans Jelinek's widely circulated series of woodcuts "The Story of Lidice"), and some were organized efforts leading to ceremonial commemorations (such as the activities of "Lidice Shall Live" committees, or the decisions by many towns worldwide, beginning with Stern Park Gardens, Illinois, two days after the news of the massacre, to change their names to Lidice).[7] Within the United States and England, *The Murder of Lidice* was one of the most influential of these gestures. The December 1942 issue of the British *Theatre*

Arts announced, "Enthusiasm for the radio as a medium for drama was quickened recently through the broadcast of Edna St. Vincent Millay's dramatic poem, *The Murder of Lidice*. The interest centred not only in the poem itself and its performance but in the emotional impact on the audience, reported over and over again."[8]

Testimony such as this suggests that the verse play served its purpose as the War Board and Millay had envisioned it. It memorialized Lidice, and it conveyed broad outlines and implications of what had happened there, for a large radio audience in the United States and other allied nations. In addition, it helped accomplish a necessary and pragmatic war aim: persuading Americans that the Germans constituted as serious a threat as the Japanese. In the fall of 1942, around the time of *Murder of Lidice*'s first airing, one public opinion poll showed that "a third of the people interviewed were willing to accept a separate peace with Germany"; *Murder of Lidice* was a part of efforts encouraged by the governmental Office of War Information (OWI) to combat those sentiments.[9] Responses like that of *Theatre Arts* indicate that the Writer's War Board and the OWI's Domestic Radio Bureau were likely to have judged the drama's performance a success, and the War Board asserts that success in its conclusion to the preface of the drama's printed version: "We are proud of our little part in this" (vi).

Along with this wave of enthusiam and interest came antagonistic responses, some virulently so, from some men of letters who treated the play not as successful propaganda but as failed war literature. Millay had already provoked angry and scornful reactions with her earlier war-related work and public statements. Her negative reviews had ranged in tone from *Vice Versa*'s sly, laconic headline for a piece reporting her announcement that she would give up special editions of her work for the duration — "Edna Makes the Supreme Sacrifice" — to the openly misogynist revulsion of *Time*'s review of *Make Bright the Arrows*: "Millay lashes out at the warring world like a lady octopus caught in a whirlpool."[10] After the heavily publicized release of *The Murder of Lidice* these attacks, and the general controversy over the evaluation of Millay's wartime work, intensified. "In definitely bad patriotic versification (usually written by civilians)," Oscar Williams wrote in the preface to his 1945 anthology *The War Poets*, ". . . both writer and reader, while deeply concerned over ravaged towns in Belgium and Czechoslovakia, are particularly callous about what the neighbor's boy is going through on the beachhead. . . . A sham patriotism cloaks the real statement which amounts to either acquiescence or rejoicing in the fact of war."[11] The reference to Millay was implicit but distinct. Frederik Prokosch, in a prose statement for the Williams collection, was equally circumspect and equally severe: "It is mostly the 'poets' safely beyond the reach of the bombers who specialize in rhetoric about Lidice."[12]

Millay, it is important to note, struggled herself with internalized versions of the judgments critics of the time applied against her. She had been writing occasional "political poems" for many years. (Never before, though, was it with the blessing of the U.S. government; in fact, her FBI file, begun in 1923, was very bulky, filled with references to her suspiciously left-wing metaphors. Much of her earlier directly war-related work, until the late thirties, was strongly pacifist.)[13] Nonetheless, like her literary detractors, she saw literature as permanent, universal, socially useless in any immediately definable way, playful and fictive. So from the start of her poetic engagement with the Second World War, she consciously defined her propaganda poems as ephemera. Calling them "not poems, posters" and marking their deviation from her other work through visual differences in printing, she strove to emphasize their local and temporary quality. She wanted her book of interventionist war poems *Make Bright the Arrows*, for instance, to be subtitled "1940 Notebook," in order to show that it was a "book of impassioned propaganda rather than a book of verse," and she planned for it to be printed as a pamphlet rather than a bound volume. She was angered when it was "issued in the same format as her other books as if it had meant to be on a plane with them" instead of being immediately "read and thrown away."[14]

"And then the reviewers had said about it that Miss Millay had used to be a conscientious artist, but had now apparently given up the effort— dreadful things like that!"[15] This is Edmund Wilson, mimicking Edna Millay in one of his several accounts of his disturbing reunion with Millay in 1948, not long before her death. Wilson continues,

When she began talking about whether it wasn't better that the public should get Catullus even in an imperfect translation, Gene [Millay's husband] pulled her up—said, Remember that was what you thought about your war poetry: that it was important to rouse the country. I thought this was very shrewd of him and showed excellent judgment. . . . I thought of the passage in Proust where he tells how Bergotte believed, when his talent was failing, and he wrote something he knew to be inferior, that it ought to be published because it was "useful." ("Visit," 290)

Millay's voice here is twice removed, mediated through the nervous reassurances of the husband and the harsh inner judgment of the literary critic who was her former lover. But her own conflicts over the relation of her overtly political "imperfect translations" are clear. They show up in the tense rhetoric of a revealing letter she wrote defending *Make Bright the Arrows* to an old Vassar friend:

if this book had really been the book you took it to be . . . would I have done the insolent and cruel thing which it would have been to send to you and Mac a book of poems trying to incite this country to send American boys into foreign lands to fight? . . . You say that if I had three grown boys as you have I would feel differently about it. There is little doubt probably that I should *feel* differently about it, but I do not for a moment believe that I should *think* differently about it. And though I have no sons to be caught in this war, if we are caught in it, I have one thing to give in the service of my country,— my reputation as a poet. How many more books of propaganda poetry containing as much bad verse as this one does, that reputation can withstand without falling under the weight of it and without becoming irretrievably lost, I do not know — probably not more than one. But I have enlisted for the duration. . . . Thus, you see, the dearest thing in life which I possess which might possibly be of help to my country has already gone over the top, in the hope that your sons need never go to war.[16]

Justifying herself as propagandist both in the guise of the sacrificing mother and in the guise of sacrificed soldier, Millay could assume the real authority of neither. The tone of this letter may be more overbearing than pleading, but its brazen claims do not mask its strain. The conflicts involved here were severe. Millay went so far as to try to attribute to them her "complete and handsome nervous breakdown" at the war's end. "For five years," she wrote to Wilson in 1946, "I had been writing nothing but propaganda. And I can tell you from my own experience, that there is nothing on this earth which can so much get on the nerves of a good poet, as the writing of bad poetry. Anyway, finally I cracked up under it. I was in the hospital a long time."[17]

When another middlebrow poet-propagandist, Stephen Vincent Benét, died suddenly and prematurely in 1943, many public eulogies emphasized the ruin of his health under the stress of his war work.[18] Millay's "crack-up," in contrast, met with little public acknowledgement, and none which linked it directly to the war. Although this difference in publicity stems primarily from the difference between (sudden) death and (delayed and mysterious) breakdown — the one conventionally calling for public mourning, the other conventionally retreating into private hiding — it also may be referred, I think, to gender difference. Benét's death could be fit into a familiar pattern: man giving life to serve his country. Millay's "nerves" were less easily subsumed into a narrative of the noble cause.

In the absence of a public narrative, Millay generated her own. We have already seen her trying out the roles of soldier and mother; she also claimed a third position, one more squarely and famously "hers." During her years of propaganda writing, she repeatedly employed a rhetoric of ephem-

eral and racking passion to describe and justify her efforts. The famous
pose of reckless sexuality which she developed in her early volumes of
poetry seems, in fact, an immediate precursor for her postures of urgent
political abandon in the Second World War. During the late thirties and
forties it is as if she had revised her early manifesto to read: "My candle
burns at both ends; / It will not last the night; / But ah! my foes and oh!
my friends, / It makes a socially useful, anti-fascist light."

Ironically, while Millay perceived these ephemeral "posters" as antitheti-
cal to her real, permanent poetic work, her talents were enlisted for the
Lidice production by the Writer's War Board precisely because aspects of
her poetic style could guarantee a text which would "last the night" and
could provide the appearance and sound of uplifting high art. The pro-
ducer's introduction to the verse play's script affirmed that "Miss Millay's
lines had the grandeur and pity which finds its way into the world's finest
poetry. . . . 'Lidice' was produced to bring out the terrible and tender
beauty of . . . this contemporary masterpiece."[19] The preface to the pub-
lished version of The Murder of Lidice by the War Board referred to the
author of the work as a "great poet" and used that high cultural word "im-
mortal" to describe the text's project: "that this immortalizing of Lidice
might be accomplished." Still, the preface continued with a line which,
while it invoked value-laden terms of praise, declared the text's intention
bluntly: "Many will think it is one of the finest pieces of true propaganda
to come out of the war" (vi).

In her wartime situation as poet-propagandist, Millay confronted a clas-
sic double bind. Faced on the one hand with Lidice and with what seemed
to her an absolute imperative to write as "finely" and "truly" as she could
against fascism, she was haunted on the other by the spectres of bad —
coarse and false — feminine propaganda: the Great War's warmongering
"certain poetess" Jessie Pope, the uncontrolled and monstrous "lady oc-
topus" she had already been called. Public fears of propaganda since the
First World War, still lingering, were often expressed in terms which fig-
uratively associated it with women, especially women's bodies, an associa-
tion potentially highly problematic for a woman writing in support of the
Second World War effort. Propaganda's paradigmatic subject was said to
be rape, its normative method a kind of prostitution (the selling of lan-
guage as if language were a dangerously seductive woman spy or a smirk-
ing, hard-selling poster girl), its style a feminine duplicity, its goal and
impulse femininity's too-complete surrender to passion, its effect on the
female reader hystericizing and on the male reader emasculating, and so
on.[20]

A woman propagandist might herself apply these terms to her own work; Millay, for instance, wrote self-abasingly to Wilson of her "years of Painstaking and Pious Prostitution of Poetry to Propaganda" ("Epilogue," xv). When others levelled them against her, though, she risked exposure to accusations other than literary, or to a breakdown of distinction between her body of work and her body. This is perhaps best illustrated by the *Partisan Review*'s vicious attack on Muriel Rukeyser in 1943 in a review charging her with abandoning naive "*New Masses* proletarianism" for gung ho "neo-Americanism." The serious political differences at stake in this debate were phrased repeatedly, obsessively, in terms of sexual difference and sexual transgression. The review described Rukeyser's patriotic poem *Wake Island* as an enterprise in which Rukeyser "wrapped herself in Old Glory, sang the Star Spangled Banner, and chased the Marines." It reproved her for crying "Yes like Molly Bloom to the working class" and then abandoning Marxism to work for the Office of War Information, admonishing her that "indiscriminate friendship makes for promiscuity." And it concluded with an image of Rukeyser waving a poster with her own interpretation of the Four Freedoms as "Free Verse, Free Love, Free Lunch, Free-for-all."[21]

Disagreements both with and within the OWI were expressed through debates about male artists and writers as well (in the controversy over whether Ben Shahn or Norman Rockwell should produce a poster, for instance, or in arguments over MacLeish's governmental role). But women, particularly Rukeyser and Millay, came in for especially vehement, sexualized ridicule. The images of promiscuous transgression which attached specifically to the woman poet-propagandist were accompanied, too, by more general models of feminine lack, models which could apply to any woman poet — we have seen Moore, no deliberate propagandist, struggling with them — but which were mobilized with special vengeance against Millay. It was in attack on Millay that Oscar Williams wrote the lines quoted earlier, damning sentimental verse written by and for ignorant American civilians "protected by a wall of living young flesh, much of which will be mangled." Similarly, Frederik Prokosch's case against the generic phenomenon of the Lidice poem, of which Millay's was the best-known example, argued that the poems' "very noticeable passion and indignation at a safe distance may be a form of compensation for the sense of guilt deriving from inaction, a luxuriant steam bath of second-hand and third-rate emotions."[22]

Millay came to the writing of *Murder of Lidice* anticipating these kinds of objections. In her culture they surfaced frequently, and critics of *Make Bright the Arrows* had ensured that she took them personally. Her verse play on Lidice was resolutely public, unabashedly propagandistic, and intended to transmit an external narrative as given (once by Nazi, now by

U.S. radio). It nonetheless shows traces of another private and internal struggle: the need to prove its author's firsthand, first-rate relation to her task. Aspects of the play may in fact be read as the implicit workings of a "coming to writing" plot, in Nancy Miller's sense of that phrase: "by coming to writing I include the psychological and symbolic gestures that authorize the writing subject."[23] To read these moments as articulations of "the problematics of authorship" is by no means to depoliticize *The Murder of Lidice*, for only by authorizing herself could Millay hope to achieve her conventionally and explicitly political ends.

III

Foremost among the self-legitimating strategies in *The Murder of Lidice* was a claim to the power of woman's prophecy. Millay's verse drama focuses primarily on one family in Lidice before and during the town's annihilation. The sixteen-year-old daughter of that family, Byeta, bears a distinct resemblance to the passionately vulnerable young woman with exposed nerve ends Millay had represented as herself in her earlier work; she comes to occupy the crucial place in the story. Two intertwined narratives center upon her. One is an interrupted marriage plot, a history of an engagement which concludes with the church destroyed, the bridegroom-to-be dying in the street, and Byeta, the bride-to-be, dead after stabbing herself to avoid rape by German soldiers. This account in general adheres to the facts of the massacre as Millay was given them (the razed church) or, in the absence of known details, to conventions of atrocity narrative (the rape scene).[24] The other plot emerges less predictably and more excessively; Byeta breaks loose from her function as doomed, unsuspecting fiancée and begins to speak the warning which aligns her voice with her author's own venture. Through her the text emphasizes moments and processes of anticipation, hallucination, premonition.

Byeta's father is portrayed as obtaining what news of the impending trouble he can get through the limited village network of communication:

> Heydrich the Hangman died today
> Of his wounds, the men in Kladno say . . .
>
> But heavy's the price we'll have to pay,
> If he's not found, I fear.
>
> How it will turn I could not learn . . .
> But my face is gray with fear.
>
> (12–13)

But his daughter seems to obtain her information about the coming danger through a susceptibility to prophetic sensations both naturally feminine and superhuman.

> "Byeta, why is your face so white? —
> Like the moon when stars are out?
> And why do you shine so fearful bright
> On all your edges and close about
> Like fox-fire seen in a swamp at night? —
> And why do your eyes in the pitch-dark
> Gleam and glow with a green spark
> Like glow-worms glimpsed in a forest dark?"
>
> . . . .
>
> "Hush, my father, and hark!
> Do you not hear him howl?
> I have heard him howl for many a day
> But that was many a mile away
> That I heard him howl before;
> But tonight he lopes through Lidice!
> Oh, do come away from the door! —
> For he snuffs your blood through the crack of the door!"
>
> "Byeta, oh, must you say such things?"
>
> "Nay, wife: I have heard, and know all.
> The wits of our daughter never did crawl
> With the wits of others — they ride on wings —
> They ride on terrible wings."
>
> (15, 16, 17)

Moments like these, in which this script abandons all effects of "realism" and begins to sound much like "The Highwayman," generate a kind of stock radio suspense; but they serve another purpose as well. An implicit comparison is established: as the family is warned by Byeta's shrill but accurate dread, so the American audience is duly warned by the premonitory voice of the author of *Murder of Lidice*. Millay's project is equated with, and justified by, the young girl's preternatural vision. One of the functions Byeta's hallucinations could be said to play here is, then, authorial defense — a way of warding off potential criticisms (including self-criticisms) of Millay's association with the Writer's War Board, even a means of denying that she was writing "propaganda." For Byeta's visions come unprompted by any immediate, external, human source of information; they come unmediated by any social institutions (she does not need the Office of War Information to tell her what will happen to her neighbors); they are instinctive, and they are exact. To the extent that Millay

could persuade her audience to believe in Byeta, she might then in turn per-
suade them that her own thoughts "rode on terrible wings," beyond the wits
of others; that the warning came from a "deep inside" rather than from some
governmental authority; and, most importantly, that the warning was true.

"Hysterical and vituperative," Millay's friend Arthur Davison Ficke had
written of her *Make Bright the Arrows*.[25] Millay, if she had lived till 1966,
might have countered with Stephen Spender's lines from a review of that
year: "One does not think of Clytemnestra as a *hysteric*; one thinks of
her as hysterical for very good reasons, against which she warns."[26] At
the center of *The Murder of Lidice*, Byeta articulates the very principle
of "for-very-good-reasons," of a hysteria which shows itself only under
the restraining orders of history. Of course, hysteria — by its (feminine)
nature marked as both inward and outpouring — threatens always, once
posited, to elude or exceed the bounds of history's good reason; it does
so in the rest of Spender's review, in which Sylvia Plath's warnings, unlike
the always sober Wilfred Owen's, only seem, Spender writes, to concern
history or any outward reference: in the end "her femininity is that her
hysteria comes completely out of herself" (26). Byeta's function, her "task,"
in *Murder of Lidice* is thus a delicate one. Her prophecies must all refer
to historical fact, but her prophetic power must be located somehow in,
not isolated from, her femininity. We might say, following Shoshana Fel-
man, that Byeta represents a woman warning neither "hysterically" nor
"not hysterically."[27]

My account of Byeta implies that she serves a particular need for the
woman who devised her, a need which results from a dilemma specific
to the woman writer. But the female prophet shows up not only in this
woman poet's work but in a number of its male-authored precursors, par-
ticularly in wartime radio verse plays by the founding father of that genre,
the leading poet-propagandist Archibald MacLeish. Indeed, the Cassan-
dra figure is a stock role in scripts of this type, texts — often written and
very often produced by men — which seek to encourage the war effort by
giving extended play not to the realism of "boys on the beachhead" but
to female voice and to the calling up of that image which signifies total
war: a hurt and ravaged woman's body.

"Patriarchal poetry is the same as Patriotic poetry," wrote Gertrude
Stein, "is the same as patriarchal poetry is the same."[28] The resemblance
between Millay's and MacLeish's female radio verse prophets does not
necessarily or entirely prove Stein's wry formulation right. Distinctions
will matter here. MacLeish's textual identification with a feminine, even
a hysterical, position in warfare — a strategy with definite sexist effects, but
very different nonetheless from the civilian Oscar Williams's wholehearted

identification with the fighting soldier — suggests that patriotic and patriarchal poetry in 1942 took a surprising variety of forms. And Millay's Byeta differs from her precursors in important ways, though in the end this patriotic poem too will require the authority of the patriarch.

IV

Archibald MacLeish's passionate pro-intervention stance, and his conviction that writers could play a key part in articulating war and peace aims, led to Roosevelt's establishment of the Office of Facts and Figures (OFF) in October 1941, with MacLeish at its head. In 1942, after protracted ideological struggles which Allan Winkler has detailed, the OFF was subsumed into the newly created Office of War Information, and MacLeish resigned to return to his post as Librarian of Congress. Throughout the war, he offered an influential and controversial model, certainly well-known to Millay, of the liberal poet turned public man and propagandist.

Shortly before this period of governmental involvement, in 1937, CBS radio produced MacLeish's *The Fall of the City* with a cast that included Orson Welles and Burgess Meredith. The play was anti-isolationist, and it offered a warning against fascist tendencies in the United States; it was spurred by MacLeish's sense that there were many Americans who, "left to themselves, would invent their conquerors and invite oppression as a way of life." MacLeish wrote in a retrospective preface to the script that it was "the first verse play written for radio."[29] (An earlier foreword, written in 1936, pays tribute to some British precursors but retains the claim to priority on the American radio scene.)[30] The opening lines of *The Fall of the City* may be read, then, as the (or among the) inaugural gestures of the subgenre Millay would take up five years later. Here the "verse play written for radio" announces itself, establishing its distinctive limits and potentials, its shaping forms.

Not surprisingly, it commences with strong emphasis on the technology upon which it depends, calling attention to the *radio* in the radio verse play. The opening speech is given to "The Voice of the Studio Director (orotund and professional)" who speaks a loose free verse calculated to simulate the usual nightly radio news show: "Ladies and gentlemen: / This broadcast comes to you from the city. / Listeners over the curving air have heard / From furthest-off frontiers of foreign hours—" (69). But this invocation of the powers of radio is almost immediately overtaken by a different kind of speech, one which seems to veer beyond all science and human machinery, calling attention to the *verse* in the radio verse play. Abandoning its initial "Voice of America" effect, the play begins to transmit the signals of a voice of hysteria. The orotund gives way to the oracular; the knowing anchorman (and his surrogate, the announcer broadcasting from on the scene) surrender to a different kind of vatic presence, more incoherent and more lyric. Hers is a distinctively Byeta-like voice. Using, as MacLeish put it, "the everywhere of radio as a stage and all of history as a time," *The Fall of the City* stages "the imagined city of Tenochtitlán where, before Cortez conquered it, the dead woman appeared at noon at the tomb's door to prophesy" ("Preface," 68):

> THE VOICE OF THE STUDIO DIRECTOR:
> For three days the world has watched this city—
> Not for the common occasions of brutal crime
> Or the usual violence of one sort or another
>
> . . . .
>
> No: for stranger and disturbing reasons—
>
> . . . .
>
> The terror that stands at the shoulder of our time
> Touches the cheek with this: the flesh winces.
> There have been other omens in other cities
> But never of this sort and never so credible.
> In a time like ours seemings and portents signify.
> Ours is a generation when dogs howl and the
> Skin crawls on the skull with its beast's foreboding
>
> . . . .
>
> We take you now to the great square of this city . . .
>
> . . . .
>
> (*The shuffle and hum of a vast patient crowd*
> *gradually rises: swells: fills the background*
>
> . . . .
>
> *A woman's voice comes over the silence of the*
> *crowd: it is a weak voice but penetrating: it*
> *speaks slowly and as though with difficulty.*)
>
> THE VOICE OF THE DEAD WOMAN:
> First the waters rose with no wind . . .
>
> . . . .
>
> Then the stones of the temple kindled
> Without flame or tinder of maize leaves . . .
>
> . . . .
>
> Then there were cries in the night haze:
> Words in a once-heard tongue: the air
> Rustling above us at dawn with herons.

Now it is I who must bring fear:
I who am four days dead: the tears
Still unshed for me — all of them: I
For whom a child still calls at nightfall

. . . .

Nevertheless I must speak painfully:
I am to stand here in the sun and speak:

(*There is a pause. Then her voice comes again
loud, mechanical, speaking as by rote.*)

The city of masterless men
Will take a master.
There will be shouting then:
Blood after!

(*The crowd stirs. Her voice goes on weak and slow
as before.*)

Do not ask what it means: I do not know:
Only sorrow and no hope for it

. . . .

THE VOICE OF THE ANNOUNCER:
                                        She is gone.
We know because the crowd is closing.

. . . .
We hear the releasing of held breath —
The weight shifting: the lifting of shoe leather.
The stillness is broken as surface of water is broken —
The sound circling from in outward.

                                        (69, 72–73)

The play ends, confirming the dead woman's prophecy, with the confused
city overtaken by a conqueror whom the people recognize is nothing but
a hollow suit of armor with its arm rising, but whom they worship as
their master nonetheless.[31]

What does the prophetess *mean*, and why will she keep showing up,
almost as if the genre "radio verse play" derived from or depended upon
her presence? First of all, in this allegory of dictatorship, she means trouble.
Disruptive as history and irrational as fascism (which for MacLeish is the
epitome of irrationalism), she constitutes a kind of Cumaean fifth column,
the sign that the city is already invaded by unreason long before the con-

queror arrives.[32] She also signifies, conversely, the innocent victim of fascism, though not because she will herself be hurt by it (posthumous, she is beyond its pale, disinterested). Her appearance signals a historical crisis so urgent it invades the most sheltered enclave, a young wife's grave, and a threat so terrible that even the shyest girl ghost's voice will be taken over by its mechanisms. When her own wavering but "penetrating" lines concerning dawn and herons transform into a forced prophecy-machine, she might be said, too, to signify the threat of fascism to lyric poetry, the spectre of a poetry no longer allowed its privacy but incapable of its own forceful or resistant public utterance.

If she represents lyric poetry, she also, more simply, represents womanhood. Her femininity carries an unspoken message: when the city of masterless men takes a master, women will suffer. The threat of fascism to women is reinforced more explicitly later in the play, when the corrupt, panicked priests of the city attempt to stave off the conquest by sacrificing a bare-breasted young girl.

The second antifascist verse radio play MacLeish produced one year later, *Air Raid*, makes the point even more clear. Inspired by Picasso's *Guernica*, the images of which, MacLeish wrote, "few living men or women — particularly women — cannot bring . . . to mind," the play depicts Guernica in the moments before the bombing as a town of threatened women:[33]

> In old days they watched along the borders:
> They called their warfare in the old days wars
> And fought with men and men who fought were killed:
>
> We call it peace and kill the women and children.
>
> Our women die in peace beneath the lintels of their doors.
> (101)

Most of *Air Raid* consists of Guernica's women's voices, gossiping, joking, chiding men in naively pacifist terms for "wasting their time on war . . . / Only boys and men like boys believe in it" (105). Finally persuaded by a "Voice of a Sergeant" that "this enemy kills women / meaning to kill them! / . . . I say it may be thought / *He makes his wars on women!*" (117), the women rush out under the planes shrieking "Show it our skirts in the street: it won't hurt us! / Show it our softness . . . our weakness / . . . our womanhood!" (122). As the play concludes they scream under the bombs, "It's us don't you see us!" (Here too the threat to women is a threat to lyric; one recurrent motif throughout the play, a woman's voice singing, metamorphoses in its final instance into the mechanical sign of the air raid: "A siren sounds in the distance like a hoarse parody of the Singing

Woman's voice, rising, shrieking, descending" [123].) Susan Gubar has argued that many Anglo-American women writers in the Second World War, identifying fascism and male domination, conceived of the war as a general "blitz on women."[34] MacLeish's verse radio plays of the late thirties emphasize violence against women in cities of men (violence not only by foreign bombers but by protofascist "priests" at home) to such an extent that they might almost, in the absence of the male author's signature, be mistaken for one of Gubar's examples.

Almost. Though for extended periods in these verse plays MacLeish writes propaganda "like a woman," he writes it, in the end, very much as and like a man. As a man, he seems in part to use the concept of the war on women in order to grasp and also mask the equally or even more threatening concept of civilian *men's* powerless vulnerability, their possible subjection to the same blitz or master in total war or in totalitarianism. (*Air Raid*, for instance, though it focuses throughout on women's speech, ends, interestingly, with the fading voices of male victims in the aftermath of the bombing.) At the same time, like a man — I use those words here not to gesture toward some essential sexual difference but to invoke exactly that culturally imposed sense in which the phrase is usually employed, as in the bucking up of boys — like a man, MacLeish in a variety of ways backs off from the principle of a femininity at once both vulnerable and powerful that he represents in the voices of his "Singing Woman" or his prophetess. Both *Air Raid* and *The Fall of the City* invoke that lyricized femininity only to subordinate it finally under the reassertion of a strongly masculine and historicized authority.[35]

In *Air Raid* this occurs when the women (whose voices up till then have been given so much play) need the sergeant to tell them what for; he brings them warning of the coming raid, "issued by men of experience, / Persons of sound sense" (117) which they fail to heed. Earlier, in a scene between two doomed lovers much like Millay's Byeta and her fiancé, MacLeish's girl tells her man:

> Tell me we're happy. No but say we are.
> How can I know we are unless you tell me?
> How can a woman know the world is good?
> Which is the world and which is her and which is
> Things she's known for sure that never happened?
> She can't tell. She can't and be a woman.
> Can a cupful of water tell you the taste of well-water?
>
> (110)

In this formulation, femininity means something profound, but its meaning inheres in a woman only to the extent that she can't herself figure it out; her essence is particular, but only insofar as she fails to distinguish it from everything else. "She can't tell. She can't and be a woman," and the prophetess's femininity, too, in *Fall of the City*, seems contingent upon and constituted by the wavering uncertainty, that inability to tell, with which she speaks her warning: "Do not ask me what it means: I do not know" (73).[36]

The male messenger who follows her does know; he enters to announce the conqueror's threat in militarily pragmatic and specific terms. In 1941, three years after the production of this play, MacLeish would attack the wartime tendency toward "prophecies of defeat, prophecies of negation, prophecies not of the things which men can do but of the things which men cannot do."[37] The creepy prophetess of *Fall of the City* can speak only in the terms MacLeish decried: "victims prophesying with the tongues of victims. . . . victims shameless in their cowardice as victims."[38] And so this interventionist play demands another more virile prophet, one who can remind his audience of "the things which men can do."

The voice of the messenger works somewhat in this way, the voice of the general who urges the crowd to fight even more so; but most of all it is the voice of the radio announcer (played in the original broadcast by Welles) which performs this function. In the 1936 forward to the play, MacLeish had encouraged his fellow poets to try the genre of the radio verse play precisely on the grounds that a central, exemplary, regulative (and, I would argue, implicitly male) consciousness was built unobtrusively into radio's very structure:

For years modern poets writing for the stage have felt the necessity of contriving some sort of chorus, some sort of commentator. There is no occasion here to go into the reasons: they are compelling enough. . . . The commentator is an integral part of radio technique. His presence is as natural as it is familiar. And his presence, without more, restores to the poet that obliquity, that perspective, that three-dimensional depth without which great poetic drama cannot exist. (xi)

The dead woman's prophecies have visceral force — "Blood after!" — but the male announcer alone can apply cogent analysis, exert the power of demystification, help shape morale. Only he recognizes that the conqueror's armor is empty. She gets some good lines, but he provides perspective, and *presence*, and the radio play's own version of the "male gaze": the male mike.

What the male announcer announces is history in the making. If, on the one hand, history invades and violates that isolated sphere of the lyric and domestic which was formerly as sealed as a woman's tomb, it also newly envigorates it. The history, or the war, in the radio verse play makes

poetry a man again: active and forceful and capable in the world of power-
ful men. It makes the verse play public speech, not private, and saves it
from the fate MacLeish lamented as the legacy of nineteenth-century poets
in his 1938 essay "Public Speech and Private Speech in Poetry." Arguing
there that in the nineteenth century poetry lost its public clout, MacLeish
asks why:

Were the poets emasculated? . . . Or was it the rise of the novel? Did the greater
muscularity and suppleness of prose move so easily in the world that the poets,
in pique or in despair, were forced to leave it? Or was it perhaps some change
in audience? Did the women's audience created by the Industrial Revolution among
the women of the middle classes . . . create in turn a poetry for women? Did the
middle-class women, exiles themselves . . . from a world in which, a generation
back, they had been workers, make companion exiles of the poets?[39]

In order to combat the rise of the novel, here figured as an erection, poetry,
MacLeish argued, needed to recover its ability and will to "move in the world,"
to refer to history and to effect it. The speaker-as-radio-announcer, send-
ing his immediate dispatches from points of crisis as it happens, guaran-
tees that power, and certifies that this verse play will be poetry for men.

In *The Fall of the City*, then, destabilizing feminine prophecy (in the
service of conveying the threat of total war and fascism) is subsumed finally
into stabilizing masculine perspective (in the service of encouraging a total
war effort against fascism). This pattern — some kind of textual leaning
toward the "feminine," some countermeans of asserting the morale of
manhood — will show up again in other male-authored texts I discuss in
later chapters. If its recurrence suggests persistent gender instabilities in
all constructions of (poetic) identities, it suggests too the specific torsions
to which modern warfare subjected gender roles and relations — the poten-
tial breakdown of distinction, for instance, between those marked as
defenseless and those marked as defenders. One could read the gendering
mechanisms in MacLeish's radio plays with an opposite emphasis from
mine here, starting with acknowledgement of their inscriptions of mascu-
line control and then proceeding to show how the feminine "victim's tongue"
undermines them. I have chosen the reverse strategy for two reasons: first,
because in general a home-front culture increasingly dominated by mili-
tary ideology demanded, reinforced, and read for myths of manhood, not
moments where masculinity was called into question; second, because the
notion of male authority over war and about war, despite any number
of local subversions by some male poets, had potentially strong exclu-
sionary and chilling effects for those American poets who most concern
me here, the women.

V

I cannot prove Millay knew *The Fall of the City* and *Air Raid* before writing her own radio verse play, but it seems to me extremely likely she knew them well. They had virtually established the still new and narrow genre she was attempting in *The Murder of Lidice*, and MacLeish in the early forties was a highly public figure. Her play contends, however, with models of gender, knowledge, and action in total war which were generally in the air, not just concentrated in MacLeish's slots of airtime.

Compare Millay's Byeta's love scene to that of the girl in *Air Raid*, the one who likened herself to well water. To her fiancé Karel's lovemaking and dreams of the future, Byeta replies, already discerning doom, with lines like "I am afraid," "one can never know," "Ah, yes, but we may not be here" (8–9). She is rendered ignorant enough to invite pathos. But at the same time she is rendered alert enough, expert enough at foreboding, to alter the scenario given MacLeish's Guernican women (in which femininity remains, up to the very moment of women's deaths in the war upon them, utterly in the dark) or to his prophetess (who, possessed by prophecy and history, has no self-possession).

Byeta differs from these models in this way: she is a woman who *can tell*. Her own self-possession, and *Murder of Lidice*'s investment in it, is signaled most clearly by her ultimate fate. Killing herself (by stabbing herself in the throat), *she* decides to silence and to fulfill her own prophecies, proving that she alone puts on her knowledge and her power, without direct violation. She cannot be raped.

Another trace of feminine production, and of the production of femininity, occurs in *The Murder of Lidice*. In addition to its central prophetic daughter, the play is full of images of mothers and maternity. The Lidice narrative proper begins, for instance, from a Czech mother's point of view, with a series of stanzas recounting her meditations as she watches out a window for her children, one of whom is Byeta. Almost the entire story of the town in the weeks before its destruction is told through mother-daughter dialogue: Byeta's hysteria, mother's reassurance. The representation of vulnerable maternity is, of course, a staple of war propaganda generally. In a final metaphor, however, Millay politicizes motherhood in a way which emphasizes not so much the mother's vulnerability as her efficacy.

MacLeish's female Guernica had cried out for male protection, for the vigilance and intervention of American fighting men. Millay's Lidice, in contrast, is represented in these lines near the play's conclusion not as woman but as child, with the world as its mother:

> The whole world holds in its arms today
> The murdered village of Lidice,
> Like the murdered body of a little child,
>
> . . . .
>
> Tortured, mangled, stained and defiled,
>
> . . . .
>
>
> And moans of vengeance frightful to hear
> From the throat of a whole world, reach his ear—
> The maniac killer who still runs wild—
>
> . . . .
>
>
> Sacred vengeance awful and dear,
> From the throat of a world that has been too near
> And seen too much, at last too much—
>
> . . . .
>
>
> And terrible sobs unreconciled.
>
> (31)

The image of the world as mourning mother is followed in the printed version of the text by a final image of America as negligent mother:

> Careless America, crooning a tune:
> Catch him! Catch him and stop him soon!
> Never let him come here!
>
> (31)

Two initial choices, then: the croon or the moan. If both kinds of maternal voice are powerless (the croon apathetic, the moan only pathetic), they also promise incipient power (the moaner insists on vengeance and protection, and the careless singer of lullabies is called upon to carry it out). This power is both conferred upon and demanded of the United States, in alliance with the "World," as if the nation were a watchful woman, or were a nation of watchful women.[40] (It is worth noting the limits of this feminist move: maternal/political power is given to American and "World" women only at the expense of infantilizing the adults of Lidice themselves.)

My point is not that male writers do not portray their own nations as mothers (for of course some do) but that for Millay, as an American woman on the home front, the stakes in that move were especially high. Maternal metaphor allowed her to represent women in active political engagement, and to represent active political engagement as womanly—to claim women's right, power, and responsibility to speak of and to act knowingly and protectively in the war effort. It allowed her to imply, in short, that the Second World War was not only a war on women but a war of women.

Certainly some male-authored U.S. propaganda of the period operated similarly, with the aim of mobilizing women specifically.[41] But what is striking about these final maternal images in Millay's work is how unmotivated by deliberate governmental plan they seem, how much more freighted with "private" anxiety and desire. When they are omitted, as they were in part in *The Murder of Lidice*'s radio production, the play's proclaimed political agenda remains undisrupted.

Two varying printed versions of *The Murder of Lidice* are extant. One, which I will call the script, was published in Margaret Cuthbert's *Adventures in Radio* in 1945, in the section of the book reprinting radio plays under the heading "Listen and Learn." The second, which I will call the text, was printed as a separate volume by Millay's regular publishing house in 1942. The Cuthbert version seems to be based on NBC files; Cuthbert herself worked for NBC, and the script here includes material specific to the actual radio production itself: Alexander Woolcott's introduction to the show, music cues, and so on.

In the text as it was printed by Harper & Brothers the aim and power of "sacred vengeance" is given to a moral mother.[42] But in the script as it was actually produced, the right to vengeance reverts to the one who claims it as His own. In place of the exhortation to "Careless America," the NBC version concludes with a version of battle hymn:

TELLER.   Ah, not in vain, ye sufferers
            Ye martyrs of the world, your pain!

CHORUS.   Woe to the offender

TELLER.   Not in vain
            The terror and the pain!

CHORUS.   Woe to the offender — woe to the offender.

TELLER.   Vengeance, mighty angel of the Lord
            Draws now his sword. (Orchestra: Finale . . .)
                                                    (254)

These lines may have been composed by Millay, or they may have been added by NBC staff in the course of the radio production. Perhaps "Careless America" was a later addition, motivated in the months between the radio play's production and the printing of the text by Millay's increasing exasperation at the American war effort; perhaps it was there from the start but vetoed by the radio producers on dramatic or political grounds. Whatever the motivation and origin of the radio script's alternative "battle hymn" ending, its effect is clear: the final word is given to a (male) Lord.

This closure effaces Millay's inscriptions of specifically feminine knowl-
edge and action, bringing to the fore another model of power which has,
in fact, been present in the verse play all along.

For Millay's script subsumes its "watchful mother" frame within a broader,
distinctively paternal, one. And if it offers its prophetess somewhat more
scope and power than MacLeish's, it too subordinates her telling to male
voice, in this case to the voice of a character called *The* Teller. The play
in both its versions begins with a device reminiscent of and perhaps bor-
rowed from Thomas Hardy's *Dynasts*, a preface in which extragalactic
spirits, a First Voice and a Second Voice, mourn the state of the planet
Earth. An unseen third presence provokes the First Voice's question, "Who
enters? Who are you?"

> (Second Voice)
> I know. It is the Teller of the Tale.
>
> (First Voice)
> Ask him: shall Wrong prevail? . . .
>
> (The Teller, slowly, thoughtfully)
> Wrong? Wrong? — Oh, no!
> No, — not for long . . .
>
> (Second Voice)
> Why came you here? . . .
>
> He comes to tell a story.
>
> (2)

At this point the "Teller"'s voice takes over for the duration of the play.
Millay planned it that way, and the gender markings for the Teller — "Ask
him" — are very clear. Unlike Hardy, who deliberately "abandon[ed] the
masculine pronoun in allusions to the First or Fundamental energy," Millay
grounds her governing voice in masculinity.[43] One male narrator is meant
to control the "tale," archaic as a scop, reassuring as a storytelling daddy,
up-to-date as Edward R. Murrow, authoritative as God.

For MacLeish, we might say, the "verse" in the verse play leans toward
private form — the lyric — and is mitigated by the matter-of-fact historicity
of the radio commentator; but for Millay, the "verse" in the verse play
leans toward communal form — the folkloric and epic — and is accentuated
by the intonations of the Teller. That accentuation is either heightened or
muted, depending upon which edition of Millay's play one consults.

This record makes clear that in the original radio production various
actors were responsible for the dialogue inside the Teller's tale. A woman,

for instance, spoke Byeta's prophecies. The framing device of the Teller's Voice was muted for the sake of dramatic realism. It is worth noting, however, that the only actor to whom the "Master of Ceremonies" of the radio program, Alexander Woolcott, referred by name in his introductory remarks is Paul Muni, who played the Teller. In the days after the broadcast, reviews of the production often mentioned Muni alone. In part, of course, this reflects nothing more than Paul Muni's reputation; but I would argue too that Muni's star status was reinforced in the Teller's part. Despite the distribution of lines across the cast, the verse play retained to some extent its effect of a single governing voice.

In the Harper & Brothers text, the one authorized as Millay's official version, that effect is even more pronounced. There the Teller's story is presented seamlessly as *his* tale or ballad. Byeta's hysteria speaks only through him; he quotes her, in quotation marks, but his "own words," unmarked, comprise the text. Over and above the play's crowd of voices, his controlling ballad-narrative establishes a unified authorial (and specifically poetic, as opposed to dramatic) agency.

In part, he seems to be there to assure a certain closure of the still uncertain war ("Ask him: shall Wrong prevail?" " . . . Oh, no! / No,— not for long." [2]); in this he differs strikingly from the equivalent spirits in Hardy's more pessimistic and ironic verse war epic *The Dynasts*, where the indifferent and inadvertent aspects of the Immanent Will are stressed. But the Teller also seems to be there as representive of another Immanent Will: not God's, or Right's, but Millay's. He certifies the text as a masterful, pretechnological, single-voiced production. Behind the Teller stands the Writer (not the Broadcaster): the Writer not as pulp scriptwriter, but as the "great poet" the Writer's War Board calls her. Radio producer Wynn Wright might betray, perhaps, a hint of ambivalence toward that effect of the "great" in his account of the play's staging:

The problem in producing "Lidice" was to keep the accent of greatness and yet put that quality into the dynamic flow and tension of spoken drama.
    Everyone who has tried to produce blank or rhymed verse knows the pitfalls. There is either the old stagy ranting, or the modern matter-of-factness, both of which obscure or exaggerate the poet's meaning. (237)

But in the printed text, that "accent of greatness," the signal of the presence of "verse," is allowed full pronunciation, its powers claimed in the Teller's capitalized name.

Muni's telling seems designed, therefore, to demonstrate the authority of Millay's writing. But it also, of course, calls that authority into question. The Teller's role suggests that intention and control are marked primarily in this play as masculine. "Depth," "obliquity," "three-dimensionality" remain even in this female-authored text the properties of male voice. A reading of the traces of a woman's "coming to writing" in *The Murder of Lidice* must stop short here: in order to speak most effectively for the women of Lidice, this American woman felt it necessary to speak first and last as a man.

The actual women of Lidice, 143 of whom survived the Ravensbruck concentration camp and returned to find the town destroyed and all the men and almost all the children dead, have spoken for themselves. Active first in efforts to find out what happened to the deported children, they went on to campaign for the rebuilding of the town and the establishment of its memorial rose garden (with its central statue of a grieving woman), and still later to participate, individually and in representative groups, in international conferences of women for peace and disarmament.[44] Compared with their own eloquent testimony and activism, Edna St. Vincent Millay's verse play now seems awkward, uncompelling, pretentiously "high-minded."[45] In the light of their testimony, however, the urgency of Millay's project in 1942 seems all the more apparent.[46]

Part Two

Women Poets and the Epistolary War Poem

3

The Masculine V-Letter

In the first place let us draw what all letter-writers instinctively draw, a sketch of the person to whom the letter is addressed. Without someone warm and breathing on the other side of the page, letters are worthless. But . . . those three dots mark a precipice, a gulf so deeply cut between us that for three years and more I have been sitting on my side of it wondering whether it is any use to try to speak across it.
Virginia Woolf, *Three Guineas*[1]

Yet the letters were not about me at all. Nothing I recognized about myself. The image of a woman seen from far away, blurred and indistinct. It could have been anyone he was talking about, the image of a woman seen through the telescopic sight of a gun, an image of someone seen from a great distance, her movements both clear and incomprehensible.
Deena Metzgar, *The Woman Who Slept with Men to Take the War Out of Them*[2]

I

During war, a woman receives a letter from a man—a letter "from the front." During war, a fighting man "writes home," or someone else must write home for him. These images are familiar now, and they were everywhere in United States in the early forties. Judging from the frequency with which the image of a woman with a letter in her hand, or of a man writing to mother or sweetheart, occurs in best-selling novels, radio broadcasts, films, and advertisements during the Second World War period in the United States alone, we may conclude that the letter scene stands as one of the most common "inherited myths" by which American women's and men's experience of war in the twentieth century is memorialized in American mass culture.[3]

While American Second War representations of total war such as MacLeish's *Air Raid* and Millay's *Lidice* de-emphasized the difference between combatants and noncombatants, another strain of war writing primarily by younger men, epitomized in the "recognition scene"[4] that centered on the soldier's letter home, strongly reinscribed that gap. This was particularly true in the United States. The scene of the war letter represents the American woman in a particularly tangential relation to the war "overseas," a war whose implications come to her only via someone else's writing. American women writers sometimes used that scene of correspondence to confront and explore — more overtly than Millay or Moore — their peripheral status in the tradition of war literature, still much in force, which tied the ability to write to direct experience, or at least the adequate simulation of direct experience, of combat. Could women recognize or represent themselves *as authors* in the world of letters within a plot that so stubbornly defined them as letter-readers, or even simply as letter-receivers? When Jane Cooper argues that the war silenced many women writers, herself among them, who felt their inability to participate "in any direct way, only through association," she concludes with the image of war correspondence: "The men's lives seemed more central than ours, almost more truthful. They had been shot down, or squirmed up the beaches. We had waited for their letters."[5]

Women poets' uses of epistolary forms will be the subject of my next two chapters. In this one I want to focus first on some male poets who put forward influential versions of the war-letter–writing scene, since it is to these poems that Brooks and Rukeyser respond. The epistolary war poem became a kind of fad in the early forties, in part, I argue, because it could both affirm an alliance between men and women and confirm the true centrality of men's position, of the "man's hand," in that alliance. It offered, too, a way of writing a "soldier poem" for a "total war," a poem which could at once reclaim the proven stance of the Great War poet combatant and revise that stance to include traces of a moderate, modified patriotism. This chapter's path will be circuitous, moving from the work of young male soldier poets of the Second World War (particularly Karl Shapiro) back to that of their predecessors, both combatant (Wilfred Owen) and civilian (the young Ezra Pound and Wallace Stevens), and then forward once again. Their strategies are very different, the positions of the authors sometimes radically opposed, but all these texts can be said in one key way to form a coherent line of twentieth-century war poetry: they constitute a series of dispatches from a front united in its appeal to masculinity.

II

Waiting for men's letters is, as Jane Cooper emphasizes, a marginal function for a woman in war. But forties representations of the woman letter reader often granted her nonetheless a kind of sentimental centrality, as object of affection or as sturdy receptacle for memory or information.

One popular scene of female reading at this time sanctified a form of female spectatorship in order to render the Second World War meaningful. It suggested that without the woman back home to read the letters, the squirming and the shooting would not matter.

Consider an emblematic version of the woman-as-reader, a doublespread Goodyear advertisement published during the war which Paul Fussell has described and discussed. The ad shows a middle-aged woman standing in the doorway of a house with a telegram in her hand. The copy goes like this:

What can you say to those whose hearts bear the aching burden of this conflict? That their sons have died in a noble cause . . . ? No, you can't say these things and have them really mean anything. You can't say anything — you can only do. You can only bend a bit more grimly to whatever task is yours in these stern times.[6]

Fussell uses this advertisement to contrast the grand linguistic flourishes with which both the British and American press exhorted the public in the First World War and the cynical emphasis in the later World War on "sheer unverbalized action":[7] You can't say anything. But if this Goodyear copy reflects the Second War home-front culture's subdued, deflated sense of the uses of speaking, its visual scene provides a reassuring and positive image, in the face of historical threat, of both its subject, a woman, and its action, reading. By transforming the opening of a telegram into personal, melodramatic incident, the advertisement domesticates public conflict, and in the process affirms that reading matters; that it is more than simply vicarious ("whose hearts bear the burden of this conflict"); that social and communal bonds depend on what words say. Because both the woman reader and the soldier memorialized in the telegram are represented as loved and as bound together by familial ties, the act of reading is given dignity and pathos.

At the same time, reading tames the woman, tethers her to the doorstep and the mailbox. It is unthinkable that she should be away from home when the mail arrives, or tear up the telegram without opening it, or respond callously instead of bearing her aching burden. She must be, and is, a silent "bearer of meaning, not maker of meaning," in Laura Mulvey's famous phrase.[8] Although the advertisement registers ambivalence about the possibilities of achieving and maintaining "linguistic command" or *making* meaning, it leaves no doubt about who is to *bear* it, both as sufferer and source. The woman's function is the same whether the mail brings an announcement of love or her loved one's death: she is the preserver, the agent of continuity, the one who remembers and yet remains physically unharmed by her family's and her society's traumas. The threshold on which she stands is a precarious place, infiltrated by violence with the delivery of the telegram — but behind her lies the inviolate realm of the American home, where some kind of meaning inheres.

The primary purpose of the Goodyear copywriters was to sell tires and boost the war effort, not to provide a positive representation of reading or of the writer's enterprise.[9] But it was a matter of concern for literary men, especially young men in the military, to find culturally representative and affirmative images not only of the Second World War but also of the acts of reading and writing about it, and many did so by turning to poetic versions of the "letter from the front." Unlike novels, films, and visual advertisements, which could treat the letter or its sinister inverted form, the telegram death notice, within a larger representational structure of setting, character, and either implied or explicitly developed plot, these poems are presented as the death-defying artifacts themselves, as letters written in the voice of the soldier to an imagined female reader.

A survey of literary magazines and major "war poetry" anthologies of the period reveals both the popularity and the uniformity of such poems.[10] The "letter from the front" form seems to have attracted younger men of letters partly because it allowed them to reconcile and display their dual roles as soldiers and as poets. Even more importantly, it allowed them both to interrogate and to affirm the idea of "linguistic command."

The poem as letter is first of all ostensibly private disclosure, removed from public discourse. It purports to be an occasional poem, a record of an actual experience and actual emotions. This simple pretense was valuable fiction for young men taught by their fathers' war experience, and their fathers' war literature, to be suspicious of ideas of heroism and patriotism and their expression in collective national rhetoric. The letter form permitted them to claim that first qualification of the war poet as Siegfried Sassoon defined it: "backed by . . . experience as an infantry soldier." At the same time, they could maintain a typically skeptical stance toward the second term of Sassoon's definition: "and . . . an originality and nobility of style."[11] Letter form assures its readers: *I am not in any way trying to be noble; I am common, private, in uniform; any soldier could write this, and everyone does.* The popularity of the letter poem reflects a desire on the part of these poets to develop genuinely domestic and democratic masculine forms, forms which would partake in what Paul Fussell has called the "principle of anonymity [which was] one way of sanctifying the war."[12] Thus Sergeant Karl Shapiro's soldier/speaker in his influential "V-Letter" exhorts a drab and modest, but powerful, woman reader: "Teach me to live and die / As one deserving anonymity . . . / [Not] the general cause of words, the hero's stance . . . "; William Meredith's speaker in

"Love Letter for an Impossible Land" writes that the sight of sailors and planes in a Pacific harbor leaves him "stammerer, inept to say / why in their simple duty there is pain," and so on.[13]

But while these war-letter poems consistently, even automatically, undercut heroic maxims and call the making of meaning into ironic question, they also provide the soldier poet's best outlet for a reformed and chastened public discourse. Within the incontrovertibly modest boundaries of a "personal letter," the poem could safely reclaim its right to *say something*, to define a meaning for the war and declare a rhetorical purpose for itself. Compared with other examples of the poets' work, Shapiro's, Meredith's, and many other poems of this type all arrive at moments of uncharacteristic fervor. Not surprisingly, in Oscar Williams's large collection of prose statements by poets on poetry and war one of the few attempts to present a convincing, positive metaphor for the war poem is Shapiro's image of a self and a poem fused at the center of a "great configuration . . . reduced in size but not in meaning, like a V-Letter."[14] What I will call V-letter form let soldier poets have their humility and transcend it too, just as it let them infuse their poems with patriotic and/or moral ardor without glorifying war too much. It allowed published poetry the "latitude" of patriotism which Oscar Williams stated was the privilege of the soldier's private letter alone:

The poet who gives his life in battle most certainly has the privilege of writing [patriotic] verse. But has the civilian reader exactly the same right to confine his thoughts of war to such sentiments? . . . It is much as if a soldier wrote home to his mother that he was safely behind the lines when he was really in action, in order to save her from worry. But published poetry does not have the same latitude as a private letter; it is always better when it is strictly truthful.[15]

The V-letter's complex structure of first denied and then modified or muted affirmation permitted poets to suggest meanings which could redeem, justify, and provide impetus for the Allied cause while at the same time adhering to the "strict truth" which, in the modern war poetry tradition, had become synonymous with recognition of the brutal and unheroic nature of combat. Like W. H. Auden's "ironic points of light" that "flash out wherever the Just / Exchange their messages," letter poems were energized by the tension between an "affirming flame" and a world "beleaguered by . . . negation and despair."[16]

Auden's speaker in "Sept. 1, 1939," from which the above lines are taken, says that these simultaneously just and ironic messages are composed "of Eros and of dust." It is no accident that in their search for a structure which could simultaneously contain prowar and antiwar sentiments, the

literary soldiers of the 1940s invented, or rather rediscovered and trans-
posed into epistolary form, the war poem as heterosexual love poem, rein-
troducing a comfortable, mainstream erotic tradition — the conventions of
English and European love poetry dating back to Petrarch — into the dusty,
barren, no-man's-landscape of modern war literature. Nor is it a coinci-
dence that a classic war poem of this type, Shapiro's "V-Letter," uses a
familiar Petrarchan convention, the *blason* or catalogue of praises.

In "V-Letter," it is true, Shapiro deflates the conventions of "romantic"
love poetry as much as those of patriotic war poetry, but here again he
scuttles conventional terms only to reaffirm a value which survives skep-
tical interrogation: the woman addressed, seen in the "ugliness of light,"
turns out to be not less but "more goddess-like / than silver goddesses on
screens" (227), just as the Second World War is more heroic, in its mun-
danity and cynicism, than any idea of heroism. But the woman reader
imagined in Shapiro's "V-Letter" is still a projection, still, as Ann Rosalind
Jones has defined the role assigned to the lady in the Petrarchan mode,
"the opaque target of the masculine gaze."[17] Like the maternal reader in
the Goodyear ad, the sweetheart readers imagined in V-letters are emo-
tional *repositories*, but have no means of, and no need for, verbal expres-
sion; these poems are not dialogues. In a world in which only unexplained
actions seem necessary and possible, soldiers and male poets are shown
struggling with the fear that "you can't say anything." But the women ad-
dressed simply have nothing to say. The highly artificial love language of
Shapiro's *blason*, and the image of a woman confined by that language
to the position of silent but reassuring object, provide a stabilizing struc-
ture or home base both for the war itself and for the soldier's poem as
it struggles to do the war ironic justice.[18]

The alliance of bugles and *blasons* (both muted) in the 1940s letter
poem was a logical and probably inevitable strategy for Second War sold-
ier poets. From Criseyde to Luciana's desertion in *Catch 22*, from Love-
lace's Lucasta to Ingrid Bergman in *Casablanca*, men have rendered war
meaningful by validating the woman in the margins as faithful symbol,
or made it meaningless by degrading her as sinister traitor. Western war
poetry from its earliest origins, and particularly in the English tradition,
has enacted its arguments about the nature and meaning of war within
scenes of female spectatorship, one modern form of which is the scene
of female reading. Thus when literary men sought, hesitantly and self-
consciously, to legitimize the Second World War, they turned to poems
which promised alliances between men and women. In doing so they were
making a very old move, but one that seemed novel in literary circles.

V-letters were, in one sense, updated versions of old chestnuts, with only a thin veneer of irony—and this partly explains their popularity as content-anthology pieces. In general, they move from a tough and "inarticulate" initial stance to passionate rearticulation, as, to take a relatively crude example, the Canadian poet Earle Birney's "On Going to the Wars" progresses from sardonic negations ("I do not go, my dear, to storm / The praise of men; this uniform / May shine less gay in gas and mud . . . ") to lines like "I, too, let's say, a travail owe / dear, I'll not survive to see / you bricked within a ghetto slum / in Canada, by booted scum."[19] Birney's poem ostensibly undercuts the posturing of its namesake, Richard Lovelace's "To Lucasta, going to the Warres," but by its end, in one respect at least, it comes close to imitating Lovelace uncritically. Twentieth-century wars can never pretend to be gentlemanly, but they might still be heroic, they might still be honorable, and they can be made so by brave acts of style exactly like the Cavalier poet's.

It will be worthwhile here to pause and examine "To Lucasta" for a moment, since Lovelace's classic dramatic scene of soldier's leavetaking is the paradigm of the poem as soldier's spoken message, one which renders the male speaker's war-making both innocent and potent by appealing to a woman ally. The speaker in "To Lucasta" resolves the disruptive sexual tensions provoked by what a woman says by subsuming them into a larger cause and a louder, smoother rhetoric of honor: "Tell me not, Sweet, I am unkind . . . / I could not love thee, dear, so much, / Lov'd I not Honour more."[20] The poem comforts its imaginary muse by silencing her. The victory it records is preliminary—to be followed by victories on actual battlefields—and figurative, a victory *of* figuration. The speaker manages to solve the problem of the threat women pose to the system of honor (which is here synonymous with war) by incorporating the feminine into the system through figurative means, in this case allegory; Honour becomes a personified other woman, war an alternative kind of sexuality which is fueled by, not countered by, carefully controlled heterosexual energies:

> True, a new mistress I now chase,
> The first foe in the field;
> And with a stronger faith embrace
> A sword, a horse, a shield.
>
> Yet this inconstancy is such
> As you too shall adore . . .
>   (92)

Birney uses a similar strategy when, in the odd lines quoted above, he links his male speaker with his female spectator by making childbirth a metaphor for war: "I, too, let's say, a travail owe . . . " "You too," Lovelace says; Birney says "I, too, let's say," and although those last two words, in typical Second World War fashion, tone down the metaphor to follow, both poems use trope to prove that what men do in war is not separate from but intrinsically connected to women's lives and women's bodies. Women are not at cross purposes with war-making or poetry-making in these poems; for both activities they are perfectly willing to provide raw material.

The connection between men and women, the eradication of distance brought about by a masculine linguistic feat in front of a cooperative female audience, is the single major impulse of the V-letter poems of the forties, perhaps spelled out most clearly in Seldon Rodman's V-letter on V-letters not surprisingly titled "V-Letter to Karl Shapiro in Australia": "Distance unites us, war engenders love / No less than hate . . . "[21] V-letters reached back to Lovelace, past the threats of a modern world, to a time in which war, women, and language seemed to have been simpler and more malleable. At the same time, letter form never allowed the reader to forget its modernity; unlike Birney's unusual leave-taking/speech-making scene, most proper "V-letters" called attention to their epistolary nature, their status as imaginary written documents in a mechanized age. The V-letter was Lovelace on microfilm, or "To Lucasta" by way of Wilfred Owen.

III

The works of the British Great War soldier poets, as I have already argued, offered far more compelling and immediate models for war poetry in the forties than earlier English poetry. (I use "soldier" here and throughout as a kind of shorthand, meant to comprehend both officers and enlisted men as well as combatants of various sorts — sailors, pilots, etc.) No matter how much their content, or even their stylistic maneuvers, recall the Cavaliers, V-letters derive their forms from Great War soldier poems; let us for a moment look at some of those poems more closely. The First World War antiwar soldier poets' primary means of obliterating their culture's myths of honor was to transform the narrative framework of the war poem as soldier's message from a speech-giving scene to a letter-writing scene, from address to a female spectator to address to a female reader. One crucial way, that is, in which the modern soldier's war poem had undercut the grand tradition of English war poetry was by changing the way in which men could be said to talk to women about war: by changing the method of transmission.

The shift to the female reader rather than the female spectator as imagined audience allowed several important changes to occur. First of all, it placed primary focus on the record of shattering experience of war rather than heroic bravado. Second, it highlighted the participation of male and female protagonists in a gigantic and mechanical process, across long distances, which made actual contact between them an impossibility or eradicated its power. Third, most importantly, it placed bitter emphasis on the ignorance of the woman who served synecdochically as a figure for the poet's audience, and insisted on a disjunction, not a gratifying identification, between poet and reader. The soldier poet's ironic power, in World War I antiwar poems, is presented as coming not from his intentions or his linguistic mastery but from knowledge derived from an experience which nearly destroys his ability to intend or create.[22] His poem becomes an act of reconstruction after the fact, opposed in every way but its assumption of a female audience to Lovelace's speaker's "before the fact" fiction-making. And the woman as reader, who has no direct experience of the war and therefore no immediate access to anger or irony, can undergo nothing but a difficult, postponed, and guilty experience of interpreting, only to be condemned for it.

Letters enter anti–Great War poems in order to deny simultaneity, to accentuate the temporal and spatial distances between soldier/author and civilian/reader. Wilfred Owen will again serve as an example here, since his influence was especially strong in the forties. The language of letters we find in poems like "The Letter," Owen's only real V-letter, or his "S.I.W.," bears little resemblance to the modest, self-deprecating diction of forties V-letters, with their clear wish for or promise of heterosexual unions. The moments where letter writing occurs in Owen's work seem gimmicky and strained. Their function is to represent a system of official euphemism, and to call painful attention to the poem's act of exploding that euphemism.

"S.I.W." (the letters stand for "Self-Inflicted Wound"), for instance, insulates a small section called "The Poem," which explains a soldier's secret motives for killing himself with his own gun, from the infected rhetoric of war exemplified by letters. Here is some of the first section, called "The Prologue":

> Each week, month after month, they wrote the same,
> Thinking him sheltered in some Y.M. Hut,
> Because he said so, writing on his butt
> Where once an hour a bullet missed its aim
>
> . . . .
> "Death sooner than dishonour, that's the style!"
> So Father said.

And here, the last section in full, "The Epilogue":

> With him they buried the muzzle his teeth had kissed
> And truthfully wrote the Mother, "Tim died smiling."[23]

The true "Poem" wedges in the space between before and after, between the mindless prologues and censored epilogues which are the verbal domain of the patriarchal family and its war, run by Father and supported willingly by Mother. Compare "The Letter," with its clash between written and oral modes, where experience of the present breaks violently through written formula, rupturing it irrevocably:[24]

> With B.E.F., June 10. Dear Wife,
> (O blast this pencil. 'Ere, Bill, lend's a knife.)
> . . . We're out in rest now. Never fear.
> (VRACH! By crumbs, but that was near.
>
> . . . .
>
> Guh! Christ! I'm hit. Take 'old. Aye, bad.
> No, damn your iodine. Jim? 'Ere!
> Write my old girl, Jim, there's a dear.)
>
>   (60)

Note, here, the shift of the term of endearment—Lovelace's charged "dear"—from the wife to the soldier comrade at the end. This soldier's self-censorship in the letter to his wife, like the suppression of the facts in the letters home in "S.I.W.," may be said to be grounded in familial affection. At the same time, however, the deliberate ignorance of the women in these poems, in compliance with "Father" and a system of institutional censorship, is bitterly satirized. Moreover, the patronizing exclusion of women from the truth serves to reinforce male bonding. Both poems contain not only figures of duped women readers but also scenes of surrogate writing: the collective authorship of the final lie home to Mother, and the hapless Jim left with the unfortunate task of finishing the letter. But although these surrogate soldier writers remind us that war poems are not only read but also written by survivors, after the moment of primary experience they struggle to record, it is the female readers, once again, who bear the brunt of secondariness and the major share of culpability for distance. Trapped at the "rear," they cannot take up dead men's pens and write for them, as Jim—and of course Owen himself—can.[25]

These epistolary moments in Owen's poems are part of a larger critique of the ignorant spectator as instigator of war—and that spectator, as I have said, is generally represented as female. The critique is complicated and ambivalent, but nonetheless it dominates Owen's work. Even when Owen's narrators seem to ally themselves with women, onlookers and readers, the poems covertly reinforce the bonds between military—and literary—men. Take, for example, "The Send-Off," his ironic reworking of the "On Going to Wars" scene. The first part of the poem represents men's "grimly gay" leave-taking for the front, their bodies decorated with white flowers by women, "As men's are, dead." "They were not ours," the poem concludes, and then, laying open the split between what war means and what women mean, "We never heard to which front these were sent / Nor there if they yet mock what women meant / Who gave them flowers" (46).

Interestingly, here Owen's speaker's use of the first person plural—"We never heard"—links his authorial persona to the blithely ghoulish flower-throwing women left behind; he is implicated in "women's meaning." In an earlier draft, that meaning is even more directly linked to him, in lines like *our* false, mournful flowers" (italics mine), "We never heard . . . how soon they found out what we meant," "what we mourners," and "what cowards meant who gave them flowers."[26] This is one of many moments in his war writing where a kind of survival guilt might be said to register. But the poem in its final fair copy also demands that we read that "we" ironically, recognizing its opposite meaning of "*you* women—not me" and acknowledging the poet's status as surrogate mocker, stand-in for dead comrades. "The Send-Off" reasserts Owen's central place in a community of soldiers even as it denies it.

There seems to be no cure, in Owen's work, for women's bad seeing, bad writing, bad *meaning*. His "Dulce et Decorum Est," as I suggested in chapter 1, makes this especially clear, since it directly confronts the woman war poet. In its earliest drafts titled "To Jessie Pope etc.," in a second draft, "To a Certain Poetess," the poem attacks Jessie Pope's patriotic verse with an open *ad feminam* accusation unmatched in Owen's work by any similar critique of a specific male authorial opponent.[27] (Fred D. Crawford has noted that Owen possessed a copy of the anthology *Soldier Poets* in which a poem by Major Sydney Oswald of the King's Rifle Corps celebrating three soldiers who died at Gallipoli is entitled "Dulce et Decorum Est Pro Patria Mori."[28] But Owen never called his poem "To Sydney Oswald," or "To a Certain Soldier Poet.")

Owen's "certain poetess" resembles the "Little Mother" whose patriotic pamphlet Robert Graves reprints in *Goodbye to All That*; she is related, too, to the sinister (though not scribbling) women addressed in Sassoon's "Glory of Women" and many other antiwar poems of the Great War period.[29] As in the American tradition Nina Baym has described in her "Melodramas of Beset Manhood," female authors in the Great War canon of soldier poetry are assumed to represent "the consensus, rather than the criticism of it," and the "encroaching, constricting, destroying society is represented with particular urgency in the figure of one or more women."[30] Repeatedly, soldiers' antiwar poems of World War I stage themselves as melodramas of beset manhood, with only the geography of Baym's model altered, for there was no alternative wilderness into which to escape, only the No-Man's-Land of the trenches.

In the final version of Owen's poem, the topical allusion to Jessie Pope in the title disappears, but in its place the famous allusion to Horace carries with it its own traces of a specifically female spectator as war's perpetrator. The line from Horace is in Ode 3.2, in which the exhortation that "it is sweet and glorious to die for fatherland"—Owen calls it "the old lie"—is immediately prefaced by the image of women anxiously, and voyeuristically, watching their men fight on a battlefield.[31] The "old lie" as Owen represents it coming down from Horace is thus not simply a disembodied ruling notion but a rhetoric peculiarly feminine, ignorant and instigatory, spoken and published only from safe parapets and behind enclosed walls, carrying a barely hidden vicarious pleasure.[32]

Owen himself, as Dominic Hibbard has pointed out, promulgated a version of this old lie, in the poem entitled variously in various drafts "The Ballad of Peace and War," "Ballad of Kings and Christs," and finally "The Women and the Slain." In one section of an early draft of this poem (written in 1915 or perhaps even 1914), a stanza "declares," as Hibbard puts it, "with no hint of irony that it is 'sweet' and 'meet' to die for brothers."[33] In later drafts, however, that notion is ironized, and the satire is accomplished through a move entirely characteristic of Owen. The glorification of patriotic death is put into the mouth of "women," who romanticize soldiers as versions of Arthur and Christ; then in turn the voices of the male "slain" debunk it savagely and wearily.

In a letter to his mother in 1917, Owen characterized the idealizing impulse in the poem as "a mote in many eyes, often no other than a tear . . . a distorted view to hold in a general way. For that reason, if no other, I won't publish in any way the Kings and Christs."[34] But Jon Stallworthy points out that the poem shows up in two tables of contents Owen drew up for his projected book in 1918.[35] The "mote" was apparently not so easily excised, but one clear way to contain it was to place it entirely in women's eyes. Women, Jessie Pope among them, bear all the ironic blame; the slain—Owen will eventually take his place among them—retain no trace in their voices of the internalized struggle with idealization and celebration which was in fact, to the end, Owen's own.

As recent feminist work has shown, women's actual reading and writing of texts during this war was often, of course, far more varied, contradictory, self-conscious, and resistant than Owen's example of Jessie Pope suggests; this point needs to be made baldly, since women's Great War signifying practices still tend to be reduced in all too many accounts to the distribution of white feathers.[36] Perhaps the single most influential anti–Great War poem by a woman, Amy Lowell's "Patterns," exploits the letter-receiving scene for elegiac and heavily ironic ends, and does so, significantly, in order to align rather than separate the experiences of men and women in wartime, and to criticize women's positioning behind the parapets as much as men's positioning outside them.[37] And Eleanor Farjeon's "Easter Monday: in memoriam E. T." accentuates the ironic "gulf so deeply cut" as fiercely as any of Owen's poems, but in order to represent the woman letter writer's/ letter reader's burden of grief, her intolerable knowledge, in the aftermath of poet combatant Edward Thomas's death, of what she cannot know.[38]

Particularly interesting (and still largely buried) are the theoretical statements about women's war writing, reading, and "meaning" which some women made at the time, answering back to men of (war) letters. Two good examples are Alys Eyre Macklin's introduction to the *Lyceum Book of War Verses* (1918) and a remarkable treatise on women's war poetry published the next year by Lilian Rowland Brown. Both these essays implicated militarism as *men's* old lie; both claimed pacifism as women's natural position. At the same time, however, unlike some other radically pacifist texts by Great War women, both concluded with spectacular repudiations of pacifism in the name of a necesary war effort. Brown praised the war poetry of women as "no mean asset in . . . the survival of the fittest"; Macklin reversed her antimilitarism with a final "we will continue to smile an unfaltering 'Adieu' to our nearest and dearest as we speed them over the sea to do their bit for King and Country."[39]

These martial closures suggest something of the disciplinary force of patriotic and military ideology in civilian Great War life. For Great War soldier antiwar poets, bitterly ironizing the "letter home" was one way to counteract such moments of closure which sped men once again overseas. Their soldier poems aimed for the effect Virginia Woolf described in her 1917 review of Siegfried Sassoon's war poems: "such loathing, such hatred accumulates behind them that we say to ourselves: 'Yes, this is going on; and we are sitting here watching it,' with a new shock of surprise." And, Woolf went on, another result ensued in the reader, across the gulf between front and home: "an uneasy desire to leave our place in the audience."[40] Uneasy desire, because dangerous; uneasy, for women, because impossible; uneasy, because only partial. In the context of finally unfaltering "Adieus" like Macklin's and Brown's, the pressures which led anti–Great

War poet combatants like Owen to put forward damning images of com-
munication to and from the front, to and from men and women, seem
obvious and inescapable.

IV

That place of uneasy desire occupied by those who comprise the sup-
posed "audience" in war is not limited to women alone. Male noncombat-
ants sit there watching too; "civilian" and "woman" are not identical or en-
tirely coterminous categories. One particular group of men who were
civilians in the Great War, the famous modernist poets, exerted an influence
on Second World War literary soldiers as strong as that of the Great War
soldier poets; before returning to the vogue of Second War V-letters, I
want therefore to consider briefly two notable examples of early mod-
ernist engagement with war-related epistolary form, Wallace Stevens's "Let-
tres d'un Soldat" (1917–1918) and some of the poems in Ezra Pound's
Cathay (1915).

Both Pound and Stevens were, of course, very much contemporaneously
present in the Second World War literary scene, and young American
soldier poets often defined themselves and were defined in strenuous op-
position to both men, particularly to Pound. Karl Shapiro, for instance,
strongly objected to the 1949 Bollingen award to Pound's *Cantos*. His
representations of his Jewishness in poems like "V-Letter" actively combat
the virulent anti-Semitism of Pound's discourse.[41] The soldier's letter to
John Crowe Ransom at the *Kenyon Review* in 1944 which prompted
Stevens's response in "Esthetique du Mal" explicitly rejected "poets of charm-
ing distemper like Wallace Stevens" and praised instead "commandos of
contemporary literature" like Shapiro.[42] Clearly, for that reader Shapiro
and Stevens occupied two entirely separate positions and represented
sharply differentiated traditions. Still, the general influence of the modern-
ists on the new generation of "contemporary commandos" is unmistak-
able, and Pound's and Stevens's early turns to the war epistle are usefully
compared to the later V-letter.

I cannot offer in this limited space a full reading of either Pound's *Cathay*
or Stevens's "Lettres." They share several striking aspects on which I will
concentrate. Each estranges and renders slant the war letter genre through
a series of "translations," lyricizing it and to some extent making it ahis-
torical, or less historically specific, or transhistorical. Each either speaks
from or seeks out, and finds positive meaning in, the place of the feminine
(i.e., the place of the *civilian*) in ways which differ significantly from the
anti–Great War soldier poets' demarcations of their linguistic terrains
which were beginning at around the moment of *Cathay's* publication, and

were well in place by the time Stevens composed his "Lettres." At the same time, this "feminization" is accompanied and finally counteracted by a reverse pull toward a brutal, realistic, "masculine" irony entirely in line with the conventions of the antiwar soldier poetry developing at the time; each of these poets finds some way to reenlist himself in the textual front ranks.

Pound's *Cathay: For the Most Part From the Chinese of Rihaku, From the Notes of the Late Ernest Fenollosa* is, as Hugh Kenner has disclosed, "largely a war book, using Fenollosa's notes much as Pope used Horace or Johnson Juvenal, to supply a system of parallels and a structure of discourse."

Its exiled bowmen, deserted women, levelled dynasties, departures for far places, lonely frontier guardsmen and glories remembered from afar, cherished memories, were selected from the diverse wealth in the notebooks by a sensibility responsive to torn Belgium and disrupted London; and as "The Jewel Stairs' Grievance" is "especially prized because she offers no direct reproach," so *Cathay* essays an oriental obliquity of reference . . . [43]

Kenner's vocabulary and simile here feminize Pound distinctly. "Sensibility" and "responsive" are words with valences at least slightly feminine, and in the end the volume is especially prized not only as like but *as* the "oriental" lady who, eyes and language downcast, offers no direct reproach. In these respects Kenner follows Pound, who willingly adopted feminine positions and voices at moments in *Cathay*. Speaking the war poem in Chinese, speaking it translated, was one way for Pound the noncombatant to speak the language of femininity in wartime without risk. As translator he could protect himself, exploring his civilian situation without exposing too much; as translator, he could also prevent the *Cathay* poems from in any way, however inadvertently, feeding the war machine. Even in late 1914, certainly in 1915, the gulf between England's "two nations"—front and home—was yawning, and soldiers' antiwar poetry was building that gap into its ideological and polemical structures. Choosing a third nation, the emblematically foreign China, Pound could write poems sympathetic to the values and experiences of those "left behind" without betraying the "frontier guard."[44]

Read next to Owen's "The Letter" or "S. I. W.," Pound's "The River-Merchant's Wife: A Letter" seems a discreet defense of the noncombatant, a validation of what she (and he) feels and knows. This poem about dedication to absence allowed Pound to affirm delicate feeling and an ethic of care and relation which extended beyond the brotherhood or combatants in wartime (qualities linked to the sensibilities of art); it allowed him to represent elegiac grief without gush, since the Chinese effect of the poem lies in large part in its tightly stressed reticence. Since the letter's strongest implication is of a deep, almost unspoken erotic and affectionate bond between the absent man and the waiting woman, a bond which seems to carry some kind of vital knowledge outside social convention, it seals the gap which a text like Owen's "The Letter" opens between the genders.

The exotic Chinese setting of "The River-Merchant's Wife" calls the modern English reader's attention to the patriarchal obedience structure which has shaped and constrained the wife's voice. This poem, like many Western texts, exploits the Western projection of sexual oppression onto the "Orient"—but only in order to deny it. The wife's arranged marriage is, her letter "artlessly" reveals, a love match after all. One of the rhetorical effects of this move in the context of Great War discourse is to repudiate charges that women cheerfully wave "adieu" out of resentment, vicarious glee, or aggression; another is to locate women's renewing loyalty to men *outside* systems of sexual inculcation and familial arrangement, to recover a pure heterosexual alliance untainted by war's gendering systems. Kenner argues that the *Cathay* poems "paraphrase an elegiac war poetry nobody wrote"; but I would argue that in its defense of women and of remaining bonds between men and women "The River-Merchant's Wife" bears strong resemblance to any number of Great War poems written by women, including Farjeon's "Easter Monday" and Lowell's "Patterns," in which adieus are shown to falter and significant connections to persist.[45]

The river-merchant's wife's position was, in fact, to some extent Pound's own.[46] He was, after all, sending typescripts of some poems in *Cathay* as literal letters to the front, to Gaudier-Brzeska. (After the book came out in print his friend wrote from the Marne that he kept it at all times in his pocket.) Pound's choice of poems to send to the trenches in manuscript is interesting, for he selected not examples like his "River-Merchant's Wife" which represent some version of his own situation, that of the one "left behind," but poems which explore the position of his correspondent, the ones which speak in the voice of combatants—the sorrowful, obliquely outraged "Song of the Bowmen of Shu" and "Lament of the Frontier Guard." Gaudier-Brzeska very much appreciated these choices; "the poems," he wrote after receiving them, "depict our situation in a wonderful way." "Our situation" means primarily, I assume, the condition of trench warfare, the implied combatants' "we" excluding the civilian Pound even as the praise of Pound's poems, and that simple verb of realism "depict," embrace him into the corps.[47]

In *Cathay* as a whole, then, speaking the war poem in Chinese, speak-

ing it translated, was one way for Pound the noncombatant to speak with-
out obvious falsehood or reprisal the one language of masculinity in war-
time which seemed to matter: the language of the soldier. He could do
so through Rihaku (Li Po) without making illegitimate or exploitive claims.
Instead of the audacity of dramatic monologue, he offered the simple
mediations of the interpreter. Depicting men's war "in a wonderful way,"
he confirmed his own poetic manhood.[48] In Pound's "non-Chinese" Great
War poems, that confirmation is even more pronounced; the delicately
fetishized women and discreetly semieroticized male bonding in *Cathay*
are replaced by gender in extremity.[49] Parts IV and V of "Mauberley," with
their critique of the "dulce et decorum" formulation, openly enlist in the
ironic "war poem" tradition of the soldier poets. Any reader who doubts
the heightened and declared *masculinity* of that tradition in Pound's hands
should consult the famous line concerning the "old bitch gone in the teeth,"
one of the most overtly misogynist moments in twentieth-century war
literature.

Wallace Stevens's poetic engagement with Great War letter form was
more direct and topical, at least at first, than Pound's, but no less "trans-
lated." Stevens's "Lettres d'un Soldat" pays tribute to and draws upon a text
which represents that most populist type of wartime and postwar episto-
lary publications, the collection of a dead soldier's letters home. Making
the title of this prior text his own, Stevens signals with his bow to and
appropriation of Eugene Lemercier's *Lettres d'un Soldat 1914–1915* that
any speaking which occurs here will happen in two voices: that of a (dead)
soldier and that of a (dead) Frenchman. I will return to the question of
what "France" or "French" means for these poems, and of how it compares
to Pound's Great War "China"; for now let us consider the ways in which
"Lettres" inscribes the soldier.

The sequence has a complex textual history with one general teleology:
poems and other apparatus fall away at each stage, each new editing mov-
ing the remaining poems further from the politics and topoi of the war
and further toward an insulated modernist lyric privacy.[50] "Lettres d'un
Soldat" began as thirteen, or perhaps seventeen, poems composed in man-
uscript in the summer of 1917 shortly after Stevens read the then newly
published collection of Lemercier's war correspondence.[51] (He read it in
French, but the book had appeared quickly in two separate English trans-
lations, prefaced in each edition with a short essay by André Chevrillon.)[52]
Originally, each of the poems began with a dated epigraph from one of
Lemercier's letters, with the epigraphs charting an unbroken chronolog-
ical progression from the soldier's enlistment to his death. In March 1918,
Stevens met with Harriet Monroe to condense the sequence to nine poems

published in *Poetry* that May. Three of the poems from *Poetry* and one from the manuscripts found their way into later editions of *Harmonium*; by this time they were minus the epigraphs and without any overt relation to each other or to Lemercier's writing. My discussion will focus on the entire manuscript sequence as A. Walton Litz has reconstructed it, since it is here that Stevens openly takes on the letter and the soldier; it is, though, important to remember that in the longer history of the poems both their epistolary structures of address and their martial and topical contexts are gradually abandoned.[53]

This lyricizing impulse moves beyond Lemercier's history, but it is also the original soldier's own. Adapting Lemercier's letters, Stevens could, as Glen Macleod has put it, "imaginatively join . . . in the spirit of the war effort," compensating for his own sense of frustration and inadequacy at not being more directly involved.[54] But going to war with the particular figure of Eugene Lemercier as comrade and mentor meant imaginatively joining only in order to go imaginatively A.W.O.L.; Lemercier's appeal for Stevens undoubtedly lay in the delicate sensibility, perhaps most of all in the capacity for aesthetic transport, brought by the resigned, romantic young artist to the battlefront and preserved there to a surprising extent. Stevens's manuscript sequence begins with a poem called "Common Soldier" which concerns the combatant's subjection to the commonplace.[55] As the poems pursue Lemercier, however, the soldier precursor is quickly reestablished as uncommon man. He is not only uncommonly brave but also uncommonly possessed of exceptional visions decidedly imagist in manner and tenor.[56]

Stevens's lyrics offer themselves as pastiche of Lemercier; their two voices slide into one another, breaking down the isolation of the discrete personal letter.[57] This dynamic implies that Lemercier and Stevens own the same style or speak the same language, the one style and language which really counts: the dialect and attitude of *lyric.* "The subjective being," Theodor Adorno writes, "that makes itself heard in lyric poetry is one which defines and expresses itself as something opposed to the collective and the realm of objectivity."[58] Thus Lemercier makes himself heard, describing "la majesté da la nuit" or "la sécurité des petits animaux des bois" in opposition to the collective drudgery, anxiety, and terror of his surroundings; and Stevens in turn hears Lemercier, remakes him heard, in just this way, attending to, expanding, and isolating the lyric possibility of "his" (or "their") voice.

"Their" here incorporates not only Stevens and Lemercier, the modernist male poet and the model male soldier, but another — for the language of lyric both seeks out and speaks from the place of the "feminine." In

Stevens's second poem, which begins the sequence in its published *Poetry* version, the emergence of this inclination toward the feminine (as a glimpse from the trenches of the figure of Venus, that "mysterious" and "multiform" beauty) constitutes the central action and the key desire. Lemercier's letters enact this response to the woman(ly) not only thematically but structurally, in their literal direction of address; the title of the English translation Stevens recommended to Harriet Monroe makes this clear: *A Soldier of France to His Mother.* "Lemercier placed a great value on writing," Glen Macleod comments. "To write a letter to his mother was to be with her."[59] In Owen's letter poems, the mother represents the one from whom truth is kept. In the Lemercier collection, all truths come via the mother and all are elicited by her. Lemercier may serve to remind us that Owen himself sent his war poems to his own mother from the front, not just censored field postcards, and Stevens, following Lemercier, accentuates the soldier's alliance with the woman back at home. For Stevens, recuperating the maternal in the war "lettre" means recuperating both romantic subjectivity and a principle of pity explicitly identified as feminine. If the poetry of war is in the pity, the pity in turn seems to derive from a maternal, not a fraternal, aura: "The moon is the mother of pathos and pity," begins the seventh poem "Lunar Paraphrase."[60]

Speaking the war poem in the tongue of Lemercier lets Stevens say "chère Maman" and retain a strong masculinity — lets him have both mama and combat. More readers than Stevens found in Lemercier a distinctive closeness to the maternal, and read this affiliation as a trait distinctively and admirably French. In the British edition of Lemercier's letters, an extra introduction by a man named Clutton-Brock was appended. It was specifically designed to prepare Englishmen for the "very French" aspects of the text, "very unlike what an Englishman would write to his mother, or indeed to anyone." Clutton-Brock's remarkable preface is worth quoting at some length:

Many Englishmen, if they could have read them before the war, would have thought them almost unmanly; yet the writer distinguished himself even in the French army. . . . He does not write as a matter of duty, and so that his mother may know that he is still living; rather, he writes to her so that he may ease a little his desire to talk to her. We are used to French sentiment about the mother; it is a commonplace of French eloquence, and we have often smiled at it as mere sentimental platitude; but in these letters we see a son's love for his mother no longer insisted upon or dressed up in rhetoric, but naked and unconscious, a habit of the mind, a need of the soul, a support even to the weakness of the flesh. . . . The most loving of English sons would not often rather talk to his mother than to anyone else. . . . [But Lemercier] tells her the deepest thoughts of his mind, know-

ing that she will understand him better than any one else. That foreboding which
the mother felt in Morris's poem has never come true about him:

> Lo, here thy body beginning, O son, and thy soul and thy life,
> But how will it be if thou livest and enterest into the strife
>
> . . . .
>
> . . . and yet twixt thee and me
> Shall rise that wall of distance that round each one doth grow,
> And maketh it hard and bitter each other's thoughts to know?

This son has lived and entered into the strife indeed; but the wall of distance has
not grown round him; and, as we read these letters, we think that no French
mother would fear the natural estrangement which that English mother in the
poem fears. The foreboding itself seems to belong to a barbaric society in which
there is a more animal division of the sexes, in which the male fears to become
effeminate if he does not insist upon his masculinity even to his mother. But this
Frenchman has left barbarism so far behind that he is not afraid of effeminacy;
nor does he need to remind himself that he is a male. There is a philosophy to
which this forgetfulness of masculinity is decadence. . . . No one could be further
from such a philosophy than this Frenchman.[61]

A decadence which is no decadence, a forgetfulness of masculinity which
is the essence of reformed masculinity, no more "natural estrangement"
(in its place, something positively unnatural?) from feeling, from ideality,
from the "naked, unconscious" semiotics of *maman*: Lemercier offered all
this, and the name for what he offered was "French."[62] Much as Pound
manipulated the sign "China" in *Cathay*, Stevens exploited in his "Lettres"
the kind of projection onto French national character which Clutton-
Brock articulates, using the Frenchman to explore alternatives to the usual
constructions of masculinity in Anglo-American discourses of war.

Moving toward *maman* functions in the sequence as a whole, however,
not as a destabilizing approach to the "semiotic" but as a reassertion of
a very familiar symbolic martial order.[63] In the eighth poem, a sonnet
which begins with an epigraph from Lemercier celebrating his contempla-
tive connections with his "Bien chère Mère aimée," love for the mother
is replaced and superceded by relation to "another mother," in a move iden-
tical to Lovelace's substitution of his new mistress Honour for his old one
Lucasta:

> There is another mother whom I love,
> O chère maman, another, who, in turn,
> Is mother to the two of us, and more,
> In whose hard service both of us endure
> Our petty portion in the sacrifice.

> Not France! France, also, serves the invincible eye,
> That, from her helmet, terrible and bright,
> Commands the armies; the relentless arm,
> Devising proud, majestic issuance.
>
> (313)

Despite the deliberate refusal of a narrow patriotic or nationalistic read-
ing of the "mightier mother"—"Not France!"—this maternal allegory has
a much more conservative function than any moment in Pound's *Cathay*.
It justifies the war in the name of something higher, confirming Wilfred
Owen's worst fears about the operations of appeals to the feminine in mar-
tial discourse. This "other mother" might confirm a woman reader's fears
as well, for like the allegorical female figures Marina Warner has described
she represents an ideal "through a series of forgettings; to accept her as
a representative . . . we must forget the place of women themselves, the
history of the female condition."[64] The positive "forgetfulness of masculin-
ity" in the "Lettres" is accompanied, that is, by a negative forgetfulness of
"women themselves," an amnesia much more symptomatic in Stevens's
text than in Lemercier's. Repeatedly, in fact, Stevens's "Lettres d'un Soldat"
enacts a series of forgettings of actual women to whom Lemercier attends;
the first poem, "Common Soldier," for instance, ignores the description
of the plight of women refugees in the letter from which it takes its epigraph,
and the specific "Mère aimée" Lemercier addressed becomes in Stevens's
hands first any lyricist's maman and then a mere stand-in for the mightier,
notional, entirely allegorical Mother.[65]

But by the end of the original sequence "Lettres d'un Soldat," under the
pressure of a typical Great War ironic narrative of disillusionment which
is brought on by (and brings on) the soldier's death, even this Mother—
and with her, the hermetic lyric impulse itself—are rejected. In the tenth
poem, for instance, the epigraph from Lemercier reads in translation,
"Last night, on coming back to the barn, drunkenness, quarrels, cries,
songs and yells. Such is life!" The poem which follows is a comic, awful
repetition of the drumming drunken songs of male hostility and cam-
araderie: "John Smith and his son, John Smith, / And his son's son John,
and-a-one / And-a-two and-a-three / And-a-rum-tum-tum, and-a." Omit-
ted are the next lines of Lemercier's letter: "But when morning came and
the wakening from sleep still brought me memories of this, I got up before
the time, and found outside a friendly moon . . . and a dawn which had
pity on me" (151). The poem's force depends on the suppression of this
scene: no mother, no pathos, no pity, no moon. All that remains is an
unchallengeable replication of the patriarchal/ homosocial rounds, one John
Smith falling into line after another. The only feminine figure in the re-

mainder of the series is, not surprisingly, a spectator not solacing but (im)passive and demonic; in the final poem, "Death was a rider beating his horse, / Gesturing grandiose things in the air, / Seen by a muse" (314).

As strongly, then, as moments in the individual poems enact a lyric pull toward private feminine feeling, other moments counteract that drive, either by converting it into public allegorical justification of the war or — the sequence is intensely contradictory in ways entirely characteristic both of Stevens and his culture — by subsuming it into an overriding ironic narrative which functions as critique of that war. Both these countermoves, and particularly the second, depend upon identifications not filial but fraternal. An insider's brotherhood is declared in the epigraph of the volume of Lemercier's *Lettres* taken from one of his notes to his mother: "You do not know the things that are taught by him who falls. I do know." It is declared, too, in Stevens's epigraph to his own "Lettres," taken from the French preface to Lemercier's volume by André Chevrillon:

to fight at the side of his brothers, in his own rank, in his own place, with open eyes, without hope of glory or of gain, and because such is the law: this is the commandment of the god to the warrior Arjuna, who had doubted whether he were right in turning away from the Absolute to take part in the evil dream of war. . . . Plainly, it is for Arjuna to bend his bow among the other Kshettyras. (11)

Speaking the war poem as Lemercier allowed Stevens to affirm, through the authority of the soldier, his own turn toward the (feminine) absolute of lyric contemplation; but also, more importantly, it allowed him access to his own place as Arjuna bending his imaginary bow at the masculine side of the brothers, writing "letters" addressed to a mother rendered ignorant and absent: "You do not know. I do know."

V

"We both know" is in one sense the implicit refrain of Second World War V-letters. Asserting significant bonds between the male soldier and his woman reader, the V-letter suggests the possibility of a positive, liberating social consensus underlying or emerging out of the military struggle. At the same time these representations of mutuality hold conventional wartime gender divisions (the male protector, the waiting woman) firmly in line. The promised consensus will be epitomized in the nuclear family; in place of the melodramas of beset manhood which dominated the Great War soldiers' literary scene, V-letters offer melodramas of beset domesticity, as in these lines from Karl Shapiro's "V-Letter.":

You turn me from these days as from a scene
        Out of an open window far
Where lies the foreign city and the war.
You are my home and in your spacious love
I dream to march as under flaring flags
        Until the door is gently shut.
Give me the tearless lesson of your pride,
                Teach me to live and die
As one deserving anonymity,
The mere devotion of a house to keep
                A woman and a man.

Give me the free and poor inheritance
        Of our own kind . . .

                                        (228)

At the same time, in place of the twice-told-tales of Pound's Chinese
or Stevens's French characters, V-letters represent themselves as communi-
cation undergoing no translation (except the mediations of wartime pos-
tal technology—which only emphasize instead of defamiliarizing the
message's "reality"). The effect of the authentic soldier's voice is height-
ened. The link between the speaking soldier and the writing soldier is
strongly asserted, and the subversive possibilities of role shifting which
Pound's and Stevens's pastiches suggest are implicitly rejected.

Less "translated," then, and less ironized, Second War V-letters nonethe-
less converge with both "war poem" traditions I have been tracing out of
the Great War—that of the poet combatant and that of the male modern-
ist civilian—in one key way. Once again they speak from the position
of the soldier, a location simultaneously a privilege and a burden, both
reserved for men. The writers of forties V-letter poems solved certain
dilemmas posed by their Great War literary inheritance by re-creating a
modestly idealized female spectator, but they also took from the First
World War poets, particularly the poet combatants who were their most
direct precursors, a model of war poetry as the display of the prowess of
a soldier poet in command of whatever words could be said and of his
own part in the conflict. "I love you first because you wait," Shapiro's
soldier writes in his "V-Letter," "because / For your own sake, I cannot
write / Beyond these words."

        . . . And in the dark of absence your full length
        Is such as meets my body to the full
                Though I am starved and huge.
                                        (227)

V-letters are not only victory-letters but also *virility* letters. Their complex mix of affirmation and negation suggests that the poets who wrote them wished to claim for themselves the attributes of Wallace Stevens's allegorical "figure of the youth as virile poet" in his Second World War period essay of the same title: "that special illumination, special abundance, and severity of abundance, virtue in the midst of indulgence and order in disorder that is involved in the idea of virility."[66] Young literary men in the Second World War seem in their V-letters to have understood literary history much as Stevens invokes it in this essay. Although the large body of Second War soldier poetry includes varied, conflicted, and sometimes extremely anxious representations of masculinity, the popular V-letter form specifically presents a simpler view of manhood in wartime. Through the V-letter, the soldier poet might demonstrate a strong, masculine force of personality, might stamp his image on the Second World War in the same way that, Stevens says, Milton's "severe and determined" (starved and huge?) face became the face of the seventeenth century for later readers. "The centuries," as Stevens put it and as V-letters, in the end insisted, "have a way of being male."[67]

4

(Not) Playing with Mimesis

Gwendolyn Brooks and the
Stuff of Letters

I

The device of the dramatic monologue or "transferred voice"[1] which
Pound and Stevens had employed during the Great War offered civilian
women poets one obvious way of crossing the gap between themselves
and soldiers. But few literary women besides Gwendolyn Brooks took on
the persona of a male soldier in order to write Second War poetry. Brooks
seems to have felt unusually comfortable, for a woman poet of the early
1940s, with putting on such a guise. Take, for example, her instructively
breezy account of the composition of her long poetic sequence "Gay Chaps
at the Bar" (1945), in a retrospective interview:

When I start writing a poem, I don't think about "models" or what anybody else
in the world has done. . . . I like to refer to that series of soldier sonnets . . . [I
wrote] in off-rhyme, because I felt it was an off-rhyme situation — I did think of
that. I wrote it because of a letter I got from a soldier who first included that
phrase in what he was telling me; and then I said, there are other things to say
about what's going on at the front and all, and I'll write more poems, some of
them based on the stuff of letters that I was getting from several soldiers, and I
felt it would be good to have them all in the same form, because it would serve
my purposes throughout.[2]

"The stuff of letters I was getting from several soldiers": this is an ex-
traordinarily offhand and relaxed phrase. "Stuff": raw goods, the matter
or substance awaiting literary elaboration and literary form. "Stuff": fabric,
rough textile material. "Stuff": stolen property. "Stuff," as dismissive slang:
worthless discourse or writing, coupled with nonsense. "Stuff," in its earliest

109

meanings in English: a body of soldiers; munitions of war; the quilted underside of defensive armor. Brooks's versions of the writing of "Gay Chaps at the Bar" is remarkable for its casual insistence on the ease with which, she claims, she could draw upon this "stuff of letters."

Brooks has, she says, appropriated whatever is worthwhile in these men's voices, transforming them into a unified sonnet sequence. She has begun as a passive receiver of letters; the poem's epigraph, from a letter by Lieutenant William Couch which provides the title phrase "gay chaps at the bar," acknowledges as much. But she has proceeded, by her own account, as the active shaper of raw stuff, the producer of the letter-as-sonnet. The body of the actual sonnet series "Gay Chaps" seems to corroborate this retrospective description: it retains no overt traces of its origin, as Brooks has described it, in the woman addressee's reception of letters and the woman reader's reading. Instead, it simply assumes the authorial voice of the V-letter, and at moments, beyond that, it erases the writing of the letter as well, in order to dramatize the spoken monologue of the soldier. Completely violating all home-front taboos against women's literary impersonation of men in uniform, the sequence demonstrates throughout what Margaret Walker, in a review of Brooks's wartime work, called the "veteran aplomb" of Brooks's sonnets — veteran, here, in every current sense of the word.[3]

"I don't think about 'models' or what anybody else in the world has done," Brooks says ingenuously in the interview quoted above. But to write in 1944 as if composing "the stuff of letters" was, as I argued in my previous chapter, to perform a highly formulaic literary activity, one no less rule bound and determined than abiding by the strictures of the sonnet. "Gay Chaps" may be read, in fact, as a strenuous engagement with convention. In this chapter, I focus first on the "rhyme," not the "off-," in "Gay Chaps"'s "off-rhymes": that is, on the poem's tactics of imitation, its exact and exacting compliance with and replication of the masculine models of war literature, of war and literature, before it. "Gay Chaps" follows the gendered structures of the soldier's poetic V-letter to the letter. As I engage the poem, I employ, then, an idea often invoked by feminists in recent years, the concept variously called "repetition," identification," "role playing," "masquerade," and, most frequently, "mimicry," "mimeticism," or "mimesis," following Luce Irigaray:

For how can we introduce ourselves into such a tightly-woven systematicity? There is, in an initial phase, perhaps only one 'path,' the one historically assigned to the feminine: that of *mimicry.* . . . To play with mimesis is thus, for a woman, to try to recover the place of her exploitation by discourse, without allowing herself to be simply reduced to it. It means to resubmit herself . . . to ideas about herself, that are elaborated in/by a masculine logic, but so as to make "visible," by an effect of playful repetition, what was supposed to remain invisible: the cover-up of a possible operation of the feminine in language. It also means "to unveil" the fact that, if women are such good mimics, it is because they are not simply reabsorbed in this function. *They also remain elsewhere.*[4]

Irigaray's concept of play with mimesis has been employed in different, and sometimes even partially contradictory, ways by American feminist literary critics and theorists. I use the term, broadly, to mean the repetition of a dominant form in such a way as to comply overtly with its structures but to expose its exploitations and to suggest the possibility of covert insubordination. In the end, then, I am concerned with identifying deviant qualities in "Gay Chaps," with finding whether and where, as it engages the normative conventions of the V-letter, it may be read as transgressive, duplicitous, or both.[5]

"May be read" is the important phrase here, for all meanings are, of course, negotiated in reading, in reception; it takes two to play with mimesis. Brooks's assumption of the male soldier persona itself has no inherent or necessary significance; for people coming upon these poems in many other contexts, the sequence might in no way articulate its distance or difference from the forms it repeats. My aim here is to suggest some stress points where, in the context of the sexual discourse of war I trace throughout this book, the "ambivalence of mimicry" and its gendered implications in "Gay Chaps" may be, for us, most readily pronounced.[6]

What did it mean for a woman poet in the home-front culture of the 1940s (a culture whose inhibitions and injunctions against just such a move I have detailed in previous chapters) to mimic the masculine soldier, to introduce herself into the tightly woven system of the stuff of men's letters, with such apparent freedom? How was she able — *was* she able — to overcome her situation of exclusion, to challenge the conviction that the poem about men's bonding and men's wounding on the battlefield was "men's stuff" only? How did it matter that this woman poet into whose texts I read the play of mimesis was Black? In this chapter I intend to ground a reading of the "mimicries" of "Gay Chaps" within a historical and cultural context which stubbornly complicated (and complicates) any theory and any practice of feminine miming. Brooks's Second World War poems themselves repeatedly take up the problem of the politics of mimicry, raising a number of additional questions about the powers and the limits of "playing with mimesis": *Why* mimesis? *How?* To what end? Whose game is this? What has been covered up? And how playful can this repetition be?

In working toward answers to these questions, we will need to examine the various audiences to whom "Gay Chaps at the Bar" appears to have been addressed and the varying contexts in which the text was likely to have been read. "Gay Chaps"'s relations to the Anglo-American masculine tradition of modern war poetry which I have been tracing in the previous chapter will be obvious — as will its openly declared, deliberately enacted links to sonnet tradition. But "Gay Chaps" needs also to be read within two other equally, or even more, pertinent contexts.

As its double publishing history makes clear — the two initial poems of the series were published first in *Poetry* in November 1944, then in *Negro Story* in March 1945 — "Gay Chaps at the Bar" situates itself not only within American modernist culture but also, firmly, within a specifically Black tradition of literary protest against overt and hidden American racism and of literary agitation for Black freedom and equality.[7] Its ironies derive as much from Claude McKay's "If we must die" as from Wilfred Owen's "Dulce et decorum est," its representations of violence as much from antilynching as from antiwar poems. Readers in the forties familiar with Black literary journals might have recognized its particularly obvious connections to several contemporary poems published in *Negro Story* just months before "Gay Chaps" appeared there. Moreover, these soldier sonnets bear an equally strong relation to sources and analogues which are not poetic but journalistic: certain rhetorical conventions, themes, and images which predominated in major popular Black newspapers such as Brooks's hometown *Chicago Defender* during the Second World War.

When "Gay Chaps" and the volume of which it was a part, *A Street in Bronzeville*, are read within the context of Black discourse on the home front, Brooks's choice of a male persona, and her strategies of representation of that masculine figure, may be understood as typical rather than unusual, and as political practices: tactics designed to expose and protest discriminations not of sex but of race. The soldier poems in *Street in Bronzeville*, with titles like "the white troops had their orders but the Negroes looked like men"[8] and "Negro Hero," engage in a project shared by a wide range of literary and nonliterary texts by Black authors, a set of tasks which was recognizable, familiar, and imperative for readers of the wartime Black press. Mixing patriotism and protest, Black representations of the American war effort, of which "Gay Chaps" was a representative example, sought to write the Black soldier into the record of war; to recognize the fact of his presence at the Second War's fronts; to give voice to his experience; to reveal and to correct the terms of his exclusion from both heroic and antiheroic modern mythologies of warfare; and, most generally and most vigorously, to expose the contradiction between democratic ideology and racist practice in the United States.

Of the poems in the "Gay Chaps" series, the seventh sonnet, "the white troops had their orders but the Negroes looked like men," most clearly carries out this project. The poem represents the introduction of Black troops into an insular white military unit. It focuses on the response of the white soldiers, who had "supposed the formula was fixed," devising neat categories, boxing "their feelings properly, complete to tags— / A box for dark men and a box for other." "But," the poem adds, bemused, "when the Negroes came they were perplexed. / These Negroes looked like men." The white soldiers, examining their black-and-white conceptual frameworks,

. . . would often find the contents had been scrambled. Or even switched. Who really gave two figs? Neither the earth nor heaven ever trembled. And there was nothing startling in the weather.[9]

The pose here is matter-of-fact, the tone dry; this is the story of a crisis which is not a crisis, a radical shift in which nothing moves. The poem plays out what we might call a mimesis of whiteness as well as of maleness, entering the point of view of the white male who is already indoctrinated by and implicated in a racist system. From this vantage point, the figure of the other who enters the scene, one formerly excluded from the military circle and from manhood on the grounds of his Blackness, starts to look suspiciously like, act confusingly like, be disruptively like, and die unremarkably like any (white) man. This "scrambling," from a covert, implicit Black perspective, is both desirable and fearful; if it represents the positive, casual transformation of white men's ideas as they fight side by side with Black men, it also suggests, with its eerie and grotesque imagery of confused boxes and misplaced tags, nightmares of dismemberment and entanglement, in which men's body parts on the battlefield may terrifyingly get mixed up with each other. The uncanny quality of the end of the poem derives in large part from its juxtaposition of the rhetoric of racial progress with an unflinching, devastating representation of combat death and injury.

Here, as elsewhere, Brooks combines a heroic antiracist affirmation — the assertion of the Black soldier's right to presence, and recognition, in battle — with an equivalent anti-heroic, antiwar negation: the right to battle is the right to be butchered. Like the masculine V-letters of the forties, Brooks's war poems are energized by the conflict between mythologizing the war as just and revealing its hidden undersides, its lies and mutilations; Brooks, however, works within the conventions of wartime Black discourse to extend the boundaries of those undersides, comprehending not just the brutality of mechanized warfare but the brutality of institutionalized racism.

The ironic strategies of "the white troops had their orders" work in solidarity with the deployment of political irony on the subject of the Black man's relation to the war machine in countless Black wartime texts, ranging from the war poems of literary men such as Langston Hughes, Owen Dodson, and Melvin Tolson to the famous popular calls to arms in the Black mass media: "Remember Pearl Harbor, and Sikeston [the site of a lynching in January, 1942] too." "Should I sacrifice to live 'Half American'?" "Let . . . colored Americans adopt the double VV for a double victory. The first V for victory over our enemies without. The second V for victory over our enemies within."[10] This last slogan, the widely influential "VV" campaign initiated by one of the most prominent Black newspapers, the *Pittsburgh Courier,* with its radical doubling of a dominant symbol, its subversion through replication, provides a sharp reminder that "playing with mimesis" is a strategy for dealing with oppression which is limited neither to "feminine" nor to "literary" practitioners.[11]

An obvious answer, then, to the question of why it was that "Gay Chaps" could, with such seeming ease, transgress the taboo felt among literary women on the home front against speaking as and speaking for soldiers is that the questions of inclusion and exclusion, of identity and difference, which most preoccupy this poem are, simply, questions of race, not questions of gender. This answer is appropriate, since it calls to task a reductive feminist reading which cannot take into account the fact that for Brooks and for the poem there are other matters at stake, alliances and struggles other than the dynamics of sexual difference. But the answer is also inappropriate, since it implies that a war poem might either "represent women" or "represent Blacks," "represent gender" or "represent race," but not do both, and since it ignores the fact that, while Brooks wrote of, for, and with Black men, she remained a Black woman.[12]

As titles such as "the white troops had their orders but the Negroes looked like men" or "Living Like a Half Man" (a war story in the NAACP's journal) suggest, Black discourse in general in the home-front media was by no means indifferent to gender. In fact—and in this aspect it does not differ from its dominant white counterpart—the constructions and crises of masculinity in wartime might be said to be one of its major subjects.[13] In the pages that follow, I wish to examine several of Brooks's war poems where gendering—what makes a man in wartime, what makes a man not a woman—becomes an open issue. It is in these places that Brooks's simple participation in or imitation of masculine poetic V-letter form threatens to break down. There identification strains or even stops, and there, perhaps, the play of mimesis might start.

II

Before considering "Gay Chaps" in detail, I want to look at two other short war-related works by Brooks in which sexual differences are exposed with particular acerbity. Any overly complacent sense of alliance between American Black men and women for the Second World War's duration collapses in the face of a document like Brooks's 1951 essay "Why Negro Women Leave Home." Published in *Negro Digest* a year after a piece entitled "Why Men Leave Home" by a professor of sociology, St. Clair Drake, and three months after "What's Wrong With Negro Women?" by a prominent member of the Black community, Roi Ottley, Brooks's essay was part of an ongoing debate in the pages of *Negro Digest* over the causes and cures of fractures and "instabilities" in the postwar Black family.[14] Brooks may have been immediately provoked to response by Ottley's particularly galling "case against Negro women"; but it is Drake's piece, whose title she so clearly usurps and reverses, which we will find especially pertinent here. For Drake's essay is finally a war story. Its rhetoric is drawn directly from the heroic and ironic masculine war narratives I have described previously, and it grounds its authority at a central moment in an appeal to a masculine consensus represented, not surprisingly, by a man's war poem.

Drake's various explanations for "why men leave home" are not only confusing but incompatible. His first argument, based on social and economic factors, emphasizes racial difference: Black men abandon their families because an oppressive system denies them access to jobs. But his second argument, based squarely in a theory of male sociobiology, erases racial difference: "Negro men leave home not because they are Negroes, but because they are men. . . . For almost a million years after humanity emerged from the purely animal state . . . women . . . stay[ed] close to camp . . . with men bringing home the bear or kangaroo." A third explanation mediates somewhat between these two positions, the cultural and the biological: "Every war . . . has uprooted the males and set the pattern of wandering ever more deeply." The unexpected proof-text for this point, the clincher to Drake's own case, quoted at length, turns out to be Alfred Lord Tennyson's representation of male bonding in wandering. "Tennyson," writes Drake, "tells us what *Ulysses* did after he came back from the battle of Troy. Nothing could be more boring than to stay quietly at home with his faithful wife." Here the unmendable gap between men and women which modern masculine war literature repeatedly lays open recurs once again with a vengeance; it functions, for Drake, less as a revelation of a culture's lack than as a genuinely desirable male escape hatch. "A lot of G.I.'s," Drake concludes, "must feel this way today."[15]

Brooks's response to Drake, from its first sharp insistence on a race-marked title ("Why Negro Women," not "Why Women Leave Home"), strongly revises his essay's mythologies of the flight of the male. For her, too, the war — not "war" as an ahistorical abstraction, but a historically specific Second World War — has had decisive, lasting effects. But those disruptions have radically shaken and altered the life of the Black *woman* whom Drake had represented as passively stable. It is *her* new demands which threaten the status quo, her transformations which galvanize the changes in the postwar family:

Many a woman who had never worked before went to work during the last war. She will never forget the good taste of financial independence. For the first time, perhaps, she was able to buy a pair of stockings without anticipating her husband's curses. . . . without risking a hysterically shouted inquiry. . . . She could buy their child a new overcoat without planning an elaborate, strategic campaign, or undergoing the smoke and fire of a semi-revolution. . . . She felt clean, straight, tall, and as if she were a part of the world. . . . Women who cannot [continue to] obtain such regard will increasingly prefer to live alone.

No poem comparable to Tennyson's finds its way into this essay by a woman poet — only a sly, revisionary trivialization of Drake's image of the male as Ulysses: "Many a husband, in these bewildering, unsettled times," Brooks writes simply, "is frankly at sea."[16]

Perhaps the intensity of the sexual antagonism in Brooks's essay and its predecessors in *Negro Digest* is a distinctly postwar phenomenon, a reflection of late-forties anxiety more than wartime hostility. Still, the forcefully plain rage of this debate, the acrimoniousness of the divorce between the genders which it enacts, casts its shadow back over Brooks's apparently undisturbed espousal of the cause of the Black soldier in wartime poems like "Gay Chaps." Let us return, then, to the war period proper and to the war poems Brooks wrote in the heat of the national military conflict, and again let us momentarily postpone consideration of "Gay Chaps," in order first to examine the myths of gender in the one poem in *Street in Bronzeville* which most vigorously and conventionally played soldier's advocate.

III

The poem, "Negro Hero," represents Dorie Miller, a ubiquitous figure in Black publications on the home front in early 1942. For readers who do not remember him or who have never heard of him, the gloss provided with the poem's first publication in *Common Ground* in 1945 will be helpful:

Dorie Miller, hero of Miss Brooks' poem, is the young mess attendant [the Navy would not allow Black men to serve as anything but kitchen help, and would not instruct them in the use of guns] who won the Navy Cross at Pearl Harbor for his 'distinguished devotion to duty, extraordinary courage and disregard for his own personal safety during the attack.'

Miller manned a machine gun on the U.S.S. Arizona after members of the air crew had been put out of action and shot down four Japanese planes, then carried his wounded captain to safety under the whistle of enemy bullets. He has been missing in action in the Southwest Pacific since Dec. of 1943. [Miller was killed in the Makin battle.][17]

Because, as many articles in the Black journals stressed, Dorie Miller's transgressive heroism was noted only grudgingly and belatedly by the Navy and by the white-run media, he came quickly to stand for the essence of untapped or unsung Black powers of war-making and war-story-making. In the inaugural issue of the important Black literary journal *Negro Story* in 1944, for instance, the editor Alice Browning called for original submissions in these terms: "No one can deny that the Negro writer has an all-important role to play in presenting new characters which are emerging from the scene as well as an interpretation of the scene itself. The Dorie Millers . . . have been untouched as fiction material."[18]

Brooks's poem answers this challenge to produce a fictive Dorie Miller. Rather than claiming to "present" a "new character," however, "Negro Hero" centers on the politics of *re*-presentation: Dorie Miller's story has already been told, has already been appropriated and circulated. The poem charts, in the Negro hero's "own voice," his transactions — and the transactions of the woman poet who writes his lines — with those official versions of his masculine experience.

"Negro Hero" begins and ends with conflict between men; with a fight, in that famous arena of male *agon*, Pearl Harbor, *for* masculine power and *over* masculine power; with a tense struggle in which, as in "the white troops had their orders," Black men's and white men's bodies come into wrenching, violent, revolutionary contact:

> I had to kick their law into their teeth in order to save
> them.
> However I have heard that sometimes you have to deal
> Devilishly with drowning men in order to swim them to
> shore.
> Or they will haul themselves and you to the trash and
> the fish beneath.
> (When I think of this, I do not worry about a few
> Chipped teeth.)
>
> (19)

These are the opening lines. Concluding, too, the poem emphasizes the Black man's ambivalent relation to a white man's law which purports to be universal and liberating but which is, perforce, repressive and exclusionary; and again the poem unleashes, even as it contains, the revolution which occurs in the United States when a Black man lays his hands on formerly white-male-controlled machines of violence. The scene seems to have nothing directly to do with women. What frames and dominates the plot of "Negro Hero" is the subject of male homosocial relations,[19] and in this the poem adheres faithfully to the discourse on Miller, largely written by Black men, in the home-front Black press.

But the subtitle of Brooks's poem — "to suggest Dorie Miller" — hints at a possible deviance from standard representations. To *suggest* Dorie Miller rather than speak for him, to claim and disclaim his voice in the same breath, to insist on the imaginary nature of the poem and on the limits of identification, to post a caution sign at the dramatic monologue's entrance: Why this extreme authorial scrupulousness? The subtitle might be a mark of decorum; it keeps the female-authored text at a respectful distance from its famous male hero. In that margin, though, we might read not just deference but difference, the hidden presence of a femininity in at least an uncomfortable, if not an actively critical, relation to the art of military homage. Perhaps the subtitle is meant to ward off accusations of slander, to preserve Miller's reputation in spite of the poem — to disclaim something in particular. If so, that trouble spot might well be the two stanzas at "Negro Hero"'s center, where the ostensibly sexually indifferent man-to-man race rhetoric of the rest of the text gives way momentarily to open figures of gender.

Dorie Miller's behavior on the deck of the U.S.S. *Arizona* on December 7, 1941, did not need to be explained. That much was clear to almost everyone who produced a version of his story in the home-front media. Dominant fictions of wartime masculinity constructed military heroism as impelled by an unreflective instinct for loyalty — to the male brotherhood of the armed services, to the national cause — whose intrinsic rightness was necessarily self-evident. Major Black newspapers, despite their "combined criticism-and-support approach," provided no significant exceptions to this particular rule.[20] Thus the strikingly explanatory impulses of the midsection of "Negro Hero" come as a surprise. In its third and fourth stanzas, the poem ceases its narrative of racial antagonism and combat heroism to render, in compacted form, two theories of war-making. The speaker puts forward two reasons for his actions, each of which consists of a figural definition of masculinity.

The first presents the image of the soldier-as-really-a-child, whose

ferocious combat urges seem half-feral and half–spoon-fed. The second
presents the image of the soldier-as-Real-Man, who chooses his battles
with full self-awareness beyond instinct or indoctrination:

> It was a tall time. And of course my blood was
> Boiling about in my head and straining and howling
>   and singing me on.
> Of course I was rolled on wheels of my boy itch to get
>   at the gun.
> Of course all the delicate rehearsal shots of my child-
>   hood massed in mirage before me.
> Of course I was child
> And my first swallow of the liquor of battle bleeding
>   black air dying and demon noise
> Made me wild.
>
> It was kinder than that, though, and I showed like a
>   banner my kindness.
> I loved. And a man will guard when he loves.
> Their white-gowned democracy was my fair lady.
> With her knife lying cold, straight, in the softness of
>   her sweet-flowing sleeve.
> But for the sake of the dear smiling mouth and the
>   stuttered promise I toyed with my life.
> I threw back! — I would not remember
> Entirely the knife.
>
> (48–49)

How are we to read the relation of these conflicting accounts of the hero's
motives? One possibility is suggested by Harry B. Shaw, in a recent article
on the representation of men in Brooks's early poetry:

In the reflection on the news coverage, the mild sarcasm of the persona becomes
evident with the repetition of "of course" in the [first stanza quoted above]. Even
in an act of heroism, the Black man was denied his full accord as a man. . . . The
implication is that whereas a white soldier performing similar feats would have
been described as manly, the Black man's acts are attributed to . . . being a child
wild with the first taste of battle.[21]

For Shaw, the Negro hero does not "speak" the story of his "boy itch"
so much as read it. Or rather, he rereads it, with an inflection — "mild
sarcasm" — which signals his differences from the racist accounts of the
white press that he mimics. The second stanza corrects the first, replacing
the false representations of white news coverage with the uncovering power
of true representation: there, in the revelations of a man who is no boy

("It was kinder than that, though), the Negro hero's self-disclosure and the discourse of the *Black* press perfectly converge.

I would like to propose another interpretation,[22] one which would understand the conflict of these two versions of the hero not as a struggle *between* public white rhetoric and private Black reality but as a struggle *within* a divided self. The second stanza's myth of masculinity and heroism does not, I would argue, replace or supercede the first. Rather, two figures of male war-making, both owned by the hero, remain in disconcerting suspension: one offensive, one defensive, one boyish, one manly, one of suddenly discharging aggression and one of stoic, planned self-sacrifice, one entirely dislodged from and one in conflicted relation to patriotic and ideological justification. To my ear, the tone of the "of course . . . of course" stanza sounds less sardonic than confessional or meditative; its "mild sarcasms" rebound directly, self-critically, back onto the speaker. The two stanzas taken together provide a startlingly subversive representation of maleness — fragmented, qualified, ambiguous.

I would suggest further that the Negro hero's critical, indeterminate relation to popular assumptions about what constitutes a man and about what causes heroism reflects his female author's alienation from those stereotypes of military masculinity. The stanza which begins "It was a tall time," for instance, differs markedly from most male-authored Second War poems, not so much in its recognition of a spontaneous or conditioned masculine aggression as in its trivialization of that aggression: the male warrior is "child," his bloodthirstiness a "boy itch." "Negro Hero" does not equate boyishness with an innocence beyond killing, as Randall Jarrell's narrator seems to, for example, in "Eighth Air Force." Rather, the poem implies here that male war-making is a form of channeled immaturity. What moves Harry Shaw to contain the implications of this "boy itch" theory by reducing them to the aspersions of white racist journalism is, perhaps, what made Brooks cover herself with that modest disclaimer, "to suggest Dorie Miller." For Shaw would preserve as a given what Brooks — and her Negro hero — are willing to explore as a question: the model of the mature male as stalwart, coherent, inherently sound. Conventionally, "to think about masculinity," as Peter Schwenger puts it, "is to become less masculine oneself."[23] Brooks, daringly, represents her Negro hero as a thinker about masculinity. In the context of the popular Black press's hungry glorification of Miller, in the context of the popular white press's anxious assertions of the manliness of Every Soldier praised for heroism, this seems a bold move.[24]

"If women are such good mimics," Luce Irigaray writes in her definition of playing with mimesis, "it is because they are not simply reabsorbed in this function. They also remain elsewhere" (76). In "Negro Hero," we can sense the presence and the pressure of that "elsewhere" most distinctly in the critique of masculine heroism as "boy itch" which issues momentarily, surprisingly, out of the masculine hero's own mouth. But what about the lines which follow, in which Brooks becomes an even better mimic? Is it possible to read any signs of an "elsewhere" in the representation of the Negro hero's relationship with democracy, which reduplicates with punitive accuracy the most misogynistic figures of the masculine tradition of war poetry?

> I loved. And a man will guard when he loves.
> Their white-gowned democracy was my fair lady.
> With her knife lying cold, straight, in the softness of
>   her sweet-flowing sleeve.
> But for the sake of the dear smiling mouth and the
>   stuttered promise I toyed with my life.
> I threw back! — I would not remember
> Entirely the knife.

This iconographical Democracy recalls the allegories of war as courtship by Lovelace and Birney which I discussed in the previous chapter; with her hidden knife, she recalls, even more obviously, Wilfred Owen's ironic method of rendering heroism meaningless by debunking the myth of the hallowed female spectator. This is an old device we have seen before: calling a spurious ideal — in this case, "democracy" — into question by displacing the noble cause's hidden evils onto the figure of a villainous woman traitor. Euphemism and complicity concentrate for the Negro hero in a woman's body, exactly as they do for the male protagonists of numerous antiwar masculine narratives.

But "Negro Hero" responds to at least two bodies of writing; if the Negro hero inherits his woman problem from traditions of rage and irony in modern Anglo-American war literature, he inherits it, as well, from equally searing traditions of rage and irony in the Afro-American literature of lynching. It is, we must note, a *white* woman problem; Democracy is the idealized, protected, sham "fair lady" of Petrarchan tradition and the slave plantation. "Fair" in this context is, of course, a scathingly ironic pun: this bleached, overvalued object of desire is an icon of her culture's systematic unfairness. The "dear" of the "smiling mouth" works similarly. Charming, seductive, with a whole machine of torture ready to activate at her cry if not her will, at once disarmingly vulnerable and menacingly powerful, the white woman as a figure for American culture's combination of appeal and concealed violence makes frequent appearances in Black Second World War rhetoric.[25]

"Negro Hero," like many other Second War texts by Black American authors in complex relation to the patriotism of the dominant culture, evokes the rape-cry-and-lynching narrative in order partially—but only partially—to revoke it. The Black man here knows what he's getting into; the female Democracy's attractions persist, are in some sense worth it; he refuses to "remember / Entirely the knife." The text mutes its militance in the service of a different notion of race pride, one which emphasizes respectability and takes a man's ability to protect his womenfolk—and Democracy is, in fact, must be, his woman—as the key measure of his dignity. (Note, however, the persistence even in this stanza of words which evoke a childish, boy-itch aggression, threatening that dignity: "I *toyed* with my life," or "threw back," with its connotations of reversion.)

Though Democracy as she figures in Black visual representations of the war period (such as editorial cartoons, where she appears repeatedly) is consistently, undeniably white, in some poetic versions by Black male authors her race is inexplicit.[26] The fact that in "Negro Hero" her color, as well as her value, are fixed as "fair" is of critical significance for an understanding of the stakes involved in this particular act of mimesis. Whatever her femininity means for Gwendolyn Brooks, one thing is certain: she is not this woman. The fairness of the lady reminds us that even as this Black woman poet faithfully reproduces a masculine system of representation, even as she copies precisely a cynically, brutally misogynist allegory, she will not herself wholly bear the brunt of *this* figure that she replicates. Invisible, repressed, the Black woman indeed remains elsewhere in this story.

The painful dimensions of that elsewhere are mapped, and the rage which floods out of that elsewhere is loosed, in Brooks's "Ballad of Pearl May Lee" (which gives Pearl May Lee's version of her lover's seduction by a white woman who then cried rape), and in other poems which surround the soldier poems of *A Street in Bronzeville*. But rather than surveying that Black feminine "elsewhere," I want to return to more familiar and problematic ground: to "Gay Chaps at the Bar," and to its perfect mimicries of the masculine stuff of letters.

IV

From the start, "Gay Chaps" links itself directly and indirectly both to soldiers' letters and to soldier poetry. Its title and epigraph derive explicitly, as I have said, from a letter to the author from a "Lieutenant William Couch, in the South Pacific." After an opening dedication to Brooks's brother ("souvenir for Staff Sergeant Raymond Brooks and every other soldier"), words from one of Couch's letters immediately follow: " . . . and guys I knew in the States, young officers, return from the front crying and trembling. Gay chaps at the bar in Los Angeles, Chicago, New York. . . . " More implicitly, but in ways which would probably have been legible to many regular readers of the wartime *Negro Story*, the poem reworks another text written by Couch — not a letter from the front, but a war poem printed in that journal five months before the first publications of the sonnets which would comprise "Gay Chaps." Here, too, the governing figure of the "bar" occurs:

To a Soldier

Here
        where the cock sounds his synchronized song
        in a sunless morning
        and the caravans of young move towards the
        battlefronts . . .

(O, brother say!)

        The planted cannon replies to the
        last word, living urge of flesh
        that aimlessly scratched the ground with
        bayonet point
        or, valiant, alert, stealthily moved into hell

(O, brother)

        but this is a neat note
        and we shall not shed tears
        home from the bar in silence . . . [27]

Couch's poem presents itself as the painful, self-limiting address of a soldier to a soldier, of a brother to a brother; it counters its own calls for authentic response to the horror and alienation of the battlefield ("O brother say!") with the tight-lipped obligations of masculine self-censorship ("but this is a neat note / and we shall not shed tears"). Brooks's "Gay Chaps at the Bar," taking up from Couch both the subject of the soldier's language and the central bar image, inserts itself within this straining dialogue, interrupting what brothers have to say to brothers with what promises momentarily to be a *sisterly* response ("souvenir for Staff Sergeant Raymond Brooks").

From the first word of the first sonnet, however, it is clear that the poetic voice of "Gay Chaps" will answer back as the voice of a brother —

or rather, of brothers, since the poem has multiple speakers; it represents
the collective voice of the veteran combatants which Wilfred Owen, in
his "Insensibility," had called the "We Wise."[28] The "souvenir" *for* soldiers
promptly metamorphoses into the memory *of* soldiers (that is, owned *by*
soldiers). Like the troops in the British Great War poems which inaugu-
rated the modern literary tradition of war poetry, the "We" of "gay chaps"
are angry recorders of an aftermath. The poem is structured around a
clear ironic contrast between after and before, front and home:

gay chaps at the bar

. . . and guys I knew in the States, young officers, return
from the front crying and trembling. Gay chaps at the
bar in Los Angeles, Chicago, New York . . .

We knew how to order. Just the dash
Necessary. The length of gaiety in good taste.
Whether the raillery should be slightly iced
And given green, or served up hot and lush.
And we knew beautifully how to give to women
The summer spread, the tropics, of our love.
When to persist, or hold a hunger off.
Knew white speech. How to make a look an omen.
But nothing ever taught us to be islands.
And smart, athletic language for this hour
Was not in the curriculum. No stout
Lesson showed how to chat with death. We brought
No brass fortissimo, among our talents,
To holler down the lions in this air.

(64)

This sonnet may be read as an extended meditation on and transforma-
tion of the conventional meanings of two word-kernels: "bar" and "order."[29]
Each has a doubled range of associations, one related to alcohol and to
heterosexual pleasure, the other to struggle and to prowess in conflict.
Thus to be "at the bar" means, in the poem's world of *before*, "to be in
the place where one knows how to drink, to seduce and tantalize women."
But in combat and its aftermath, the bar takes on a range of other sinister
meanings; a blockage or obstacle, a marker of lines, it signifies not only
the "color bar" of racist structures which the Black soldier breaks through
into battle but also, as in the crossed "bar" of Tennyson's famous poem,
judgment and death.[30] "Order" begins as a verb indicating sure posses-
sion of language in the context of the barroom, and adds in the later part

of the poem an additional military denotation, a more potent command; the sonnet ends, however, in an explicit denial of the efficacy of men's language. It concludes, on the battleground, after the carnage, with a series of nothings, nos, nots, inhibitions, losses.

At the outset of this group of sonnets, both "bar" and "order" summon suggestions of control, of competence, of male power—only for the first poem to dispel them. The epigraph which begins the poetic series establishes an image of shattered masculine selfhood and a pattern of traumatized return ("return from the front crying and trembling") which underlies the entire sequence. Only in the second poem, "still do I keep my look, my identity," does Brooks focus on the death of a soldier, with a characteristic combination of grim depiction of rigor mortis and loving insistence on the dead man's individuality.[31] The subject of the eleven other sonnets, over and over, is the veteran's stunned survival and his "incompleteness," his resumption, as the third sonnet puts it, "on such legs as are left me, in such heart / As I can manage."

This hint of amputation recalls Owen's "Disabled," a comparison which reveals one important way in which "Gay Chaps" repudiates as well as duplicates the conventions of the modern masculine soldier poem. "Disabled"'s war-wounded protagonist notices with bitterness how the same women's eyes which had goaded him to war "passed from him to the strong men that were whole."[32] "Gay Chaps" records a similar transition from masculine power to impotence, but although the first sonnet places women in the barroom to gaze at the men in their glorious displays of nightlife style, it absents women entirely from the battlefield and its aftermath. It refrains—and this is crucial—from including a female spectator in the second half of the poem, and does so, I believe, to resist the image of the demonic, instigating female gaze which for Owen and other literary men in the ironic tradition constituted the beginning and the end of aggression.

This strategy of omission, within what otherwise reads as a strikingly oppositional and anti-heroic Second War poem, serves two functions. In its representation of trauma without emasculation, its refusal of symbolic castration, its insistence on the continuing dignity and authority of the veteran, it mounts a defense of the soldier. But it also, of course, defends the woman who defends the soldier. Transforming the "stuff of letters" written to a woman into a dramatic veteran's chorus speaking to no one, "Gay Chaps at the Bar" from its first poem certifies that this act of mimesis, this masculine masking, will be undertaken in a spirit of feminine humility, that it has been motivated by the energy of empathy, and that when the soldier says "I am incomplete" (66) he is not the victim of untoward female glee.[33] One distinct sign of that commitment is the curious disappearance of women from the opening sonnet at the moment at which it first represents the consequences of combat; present neither as readers of soldiers' letters nor as spectators, women vanish, exempted from the antagonisms of sexual difference in wartime and from the war poem's pressures of address.

The sequence's first poem, "gay chaps," seems to shy away, then, from the central image of the culpable modern female spectator whose various shapes I have traced in earlier chapters. But that figure, barely suppressed, soon reappears at the heart of the fourth sonnet, the one entitled, aptly, "looking." In "looking" alone, among those "soldier sonnets," the subject of the poem becomes a woman's subjectivity. As its title suggests, this sonnet explicitly explores the situation of the woman who, left behind in war, looks on; enacting a paradigmatic wartime plot, it grapples with questions about the politics, the ethics, and the efficacy of women's language and of the female gaze:

> You have no words for soldiers to enjoy
> The feel of, as an apple, and to chew
> With masculine satisfaction. Not "good-by!"
> "Come back!" or "careful!" Look, and let him go.
> "Good-by!" is brutal, and "come back!" the raw
> Insistence of an idle desperation
> Since could he favor he would favor now.
> He will be "careful!" if he has permission.
> Looking is better. At the dissolution
> Grab greatly with the eye, crush in a steel
> Of study—Even that is vain. Expression,
> The touch or look or word, will little avail.
> The brawniest will not beat back the storm
> Nor the heaviest haul your little boy from harm.
>
>   (67)

"Elsewhere of 'matter,'" Irigaray writes in "The Power of Discourse," beginning to map the imagined terrain which edges against and lies beyond the realm of masculine discourse. She proceeds to elaborate on what she means by "matter": "mother-matter-nature" (77). Irigaray's formulation of the mother's relation to mimesis is worth quoting at length at the outset of a discussion of "looking," for it bears on what the "matter" is within the representation of the maternal in this soldier sonnet. "If women can play with mimesis," Irigaray continues, "it is because they are capable of bringing new nourishment to its operation. . . . "

Because they have always nourished this operation? Is not the "first" stake in mimesis that of re-producing (from) nature? Of giving it form in order to appropriate it for oneself? As guardians of "nature," are not women the ones who maintain, thus who make possible, the resource of mimesis for men? For the logos? (77)

Women, Irigaray suggests, are in one sense the makers and founders of mimesis: it is women, the first reproducers, who are supposed to provide and tend the fertile ground of the "natural" upon which all linguistic and cultural reproductions build. Nurturer and embodiment of the "real" from which all figurations turn and to which all realisms attach, the woman-as-mother selflessly empowers the symbolic order. Brooks's "looking" develops, in part, a similar mythology of feminine relation to systems of representation mastered by men. Effective language, in this sonnet, is imaged repeatedly as masculine; words with clout are either "male" themselves ("brawny" and "heavy," like a burly Marine), or they are fed, with maternal affection, by a woman to a man. The woman's word, an apple handed to the son so he can chew it "with masculine satisfaction," is no forbidden fruit; this is not Eve's apple, not a challenge to the logos, but the word as *snack*, offered by a mother (or by a woman acting, in wifely or girlish submission, like a mother) who properly maintains her position as natural resource.

"Looking" represents this order of things, however, only in a state of acute disruption: "You have no word for soldiers to enjoy." The tone here, at the start of a series of melancholy and deprecatory imperatives, bears a close resemblance to the inflections of voice in the growing wartime genre of advice literature for soldier's families, whose dual purpose was to recognize new anxieties and promote a new kind of emergency good manners. The crisis of the war disturbed, redefined, even sometimes drastically altered, women's understanding, and their culture's understanding, of their roles as nourishers of the symbolic order; "looking" records and responds to that upheaval.

Like some of the most interesting examples of home-front advice literature (a body of texts which Susan Hartmann has categorized, memorably, as "prescriptions for Penelope"), "looking" wavers ambiguously between prescription and description, between speaking to and speaking for its female subject.[34] It may be read either as a removed — even condescending — scolding, or as a self-revealing monologue only barely masked by the guarded use of "you" instead of "I." The form of address maintains, of course, the fiction of mimesis, keeping the woman at a careful distance in a poetic sequence whose decorum demands the consistent perspective of the masculine soldier. But the choice of the second person as governing pronoun takes on other ramifications, both aesthetic and political, when we read it, in a female-authored text, as a strategy of feminine *self*-representation.

This kind of address to a feminine second-person occurs in *A Street in Bronzeville* not only in this "soldier sonnet," part of a larger group of poems whose clear project is to mimic men, but also in what is perhaps Brooks's best-known dramatic monologue in a female voice: her representation of "The Mother." Barbara Johnson has illuminated the operations of the apostrophe to a "you" in the famous opening line of that poem, "Abortions will not let you forget":

The "you" can be seen as an "I" that has become alienated, distanced from itself, and combined with a generalized other, which includes and feminizes the reader of the poem. The grammatical I/thou starting point of traditional apostrophe has been replaced by a structure in which the speaker is simultaneously eclipsed, alienated, and confused with the addressee.[35]

It is not, I think, accidental that "looking" shares with this poem about abortion the eclipses, alienations, and confusions of a self-objectified "I/ you." To willingly give up a son to the military in wartime can feel like a failure of nurture, like a murder of one's own child. "*Any* death of a child," Johnson writes, may be perceived "as a crime committed by the mother, something a mother ought by definition to be able to prevent" (198). In the face of the fear of that crime, and in the struggle between senses of guilt and of innocence, of coercion and of choice, maternal selfhood in both poems splits and blurs.

But here the two poems begin to differ, for if "The Mother," the abortion poem, violates taboos by too nearly severing abortion from criminality, "looking," the war poem, risks transgression if it too closely links maternal sacrifice to criminal negligence. In the forties, having an abortion was forbidden; letting the son of age be drafted or enlist was mandatory. Abortion would be done in secret; mother-son separation in the name of patriotism might be conducted with a show of public pride. At the same time, voluntary abortion was in some part an assertion of decisive will, while maternal sacrifice was in some part, as "looking" makes clear, a capitulation to the unpreventable. Brooks herself describes this difference sharply, in a comment on the persona of her abortion poem: the woman who aborts a child, she writes, is "hardly your crowned and praised and 'customary' Mother; but a Mother not unfamiliar, who decides that *she*, rather than her World, will kill her children."[36]

These distinctions underlie several important differences in the function and effect of the structures of address in the two poems; they help to explain why the feminization of the reader which Johnson describes seems startling in "The Mother" but conventional in "looking," and why "The Mother" can move from the second person to a female "I," while "looking" does not and cannot. The mother in the soldier sonnet, crowned and praised and customary, remains from start to finish locked within the systems of war and gender Nancy Huston has neatly summed up: "Women are required to breed, just as men are required to brawl."[37]

"Looking" exacts this maternal service, but it also enacts the ways in which it takes its toll. In wartime, the poem suggests, linguistic systems which the mother used to nourish collapse; an alternative is then proposed — a maternal look — which scarcely suffices better. Unlike the masculine loss of words in "gay chaps," which is represented with clear irony and outrage, the feminine *lack* of words in "looking" seems guilty, the anger associated with it far more internalized and self-reflexive. The same holds true for the feminine look the poem counsels; here the female spectator, both the one who looks on and the one who is looked at looking on,[38] struggles, anxiously and painfully, under the pressure of the advice which constitutes and represents her, to put on the right maternal face for the soldier.

But "even that is vain." "Looking" suggests the vanity of expression in a double sense. Not only will the possible arranged gestures for the woman on the threshold — words or looks — "little avail" against the buffeting storm of the war, but that woman's expressions will also, in a sense, exist in vain, in *vanity*, signs of a constant awareness, as if she held a mirror up to her face, of the etiquette of feminine wartime response. It is in this representation of self-consciousness, I would argue, that we might find the most distinct traces of a critical feminine difference in this soldier sonnet. For the sad, odd rhetoric of advice-giving maintained throughout the poem raises a subversive possibility. If the proper feminine language and posture in the scene of parting do not surface unbidden from an originary reservoir of maternal feeling, if they may or must be stylized and scripted, then even mother-love itself, that most natural of resources, might be susceptible to, even composed of, mimicries.[39]

In the end, though, "looking"'s subversive anxieties give way to a more conservative emotional appeal, a pathos best understood in the context of the very popular discourse in the mass culture of the forties which Mary Ann Doane has called "maternal melodrama." Like the wartime films Doane analyzes in her *The Desire to Desire*, "looking" enacts a scenario of mother/child separation, focusing on what Doane calls

the contradictory position of the mother within patriarchal society — a position formulated by the injunction that she focus desire on the child and the subsequent demand to give up the child to the social order. Motherhood is conceived as the always uneasy conjunction of an absolute closeness and a forced distance. The scenario of 'watching the child from afar' thus constitutes itself as the privileged tableau of the genre. . . . (74)

And like the "weepies" Doane describes, "looking" exhibits "a distrust of language, locating the fullness of meaning elsewhere," aiming to "recover for meaning what is outside meaning" by affirming the primacy of "non-linguistic registers" (85). Although, as I have said, "looking" makes the maternal look and gesture problematic by asserting their vanity, opening the possibility of a critical distance between the mother and her son, the mother and her motherhood, and the reader and maternal ideology, its closing lines accomplish the end defined by Doane: "The pathos which plays a dominant role in maternal melodrama works to close the gap between spectator and text" (178). The excessive language of pathos in Brooks's lines — "The touch or look or word, will little avail, / The brawniest will not beat back the storm / Nor the heaviest haul your little boy from harm" — the *woman's* language, "your little boy," confirms the presence of a spontaneous motherly grief, and affirms a maternal and filial bond which cannot be undone. In an exact reversal of the movement in "gay chaps" from masculine verbal potency to verbal impotence, "looking" gestures finally toward a redemptive silence, rooting it in boundless, inexpressible maternal power of feeling. This recuperation of the "spontaneously" maternal is, however, drastically limited, both by the poem's governing structure of negation and by maternal melodrama's stereotyped script.

In the midst of a series of poems which mimic masculine representations of soldiers' experience, "looking" anatomizes the position of the female spectator from "inside" — a second-person inside which tends disturbingly, until the final words of the poem, to fuse and be confused with roles externally imposed. It comes as no surprise that the one figure of feminine subjectivity and interiority these well-mimed soldier sonnets are able to admit takes the shape of a mother. The maternal self-consciousness which "looking" renders is far less transgressive and far more permissible within the war poem than other forms of more sexually narcissistic feminine self-regard. Irigaray ends her survey of the "elsewhere of matter" with a warning about the limits and the vulnerability of the mother's position: "Mother-matter-nature must go on forever nourishing speculation. But this re-source is also rejected as the waste product of reflection, cast outside as what resists it. . . . Besides the ambivalence that the nourishing phallic mother attracts to herself, this function leaves women's sexual pleasure aside" (77). No sooner has "looking" with finely tuned ambivalence played out the scene, so central to war systems, in which soldier and mother must simultaneously embrace and detach than the troubling question of the "elsewhere of female pleasure" surfaces, with a disturbingly familiar ring, in "Gay Chaps at the Bar."

The next sonnets in the sequence depict desirable women, lovers of soldiers, who live wholly in the realm of a surface aesthetic which is unable to recognize, and which attempts to repel, the deep disturbances that war causes in past and distant places. Two companion pieces, "piano after war" and "mentors," share an identical pattern. In both, a soldier speaker who envisions his survival after war's end rejects the imagined seductive image of a present woman for the company of dead, remembered fellow soldiers. He swears to imprison himself in recall — not to "thaw," not to "rejuvenate," not, in a real sense, to survive: "I swear to keep the dead upon my mind" (69).

The female objects of desire — and objects of the punishing repudiation of desire — in these poems are represented as sirens, in keeping with the older ironic, anti-heroic war poetry tradition upon which this sonnet series so insistently calls. Femmes fatales, they tempt soldiers and civilizations to ignore history, to forget the truth about military conflict, to dally in the realm of trivial detail. They wear flowers in their hair and dance at banquets, or play piano "on a snug evening" with "cleverly ringed" fingers. Possessing no observable self-knowledge or knowledge of destruction, they produce a powerful but superficial form of art without war.

Through these female figures, "Gay Chaps" takes up a question central to many texts within the developing canon of war literature in the Second War period (the war poems of Richard Eberhart and Richard Wilbur come immediately to mind): the place of aesthetic impulses in the war poem and in a world at war, or, as we might say, the proper aesthetics of war.[40] Other texts written before and after this one embody the threat of an aesthetics which cannot incorporate pain in women. The veteran Krebs in Hemingway's paradigmatic "Soldier's Home," for instance, is represented as feeling this way about girls on his return: "He liked the look of them. . . . But the world they were in was not the world he was in. . . . They were such a nice pattern. He liked the pattern. It was exciting. But he would not go through all the talking. He did not want one badly enough. He liked to look at them all, though. It was not worth it."[41] The speaker of Brooks's "piano after war," imagining himself haunted by the ghosts of soldiers, deadened and unable to respond to the attractions of the woman who serenades him, shares Krebs's world. Both texts place themselves within the broad field of home-front cultural discourses which represented the ex-soldier's alienation. Both engage, too, in a common literary project: testing the power and the failure of aesthetic pleasure in wartime through stories about breaches between patterned women and battered men.

But there the resemblance ends. "Soldier's Home" and "piano after war" disclose an identical subject, the estranged veteran; they do so, however, in acutely divergent ways. I want to pause here briefly for a closer look at their differences in form and style, for in those disparities we might locate in Brooks's sonnet a potentially severe disruption of the orderly processes of imitation and identification, exposing—if only momentarily—visible, crooked seams in the ostensibly smooth mask of the soldier.

The language of the narrative passage from "Soldier's Home" is curt, stuttered, telegraphic; it enacts exactly Kreb's traumatized resistance to aestheticism and the feminine. This is, of course, classic Hemingway style: the art hiding its art, the masculine reticence which signifies, even as it suppresses, a hidden depth, the famous iceberg effect Hemingway described as "7/8 of it under water for every part that shows. Anything you know you can eliminate, and it only strengthens your iceberg."[42] In this description of Krebs's frozen impassivity, form and content perfectly coincide.

"Piano after war," in contrast, strives after no iceberg effect; in fact, this sonnet courts melting, demands a thaw, revels in a liquid musicality:

> On a snug evening I shall watch her fingers,
> Cleverly ringed, declining to clever pink,
> Beg glory from the willing keys. Old hungers
> Will break their coffins, rise to eat and thank.
> And music, warily, like the golden rose
> That sometimes after sunset warms the west,
> Will warm that room, persuasively suffuse
> That room and me, rejuvenate a past.
> But suddenly, across my climbing fever
> Of proud delight—a multiplying cry.
> A cry of bitter dead men who will never
> Attend a gentle maker of musical joy.
> Then my thawed eye will go again to ice.
> And stone will shove the softness from my face.
>
> (68)

The visual imagery of "piano after war" replicates exactly the conventions of ironic masculine war poetry: the male gaze objectifies a woman who is both seductive and sinister. But the poetic *voice* flows oddly counter to that perspective—pretty, polished, musical, it aligns itself with those manners and values which home-front culture and the poem itself define as feminine. Once again Mary Ann Doane's work on forties cinema is pertinent: in the classic "woman's film," the love story, Doane writes, music is "the bad object . . . the site of overindulgent or excessive affect . . . constrained by its confinement to female subjectivity" (103). Here, as "piano after war" represents the veteran's paranoia in audaciously lyric, excessively melodious language, content and style rupture and work openly against each other.

The self-conscious Shakespearian rhetoric of a line like "That sometimes after sunset warms the west" suggests another context for interpretation of the poem's form and diction: "piano after war" raises, more insistently than any previous part of the "Gay Chaps" sequence, the question of the soldier's relation to the *sonnet*. Brooks used sonnet form habitually and expertly throughout the forties; Stacy Carson Hubbard, in her groundbreaking analysis, has described the dynamics of form in another sonnet, "First fight. Then fiddle," published in Brooks's next book which also opposes combat to the lyric and to music:

Like a jazz riff, it undoes and redoes its own chosen model, stopping short where the line extends, racing past where the rhyme calls halt, and plying the stiffness of iambic pentameter with syntactical interruptions and occasional dactylic and spondaic intrusions. . . . This counterpointing of the sonnet's formal devices works to ironize from within both the poem's relation to literary tradition and to nondiscursive action.[43]

In comparison to the nervy energy of "First Fight. Then Fiddle," "piano after war"'s relentlessly pretty negotiations with sonnet form seem placid and listless. Here, perhaps, the conservative pressures inherent in the particular mimetic project of "Gay Chaps" may take their toll. The struggle over which must have priority, war or poetry, is represented in "First Fight" as a productive argument within the self, an ironic tension worked out vigorously within the voice. But "piano after war," caught inside the reactionary sexual conventions of the dominant masculine ironic war poetry tradition, seems to divide these values and attributes between men and women, creating oppositional categories rendered as inert and essential, deploying all its irony at the expense of the female "other." Since its claims to represent male experience depend on stigmatizing a "feminine" lyric impulse which is, in fact, its own, "piano after war" might be said to fail miserably, interestingly, performing and enacting a crisis of mimesis.

How, then, to judge that "failure"? After all, the tricky play with mimesis as Irigaray formulates it works only to the extent that it manages to open a gap between style and essence, the "here" of the text and an "elsewhere." Otherwise it ceases to be playful or critical, becoming instead simply docile, sober: complicit mimesis itself. Couldn't this "failing," then, constitute the success of "piano after war"?

Perhaps, but finally, like "looking" with its appeal to maternal pathos, "piano after war" aims less toward a radical crisis in gendered structures than toward a liberal conciliation. It is important to note that the piano-playing scene on which the poem centers takes place within a dramatic monologue and in the future tense: "On a snug evening I shall watch her fingers." The veteran's denial of a feminine aesthetics is represented not as accomplished fact but as desperate fantasy, a process of shifting from longing to mistrust, from opening to foreclosure, from the will to survive to a deliberate deadening, which exemplifies the trauma of the soldier. The dynamic of "shall," its willed projection into the future, implicitly raises the possibility that the speaker might move beyond his impassivity, might heal; the woman's music—a music the poem itself, the speaker's desire itself, releases — might, however suspect, be an integral part of that process.

Moreover, as in all Brooks's poems, a reading of sexual differences in "piano after war" is complicated, if not altered, by the presence of other factors: differences of race and color. The female figure here is not obviously a "fair lady" like the Negro Hero's paramour; she is not racially marked with categorical certainty. But in the context of the entire collection of poems in which "Gay Chaps" was the concluding sequence — a book preoccupied, as Gloria T. Hull puts it, with "the browns, blacks, tans, chocolates, and yellows of Afro-American color . . . especially as this schema victimizes [Brooks's] darker-skinned female characters[44] — this woman's racial ambiguity demands and frustrates identification. "On a snug evening I shall watch her fingers, / Cleverly ringed, declining to clever pink, / Beg glory from the willing keys": Are these the fingers of a Black or a white woman? The reduction of the female body down to this one small detail seems carefully designed to collapse the usual fine light and dark distinctions of heroine description, to suggest, cautiously, women of two races.

In *Street in Bronzeville* as a whole, however, Brooks's poetic voice characterizes itself not only by lush musicality but also, as Barbara Christian puts it, by "harsh cutting edges."[45] And in that volume the poems repeatedly chart distinctions between privileged women who obey the standards of the upper middle class and poor women who can't or won't, between light- and darker-skinned women, between Black and white women. In this larger context, "piano after war"'s lady of the rosy-fingered sunset with lyric power at her fingertips wields only limited power and bears only limited guilt.

Still, within the more narrow compass of "Gay Chaps at the Bar," the failure of coherence between subject and enunciation in "piano after war," its odd disjunctive breaks between a mode defined as feminine and a perspective resolutely masculine, raise pressing questions about the possibilities of cross-gender identification and about the gender of voice and style.[46] Those contradictions escalate and multiply in two heavily stylized later poems in the series, "love notes" I and II. The "love notes," as their generic titles make clear, openly confront the conventions both of the courtly love sonnet and of forties V-letter form. Here, finally, the "stuff of letters" from front to home, man to woman, is mimicked directly, but reworked in ways which disturb the norms of both Petrarchan tradition and its modern wartime counterpart. In these two poems, the focus shifts from character and dramatic scene (as in the earlier sonnets) to sheer rhetoric; the gendered conceits of the love note are mustered and disrupted one after another in a highly mannered display of stylistic ingenuity:

love note I: surely

Surely you stay my certain own, you stay
My you. All honest, lofty as a cloud.
Surely I could come now and find you high,
As mine as you ever were; should not be awed.
Surely your word would pop as insolent
As always: "Why, of course I love you, dear."
Your gaze, surely, ungauzed as I could want.
Your touches, that were never careful, what they were.
Surely—But I am very off from that.
From surely. From indeed. From the decent arrow
That was my clean naïveté and my faith.
This morning men deliver wounds and death.
They will deliver death and wounds tomorrow.
And I doubt all. You. Or a violet.

(73)

love note II: flags

Still, it is dear defiance now to carry
Fair flags of you above my indignation,
Top, with a pretty glory and a merry
Softness, the scattered pound of my cold passion.
I pull you down my foxhole. Do you mind?
You burn in bits of saucy color then.
I let you flutter out against the pained
Volleys. Against my power crumpled and wan.
You, and the yellow pert exuberance
Of dandelion days, unmocking sun;

The blowing of clear wind in your gay hair;
Love changeful in you (like a music, or
Like a sweet mournfulness, or like a dance,
Or like the tender struggle of a fan).

(74)

Critics have frequently, and usefully, read these two sonnets as extended manipulations of one controlling metaphor: woman-as-flag, or flag-as-woman, a figure related to the female Democracy we viewed through the eyes of the Negro Hero.[47] Like the Black soldier in that earlier poem, the speaker of the "love notes" strongly resembles the unrequited lovers of Renaissance sonnet tradition, vacillating, in eloquent alternations, between bitter despair and compensatory idealization. The flag/nation/lover here bears all the defining features of the Petrarchan lady; "she" is both the object of desire, tyrannical and fickle, who thwarts the speaker's needs with careless cruelty and the chaste object of love whom he vows to serve faithfully. The wit of the "love notes" lies primarily in the way they translate received gestures of poetic courtship — in particular, the motivating ambivalence which seems to drive love sonnet tradition — into the battlefield, harnessing that familiar rhetorical volatility to express the emotional and intellectual struggle of the Black soldier.

To render democracy as a female figure is one thing. To collapse a woman into a flag goes one step further, reducing the representation of the soldier's allegiance to an almost entirely abstract sign-system, a pure semiotics of war, democracy, and gender. The "love notes" thus constitute "Gay Chaps"'s most condensed and sharpest engagement with the "stuff" of love and war poetry. Combined, they replicate a system in which the brandishing and embellishment of a female figurehead go always, inexorably, hand in hand with her punishment. Both poems invoke the intimate, hopeful modes of address of the Second War V-letter; each offers tempered declarations of the faithfulness of lovers to each other, of soldiers to their cause, of nations to their defenders. But the predominant tone, until the second sonnet's attempt to recuperate the lover at its close, is one not only of doubt but of active hostility.

Like the governing metaphor, "Woman's face is a shield," which Nancy Vickers has analyzed in Shakepeare's *Lucrece*, the link of woman to flag in the "love notes" draws on the double meaning of the traditional *blason* whose workings I have already traced in the conventional V-letter poems of the forties: its association with military heraldry as well as with the poetic catalogue of praise — or blame — of a woman's body. In the "bits of saucy color" worshipped and scorned by Brooks's soldier, as in the "heraldry of Lucrece' face" glossed by Vickers, "the colors of [a woman's flesh] . . . are indistinguishable from the 'colors' of heraldry—which, in turn, are indistinguishable from the 'colors' of . . . rhetoric," and the consequence of these conflated figures is identical to that described by Vickers for the raped Lucrece: "a stylized fragmentation and reification of the female body that both transcends the familiar clichés of the battle of the sexes and stops the reader short . . . the female body is mastered through polarized figurations that can only denigrate or idealize."[48] The gendered tropes in "Gay Chaps at the Bar" end here, in a pair of "love notes," more hostile than wistful, which unsparingly mimic misogyny. What, then, are (and were) the political effects of that mimicry? Could this indictment of the "insolent" and "changeful" Democracy-as-woman avoid rebounding onto real women—including (and beginning with) the author herself?

Once again, the misogyny enacted here is first of all in the service of a protest against racial oppression. This represented soldier, as Elizabeth Young has put it, has received a "Dear John" letter from the nation.[49] And so the "Love Notes" strip bare the consoling idealizations of dominant forties V-letter form, of poems in which the needs of the girl back home and the needs of the national government so seamlessly and comfortably entwine. These two ironic poems generally refuse the sentiment which poems like Karl Shapiro's had reintroduced into the modern ironic war poetry tradition; they choose to emphasize violence—sexual violence, too—over violets.

We can read the mimicry of male sexual antagonism here, then, as part of a critique of U.S. racism, one accomplished through a turn back toward the harsh protest misogynies of earlier Great War poetry and away from the self-congratulatory morale-building of the current V-letter-as-sweet-love-letter vogue. But in "Gay Chaps at the Bar" overall, the ironic tradition of modern war poetry is also subjected to revision. By the end of the sequence all gender distinctions collapse. That collapse, as the series represents it, is a sign of reconciliation—but it is also, finally, in this war poem, a symptom of catastrophe.

On the one hand, these sonnets' adroit mimicries function to secure and and exemplify universal empathy for the soldier. Poems like the "love notes," "mentors," and "piano after war" are, on the one hand, patently imitative of—even obedient to—the authoritative tradition of the modern masculine ironic war poem as it came out of the First World War; they render a world laid to waste by war by opening up a conventional gap, a wasteland, between men and women. But they also, by the sheer, known fact of their Black female authorship alone, swerve from that tradition. The "Gay Chaps" sequence displays a triumphant power of sympathetic identification which allows Brooks as author, not just reader, to become her soldiers — even to the point of giving voice to their sexual anxieties about and antagonisms with women. Paradoxically, Brooks mends the split between the woman and the literary soldier by writing war poems which insist upon that split. In effect, her demonstrable ability to mimic perfectly a modern masculine war poem subverts the gender division upon which such poems have been predicated, defending women against the attacks of the war poetry tradition by proving a feminine capacity for fellow-feeling, for the "right stuff."

But in its final poem, on the other hand, "Gay Chaps at the Bar" offers a bleaker representation of the power of mimesis. "the progress" depicts American Second World War society, both military and civilian, as a culture of mimicry, in which everyone — of all races, men and women — must assume the requisite alien masquerade:[50]

> And still we wear our uniforms, follow
> The cracked cry of the bugles, comb and brush
> Our pride and prejudice, doctor the sallow
> Initial ardor, wish to keep it fresh.
> Still we applaud the President's voice and face.
> Still we remark on patriotism, sing,
> Salute the flag, thrill heavily, rejoice
> For death of men who too saluted, sang.
> But inward grows a soberness, an awe,
> A fear, a deepening hollow through the cold.
> For even if we come out standing up
> How shall we smile, congratulate: and how
> Settle in chairs? Listen, listen. The step
> Of iron feet again. And again   wild.
>
> (75)

Here the "world elsewhere" is figured as a hollowness inside, mimesis as a deadening outward conformity imposed by militarism — even more harshly on men than on women. The extent to which all distinguishing categories collapse is suggested by the implicit reference to fascism as well as militarism in "the step of iron feet again"; fascism, often represented in American women's Second War writing as an *exaggeration* of gender or other divisions, here is figured rather as a universal mechanical invariability. Across the wide white space in the last line, possibilities project themselves — wildness, resistance; but the repetition of "again. And again" suggests that in totalitarian total-war–making wildness is indistinguishable from iron uniformity.

In the light of this last poem, the "uniform" structure of the sonnets in this series, each with its own subordinated small letter title, comes to seem a kind of parody of the endless repeating round of salutes and songs represented here. "Brooks manipulates the image of the sonnet as confined and structured," writes Stacy Hubbard, "so as to highlight the paradoxical nature of those forms and rituals (poetry, war, funerals) which both define, immortalize, and kill."[51] In "the progress," not only the war poem but all sanctioned behavior in the war culture are represented as capitulation in paradoxical forms; if ritual can render you, like Brooks's mother, "crowned" and "praised" and "customary," it can also kill you and your kind. As Brooks herself put it, in a poem entitled "Revision of the Invocation (The Negro: His Pleas Against Intolerance)" which won *Negro Story's* literary prize in 1945,

> . . . Where massive horror is rhythmic in the world
> This is game-playing.
> But the toys are all grotesque
> And not for lovely hands; are dangerous,
> Serrate in open and artful places.[52]

In such a world, at such a time, this poem and the final sonnet in "Gay Chaps" imply, playing with mimesis is no game. It is, as adults say to children, like playing with matches, or, as adults say to adults, like playing with fire.

5

The Letter and the Body

Muriel Rukeyser's "Letter to the Front"

> The word spoken across
> Distance and loneliness —
> Communication to the flesh.
> . . . .
>
> And then I remember the page
> Of other words for death.
> Then I remember the voices,
> The voice not recognized
> Or overheard too soon;
> Rejected offerings,
> Letter and telephone,
> And I think of the bombing weather
> Fine in the full of the moon.
> Muriel Rukeyser, "Gift-Poem," 1944[1]

> [T]he central training of women: oneself as audience. . . . In a group brought up primarily to be audience . . . [t]he role of the listener is felt strongly, and is conceived as having qualities which can evoke further action, further communication. This is the listener who is necessary . . . This is the listener who answers, traditionally, as Muse, evoker; who answers, sometimes as artist, and breaks that barrier.
> Muriel Rukeyser, "Many Keys"[2]

> She was playing the whole series of moods that are the poetic woman — the war-hating woman, the woman in love.
> Bob Ray, review of Rukeyser's "Middle of the Air," 1945[3]

I

Unlike Gwendolyn Brooks's "Gay Chaps at the Bar," which develops an extensive sequence of war poems before its "love notes" admit its buried

140

origins in the "stuff of letters," Muriel Rukeyser's "Letter to the Front" (1944) signals from the first its declared relation to epistolary models then in vogue on the home front. The title of Rukeyser's long poetic series immediately places the text to follow in the tradition of the war poem as soldier's message — but with a crucial difference. Rukeyser does not mimic the voice of the soldier; rather, replacing "from" with "to," she reverses V-letter form.

The woman's letter to an absent soldier — a text Rukeyser rewrites repeatedly from the late thirties on — was not, of course, an unfamiliar document in American Second War culture. Insipid collections of women's letters overseas flooded the home-front literary market; Margaret Buell Wilder's bestseller *Since You Went Away . . . Letters to a Soldier from His Wife* is a typical example.[4] The forties poem-as-letter-from-home has, too, more venerable predecessors. From Ovid's *Heroides* to the present, a genre Linda Kauffman defines as "amorous epistolary literature" has represented the writing of the woman left behind, enacting a script which calls, as Kauffman puts it, for "men going to war and women warring with their passions."[5]

The volume of which "Letter to the Front" was a part, *Beast in View*, is largely given over to love poems which dwell on an ancient and familiar theme of erotic abandonment: the abandonment of women by soldiers, the abandonment of women, in the absence of soldiers, to grief and desire.[6] Many of these poems develop open epistolary fictions. Like the heroines across centuries whom Linda Kauffman analyzes, the "I" of *Beast in View* transforms herself, poem by poem, "from the archetypal Woman Who Waits into the Woman Who Writes"(25). This metamorphosis, far from being inherently revolutionary or subversive, seems, within the large and long tradition of amatory epistles, almost formulaic.[7]

Waiting and writing, warring and passion. There is a personal story behind *Beast in View*; Rukeyser's lover, the German athlete Otto Boch, was killed fighting with the Loyalists in Spain, a fact which Rukeyser learned in the year before the book's publication.[8] But we need no specific biographical information to gather the details of *Beast in View*'s underlying plot. "One Soldier," "Gift Poem," and "Sixth Elegy" address themselves directly to the lover who is somewhere else, gone to war; "Mortal Girl" evokes Ovidian narrative, speaking for Leda after the swan has departed ("I wait in all my hopes, / Poet beast and woman"); "The Meeting," Penelope-like, takes up the question of the costs of feminine dedication to absence:

> One o'clock in the letter-box
> Very black and I will go home early.

Now I have put off my dancing-dress
And over a sheet of distance write my love.

. . . . (. . . . . . .

Each absence brings me nearer to that night
When I stone-still in desire standing
Shall see the masked body of love enter the garden
To reach the night-burning, the perpetual fountain.

(BV, 12)

The epigraph of the volume, from a poem by Dryden which supplies the book's title, links love and war as common pursuits with the same "beast in view," "all, all of a piece throughout." Both quests — military and erotic, public and private — end, in Dryden's lines, with failure and treason: "Thy wars brought nothing about; thy lovers were all untrue." The only hope for completion, for gratified "night-burning," is change: "'Tis well an old age is out, / And time to begin a new" (BV, ii). Beast in View offers multiple variations on this theme, strongly eroticizing the speaker's response to the soldier's distance, hinting repeatedly that his absence signals amorous betrayal, crying for a new satiation of female desire.

But this is, after all, Muriel Rukeyser writing — Rukeyser, whose first poem in her first published book had rejected the story of Sappho bereft and pleading to Phaon, turning instead to a different model. "Poem out of Childhood," Rukeyser's early portrait of the artist as a young woman, evokes the major figure of the woman writer in Ovid's Heroides — "Sappho, with her drowned hair trailing along Greek waters, / weed binding it, a fillet of kelp enclosing / the temples' ardent fruit" — only to cut it off sharply: "Not Sappho, Sacco."[9] Her poems in the thirties included long sequences based on investigations of the silica poisoning of miners and on the Scottsboro trial, and in the decades following the forties her books were filled with poems on the Civil Rights movement, on the Vietnam War, and on political prisoners around the world.[10] In Beast in View, left-wing politics, the revolutionary material of Sacco, matters as much as Sappho's lyric erotics. What's more, the two entirely conjoin. Rukeyser's war poems, like her earlier and later work, are unusually open and ardent in two ways; their candid intensities of sexual desire link with their overt political stakes.[11]

Thus Beast in View, at least as often as it appeals to mythic narratives of abandonment, insistently historicizes and politicizes those plots. The title "Long Past Moncada," for instance, dates and places the war letter it represents with careful particularity. In that poem, the lovers' longing exactly coincides with the wish for a Republican victory in Spain and with the hope for a fervent and successful antifascist struggle worldwide:

> Whether you fell at Huesca during the lack of guns,
> Or later, at Barcelona, as the city fell,
>   You reach my days;
> Among the heckling of clocks, the incessant failures,
> I know how you recognized our war, and ran
> To it as a runner to his eager wedding
>   Or our immediate love.
>
>   (*BV*, 44)

That this war/love letter, in the wake of the Spanish Civil War, is branded with the guilt of a survivor as well as burning with the expectant desire of a patient tender of home fires is made clear by its next stark self-accusation: "If I indeed killed you, my darling, if my cable killed / Arriving the afternoon the city fell . . . " (*BV*, 44). In the world of *Beast in View*, one immersed in war, the most loving letter is capable of literal killing. "When," as "Sixth Elegy. River Elegy" puts it, "the cemeteries are military objectives / and love's a downward drawing at the heart / . . . every letter bears the stamp of death" (*BV*, 83). But such letters are always accompanied in *Beast in View* by some reference to a spirit which gives life — a spirit strongly antifascist and specifically connected to a tradition of left-wing activism represented by the missing soldier: "Other loves, other children, other gifts, as you said, / 'Of the revolution,' arrive — but, darling, where / You entered, life / Entered my hours . . . " ("Long Past Moncada," *BV*, 44).

"Letter to the Front," the long poetic series at the center of *Beast in View*, seems to offer in its generic title the paradigmatic version of all the amorous political epistles in that volume; fifty pages into the book, if we recognize any poetic plot, it should be this one. The title is, however, easily misread. Two of the editors of an anthology of lesbian feminist essays on sexuality, for example, quote from the poem on their dedication page, citing it as "Letter *From* the Front."[12] The slip reflects, of course, a common desire, the need for our authors to be perfect veterans for us; but it misses Rukeyser's redefinition of the dynamics of power in the reading and writing of war poetry. The letter from the front is still, as it was in the forties, a privileged form, thought to be ideally suited for first-hand reports of historical crisis.[13] The letter *to* the front seems doomed, in contrast, to be merely minor, its only subject the cravings of one abandoned woman. But Rukeyser's "Letter To" not only transgresses the bounds of the feminine epistle, pushing it beyond the billet-doux to assert its status as serious war correspondence; it also constitutes an ironic commentary on and a subtle challenge to the primacy of the eyewitness soldier as subject and speaker of the modern war poem.

"Letter to the Front" self-consciously confronts and reenvisions conventions of both war poetry and love poetry. It does so by exploiting the conventions of a traditional "women's form," the amorous epistle, for a traditionally masculine end, the making of a theory of war. Since "Letter" adapts women's discourse for its own subversive purposes, we might say, following Irigaray, that the poem mimics a feminine voice, just as "Gay Chaps" mimes conventional masculinity. But that point should be followed with an immediate qualification, for in addition to the mocking, nuanced textual strategies Irigaray envisions as the play of mimesis, "Letter to the Front" offers open debate and militant contestation. Taking up the great subject of feminine epistolary fictions — writing's reenactment of or substitution for bodily experience — it extends those fictions to comprehend in the broadest possible terms the subject of the Second World War, exploring suffering's relation to political desire and war literature's relation to both belief and the body.

II

Lines like "If I indeed killed you, my darling" in the other poems of *Beast in View* suggest an addressee with a specific dramatic, if not historical, identity, someone individual and "real"; the reader is encouraged to interpret such moments as confessional and occasional. But "Letter to the Front," the volume's most ambitious poem, develops figures of address both more abstract and more devious. Refusing, through a variety of means, simple biographical interpretation, transforming the normative "letter from the front" form of the forties war poem, "Letter" displaces the frontline soldier into the place of reader. It also, more radically, plunges the reader into the place of the frontline soldier, immediately introducing questions of position: What is a front? What is *the* front? Why have we been "put" there? What demands does such a metaphor place on us?[14]

Disrupting the epistolary conventions which its title promises, the first poem in the "Letter to the Front" series invokes the modes of address not of a letter (homely, time-bound, occasional) but of supernatural prophecy, uncanny and free of all temporal constraint. It is not until the second poem that we encounter an "I" which resembles the "I" of customary letter writing, and not until the sixth poem — four pages into the text — that we come upon a "you." Karl Shapiro's "V-Letter," in contrast, uses both first and second person pronouns in its opening line ("I love you first because your face is fair") to establish without delay the dramatic identity of the letter writer and his addressee. But "Letter to the Front" begins by disturbing the coherence of the fiction of the letter, withholding simple imitation of epistolary structures until over halfway through the sequence.

No robbing the mailbag — or malebag — illusions obtain here. Rather than simply rendering the deictics or orientational cues of masculine V-letters backwards — say, by substituting female "I" for male "I," "here" for "there," "I could not love you (Dear) so much, loved you not Honour more" for Lovelace's endearments — the first poem of "Letter" reveals the sexual politics of those deictics, their implications for women kept in their poetic place by the smallest words, by pronouns or adverbs of place and time. The first line of the poem is not "I love you" but a radical declaration of feminine omniscience:

> Women and poets see the truth arrive.
> Then it is acted out,
> The lives are lost, and all the newsboys shout.
>
> Horror of cities follows, and the maze
> Of compromise and grief.
> The feeble cry Defeat be my belief.
>
> Now the strong agonized men
> Wear the hard clothes of war,
> Try to remember what they are fighting for.
>
> But in dark weeping helpless moments of peace
> Women and poets believe and resist forever:
> The blind inventor finds the underground river.
>
> *(BV, 57)*

The truth's "arrival" in the first line, after the letter image in the title, might briefly suggest to the reader the arrival of a letter bringing news from a conflict zone to the doorstep; the next line's "then" changes our sense of what arrival means. "Truth" in this poem is not an artifact which crosses, like a letter, from one space to another, but an intangible foreboding of events, an idea: "*Then* it is acted out." These lines, and the whole first poem, argue implicitly for an alternative mode of literary authority for the war poem, one based not on the documentation of hostilities by "newsboys" — the whole tradition of masculine authority of war experience is here lightly, with an effect of boredom, waved aside — but on a continuity of clairvoyance. The war poem as a man's record written in the aftermath of conflict is replaced and superceded by the poem as a warning, preliminary, primary and female.

Challenging common notions of both the space and time of conflict, "Letter" invokes the structures of conventional history only to revise them. Its ten poems are subtly but distinctly ordered in temporal sequence, from the years before the outbreak of fighting in Spain through the ongoing World War to the future. But its opening and closing gestures, its initial *"Then* it is acted out" and its final "I send you *now,* for a beginning" [my italics], are deliberately open-ended, calculated to push the temporal range of the war poem beyond usual demarcations of the war's duration. The series begins and proceeds with a reconceptualization of warfare much like that advocated in a recent feminist essay by Margaret and Patrice Higonnet:

When war is understood as an ideological struggle rather than strictly as a physical or diplomatic event . . . we redefine its temporal limits. Women experience war over a different period from that which traditional history usually recognizes, a period which precedes and long outlasts formal hostilities. Masculinist history has stressed the sharply defined event of war; women's time more closely reflects Bergson's concept of *durée.* . . . What holds for historical time is also true for the historical space we record. We must move beyond the exceptional, marked event, which takes place on a specifically militarized front . . . to include the private domain and the landscape of the mind.[15]

"Letter to the Front"'s transformations of the temporal and spatial grid of traditional war narrative anticipate the critical revisions called for here; its open valorization of women's powers from its first words suggests its willingness to declare itself a feminist history.

But the poem's opening demonstration of its indifference toward a "specifically militarized front," its founding affirmation of "the landscape of the mind," may also be read as response to an interpretive framework specific to the 1930s and 1940s which had nothing, seemingly, to do with gender. The idea of the "Popular Front" — of the worldwide antifascist movements of support for Spain from 1936 to 1939 and behind them the French "Front Populaire," of the vestiges and heritages of those movements in the official ideologies of the Allies during the Second World War — provided for Rukeyser and many of her contemporary readers an immediately compelling model of the war as ideological conflict. The Popular Front rhetoric which this poem draws upon and exemplifies might be understood as a combination of qualities we have seen in the war work of Moore and Millay; it combines Millay's antifascist antagonism with Moore's inward ethics, and adds to these a sense of concerted, collective, historical leftist struggle.

The title "Letter to the Front" evokes the heavily militarized, conservatively gendered structures of the V-letter — men hard at war, women safe at home. But it also evokes the fluid *durée* and private landscape of Popular Front mythology, which defined struggle as at once inward, collective, and everywhere. As we shall see, the interplay of these two contesting versions of the front—one supposedly only material and one openly ideological, one gender-specific and one mutual, one sanctioned by the state, one promoted by the Left—structures and energizes the entire poetic series.

To illustrate this, let us look midway through the "Letter" sequence at the seventh poem, which engages with particular ease a straightforward line of Popular Front rhetoric. In this poem, a sestina which begins "Coming to Spain on the first day of the fighting," the meaning of the important end word "soldiers" wavers, and eventually metamorphoses, through the course of the six stanzas and envoi. The soldiers begin as glamorous, presumably Spanish, others—"Flame in the mountains, and the exotic soldiers"; are rendered more familiar, but still marked as masculine and distant from the perspective of the speaker—"We wondered, Were they changing, / Our mild companions, turning into soldiers? / . . . The belted soldiers / Vanished into white hills that dark was changing"; and then are subsumed into a larger collective cause—"keeping / Among us only the main wish, and the soldiers. / . . . this country / Struck at our lives, struck deeper than its soldiers." The final six-line stanza draws a sharp line between the heroic certainties of combatants and the "subtle fearing" and hesitant withholding of noncombatants: "Those who among us were sure became our soldiers." But the envoi redefines the fight as symbolic and general, resolving the distinction between soldiers and others (and the myths of gender division which underlie that distinction) by erasing it entirely: "This first day of fighting showed us all men as soldiers" (*BV*, 59–60). Although in the context of this combat poem the word "men" inevitably retains traces of a specific masculinity, it is meant primarily, I think, to be read generically. The sestina's built-in "structures of permutation"[16] push toward the triumphant moment at which the Popular Front emerges full-blown into the poem, reinventing combat as universal.

Representations of the Popular Front, with their insistence on collective ideological transformation and on unity of vision and purpose, have a way of rendering gender a seemingly unnecessary category. Of course the systematic opposition of masculine to feminine, of men to women, nonetheless informs the Spanish Civil War literature of the radical tradition. It structures the confrontations, for instance, between toughened men and idiotic women in Ernest Hemingway's "The Butterfly and the Tank" or Dorothy Parker's "Who Might Be Interested"; it shapes, in Auden's notorious "Spain," the particular nature of the experience of the speaker: "Today the makeshift consolations: the shared cigarette, / The cards in the candlelit barn, and the scraping concert, / The masculine jokes. . . . "[17]

Next to the implicit masculinity of Auden's war-hardened voice of the struggle, the opening word of "Letter to the Front"—"Women"—takes on new force. In this poetic sequence, the construction of gender in wartime is not only very much *an* issue. It is very much *at* issue. In poems like the Spain sestina, "Letter" promotes a leftist vision of triumph over rigid divisions of gender and over hierarchical modes of military and political authority. But "Letter" also represents, throughout, the traumas of gender division which inhered in left theory and practice in the thirties and forties; it suggests that in the Second World War those distinctions threaten, if unchanged, to render the Popular Front indistinguishable from any other front, or the struggle indistinguishable from any warfare; and it seeks to advance a permanent revolution in the relations of men to women and of both to antifascism.[18] "Letter to the Front," like much of Rukeyser's work, enacts and demands a resistance to the disempowerment of women as well as to other forms of oppression more commonly recognized by the American Left, insisting on the salience of the category of gender for liberal and radical discourses on the war.

Look again at the opening line of "Letter to the Front": "Women and poets see the truth arrive." Many poets of the Second War period made such claims for poetry, paying tribute with their equation of poets and prophets to the body of work by a number of authors, including Rukeyser herself, who had warned against fascism during the thirties. "War seems to me," Rukeyser wrote in her prose statement on poetry and war for Oscar Williams's 1944 anthology, "the after-image of many failures to react to truth at the time that truth first happens. We confess by this war that we did not react to fascism as it arrived. But now the fact that it might be a war against fascist ideas has slipped away."[19] This was an entirely representative line of reasoning for Left-leaning authors of the Second War period. Oscar Williams himself, that expert compiler of Second War literary commonplaces, makes a similar case, for instance, in his introduction to *New Poems of 1943*: "The poets of this generation functioned, before the movement of armies, as prophets great and tormented as any before them. And like all prophets they were rejected by society."[20]

What renders "Letter to the Front"'s opening figure of the poet as prophet distinctive, however, is that the moral authority of those poets who have spoken out in advance against fascism is represented explicitly as feminine: not "poets see the truth," but "*women* and poets." The challenge to fascism is imagined here as a feminine act and a feminine power—even if it occurs in a text written by a man. "Women and poets": the poem's first audacity is its casual, almost as if automatic, association of the two together, its proclamation of their centrality, and its attribution to them both of primary intuition.

Such a claim — in the face of a canon of Spanish Civil War literature which was, as usual, heavily masculine — had liberating force, and also attendant dangers. As statements of historical fact, or celebrations of inherent moral rectitude, the arguments of lines like "Women and poets see the truth arrive" or "Women and poets believe and resist forever" are untenable. Ezra Pound and the Nazi women whom Claudia Koonz has analyzed remind us conclusively that poets and women possess neither built-in antifascist barometers nor essential predilections for radical resistance.[21] These declarations may be more productively and fairly read as critical responses to normative ideas about the truth of war. Contending with the notion that truth in warfare is pragmatic, material and immediate, a form of knowledge owned by military men on active duty, "Letter"'s first poem takes up figures usually regarded as marginal in war systems — women, poets — in order to politicize and valorize those traits conventionally associated with them. Sensitivity becomes a register of ideological complexity, emotion becomes conviction, passivity a critical intellectual distance, exclusion the necessary precondition of unhampered vision, and so on.

On the one hand, this redefinition of what constitutes truth in war represents a potentially serious challenge to prevailing conceptions of war and gender. We may, for instance, read "In dark weeping helpless moments of peace / Women and poets believe and resist forever" as a manifesto in which the dangerous energies of femininity and poetry are called forth to work their disruptive force. The "dark moments" which women and poets are "in" may be interpreted as "elsewheres" in Irigaray's sense, as figures of marginal pockets of resistance to a dominant, harmful symbolic order. On the other hand, however, this formulation sounds all too familiar. The weeping helplessness which is here the domain of women and poetry suggests the presence less of destabilizing elsewheres than of dutiful separate spheres: a nicely cordoned-off feminine realm of feeling and "believing-in" to counterbalance and compensate for the harsh realities of "strong agonized men."

It is, perhaps, due in part to this uncomfortable family resemblance between revolutionary possibility and old-hat domestic ideology that the poem abandons reference to gender in its final line, opting for a sexless image of power in marginality and of secret resourcefulness: "The blind inventor finds the underground river" (BV, 57). But questions about gender are not so easily put aside in a poetic sequence which raises them as emphatically as this one does in its opening stanzas. And in the tradition of modern war poetry, imagery of vision and blindness — as its appearances in other texts in earlier chapters of this book have strongly suggested — tends only to exacerbate, rather than resolve, the tensions of sexual division.

"Letter to the Front" offers a series of visionary moments such as the "blind inventor" line, passages in which the voice peaks, regaining temporarily the moral high ground of universalizing Popular Front style, before subsiding. Each of the poetic sequence's assertions of vision, however — each "I have seen," "I saw," or "we saw" — is haunted by anxious reminders of gendered scenarios of seeing in wartime. The script which separates the authoritative eyewitness from the passive spectator, and which associates one kind of sight with masculinity and the other with femininity, still exerts its pressures on this "letter," and the letter, in turn, responds to those structures of seeing with open feminist challenge and protestation.

The predominant recurring vision in "Letter to the Front," prefaced each time it occurs with an "I saw" or "I have seen" that is reminiscent of the claims to privileged sight of a saint or in Revelation, is the figure of a boat pulling away from a Spanish harbor. It is in relation to this sight, in the second poem, that the personalized voice of the speaker, the "I" of the sequence, is introduced: "I have seen a ship lying upon the water / Rise like a great bird, like a lifted promise" (BV, 58). In the fifth poem, which begins "Much later," the ship reappears, here marked as a remembered image reemerging in a dream:

> I saw a white ship rise as peace was made
> In Spain, the first peace the world would not keep.
> The ship pulled away from the harbor where Columbus
> Standing on his black pillar sees new worlds;
> And suddenly all the people at all the rails
> Lifted their hands in a gesture of belief
> That climbs among my dreams like a bird flying.
>
> (BV, 61)

This ship vividly recalls Whitman's many images of the self and the text as venturing vessels. Like Whitman's figure of the book as "a lone bark cleaving the ether, purpos'd I know not whither, yet ever full of faith," the white ship in "Letter" signifies a poetic project which is at once political, emotional, and textual, uncharted but destined, undertaken in a vehicle laden with secret potential meanings.[22] But this ship responds as well to a more immediate historical referent; the scene is autobiographical, and the story connected to it is part of a personalized mythology. Rukeyser's note to an earlier poem about the same ship, "Mediterranean" (1938), provides a compact version of the relevant plot:

On the evening of July 25, 1936, five days after the outbreak of the Spanish Civil War, Americans with the Anti-Fascist Olympic Games were evacuated from Barcelona at the order of the Catalonian Government. In a small Spanish boat, the

Ciudad di Ibiza, which the Belgians had chartered, they and a group of five hundred, including the Hungarian and Belgian teams as well as the American, sailed overnight to Sete, the first port in France. The only men who remained were those who had volunteered in the Loyalist forces: the core of the future International Column. (*CP,* 136–37)

This account omits two important facts: Muriel Rukeyser was part of the American contingent to the Anti-Fascist games, and although she had passionately wanted to stay and fight with the Loyalists, she was compelled to evacuate the country, as were all foreign women without nursing experience. The scene of compulsory banishment from Spain recurs again and again in the next decade of Rukeyser's work; her poetic treatise *The Life of Poetry* (1949) begins with a version of it, as if it somehow contains the origin and summation of all her writing:

I think now of a boat on which I sailed away from the beginning of a war. . . . This was the first moment of stillness in days of fighting. We had seen the primitive beginnings of the open warfare of this period: men running through the silvery groves, the sniper whose gun would speak, as the bullet broke the wall beside you; a child staring upward at a single plane. More would come; in the city, the cars burned and blood streamed over the walls of houses and the horse shrieked; armies formed and marched out; the gypsies, the priests, in their purity and violence fought. Word from abroad was coming in as they asked us to meet in the summer leafy Square, and told us that they knew. They had seen how, as foreigners, we were deprived; how we were kept from, and wanted, above all things one: our responsibility.

This was a stroke of insight: it was true. "Now you have your responsibility," the voice said, deep, prophetic, direct, "go home: tell your peoples what you have seen."[23]

Most striking about this scene is its rapid transformation of deprivation and exclusion — the situation of the American woman who is excluded categorically from eligibility for the Lincoln Brigade — into compensatory power, a singular ability to memorialize and prophesy. Something similar happens in "Mediterranean." The speaker watches from the deck of the departing ship as her male lover, who has stayed behind to fight, turns away on the shore: "At the end of July, exile . . . / . . . I see this man, dock, war, a latent image" (*CP,* 137). Her position here is identical to that of the abandoned women in the amorous epistles Linda Kauffman analyzes: "they are exiled not only from the beloved but from all solace, protection, identity . . . " (40). But in Rukeyser's poem absence rapidly converts to presence, deprivation to power, loss to purpose, and the inactive, worshipful feminine gaze is firmly rejected: "Otto is fighting now . . . / No highlight hero. Love's not a trick of light. / . . . The picture at our

eyes, past memory, poem, / to carry and spread and daily justify" (142).
Each appearance of the ship in Rukeyser's wartime work effects a similar
transmutation of the woman's shipboard look; what starts as spectator-
ship transforms itself into witness.

To witness is both to see and to actively turn oneself into a sign, to
"bear" what is seen as testimony. Thus the "white ship" in "Letter to the
Front" represents not only the site from which war is passively viewed —
a spectator-ship — but also a testifying dream symbol in and of itself,
something to be seen as well as someplace from which to see. In the image
of the witnessing vessel, the distinctions between viewer and spectacle,
subject and object, passivity and activity which structure so many of the
war narratives we have examined collapse.

If watching can become a form of witness, so, too, might that even more
removed and mediated work of the eye, reading. It is not enough, for
Rukeyser, to substitute the status of the war correspondent on the deck
of the ship for the authority of the front soldier. The war poem which
defines itself as a "letter to the front" demands a redefinition of reading
by the reader, who has already, before the text's first words, been drafted
into the front lines and granted the responsibility and authority which go
along with active duty.[24] In the following passage from *The Life of Poetry*,
Rukeyser discusses at length the model of reading which "Letter to the
Front" seeks to elicit:

> The giving and taking of a poem is, then, a triadic relation . . . we are always
> confronted by the poet, the poem, and the audience. . . . At this point, I should
> like to use another word: "audience" or "reader" or "listener" seems inadequate.
> I suggest the old word "witness," which includes the act of giving evidence. The
> overtone of responsibility in this word is not present in the others and the tension
> of the law makes a climate here which is that climate of excitement and revelation
> giving air to the work of art, announcing with the poem that we are about to
> change, that work is being done on the self. (*LP*, 187)

The act of reading here, at once a plain and an exalted task, is invested
with an extraordinary degree of activity and meaning-making authority.
Reading becomes a form of basic training, a kind of direct action, and
therefore powerful and justifiable in a time of crisis which seems to de-
mand only the most energetic forms of responsibility. Not only justifiable,
but decisively important: to read is to join in the ideological work which
is the central purpose of the Popular Front.

The conception of reading Rukeyser puts forward in the above passage,
explicitly sexless, has special implications for American women. Reading
in war, reading about war, has a strong association with femininity —

corrupt femininity, at that. It is a sign of how little Rukeyser's writing about war falls in line with the dominant modern ironic tradition that it can so enthusiastically, from the standpoint of a woman, reclaim reading as a mode of action. Think, for instance, of one famous woman reader of war in the American literary tradition, Henry James's Isabel Archer, who in her youth is inordinately, indiscriminately fond of reading martial and revolutionary narratives. Rukeyser's images of reading suggest that she wanted not so much to deny Isabel as to transform her, into a reader whose emotional, intellectual, and sexual energies would be tapped by conflict and politics instead of being falsely satiated or titillated by them, and into an actor whose loyalties in a Civil War would not be indiscriminately distributed. Isabel Archer's "deepest enjoyment" — "to feel the continuity between the movements of her own soul and the agitations of the world" — becomes, in Rukeyser's war poems, the central project.[25] The transformation of reading into witness involves an implied transformation of gender roles, for in war letters and in war poems, as the pivotal poem in "Letter to the Front" makes clear, the position of reader, more often than not, is occupied by a woman.[26]

III

The sixth poem in the "Letter to the Front" sequence marks the turn, in the fictive chronology of the series, from the late thirties to the early forties, from the Spanish Civil War to World War II, and from Europe to the United States. The traveler returns from Spain, in the words of the ninth poem,

> to the powder-plant in twilight,
> The girls emerging like discolored shadows.
> But this is a land where there is time, and time:
> This is the country where there is time for thinking.
> "Is he a 'fellow-traveler'?" — No. — Are you sure? — No.
> The fear. Voices of clawhammers and spikes clinking.
>   (BV, 65)

The wartime American society represented here is heavily militarized, yet still enervated, ignorant, and suspicious, distant from the realities of the war. Above all, it is a culture with "time, and time." This is American time; as Klaus Mann argued in an editorial in the journal *Decision*, with which Rukeyser was closely associated during the war, "we in this hemisphere have had the longest time to think and make up our minds. . . . We have already been prodigal with this time lag, which is in a sense an almost divine dispensation."[27]

It is also, as the emergence of the "girls" in the lines quoted above sug-
gests, a degraded version of women's time, like the temporal modality
Mary Ann Doane in *Desire to Desire* describes in forties "women's films,"
which "rests on the assumption that it is the woman who *has the time* to
wait. . . . A feminine relation to time in this context is thus defined in
terms — repetition, waiting, duration — which resist any notion of progres-
sion"(109). The woman who has the time to wait in this negative *durée*,
this exhausted duration with no available vision of change, has also, as
Doane points out, "the time to invest in love," to play out the classic role
of the abandoned heroine. In the World War section of "Letter," not sur-
prisingly, urgent Popular Front mythologies give way in part to what
Doane calls "the discourse of the love story" (109), and to the familiar
divided home/front structure of conservatively gendered war literature,
in which men go away to war and women dedicate themselves faithfully
to absence.

"Letter"'s judgment of that structure may be inferred in part from its
wraithlike imagery of the women on the home front who emerge in the
ninth poem, drained and barely visible, from the powder-plant like "dis-
colored shadows." (With a whole history of representations in labor ac-
tivism behind it, this image is the most critical literary counter to whole-
some home-front versions of Rosie the Riveter I have found.) But its
most extended engagement with, and critique of, dominant wartime con-
structions of gender, front and home, occurs in the one poem in the series
which works with epistolary conventions in classic form. Drawing on the
amorous epistle's capacity to represent, as Janet Altman explains, "alter-
nately, or even simultaneously, presence and absence, candor and dissim-
ulation, mania and cure, bridge and barrier,"[28] the sixth poem takes up the
question of the power of the letter in a system which enforces lags and
divisions between the fighting soldier and his waiting woman. The poem
speaks explicitly for and in the voice of the fictional woman reader ad-
dressed in masculine war poetry, as if answering a V-letter:

> Home thoughts from home: we read you every day,
> Soldiers of distances. You wish most to be here.
> In the strange lands of war, I woke and thought of home.
> Remembering how war came, I wake and think of you,
> In the city of water and stone where I was born,
> My home of complex light. What we were fighting for,
> In the beginning, in Spain, was not to be defined.
> More human than abstract, more direction than end.
> Terror arrived intact, lit with the tragic fire

Of hope before its time, tore us from lover and friend.
We came to the violent act with all that we had learned . . .

But now we are that home you dream across a war.
You fight; and we must go in poetry and hope
Moving into the future that no one can escape.

. . . .

We hold belief. You fight and are maimed and mad.
We believe, though all you want be bed with one
Whose mouth is bread and wine, whose flesh is home.

(*BV*, 61–62)

The ambivalent relation of "we" to "you" and "we" to "home" in this passage sharply contrasts with the comfortable equation of woman and home by the soldier hero of Karl Shapiro's "V-Letter": "You are my home," he writes to his woman reader, "and in your spacious love / I dream to march as under flaring flags / Until the door is gently shut."[29] Section six of "Letter to the Front" may be described, in fact, as a sharp meditation on and open challenge to the metaphor of woman as home which underlies the war letter / love letter formula. "But now we are that home you dream across a war. / . . . We believe, though all you want be bed with one / Whose mouth is bread and wine, whose flesh is home": the soldier in the V-letter as these lines portray him, like the stock male manipulator of rueful women's mythology, only wants one thing, but these sadder-but-wiser women will not, or will not only, provide it.

Soldiers of distances here are prolific correspondents — "we read you every day" — and each of their letters seems to be inscribed with longing for the stable, wholly receptive, wholly nurturing feminine landscape of home. Within this context, the woman who wishes to write back, or write in ways other than simply writing back, struggles to be more than flesh, more than home, more than simply a nourishing primal body. She has, so to speak, a front of her own; she "believes," and to do so is represented as an imaginative affirmation of marginality and defiance — an active "although" — both in relation to the violence of warfare and in relation to the wishful conventions of the war lyric as love lyric which the Second World War had spawned. What Brooks exposes through devious mimicry in her "love notes," Rukeyser here opposes with overt militance. The problem is what masculine letters do to women's bodies.

"Holding belief," the action advocated here for or practiced here by women, is represented as an excess, something more than and potentially even threatening to the minimum response craved by the soldier from the girl back home. (Among other things, it might mean a *with*holding, a woman's refusal to turn her body over to the service of a patriarchal belief system.) The phrase recurs in "Who in One Lifetime" from *Beast in View*:

> Who in one lifetime sees all causes lost,
> Herself dismayed and helpless, cities down,
> Love made monotonous fear and the sad-faced
> Inexorable armies and the falling plane,
> Has sickness, sickness. Introspective and whole,
> She knows how several madnesses are born,
> Seeing the integrated never fighting well,
> The flesh too vulnerable, the eyes tear-torn.
>
> She finds a pre-surrender on all sides:
> Treaty before the war, ritual impatience turn
> The camps of ambush to chambers of imagery.
> She holds belief in the world, she stays and hides
> Life in her own defeat, stands, though her whole world burn,
> A childless goddess of fertility.
>
> (BV, 37)

Two aspects of this awkward, resonant poem are pertinent in relation to "Letter to the Front." Here, as in "Letter," belief offers an alternative to and a salvation for the torn vulnerability of the flesh, of the body (particularly the male body, which "Letter" represents as "maimed"). The female body is transfigured into a holder, a container, of belief, through images which both suggest and deflect sexuality: here, the "childless goddess of fertility," stationary and intact, a spiritual vessel, or in "Letter," the woman who wants her body to be more than a soldier's bed, who images herself rather as a kind of seedbed of ideas. (Compare the childless goddesses in H. D.'s *Trilogy*, discussed in chapter 9.)

"Who in One Lifetime"'s final image of the goddess, fertile and childless, at once intensely in her body and wholly spirit, has a close counterpart in "Letter to the Front." At the center of the sixth poem in the series, another spiritual female figure emerges in a simile:

> Peace will in time arrive, but war defined our years.
> We are like that young saint at the spring who bent
> Her face over dry earth the vision told her flowed,
> Miring herself. She knew it was water. But for
> Herself, it was filth. Later, for all to come
> Following her faith, miraculous crystal ran.
>
> (BV, 61)

This simile performs several functions, and fulfills several needs, which we have already found to be urgent for the series as a whole: it celebrates, with its image of female premonition, the woman who sees, and it converts defilement, vulnerability, and transgression through faith into vindication and victory. It is odd to find, in a work whose implicit Judaism will be made explicit in a poem which follows later in the series ("To Be a Jew in the Twentieth Century"), that these purposes are accomplished through the figure of a Christian saint, Bernadette Soubirous, though in the poem's own historical and cultural context not as strange as it might at first seem.

Bernadette's famous vision of the Virgin Mary at Lourdes became in the United States during the Second World War a popular symbol of radical faith, innocence, and resistance, primarily as the result of the bestselling fictional account of the saint's life by the German author Franz Werfel, published in translation in the States in 1942.[30] Werfel clearly defined his novel as a Second World War book, prefacing it with an account of his attempt to flee France after its collapse in June of 1940, a journey which ended in Lourdes. His *Song of Bernadette* was remarkable as secular hagiography; its restrained, nonjudgmental retelling of the Catholic saint's life was greeted by wartime readers as especially meaningful because the author declared himself to be a Jew. Rukeyser, like Werfel, secularizes her young saint, placing emphasis on the process, rather than the content, of her act of envisioning.

The evocation of the story of Bernadette in "Letter" adds subtexts of additional meaning to the figure of the saint at the spring. Bernadette had already acquired, through Werfel's book, an association with political resistance. The poem erases any specifically theological content of the saint's life encapsulated within it, but it claims and politicizes aspects of sainthood, that state of being in which identity and belief are perfectly united. For readers who recognized the allusion, however, the story of the French peasant girl's confrontation with a beautiful vision of a "lady" might have suggested, subtextually, images of heightened, supernatural female power. The excluded religious meanings of the story intimate that the source of the healing spring, of true vision in wartime, may be imagined as a woman.

What matters most, I think, is yet another aspect of the figure: its reconciliation of abstract belief with the concrete sensation of the body. Refuting the image of the unscathed, passive female spectator, the young saint proves that female vision may be rooted in intensities of bodily struggle. The act of "holding belief," if real, the image argues, exerts stresses which are physical as well as emotional. The spring here suggests on the one

hand an elemental female well of energy, like "the woman's place of power
in each of us" Audre Lorde images as "neither white nor surface; it is dark,
it is ancient, and it is deep."[31] But it also, on the other hand, cagily re-
works a dominant trope of *masculinity* in modern ironic war literature.
Consider, for instance, the discussion by Stephen Spender of Wilfred
Owen to which I referred in chapter 2: "Owen's [warning] came out of
the particular circumstances of the trenches . . . the mud and blood into
which his nose was rubbed" ("Warnings from the Grave," 23). "Letter to the
Front" devises for its female visionary equivalent "particular circumstances,"
chastening and authorizing her vision by rubbing her face in mud.

The poetic series not only borrows from the imagery and theory of
masculine embodiment in dominant modern war literature; at moments
it claims the authority of embodiment — the capacity to link concrete and
abstract, to work for and stand for ideas with the body — as a specifically
female power. Developing, in its sequence of poems which represent the
Second World War period, a polarized symbology of gender, "Letter" in-
verts, with a powerful reversal, traditional notions of sexual difference in
wartime. It talks back to that tradition first by angrily representing Ameri-
can powerlessness, laxity, and betrayal through a series of images asso-
ciated with the masculine failure to embody desire, impotence:

> Here is the man who changed his name, the man who dyed his hair;
> One praises only his own birth; one only his own whore.
> Unable to create or fight or commit suicide,
> Will make a job of weakness, be the impotent editor,
> The sad and pathic bull always wishing he were
> The bullfighter . . .
> . . . He forever betrays. He alone is betrayed.
>
> *(BV, 63)*

At points in the poem, these opponents are directly named: Nye, McCor-
mack, Hearst, Pegler — all leading isolationists. The aggressive satire here
is not atypical in modern war poetry, as comparison with — to take a
canonical example — "Hugh Selwyn Mauberley"'s "There died a myriad, /
And of the best, among them, / For an old bitch gone in the teeth. . . . "
reveals.[32] It is rare, however, for the allegorized male body to come under
this kind of satiric attack, especially in war poetry, and the transgressive
hostility of these lines is rapidly replaced by generalized and neuter Pop-
ular Front rhetoric: "We shall grow and fight again. / The sickness of our
divided state / Calls to the anger and the great / Imaginative gifts of man"
(BV, 64).

Opposed to the imagery of impotence is a series of passages which valorize the great imaginative gifts of women in particular, grounding those gifts in the female body through figures of childbirth:

> If they bomb the cities, they must offer the choice.
> Taking away the sons, they must create a reason.
> The cities and women cry in a frightful voice,
> "I care not who makes the laws, let me make the sons."
> But look at their eyes, like drinking animals'
> Full of assurance and flowing with reward.
> The seeds of answering are in their voice.
> The spirit lives, against the time's disease.
> You little children, come down out of your mothers
> And tell us about peace.
>
> (BV, 65)

These lines suggest, with their transcription of the "frightful voice" of civilian women, the poem's commitment to that "other word" which Olive Schreiner once demanded: "It is especially in the domain of war that we, the bearers of men's bodies, who supply its most valuable munition . . . it is we especially, who in the domain of war, have our word to say, a word that no man can say for us." Like Schreiner, Rukeyser conceives of an authority for "answering" to war which originates in, instead of being threatened by or exclusive of, maternal energy and maternal occupation. Like Charlotte Perkins Gilman, she calls for what Gilman called "bee's fictions": stories recording the productive communal activities of female "hives" which could replace, and render obsolete, masculinist war narrative. Working within a long tradition of feminist thought which locates women's authority to speak about war, and to speak against war, in their ability to bear and their history of nurturing children, "Letter" articulates here a classic example of "motherist" rhetoric.[33]

The limits of this strategy are obvious, in ways the text itself may acknowledge. The woman who says, "I care not who makes the laws, let me make the sons," who defines herself wholly in terms of her womb, might well be the ideal spokeswoman for Nazi domestic ideology; the poem recognizes this, perhaps, in its description of the mothers' cry as "frightful" and in the lines privileging women's vision over women's voice which follow ("But look at their eyes").[34] The power of the strategy is equally clear. It grants the female voice an authority on the subject of war which is grounded in that prerequisite of modern war narrative, the experience of the body. It offers a visionary figure of promise and productivity to counterbalance injury and despair, emphasizing life over death: "Against this weight of time," Rukeyser writes in a wartime piece of prose, "freedom's a single fighter. Janus-faced . . . like a woman in childbirth who may in one agony discover her mother and her child and be reborn."[35] Not least, it strongly revises the plot of female abandonment in wartime, replacing the woman dedicated to absence with the wholly present mother, "full of assurance and flowing with reward." The sons taken away at the beginning of the stanza quoted above metamorphose into children restored to the womb for a new birth. The story of separation which underlies these lines is less Penelope's than Demeter's, which stresses, as Joan DeJean points out, not desertion but female endurance, and which ends in a world-salvaging reunion between mother and child.[36]

Finally, and most importantly, the rhetorical appeal to motherhood in wartime, defining the central actor in the struggle not as the male body in combat but as the female body in labor, shifts emphasis from fighting and dying to that which is fought and died *for*. This does not mean that in "Letter," women and children are the passive beneficiaries of male *agon*. The front is the arena of the male body, but it is the female body which works at the vanguard of that other, in the poem's terms even more essential front, the *Popular Front*.[37] The startling final metamorphosis of "Letter"'s white ship in a poetic series published four years later, "Nine Poems for the Unborn Child," makes this especially clear.

The speaker of the "Nine Poems" bears, as Rukeyser herself bore in 1947, a child whose paternity is hidden or uncertain; one of the mythic shadow fathers invoked for the infant is represented as "advancing, / His hands full of guns, on the enemy in Spain." Describing a moment at which doctors before labor broach the question, "If you must choose, / Is it yourself or the child?," the poem continues:

> Laughter I learned
> In that moment, laughter and choice of life.
> I saw an immense ship trembling on the water
> Lift by a gesture of hands. I saw a child.
>
> (*CP*, 286)

Refiguring the antifascist ship of "Letter to the Front" in her own body, *as* her own body, the speaker of "Nine Poems" claims an unmediated knowledge equivalent to the soldier's direct experience of armed struggle: "And in my flesh at last I saw." An unpublished poem from the same period makes even stronger claims for this figure of the mother's body as a bearer of witness, laden with social meaning:

> I thought of the far country: for this man this belief,
> I said, I would give my life, but there is no
>   giving of life
> Except this giving . . .

> there is no giving of life
> except the giving of life[38]

In the concluding pages of "Letter to the Front," a similar visionary rhetoric of maternity predominates. At one point within that assured flow of celebration, however, a kind of antipoem emerges, complicating the "Letter"'s constructions of the values of gender. It images women's bodies not as sources of strength but as places of risk, causes of enfeeblement, and dangers to poetry:

> I hear the singing of the lives of women,
> The clear mystery, the offering and pride,
> But here also the orange lights of a bar, and an
> Old biddy singing inside:
>
> > Rain and tomorrow more
> > They say there will be rain
> > They lean together and tell
> > The sorrow of the loin.
> >
> > Telling each other, saying
> > "But can you understand?"
> > They recount separate sorrows.
> > Throat. Forehead. Hand.
> >
> > On the bars and walls of buildings
> > They passed when they were young
> > They vomit out their pain,
> > The sorrow of the lung.
> >
> > Who would suspect it of women?
> > They have not any rest.
> > Sad dreams of the belly, of the lip,
> > Of the deep warm breast.
> >
> > All sorrows have their place in flesh,
> > All flesh will with its sorrow die —
> > All but the patch of sunlight over,
> > Over the sorrowful sunlit eye.
> >   (BV, 65–66)

This short lyric provides a melancholy corrective to the sequence's confident assertions of female force, introducing a new note of uneasiness and ambivalence about the access of the female body to joy, to knowledge, and to power. Here, woman's body is sorrowful, is sorrow itself:

a sadness at once deep and dismembered. For the fragmentation of body parts here once again recalls the *blason* we have been tracing through the last three chapters, whose central presence in the history of amorous poetry exerts a shaping force on the war poems of the forties which stage themselves as love poems. What women "recount," within the undersong of the surrogate poet, the old biddy, is the story of "separate sorrows" or the sorrows of separation — not only their deeply debilitating separation from each other, but also the mental and verbal fragmentation, by men and by themselves, of their single bodies into separate, sad parts: "Throat. Forehead. Hand. . . . Sad dreams of the belly, of the lip, of the deep warm breast." This list recalls the catalogue of praises, but turns it to a catalogue of woes.

There are hints of a sexuality aligned with the earlier celebration of the female body here — lines describing belly, lip, and breast, deep and warm, parts which invoke a female presence both arousing and maternally comforting, as well as lines which boldly go where no *blason* has gone so plainly before: lung, loin. But in this song of an "old biddy" — that chicken-like image of femininity as servitude and debility, a more compassionate version of Pound's "old bitch gone in the teeth" — the isolation of one part of the body from another diffuses any real possibility of bodily and sexual power. In the women's language represented in this lyric, the *blason* reduces to weak blues: female complaints.[39] The body, taken apart, retains no force.

Nancy J. Vickers's groundbreaking feminist reading of the motives and functions of the Petrarchan *blason* suggests, as I proposed in chapter 4, that the biddy's version may be read less as an opposition to the traditional workings of the catalogue of praises than as a culmination of that tradition. In Petrarch's *Rime Sparse*, Vickers argues, the response of the male "I," who figures himself as Actaeon transfixed by Diana, to the threat of the sight of a powerful and whole female body "is the neutralization, through descriptive dismemberment, of the threat. He transforms the visible totality into scattered words, the body into signs."[40] Laura's body, dispersed into small parts, may then be viewed from an adequately defended position and safely subjected to praise. In Vickers's reading, the Renaissance *blason* separates the woman's body into particular features not to celebrate her but to subdue her.

"Descriptive dismemberment" may be, then, built into the *blason* from Petrarch on; "his role," writes Vickers, "in the history of the interpretation and the internalization of woman's 'image' by both men and women can scarcely be overemphasized" (95). The negative, inverted *blason* of sorrows in "Letter," which is taken as women's own tale, proves, in one sense, the infiltration and internalization of figures shaped by male fantasies into the women's lyric and women's language. These women, in a woman's song in a woman's poem, descriptively dismember *themselves*.

But the "biddy's song" also constitutes a critique of internalization. We can read that critique first of all in the careful framing of this weary "woman's song" within the larger alternatives for female voice in the series as a whole. The biddy's words are introduced, for instance, as an unfortunate movement inward:

> I hear the singing of the lives of women,
> The clear mystery, the offering and pride,
> But here also the orange lights of a bar, and an
> Old biddy singing inside . . .
>
> (BV, 66)

They are followed by images of emergence and rebirth: "Surely it is time for the true grace of women / Emerging, in their lives' colors, from the rooms, from the harvests, / From the delicate prisons. . . . " (BV, 66). Here, firmly, is a rejection of the "delicate prisons" of women who stay inside male poetic tradition, of the *blason* and the defeated blues.

The biddy's critique inheres, too, in its granting of voice and subjectivity to the woman formerly silenced by and within the *blason*; it's a far different matter to descriptively dismember oneself than to be fragmented by another. The drunken women in the biddy's song — gay girls at the bar — are no Petrarchan ladies; their bodies, however fragmented, have "depth," are represented as more than glittering surfaces; they add to the attributes of Laura — the requisite breasts and lips — those of other women: those, since their depth is the depth of sorrow, of the *Mater Dolorosa*, or those, since their depth is the depth of pain and desire, of Lady Day.

We can read the poem's critique of internalization, as well, in the nausea and dis-ease of the women's scattered, sorrowing bodies. The chronic pain inflicted and symbolized by their *blason* takes even more acute form in the other war poem in *Beast in View* which makes use of what Vickers terms the "poetics of fragmentation" (102), the "Sixth Elegy," with its ghoulish image of a betrayed, defeated city occupied by "living dead," "half-faced, half-sexed . . . / . . . a lip, a breast, half of a hand" (BV, 80). "Sixth Elegy"'s satiric representation of a disordered, decaying body politic through a *blason* gone bad makes explicit what in the more meditative "Letter" remains covert: descriptive dismemberment is mutilation. The catalogue of a woman's body parts, which in "V-letter" poems by the male soldier poets of the forties works as a distraction from and compensation for the attacks on the male body in combat, in Rukeyser's war poems becomes inseparable from other inflictions of violence.

"All sorrows have their place in flesh": this is what the biddy's women know. "All flesh will with its sorrow die — / All but the patch of sunlight over, / Over the sorrowful sunlit eye." The momentary promise of transcendence here — "All but" — is immediately disappointed; no body part is exempt from death and sorrow, and not even the privileged eye is given final peace. The sunlight on the eye suggests a brilliant illumination, a revelation. But the imagery of the light as a patch undoes its transcendental, visionary power: eye patches keep light out, not in. This eye is not enlightened, lit deep from inside; light settles on top of it like a bandage to prevent further damage.

The melancholy eye here is the opposite of the true vision of the "women and poets" in the first poem in the series, just as the biddy's fragmented women represent the cautionary inverse of the powerful maternal body "Letter" uses to symbolize an integrated, productive body politic. Descriptive dismemberments, "Letter" suggests, are dangerous rhetorical and political choices. The task is to find a voice which unifies and empowers others and the self, instead of fragmenting and repressing them.

The figure of the poet in Western tradition most obviously associated with dismemberment — with punishment by, and triumph over, fragmentation — is, of course, *the* figure of the poet, Orpheus. It is not surprising, therefore, that "Letter to the Front" ends, in an odd, dangling apostrophe, with a voice resonantly Orphic, "subsumed," like the voices of Orpheus that Mary Jacobus traces in classic and romantic tradition, "into transcendental Nature . . . banishing rough music with the music of natural harmony":[41]

> O the future shining
> In far countries or suddenly at home in a look, in a season,
> In music freeing a new myth among the male
> Steep landscapes, the familiar cliffs, trees, towers
> That stand and assert the earth, saying: "Come here, come to me.
>
> Here are your children." Not as traditional man
> But love's great insight — "your children and your song."
>
> (BV, 67)

Here, the female Orpheus unifies front and home, far countries and familiar cliffs, and transforms them all with a power of voice and insight derived not from the maenads but from Demeter.

It is also not surprising that Rukeyser wrote, a few years after "Letter to the Front," a long poem entitled "Orpheus" in which Orpheus, "scattered. The fool of things. / . . . Sideshow of parts," his body divided into "hand, a foot, a flat breast, phallus, a foot, / shoulder and sloping back and lyre and murdered head," heals: "And all the weapons meld into his song" (*CP*, 292, 293, 298). Nor is it surprising that in her famous "The Poem as Mask," written almost twenty years later, she claimed Orpheus as herself and Orpheus's ordeal as childbirth: "when I wrote of the god, / fragmented, exiled from himself, his life, the love gone down with song, / it was myself, split open, unable to speak, in exile from myself" (*CP*, 435). Self-exile, not exile from Spain or other faraway battles, is what women in "Letter to the Front" who want to fight the war and to prevent war, to work for their beliefs with their bodies, must struggle to overcome.

IV

Words like "fragmentation," scattered parts," and "dismember" have, of course, strong literal meanings which haunt any critical discussion of war poetry and any war poem itself. Even if it holds true that in general women, defined as Others, have borne the brunt of being made into no more than bodies (or home-bodies) in the master texts of Western culture, it is also true that men have faced the fact of their embodiment in the most brutal ways on Western culture's battlefields. The prevalence of wounds, scars, disfigurements, mutilations, and amputations in texts which represent war testifies to the insistent presence of men's and women's *literally* hurt bodies in warfare. Compared to such actual dismemberments, the conceptual sorrows of the old biddy in "Letter to the Front" may seem to some readers trivial, secondary, and tolerable. We have here another version of the problem I discussed in my reading of the differences between Jarrell and Moore: the struggle to recognize adequately the pain of the soldier, the pressure in the war poem of the literal.

Even Moore's most exalted images of inward Christian warfare cannot — and do not aim to — bury the presence of the soldier's form upon the dust. At some point in all of the other war poems by women I have considered at length so far, the body wounded in warfare makes an inevitable, dramatically charged appearance. The second sonnet in Brooks's "Gay Chaps" series describes, relentlessly, the twisting and gagging of an individual soldier. Millay's *Lidice*, very much within the tradition of atrocity narrative, represents at length "the awkward limbs of the dead."

But "Letter to the Front," in contrast, consistently substitutes spiritual and mental contest for physical engagement. It insists, repeatedly, on a

conceptual fight which precedes, and takes precedence over, armed strug-
gle: "Women and poets see the truth arrive. / Then it is acted out"; "After
the change of heart there comes / The savage waste of battlefield"; "Not
alone the still / Torture, isolation; or torture of the flesh. / That may come
also. But the accepting wish. . . . " Again and again, the poem places lit-
eral combat, physical action, and physical suffering in the position of
that which may come also. When its tenth section argues that women may
be "lost surely as soldiers . . . gone down under centuries / of the starved
spirit," it equates categorically physical and spiritual death. In the fourth
section, "Sestina," the lines "The fighting / Was clear to us all at last" are
followed by "The belted soldiers / Vanished into white hills that dark was
changing." Here, characteristically, the clarity of the fight is asserted pre-
cisely at the moment when soldiers' bodies blur and disappear.

In its relative indifference to the literal body, "Letter to the Front" works
within a long tradition of epistolary fictions. "Nothing of body," as *Clarissa*
puts it, "when friend writes to friend." Rather, the letter, Richardson's
Lovelace argues, is "writing from the heart. . . . Not the heart only; the
soul was in it."[42] The letter is the medium of disembodied desire. Forties
soldier poets drew on exactly this aspect of epistolary form in their V-letters,
lyrics at once intimate and dreamily abstract, war poems as heartfelt
records of the soul. In this one sense, Rukeyser's revision of the V-letter
may be said to retain as many of the conventions of that form as it revises.

In the soldier's V-letter poem, however, the reader is left to infer, behind
the letter writer's protective manly or wistful boyish stance, the unspoken
literal danger which threatens at any point to end his soulful correspon-
dence for good: the event to which Shapiro's hero in his "V-Letter" refers,
with studied nonchalance, as "my matter-of-fact and simple death."[43]
This implicit pathos was available to Second War soldier writers in large
part because of what had *not* gone unspoken in the literature of World
War I, a body of war poetry not, incidentally, actively hostile to the sen-
timental possibilities of epistolary form; in Wilfred Owen's war poems
which use the figure of the letter, for instance, at the moment when men
are wounded letter writing stops explicitly, theatrically dead. Owen's poems,
as we have seen in chapter 4, set up the confidences of friend writing to
friend as euphemisms only. And then they disrupt them, break them off
violently, as if insisting: "In war, *everything*, always everything, of body."

"Letter to the Front," which argues throughout for the primacy of what
its third section calls "wars of the spirit in the world," works arduously
against this tradition. For Rukeyser, the most egregious errors and failures
in war and in war poetry stem not from the lack of concrete personal ex-
perience but from the refusal to think impersonally, theoretically—the

failure to recognize the war as part of an ideological struggle. The worst villain in "Letter to the Front" is a "man in the clothes of a commander," who refuses to[44]

> . . . say "for a free world,
> 'A better world' or whatever it is;
> A man fights to win a war,
> To hang on to what is his—"
>   (BV, 63)

In part, this critique of the jingoism of commanders falls neatly in line with the foot soldier's perspective which dominates the modern ironic war poetry tradition; but in larger part it also criticizes and counters that tradition's fundamental suspicion of abstraction.

Eric Leed provides a cogent summary of the powerful model of the individual's relation to war which "Letter" attempts to defy. Experience of modern war, he argues in his analysis of the attitudes of Great War soldiers, tends to be comprehended as distinctively concrete and bodily:

The knowledge gained in war was rarely regarded as something alienable, something that could be taught, a tool or method. Rather, it was most often described as something that was part of the combatant's body, like a chemical substance in the veins, a mark, a scar, a set of reflexes, a part of the individual's very potency.[45]

Strongly resisting this conception of knowledge, "Letter" argues that knowing war, and knowing how to prevent war, are alienable skills. Wisdom, in "Letter," can be taught; insight can be recognized and transmitted—as in a letter; the tools and methods necessary for the struggle can be grasped from anywhere at any time.

In this upholding of the primacy of negotiable belief over the felt experience of the body, the poem opposes not only the dominant strain of modern war poetry and war narrative but also a further reaching and compelling practice and tenet of modernism. Mimesis, in Auerbach's great Second World War study, begins with a mark on a returned combatant's body, Odysseus's scar. Its exemplar in modernity is the random, common, personal moment in which Woolf's Mrs. Ramsey measures and knits a stocking, "comparatively independent of the controversial and unstable orders over which men fight and despair; it passes unaffected by them, as daily life."[46] The particular scar on the body of a man, the particular world of women who, like Penelope, tend, weave, mend, maintain the quotidian: neither of these moving specificities much concerns Rukeyser's "Letter."

Unapologetically rhetorical and resolutely antimimetic (here we can

measure its distance from Brooks's war poems), "Letter to the Front" ex-
ploits with no holds barred the "epistolarity" of letter form — a form which,
as Linda Kauffman points out in her study of the literary love letter, "lies
at the extremes of telling, so far removed from mere mimesis that the
diegetic and performative aspects of narrative dominate the discourse"
(24). It courts and welcomes "the controversial and unstable orders over
which men" — and women — fight, and it refuses to define that fight in terms
only of despair. "One of the worst things that could happen to our poetry
at this time," Rukeyser wrote in *The Life of Poetry* in an explicit argument
against the poetry of wounding,

would be for it to become an occasional poetry of war. A good deal of repugnance
to the social poetry of the 1930's was caused by reactionary beliefs; but as much
was caused, I think, because there were so many degrees of blood-savagery in it,
ranging all the way from self-pity — naked or identified with one victim after
another — to actual bloodlust and display of wounds, a rotten sort of begging for
attention and sympathy in the name of an art that was supposed to produce ac-
tion. (*LP,* 216)

"Letter"'s purpose, at once a tribute to and a strong revision of the tradi-
tional projects of the heroines in amorous epistolary fiction, is to inscribe
and to encourage political comprehension and political desire. It attempts,
like Rukeyser's work as a whole, to convert one gendered script — "Call the
male puppet, Croak, / Call the female puppet, Shriek" ("Correspondences,"
CP, 216) — into a more hopeful and reciprocal plot:

> The woman to the man:
> What is that on your hands?
> It is also on my hands.
>
> What is that in your eyes?
> You see it in my eyes, do you?
>
> Is your sex intact? Is mine?
> Can it be about life now?
> (*CP,* 513)

Where letters in Owen's poems end with the brutal interruption of the let-
ter writer, "Letter to the Front" ends with a graceful invitation to the reader:
"signs of belief, offered in time of war, / As I now send you, for a begin-
ning, praise." "A letter," writes Janet Gurkin Altman, "is . . . an attempt
to draw [a particular] *you* into becoming the *I* of a new statement. . . .
Within the epistolary framework . . . even closural gestures have inaug-
ural implications."[47] Embracing the inaugural implications of epistolary

form, "Letter to the Front" defines itself as prospective. It is a letter *to*, not from, like the tentative signals sent by men and women across "vast distances" in Rukeyser's later Vietnam-era "Poem" (*CP*, 558).

V

"Letter to the Front" affirms in the strongest possible terms the need for and the power of abstract belief in wartime and in peacetime; but we would be mistaken to conclude that it calls simply for "nothing of body." In fact, as I have shown, "Letter" returns repeatedly to a problem it cannot and would not wholly evade: the problem of embodiment. Instead of describing the wounded on battlefields, it represents at one point, for instance, forms of injury less usual in the war poem, which are literal as well as metaphorical, concrete as well as abstract: "I hold their dead skulls in my hand; this death / Worked against labor, women, Jews, / Reds, Negroes" (*BV*, 64). Compared to its closest analogue in the literature I have discussed — Moore's promise not to hate "black, white, red, yellow, Jew, / Gentile, Untouchable" — this list is not only more politicized; it also, with its gesture toward the graphic ("dead skulls"), seeks to be and purports to be relatively *particular*.

The most famous poem in the series, the sonnet "To Be a Jew in the Twentieth Century," enacts most powerfully the struggle of the body with and for belief:

> To be a Jew in the twentieth century
> Is to be offered a gift. If you refuse,
> Wishing to be invisible, you choose
> Death of the spirit, the stone insanity.
> Accepting, take full life. Full agonies:
> Your evening deep in labyrinthine blood
> Of those who resist, fail, and resist: and God
> Reduced to a hostage among hostages.
>
> The gift is torment. Not alone the still
> Torture, isolation; or torture of the flesh.
> That may come also. But the accepting wish,
> The whole and fertile spirit as guarantee
> For every human freedom, suffering to be free,
> Daring to live for the impossible.
>
> (*BV*, 62)

The significance of this poem's representation of Jewish experience at a time when the great majority of American volumes of war poems ignored the Holocaust cannot, I think, be overemphasized. "To Be a Jew in the

Twentieth Century" offers a profound extension and reformulation of the terms of the other poems in the "Letter" sequence and of the terms of Western war poetry and dominant American home-front culture. Stressing the active work of Judaism, it reworks a traditional rhetoric of election: Jews are people who must choose to be the chosen people. Giving new substance to the word "belief" which has cropped up so frequently in "Letter," it represents that belief as rooted and exemplified in Jewish cultural and spiritual tradition. Its figure of the gift which is also torment refigures conventional imagery of war's exchanges; external battles and written, distant correspondences are replaced by an inward, invisible offering, an internal struggle to acknowledge and live by one's identity and one's principles. Finally, not least, "To Be a Jew" adds another dimension to the front which this "Letter to the Front" redefines, reminding us that in 1944 not only soldiers bore marks, scars, and wounds or capacities of vision and resistance.[48]

There is a body at the center of "Letter to the Front." It is a Jew's body. And, in this war poem, as the female saint who buries her face in mud, the fertile mother, and the old biddy make clear, it is a woman's body. "Letter to the Front"'s strongest revision of the tradition of war poetry and war letters lies here: the great questions of that tradition—if, why, how the body should be or will be put to use, put in danger, for the sake of belief—are claimed as questions, necessary and inevitable, for supposed "non-combatants."

In a tribute to Rukeyser published in 1980, Kenneth Rexroth wrote, "She does not have an ideology grafted into her head." Instead, "she has a philosophy of life which comes out of her own flesh and bones. It is not a foreign body."[49] In "Letter," both philosophy and flesh, both body and belief, or, to use Irigaray's terms, both ideas and matter are represented as available tools, available terms for women as well as men. The poetic series, resolutely ideological, strives through its figures at once both to free the politics of war from and to ground them in flesh and bone, to prove that finally, in the struggle of ideas it represents and advocates, no body is foreign.

Part Three

Making Differences:
Nisei Women Poets and the War

Preface to Part Three

It makes no difference whether the Japanese is theoretically a citizen. He is still a Japanese. Giving him a scrap of paper won't change him—I don't care what they do with the Japs as long as they don't send them back here. A Jap is a Jap.
Lieutenant General John L. DeWitt[1]

My parents . . . were not so much concerned about my having become a pacifist, but they were more concerned about the possibility of my marrying one. They were understandably frightened (my father's prison years of course were still fresh on his mind) about repercussions on the rest of the family. . . . I argued that even if I didn't marry him, I'd still be a pacifist; but my father reassured me that it was "all right" for me to be a pacifist because as a Japanese national [Yamada was born in Japan] and a "girl" it *didn't make any difference to anyone.*
Mitsuye Yamada[2]

"Experience makes men and women out of us, if we are strong enough. Last year the nisei went through an almost devastating human experience . . . a whole body of authentic nisei literature will grow out of evacuation. The story is here. We must write it ourselves."[3] These lines are taken from a women's column published in early 1943 in the *Pacific Citizen,* one of the very few Japanese American (or Nikkei) journals the U.S. government allowed to continue publication through the war years, during the period when 120,000 Japanese Americans were put into internment camps without charge, hearing, or trial. The paper had escaped suppression not only because it was printed entirely in English but also because the youthful organization it represented, the Japanese American Citizens League (JACL), had been from well before Pearl Harbor assertively pro-American and insistently all-American in its self-presentation.[4] Its stance is summed up neatly in the name of the author of the above lines, "Ann Nisei," whose nom de plume marks her assimilation into the dominant American culture ("Ann"), her autonomy (no patronymic to tie her too closely to family structures), and her cultural and ethnic alliance with a particular generation ("Nisei," the U.S.–born children of immigrants from Japan).

173

"Ann Nisei" did not—as the sometimes bitter resentments and violent reprisals against JACL leaders within the camps make clear—speak for all Japanese Americans, nor even, despite her name's claim to typicality, for all Nisei women. On one point, however, her statement may be read as representative; and in that point it constitutes a forceful challenge to the cultural codes of war and gender in the United States which I have been tracing in previous chapters. Other, non–Japanese American women might struggle in the war years with their sense of distance from the zones of actual military occupation and confrontation. But Nikkei women—either denied citizenship or stripped of their rights as citizens, forcibly exiled from their homes, exposed to humiliation and violence, their families dispersed and faced with catastrophic economic losses, imprisoned in desert camps bounded by barbed wire and guarded with machine guns in the interior of an ostensibly sheltered and sheltering nation—brought to bear on their wartime writing a traumatic, undeniable "authority of experience."

It is no surprise, then, that "Ann Nisei"'s model of camp literature, in which the burden of experience both scars the writer and breaks voice open, explicitly invokes the canon of Great War soldiers' writing: "It may be too early for any really good story of evacuation. . . . The great books of the last world war came long after 1918" (5). Often, unlike the women's war poetry I have discussed so far, Japanese American women's poetry of relocation and internment seems to stand in a line of descent from the documentary ironies of the founding modern war poets. At the same time, these women's poems, substituting the camp for the battlefield as an arena of critical experience, remap the boundaries of the American canon of war poetry.

The following two chapters, which explore some of the body of Japanese American women's internment poetry, must occupy, then, a place both pivotal and central in this volume, and must function as both normative and disruptive. Normative, because Nikkei poems of the forties uncover within the American war culture the possibility, the necessity, the inevitability—above all, the *fact*—of a *civilian* "war poetry of experience." In using this phrase, I do not mean to imply that the poems represent themselves as simple records or reportage; in fact, as I shall show, many of them insist in the most explicit and politicized terms upon the fictive and ideological structures of the language they are given to use. But repeatedly, these poems locate violent crisis at home, up close. In this sense, Nikkei women's "poetry of experience" may be read as a series of *concentrated* (I intend that word to invoke a full range of Second World War meanings) exposures of a more generalized "experience" largely hidden from view in the canon of forties war poetry: the lives and deaths of civilians, and the complex range of conflict and trauma beyond combat.

No other group of American women in the forties, however, faced anything like the sudden mass exclusion, incarceration, and enforced relocation which Nikkei women endured; no other American writers faced such censorship. And so these two chapters will differ significantly from the others which have preceded them. In a variety of ways, the poetry produced by Japanese American women against considerable odds during and about the war years resists all universalizing gestures.

In chapters 6 and 7 I focus on Nisei women's writing. At moments I also refer to poems by Issei (first generation immigrants) and by Sansei (the daughters of the Nisei). I look primarily but not exclusively at poems written in the camps, "those forbidding places," as Sansei poet Lawson Fusao Inada puts it, "without grace or distinction, graced by our presence, distinguished by our vision."[5] Two differences between these chapters and the others in this book will be readily apparent: I discuss the social structures within which Nisei women wrote at greater length and in greater detail than any other similar contextualizing moments elsewhere, and I do not limit my discussion primarily to one poet. Both these choices have seemed necessary to me. The history of internment and relocation is still not widely known, the poetry both especially buried and various. But both these choices bring with them attendant difficulties and errors which should be noted at the outset: the danger of reading Japanese American literature merely as sociological documentation, and the danger of undervaluing each individual woman's work.

It is not only difficult but also pernicious to generalize about any aspect of Nikkei culture during the war. Nikkei experiences varied subtly and drastically, depending on any number of factors. I shall, obviously, be particularly interested in differences produced by and worked upon gender roles. But the following factors, among others, also matter: time periods and geographies (life in the original "assembly centers" differed, for instance, from conditions in the later, more permanent "relocation camps," and different also was the usually later experience of individual relocation to cities or campuses in the Midwest or East; moreover, the critical turning point of registration and the loyalty oaths resulted in substantial changes); camp assignments (the course of events at Topaz, where several of the writers I consider were incarcerated, differed from that—to take an obvious example—of the camp which became marked as the center for "hard-core" resisters, Tule Lake); age and generation; whether one spoke Japanese, English, or both; cultural background (whether, for instance, a member of the second generation was only American-educated—

Nisei — or had been sent back to Japan for a period of acculturation — Kibei); political affiliations, which were not, of course, static and unchanging; economic background and — a crucial factor for women — familial situation.[6]

These chapters, limited in scope and at the same time committed to exploring a range of women's writing, will not do justice to the complexities of these variations. I do not intend them as a general summary. To present them as such would be to ignore the project which Nikkei, and especially Nisei, women writers undertook in the war years with grace and with distinction as well as with difficulty: defining differences — from Japan, from dominant U.S. culture, from their parents, from men, from each other, within themselves. In the context of statements like DeWitt's famously public "A Jap's a Jap" or Mitsuye Yamada's father's private judgment that as a girl she made no (political) difference to anyone, the making of differences in and through poetry could be, for Japanese American women, a significant means of resistance.

6

Toyo Suyemoto and the "Pre-Poetics" of Internment

I

"During the mass evacuation of the Japanese in 1942," the Nisei poet Toyo Suyemoto recalls in her 1983 essay "Writing of Poetry," "my family and I were moved out of Berkeley to the Tanforan Race Track in San Bruno, California, and that spring my dated poetry notebook shows an abrupt gap in my writing."[1] The abrupt gap where poetry stalls behind Tanforan's fences serves as a reminder of the potentially paralyzing obstacles to writing which Japanese Americans encountered during the Second World War. But Suyemoto soon went on to write a number of wartime poems and to publish them as well, seeing them into print both within and beyond Topaz, the camp in which she and her family were interned after Tanforan. My aim here is to reopen that dated poetry notebook of her war years, and to open it as a question. How should we, do we, read both the poems and the gap today?

"Pre-poetically, by necessity"[2]: Ann Rosalind Jones suggests the beginnings of an answer, in a recent essay on Renaissance women's poetry demonstrating the importance of studying

the conditions necessary for writing at all, and the ways those conditions shape the lyrics of . . . women writers. . . . Women are spoken of; they speak to. The "of" and the "to," the context and the audience, must be the starting-points for any understanding. . . .[3]

Suyemoto's wartime verse, as I will show, bears a direct and conscious relation to some traditions of women's lyric familiar to feminist critics; Jones's work, and that of other feminists on women's poetry, will be pertinent here. But the "sociotextual constraint"[4] of gender ideology exerts its

177

forces on Suyemoto's forties poems always only in conjunction with other equally salient and immediately pressing social categories—American constructions of race, ethnicity, citizenship, loyalty. In the United States in 1942 or 1944, Japs were spoken of; Japanese Americans (Issei, the first generation immigrants, or Nisei, their U.S.-born children) spoke to; and Japanese American women were spoken of and themselves spoke to always within those demarcating frameworks.

In the remaining pages of this chapter, I will first trace that "of" and "to," sketching a general prepoetics of Japanese American (or Nikkei) women's writing in internment. Second, I will consider Suyemoto's work as one example of such writing.

II

Compelled by the relocation and internment order to leave their homes taking with them only what they could carry, the Japanese Americans on the West Coast were forced to abandon or destroy their books and personal papers along with their other belongings. It was dangerous and in most cases impossible for them to keep any materials written in or marked as Japanese. Nisei daughters' memoirs of internment register these losses for their mothers with particular anguish. Monica Sone recounts her family's fearful attempt, in the panicked time after Pearl Harbor, to destroy all the Japanese objects in their home: "Mother had the most to eliminate," she recalls, "with her scrapbooks of poems cut out from newspapers and magazines, and her private collection of old Japanese classic literature."[5] "She was trying," Yoshiko Uchida writes of her mother in the days immediately before evacuation,

to discard some of the poems she had scribbled on scraps of paper, clippings she had saved, notebooks of her writings, and bundles of old letters from her family and friends. Only now have I come to realize what a heartbreaking task this must have been for her as her native land confronted in war the land of her children. She knew she would be cut off from her mother, brothers and sister until the war ended. . . . She put most of them in her trunk where they remained, not only during the war, but until her death.[6]

Those Issei women who managed to keep Japanese books lost them later when they were seized during searches in the camps. As Toyo Suyemoto testifies, not even Bibles in Japanese were left unconfiscated.[7]

Writers in the camps, crowded into extremely cramped quarters (in the early time of internment, before the permanent camps were completed, housing consisted of stables, stockyards, and pigpens), faced constant noise, discomfort, and a severe lack of privacy. Not all could adopt artist

Miné Okubo's tactic for guaranteeing time and space for work at Tan-
foran Race Track, posting a "quarantine" sign on the door of her barracks
"room," which had formerly housed a horse, and warning those who
came too close that she had hoof-and-mouth disease.[8] They lived under
surveillance; some were deprived of even the most basic writing materials.
An introduction to an important recent collection of tanka poems on
internment written in Japanese by imprisoned Issei men notes that be-
cause of the scarcity of writing paper "these short poems . . . were ideal
forms for the internees' pent-up emotions."[9] One of the poets whose work
is included in that volume "managed to write approximately 200 poems
per sheet in minute handwriting on thin rice paper stationary which could
easily be carried around without official notice."[10]

Women and most Nisei were subject on the whole to less harsh condi-
tions in the camps than the male Issei leaders in the geographically separ-
ate prison "centers" like the one where this man wrote tanka. In general,
they had somewhat more opportunity to write, but additional barriers
constrained them. Newspapers run by internees (primarily Nisei) but con-
trolled by the administration in each of the seventeen "assembly centers"
and, later, in each of the ten "relocation camps" provided a sanctioned
public forum for writing in English within camp confines. These journals
were, however, heavily censored, subject both to vigilant editing by camp
officials ("McQueen put 'seeming' in front of 'injustice' in the editorial Taro
wrote for the 4th," wrote Charles Kikuchi, who worked on the *Tanforan
Totalizer*, in a diary full of similar examples) and to outright suppression.[11]
In the Japan-hating mainstream culture beyond the camps, there was vir-
tually no outlet for Nikkei literature. Toshio Mori's collection of short
stories, *Yokahama, California*, which had been scheduled for publication
in 1941, did not come out in print for another nine years.[12] Miné Okubo
recalled later of the book she produced at Topaz, "It was so difficult getting
it published. At that time anything Japanese was still rat poison."[13] More-
over, intense conflicts within the Nikkei camp communities — particularly
during the most painful and divisive moment of internment, the "registra-
tion" or "loyalty questionnaire" imposed by the War Relocation Authority
(WRA) — could make publication even in the few available camp outlets,
or even writing itself with its requisite self-assertion, risky or infeasible.[14]

One brief text will serve here to illustrate some of the pressures on any
kind of Nikkei public discourse in the camps; it will also begin to exem-
plify the possibilities of creative and strategic resistance to those silencing
prohibitions. The brilliant tour de force "Yule Greetings, Friends!," pub-
lished in the inaugural issue of the Topaz camp literary magazine *Trek* in
December 1943 under the outrageous pen name "Globularius Schraubi,"

dances past the censors in the form of a satiric "glossary" and "etymology" of "Japa-Merican" speech in its most recent dialect, "Evacuese." The essay stages itself as a sequel to or double of a dominant text, the description by H. L. Mencken ("His Linguistic Majesty") in his *The American Language* of the assimilation of Americanisms into Japanese as it is spoken in Japan. (Mencken's study leaves little room for the fact that a Japanese in complex interaction with English is spoken by some Americans.) Mocking and subverting Mencken's summations by working the etymology from inside, insisting on the presence of a Japanese which is within, and which troubles formulations of, "*The* American Language," "Yule Greetings" substitutes for the generalizing voice of Mencken's encyclopedia a series of Nisei private jokes. Along the way it manages to work into print a biting, coded critique of internment. Here are two paragraphs from the introduction to the glossary:

What concerns us at the moment is the alingual status of Japa-Mericans in the Areas into which they were recently imported and where they are now concentrated. The term "alingual," as used here, should not be construed, of course, to mean that they are dumb or that they do not speak, even though they may be speechless under the circumstances. In fact there is a good deal of tongue locomotion going on in all the Areas. Just how they wag their tongues, and in what tongues, is a subject of profound speculation in philology and socio-psychiatry.

Dead men tell no tales. Dogs tell tales with their tails. Good dogs, however, wag them not at all when at a crucial moment, and as a result the merit of a dog is judged by the time, place, and manner of their tale-wagging. The best of them are enrolled, therefore, in the Tail-Waggers association together with such celebrities as Bette Davis . . . the basis for judging the merit of little girls is the way they wag their pig-tails. When they grow up they are judged by the way in which they wag their tongues.[15]

This remarkable passage may seem close to impenetrable to a reader today not familiar with the culture of the camps; I wonder whether it seemed so to the WRA censor. It is striking how much gets said in these lines, even as the text exposes the difficulties and dangers of saying anything at all. We can read here, first of all, a lightly coded, strong protest against WRA policy (note, for instance, the casual, oblique introduction of the word "concentrated" into the first sentence, a way of writing without writing "concentration camp"), but also a more heavily coded set of references to conflicts, under the pressure of internment, between Japanese Americans.

The next lines, with their dizzying array of puns on "tail" and "tale," depend upon a buried allusion to the Japanese word *inu* ("informer" and, literally, "dog"), a term used by some members of the community to brand others (often Nisei leaders) seen as accomodationist traitors to their own people. In the word "tail / tale-wagging" which circulates evasively, perhaps prescriptively, perhaps only descriptively, through the second paragraph are collapsed a number of possible forms of tainted or dangerous speech: collaboration with camp authorities ("telling tales"); overeagerness to please camp authorities ("wagging tails"); malicious gossip accusing others in the camps of betrayal ("wagging tongues"). For our purposes, it is important to note that this anatomy of "speechlessness under the circumstances" takes a curious punitive turn toward the feminine not entirely explained by the sheer verbal attraction of a pun on "pigtails." For women, as the odd Bette Davis reference seems to hint, "tail-wagging" is a form of sexual as well as verbal promiscuity; the passage ends by placing women's speech under especially tight surveillance.

The war and internment, as this essay on "alinguality" suggests, made writing impossible for Japanese Americans. But they also, as the essay's masked critique makes clear, made not writing impossible; protest, record, satire, communication, reflection were, more than ever, critically important. And sometimes, they made writing for the first time possible for women. Despite all the obstacles charted above and more, a vigorous, complex wartime Nikkei literary culture developed, particularly in the camps. Women played significant roles in this cultural scene. Against the "abrupt gap" in Toyo Suyemoto's poetry notebook for early 1942 we can balance her reminiscence of later war years in Topaz, in this retrospective interview:

And it took quite a lot of effort on the part of the young people to get a camp magazine going. I was asked to contribute poetry then, and it was really interesting because Miné [Okubo] would sometimes stop by and say, "Can you have a poem ready for this issue?" I said, "How soon?" "Tonight." I said, "You mean I have to write a poem by tonight?" "Oh," she said. "You can do it!" And I said, "When will you pick it up?" She said, "I'll come by at three o'clock in the morning." I said, "I won't be up then!" She said, "Well, tack it on the door, and I'll pick it up." Sure enough, I'd finish a poem, write it out neatly, tack it on the door to the barracks, and along about 3 o'clock I'd hear footsteps on the path, and I could hear Miné's voice talking to her brother, who always accompanied her, and, you know, the door opened, and a few steps, the door closed, and the poem would appear in the new issue of *Trek!* (laughter)[16]

If the laughter here signifies Suyemoto's mature amusement at the alacrity with which she and Miné carried out their literary negotiations, it also suggests the ebullience and sheer vitality of the story she has just narrated. Okubo's late night, prowling news work guaranteed an outlet for Suyemoto's poems: the anecdote conveys a surprising sense of freedom and access, of the necessary emotional conditions for creative energy – of a developing writing community for women.

Before the war, historian Sandra Uyeunten has shown, Issei values had lodged feminine propriety solely within the private household, limiting or entirely prohibiting women's public discourse. But in the crowded barracks life of the camps, as Uyeunten demonstrates, distinctions between "public" and "private" blurred or entirely broke down, and the two spheres merged into a single common world.[17] In addition, Issei women – who had for years undertaken backbreaking labor both in their homes and outside them, as domestics or side by side with their husbands on farms or in small businesses – found themselves with greatly increased time for leisure and, potentially, time for writing.[18]

The War Relocation Authority which oversaw the camps organized heavy schedules of recreational routines in its effort to keep people busy, to police their activity, and to "Americanize" the Issei properly. These included writing groups, as Lili Sasaki testifies wryly: "We were clubbed to death in all the camps: sewing clubs and poetry clubs and this and that. Right away, we put together a writer's club, artist's club."[19] George Akimoto's more gruff description of these activities links them particularly, and dismissively, to (presumably Issei) women: "The ladies would get together and play cards, mah jong or whatever. They had poetry classes and that sort of thing."[20] Certainly, camp authorities used "poetry classes" as a means of social control; but we can be alert to the corrective force implied in Sasaki's "clubbed to death" without accepting wholesale Akimoto's devaluation and trivialization of these women's gatherings. Issei women could make use of writing groups in the same way they used other "classes," including the courses which taught some of them English for the first time – strategically and creatively, for purposes of their own.[21]

Unlike those concentrated sites of "Americanization," English classes, Issei poetry groups, whether sanctioned or unsanctioned by camp officials, could also elude and resist WRA control by working in Japanese. Clubs like those in Japan dedicated to the composition of tanka and other Japanese short poetic forms were common in the camps. Other poems in Japanese were written, of course, outside group auspices. Available translations suggest to me that the poems in Japanese comprise a particularly compelling body of poetry produced in the camps – surely, in part, because of their freedom from censorship, but also because of the elegiac charge which came from claiming the Japanese language in writing; the controlled heritage of Japanese poetic forms; and, not least, the maturity and knowledge which came from years of Issei experience. Many of these poems were written by Issei women.[22]

Nisei women's literary explorations during the war took somewhat different routes than those of their mothers. The younger generation had grown up, as Valerie Matsumoto puts it, "integrating both the Japanese ways of their parents and the mainstream customs of their non-Japanese friends and classmates — not always an easy process given the deeply rooted prejudice and discrimination they faced as a tiny, easily identified minority."[23] In the prewar years, a distinct, ambitious young Nisei literary culture had developed both in spite of and in response to what it defined as "the double tyranny of community traditions and race discrimination."[24] Nisei writers wrote English columns in the Japanese vernacular papers; they founded newspapers entirely in English such as the *Pacific Citizen*, literary magazines, and journals such as *The Current Life* ("the first national Nisei magazine"); in West Coast cities, they gathered to read and criticize each others' work; from rural areas, they corresponded in the English-language sections and followed each others' writing eagerly.[25]

Women had played a limited but active part in these prewar Nisei literary circles, particularly as columnists and poets. Kenny Murase's playful, collegiate summary of the "galaxy of literary lights" on the "nisei literary horizon" in the first issue of *Current Life* (October 1940) suggests something of the extent to which young women participated in that "nisei literary world"; their names comprise a third of his particular "who's who" list. It also illustrates the implicit standards of feminine propriety which shaped the lives and work of these "leading nisei poetesses" within the close prewar Japanese American community. Lucille Morimoto, according to Murase, "appears the classic Grecian type — stately, elegant, patrician"; Molly Oyama is "an affectionate young matron"; Ruth Kurata "was wise-cracking, tomboyish hoyden — now sweet, doting Mama"; Hisaye Yamamoto is "naive, cute," Mary Kitano "pert, petite and piquant . . . twirls a mean baton"; and Ayoko Noguchi, the "winsome little country lassie," tellingly "helps Mother with cooking and house-cleaning, packs melons and vegetables."[26]

After internment, the writers who comprised the "nisei literary world" regrouped in the camps — most notably at Topaz, where a nucleus of San Francisco writers who had moved as a unit from Tanforan put out *Trek* (and later, on the verge of relocation, *All Aboard*). Nisei women continued to contribute to the newspapers and literary journals produced in English under the surveillance of the WRA. Sometimes, as at Manzanar, where women outnumbered men on the editorial board of the *Free Press* by a five to one ratio, they exercised considerable influence.[27] Women like Okubo and Suyemoto at Topaz or Hisaye Yamamoto and Wakako Yamauchi at Poston formed work-sustaining networks in the camps, offering each other inspiration and encouragement.[28]

As historians Uyeunten and Matsumoto have shown, internment and relocation precipitated radical alterations in Nisei women's lives. The destabilization of the traditional immigrant family, the "weakening of Japanese patriarchal controls,"[29] and the relative privilege granted to the American-born Nisei in the camps and in the relocation process resulted in greater autonomy for Nisei daughters. Young women were increasingly able to avoid or refuse arranged marriages. Resettlement programs geared toward removing them from the camps to jobs or campuses in the Midwest or East offered them new opportunities for travel, work, and schooling outside the Nikkei community.[30]

"Before the war," the columnist who called herself "Ann Nisei" wrote in 1943, the Nisei woman had been perceived as "vague, dull, stolid—a modernized version of her mother, and exuding withal the faint odor of cherry blossoms."

But events of the past two years have shown the falsity of this picture. Today thousands upon thousands of nisei women have relocated, alone or with their families. . . . For many of these women it was surely difficult to . . . set out on their own. . . . And yet they were anxious and eager to meet the world, expectant that they could conquer it.[31]

This proclamation of the eve of a youthful female renaissance repeats in general and gendered terms the literary claims of other essays of its type around the same period. Repeatedly, for instance, Larry Tajiri's editorial column in the *Pacific Citizen* predicted the emergence of a serious Nisei literature of internment, always fiction, always just on the verge of being written.[32] In this cultural climate, a young writer of short fiction like Hisaye Yamomoto, who had signed her columns with the pen name "Napoleon" in the years before the war, found herself not only allowed but even expected to aim toward epic literary conquest in the specific form of "the Great Nisei novel."[33]

As we trace the "prepoetics" of Nisei women's wartime writing, searching out the conditions which made writing possible, we need, however, to be wary of the *Pacific Citizen*'s overdetermined desire for novels "new" and "great" and certifiably "American," a demand which obscures and renders only "minor" the many tanka poems which were being written by Issei in response to camp experience. We need to look, as well, not only away from but also back to "the faint odor of cherry blossoms" which in Ann Nisei's essay stands as an ambivalent symbol for both Issei culture (which is not identical to Japanese culture) and the figure of the mother. For with striking frequency, Nisei women writers' memoirs of the camps locate their own enabling "prepoetics" in their mothers' poems.

"Poetry has always been something very very close to me," Toyo Suye-moto tells an interviewer, "thanks to my mother's influence," and goes on to describe her mother writing poetry ("to this day I don't know what she wrote about") and practicing her expert calligraphy after her nine children had gone to bed. Elsewhere, Suyemoto pays tribute to the "rigorous dis-cipline" of tanka and haiku forms which her mother taught her. "My mother was of a literary bent herself," Hisaye Yamamoto comments simply. In *Nisei Daughter*, Monica Sone recounts a childhood steeped in poetry learned from her mother; although, she writes, the Americanized children in her family made fun of the form, adding its common expression "nali keli" ludicrously to any English sentence, "we had to admit there was something in tanka, the way mother used it" (117-18). In Yoshiko Uchida's *Desert Exile: The Uprooting of a Japanese American Family*, the Nisei daughter's narrative alternates and interweaves with translations of tanka her mother produced under the pen name Yukari, some found by the daughter on scraps of paper or the backs of envelopes; the tanka include a powerful set of camp poems.[34]

Almost certainly, the literary inclinations of these mothers of writer daughters were unusual. Most Issei women in the prewar years must have worked too hard to think much about poetry (though many, who had come to America believing that they would one day return wealthy to Japan and found instead an inexorable round of poverty and hard labor, must also have looked back with longing to an idealized Japanese culture from which they were far removed).[35] Still, the frequency with which the mother's poems emerge in these narratives suggests something about an availability of Japanese poetry to women and an association of great Japanese poetry with women in Issei culture which could serve as an enabl-ing resource for women writing, especially women writing poetry, in the camps.[36]

In retrospect, years after the Second World War, many Nisei women authors publicly embraced that bond to an Issei literary tradition in Jap-anese, representing it as a distinctively feminine legacy mediated through and created by their immigrant mothers.[37] Their published writings dur-ing the war, however, enact a struggle as much or more to disassociate themselves from than to affiliate themselves with that tradition. After all, many of them could not read the Japanese their mothers wrote in, if their mothers wrote. And during the war they faced a pressing need to define, in public, the ways in which "tanka" was not, or—as Suyemoto's wartime poems will demonstrate—was not only or never simply, their mother tongue.

III

Toyo Suyemoto was as far as I know the Japanese American woman poet who gained the broadest reading public — though that breadth was extremely limited — outside Nikkei circles in the war years.[38] Two of her poems, sent from Topaz, were published in the *Yale Review* in 1946; after relocation, she studied verse writing in workshops with competitive admission taught by Randall Jarrell and Karl Shapiro. In addition, as her description of her work with Miné Okubo has already suggested, she published regularly while in Topaz both in *Trek* and *All Aboard*, probably the most visible of in-camp publications. Reading Suyemoto's wartime work, then, I will be tracing in part what made her work so relatively *presentable*; but I hope to reveal the resistance and critique embedded within the forms and diction of poems which appear apolitical.[39]

Brought up in a home which placed strong emphasis on both Japanese and English literary traditions, Suyemoto had begun writing poetry at an early age, had graduated from the University of California at Berkeley in 1937 with a degree in English and Latin, and had published widely in the Nisei literary magazines of the prewar years.[38] In general, her poems, almost always formal, brief, at once controlled and impassioned, resemble the work of modern female lyricists such as Wylie, Teasdale, and Millay, with their roots in the long tradition of "appetitive yet renunciatory" American women's lyrics which Cheryl Walker has analyzed.[40] The love poem "Retrospect," one of the two poems published in *Yale Review*, gives a good sense of the timbre of her work:

No other shall have heard,
   When these suns set,
The gentle guarded word
   You may forget.

No other shall have known
   How spring decays
Where hostile winds have blown,
   And that doubt stays.

But I remember yet
   Once heart was stirred
To song — until I let
   The sounds grown blurred.

And time — still fleet — delays
   While pulse and bone
Take count before the days
   Lock me in stone.[41]

Or take another, in this case prewar, example, "Japonica," from the Nisei magazine *Current Life:*

> How punctually the flowering quince
> flames after winter rain
> And brings back warmth into
> The air again.
>
> Oh, vivid scarlet points, assure
> The heart of spring's return
> Now that the barren boughs
> Can bravely burn![42]

Nothing in form, diction, or content marks these two texts as Japanese American per se, and this undoubtedly accounts in part both for "Japonica"'s polemical appeal to the prewar Nisei audience of *Current Life* and for "Retrospect"'s acceptance by the wartime mainstream audience of *Yale Review.* The poems simply assume, rather than assert, an identity without the imprint of "ethnicity," aligning themselves inconspicuously with white European American literary tradition.

But what about the poems Miné Okubo commissioned for *Trek,* written in internment with a broad Japanese American audience in mind? Has the camp experience wrung, as "Ann Nisei" would claim, a different kind of poem out of Suyemoto? The following two examples, published respectively in the first (December 1942) and second (February 1943) issues of *Trek,*[43] sound, after all, simply like further well-polished rehearsals of the flower motif of "Japonica," with its abstract paradigm of female frustration and desire:

> Gain
> I sought to seed the barren earth
> And make wild beauty take
> firm root, but how could I have known
> The waiting long would shake
>
> Me inwardly, until I dared
> Not say what would be gain
> From such untimely planting, or
> What flower worth the pain?
>
> In Topaz
> Can this hard earth break wide
> The stiff stillness of snow
> And yield me promise that
> This is not always so?

> Surely, the warmth of sun
> Can pierce the earth ice-bound,
> Until grass comes to life,
> Outwitting barren ground!

Once embedded, however, in the context to which the title of the sec-
ond lyric, "In Topaz," pointedly refers, these poems begin to read differ-
ently. Even their actual placement on *Trek*'s pages signals the impossibility
of extricating their oblique parables of loss and recovery, hope and des-
pair, from a specifically Japanese American history. "Gain" falls in the
margins of Taro Katayama's "State of the City," a prose account, with the
gaze of the censor everywhere apparent in it, of the "development" of the
Topaz compound; across from the poem lies Katayama's description of
community efforts to transform the camp's wasteland by planting trees.
"In Topaz" interrupts a history of the surrounding desert.[44] The packed
figure of "barren ground" which links both these poems invokes, with a
sharp political edge, more than the obvious extremity and deprivation of
the physical conditions of camp life — dust storms, freezing cold, and blis-
tering heat, sunbaked, unyielding dirt. It is important to bring to the *Trek*
poems, as Suyemoto's Japanese American readers at the time would have
brought to them, a sense of a whole politics and mythology of agriculture
in Nikkei experience: of an American "promised land" which kept reveal-
ing itself to immigrants from Japan as a wasteland, preventing them from
owning property in their own names, expoiting their labor; of how Issei
farmers, in decades before the war, transformed cheap unwanted Califor-
nia land into fruitful, highly profitable growing fields, from which they
had now been uprooted, and which they had now lost; of the fact that
forced evacuation took place in the spring and summer of 1942, after
planting but before the harvest; of the WRA's deliberate choice to locate
camps on desert terrain in order to take advantage of Issei skill at improv-
ing soil; of the panicked demand, in wartime agricultural crises, for Jap-
anese Americans to be released from the camps as farm workers, under
heavy supervision; of the gardens planted in front of barracks doors.[45]

The seasonal and agricultural tropes in these two poems seem innocu-
ous enough for any WRA overseer when they are read, within one lyric
strain of Western literary tradition, as *metaphors* for personal or collec-
tive crisis. But they take on a sharper, more disruptive, and far less naive
aspect when they are read *metonymically*, as part of a coded narrative of
Nikkei experience on American land. To Randall Jarrell's question dismiss-
ing nature symbolism in the war poem — "How can anything bad happen
to a plant?" — "Gain" and "In Topaz" suggest one answer. Plenty bad can
happen, when one is a Japanese American farmer in 1942.

Suyemoto is by no means alone in her use of such figures; many camp poems, particularly those in traditional Japanese forms with their own strong tradition of seasonal and natural representations, develop images of planting, withering, harvest, blooming, or barrenness.[46] In her later work for the final volume of the Topaz literary magazine, now named *All Aboard*, she pays tribute to those forms, rewriting the plot of "Gain" and "In Topaz" in poems whose names ensure recognition of their roots:[47]

> Hokku
> The geese flew over
> At dusk—I shivered, not with
> Cold, but sense of loss.
>
> Where do the geese go?
> Can they escape from autumn
> And return to spring?
>
> Let me follow them:
> The birds know better than I
> Which way leads to spring.
>
>
> Tanka
> If I could but see
> Flame-points of scarlet against
> Spring's frost-laden air!
> (There was a time, remember,
> When quince-blossoms warmed our hearts?)
> The heart must believe
> (For there is no other way)
> That spring does return—
> In time, when the winter ends
> And grass-roots keep their promise.

For Japanese American readers of *Trek* who had followed the earlier sequence of Suyemoto's winter/spring verses in quatrains, part of the drama of these poems would be in the revelation of how much and how little difference writing in Japanese forms made. On the one hand, the poems gesture distinctly toward a separate Nikkei cultural heritage, as if to issue a declaration: "'Ode to the West Wind' is not our single source." The only texts of their kind to find their way into Topaz's WRA-supervised publications, they infiltrate the pages of *All Aboard* with a sharp reminder of other hokku and tanka written in the camps which were unpublishable, and of a Japanese language, a cultural poetics markedly different from that of mainstream American culture, which could barely be employed publicly. On the other hand, the easy slippage of images and thematics from quatrain to tanka suggests that the two forms are very close to inter-changeable, their differences negligible: that essences — of loss, memory, the possibility and impossibility of recovery — transfer intact across poetic patterns, even patterns derived from ostensibly distinctive cultural tradi-tions. In Suyemoto's "Hokku" and "Tanka," the cultural difference be-tween "Japanese" and "European" forms is at once stressed and minimized; it is, perhaps, exactly in that simultaneous emphasis and erasure that we can trace a specifically Japanese American discourse.

One further feature of this sliding of images from poem to poem is worth remarking upon here. A reader of, say, Suyemoto's first tanka with-in the context of her series of *Trek* poems is likely to interpret it as a fic-tional address to the entire community of relocated and imprisoned Japanese Americans, so that in the lines "There was a time, remember,/ When quince blossoms warmed our hearts?" the quince is taken to signify collec-tive memory of the time before the figurative and literal winter desert of the camps. In several other of Suyemoto's poems, however, including the prewar "Japonica" and "Gift of Quince" published in the 1946 *Yale Review,* quince is a private sign of remembrance, a love token: "You placed a spring of scarlet quince / In my curved hand, and then I knew / This was your answer to all that / I asked of you: / The flame had never been put out. . . . "[48] This suggests an alternative reading of the quince tanka, one which locates it too as a private declaration and fixes it as "love poem."

In the tanka, then, lines between public and private loss, between per-sonal and communal utterance, waver and break down. Two forms merge: the love complaint, that "women's genre," and the lamentation of exiles. This genre-crossing, characteristic of Suyemoto's wartime work, is not un-common in women's Second World War poetry. It is quite unlike anything in comparable poems in English by Nisei male poets in the war period. Take, for instance, Taro Katayama's use of agricultural figures in his "Agronomy," published in the February 1943 issue of *Trek:*

> From seeds by steel and lightning sown
>   In Asia's darkening plain;
> From compost rich in blood and bone,
>   The dower of Europe's slain;
>
> From tillage rending hill and field,
>   Will nothing come to pass?
> Will earth no fearful fruitage yield,
>   No judgment rise with grass?[49]

The explicitly public and military preoccupations of Katayama's quatrains are clear, and not at all surprising. This poem was published at the height of WRA registration, an intense crisis particularly for Nisei men, who were forced to choose between potential enlistment in the 442nd Battalion or draft resistance. In the male-authored Nisei literature of internment—John Okada's *No-No Boy*, for instance, or poems like Katayama's "Nightmare" or "The Volunteer" ("Were it not better thus to die / . . . Than, skeptic, cling to life")[50]—this choice is the central, energizing, agonizing subject. Heightened in Katayama's *Trek* lyrics, the military conflict and the question of loyalty are muted in Suyemoto's.

But they are not entirely absent. Bending the ostensibly private discourse of her prewar "lost love" lyrics to her own wartime ends, Suyemoto inflected them with undertones of a Japanese poetic tradition, transformed them into political commentary on the economic and social losses of all Japanese Americans. Her polished "feminine" mode—the "merely private" love poem—may have made her work less threatening to the mainstream culture than Katayama's open contestations, enabling her to break (momentarily) mainstream publication barriers where others could not. Less threatening, perhaps, but no less threatened. Nothing illustrates more clearly the impossibility of and dangers to the "merely private" in the camps, or the material intensity of those conditions I have called "prepoetics," than the fate of Suyemoto's son, who died at seventeen from allergies that he contracted as an infant in the horse stalls of Tanforan.

7

Identity and Contestation in Nisei Women's War Poetry

I

It may be true, as some historians of internment have argued, that conflicts such as those we saw in Taro Katayama's poems over how to answer the loyalty oaths imposed by the War Relocation Authority were in general much greater for Nisei men than women. Women, after all, could not enlist or be drafted. No matter how assimilated into mainstream American culture, they would not be stigmatized for complying in proper feminine fashion if their parents, fearful that they would all be otherwise forced to leave the camp or that the family would be separated, urged them to reply to the loyalty questions in the negative.[1] And no matter what they answered, as Mitsuye Yamada's father told her, girls might "make no difference to anyone." Certainly the contrast between the coded privacy of Suyemoto's nature images and the crackling tension, overtly historicized, of Katayama's poems on enlistment suggests a general paradigm of gender difference in camp writing.

But that contrast is in part misleading. Some poems written by Nisei women in the forties openly confront and struggle with the subject of Nisei identity and its painful corollary, Nisei wartime loyalty, in terms which put the WRA's questions directly into question. On the whole, however, these poems were not published during the period from the war's declaration to V-J day. Either they were printed before the U.S. war began, like Chiye Mori's "Japanese-American" and Hisaye Yamamoto's "Et Ego in America Vixi," or they were printed much later, like Mitsuye Yamada's work.

In some of these poems, a direct and revisionary relation to the conventions of war literature I have been tracing in earlier chapters is readily apparent. Consider, for instance, the prewar (or more precisely pre–U.S. war) writing of the very young Nisei woman poet Chiye Mori, who published her work in the early 1930s in the Nisei journal *Reimei (Dawn)* which was based in Salt Lake City.[2] (Taro Katayama was one of the editors of that journal.) The authors involved with *Reimei* frequently alluded in its pages to the already well-developed canon of modern Anglo-American Great War writing. The preface to the second issue of the journal, for example, represents the situation of the Nisei first as advantage ("having alien, therefore clairvoyant, eyes to both East and West, we should be least vulnerable to bias"), then as disadvantage ("apparently inconsequential issues may often assume a magnified and even malignant import") — and then attempts to resolve this tension by appealing to a familiar cultural narrative of post–Great War disillusion:

We cannot participate in any nationalism, as we ourselves are not nationalists. We claim to constitute a new genre, a citizenry of humanity, (and though none of us has experienced war; or ever hope to), not unlike the liberated, disillusioned generation that came through the World War, men who now see the world "shorn of false glamour."[3]

What the World War precursors offer here is more than simply an ironic vision; they provide a means of and a model for the discrediting of nationalism. In their invocation of combatant predecessors, these young Nisei writers sound like many other U.S. authors coming of age in the thirties. Their desire to match the "liberated, disillusioned generation" with a freedom and a skepticism of their own was common enough in American culture between the wars. But the emphasis on nationalism takes on a special edge here, for the need to debunk and to reject the conventional defining powers of the nation-state was one these Nisei felt with special intensity and growing urgency.

Still, in these early issues of *Reimei* comparisons between the Nisei and well-known Great war survivors often served to prove the manliness of the young writer, so critiques of nationalist militarism went hand in hand with celebrations of combat. "War and Youth," a piece jointly authored by editor Yasuo Sasaki and a white man writing under the pseudonym Hoshina Airan, centers on their "commmon obsession" with "those reactionary documents of the last Great War":[4]

And soon we were blurting out, wildly, almost incoherently, our "war experiences" — . . . "Do you realize how much these men have in common: Remarque, Sasson [sic], Graves. . . . " War . . . is merely life accentuated, concentrated, the stimuli are manifold and intenser. Here, therefore, is manifest the opportunity to plumb the depth of the soul and to test the stoutness of the heart. (27–28)

Significant exceptions to this celebratory tone occur in Chiye Mori's *Reimei* poems. In the journal's first issue, the sixteen-year-old Mori's "Vain" had scoffed at those who "talk of war and peace / And the fate of nations."[5] Five months later, in November 1932, not long after the Japanese invasion of Manchuria, she herself took on the discourse of war. Her poem "Japanese-American" portrayed the borderline position of the Nisei not, in the manner of the journal's optimistic preface, as the site of power and knowledge but rather as a place of terrifying exposure to violence:

> Behold,
> We are clay pigeons traveling swiftly and aimlessly
> On the electric wire of international hate,
> Helpless targets in the shooting gallery of political discord,
> Drilled by the clattering shells
> That rip toward us from both sides.
> Perhaps we are merely incidental in the gunplay.
> Irrevocably set in the dizzy pour of whining bullets,
> Forced to travel up and down an uncertain line,
> The hesitating border of two countries,
> The innocent guns are held in the bloated hands
> Of idle politicians who dare not look the enemy in the eye,
> But shoot at us, and like little boys,
> Playing a game of make-believe,
> Pretend we are the foe . . . [6]

If not for its title, this poem might read like any thirties adolescent's fantasized replay of the poems of Owen or Sassoon. But Mori was a responsive and a prescient Nisei young woman, and her phrase "Japanese-American" situates the war in a present hurtling toward the future. Redefining the trenches of Great War narrative as the borders of national and cultural identity, the poem maps out no-man's-land as a specifically Nikkei terrain — not a physical space so much as a political and psychological position shared by all Japanese American men and women. If the Nisei constituted "a new genre," as *Reimei*'s preface claimed, then that genre, "Japanese-American" implies, must be in danger and at war. What emerges here is the war poem as Nisei identity poem (or the identity poem as war poem), a kind of text increasingly common in the decade between this issue of *Reimei* and the moment at which Mori found herself interned at Manzanar.

II

Another poem, this one written in the months leading to Pearl Harbor by another young Nisei woman, Hisaye Yamamoto, faced the problem of representing Nisei (and specifically female Nisei) position and identity with considerably more freewheeling confidence than Mori's. Yamamoto's "Et Ego in America Vixi" was published in June 1941. At this time, sloughing off the ironic antinationalism which had dominated earlier journals like *Reimei*, one Nisei-authored text after another sought to claim a nation, to make an increasingly hostile mainstream audience aware that Japanese Americans *were* American.[7] "Et Ego In America Vixi" suggests with its authoritatively Westernized, Latinized title that it will certify its speaker's U.S. citizenship and patriotism. And the poem does so, but not simply:

> My skin is sun-gold
> My cheekbones are proud
> My eyes slant darkly
> And my hair is touched
> With the dusky bloom of purple plums.
> The soul of me is enrapt
> To see the wisteria in blue-violet cluster,
> The heart of me breathless
> At the fragile beauty of an ageless vase.
> But my heart flows over
> My throat chokes in reverent wonder
> At the unfurled glory of a flag—
>> Red as the sun
>> White as the almond blossom
>> Blue as the clear summer sky.[8]

This poem administers its own defensive version of a "loyalty oath," but it also complicates and undermines its every self-explanatory declaration. Adapting the lyric catalogue of praises for the purposes of self-portraiture and self-definition, "Et Ego" deploys a series of descriptive phrases to characterize a distinctively Nisei femininity. Anti-"Jap" stereotypes are neatly countered here; the face in this prewar poem is proudly, appealingly Japanesey, as adjectives like "sun-gold" and the association with purple plums imply.[9] This self-blazoning seems initially other-directed and mildly seductive as well as inward-directed and affirmative, as if offering for display a catalogue of the safely exotic fascinations of the Oriental female in Caucasian culture, proclaiming: see my nice skin, nice cheekbones, nice eyes, nice hair.

The traditional inventories of the woman's body parts in the blazon, Patricia Parker argues, may be understood as linked "to merchandising and to dominion,"

to conquest of a territory traditionally figured as female and controlled by its par-
tition or division [such as the feminized "New World," America]. . . . all partici-
pate in an imagery of opening and controlling something gendered as female . . .
in a process in which ostentatious display . . . is controlled within an economy
of mastery and ownership.[10]

To what end, then, for whose mastery, does the female speaker in "Et Ego"
inventory herself? The answer becomes apparent as the poem continues:
not to permit or invite domination but to ward it off; this blazon is a
strong form of self-defense. But the rhetorical strategy nonetheless in-
volves a self-mapping of the "territory" the "I" herself comprises and at-
tempts herself to control. The implicit interrogation to which the rest of
the poem attempts to respond is: What nationality governs the territory
which I am?

First, "Et Ego" moves from face to soul and heart in order to claim a
positive Old World cultural tradition, to represent a self demurely attuned
to the Japanese aestheticism exemplified by wisteria and vase. Here, how-
ever, the poem turns, with a "but" which resembles the reversal or counter-
argument of sonnet form, and another dimension of the speaker's "heart"
is revealed, manifested as awe at the American flag. The excess here—
overflowing, even choking—suggests that this version of the dominion of
the self is core, quintessential.

But the figures of speech through which the colors of patriotism unfurl
are suspiciously equivocal. "Red as the sun/ White as the almond blossom/
Blue as the clear summer sky": how "red-white-and-blue" is this? "Almond-
blossom" hints of stereotypically Asian predilections; "red as the sun,"
even more audaciously, invokes an image of the red sun of the *Japanese*
flag in order to describe the American. Only the belated "blue" line seems
unremarkable, though even here one could imagine a more obviously
"American" comparison; the United States has no corner on blue sky.

There is, I think, an implicit argument in these hinting, Japan-haunted
similes. Rather than refute claims of American identity, they confirm
those claims. Americanness, they imply—even the central emblem, the
very sign of America—can look like, can share qualities with, can even
contain things Japanese. So, too, can reverent, committed American citi-
zens have eyes that slant darkly, a taste for Asian vases, or hair that recalls
purple plums.

Still, even as it firmly asserts Americanness, "Et Ego" disrupts the order-
ly process of patriotic inventory with its teasing refusal to separate pre-
cisely that which signifies and is signified by "America" from that which
signifies and is signified by "Japan." Following Parker, we might say that
the self represented in this poem, despite her blazoning, *through* the sub-

tleties of her self-blazoning, resists being brought under the control of distribution.[11] "Et Ego" is in part a poem about the capacity of simile, both to demarcate the self and to evade demarcation, powers infinitely more extensive and flexible than those contained in the "yes" or "no" answers Yamamoto would face on the WRA questionnaire two years later.

III

In Mitsuye Yamada's *Camp Notes,* written in part during and shortly after internment but not printed until 1976 (by the feminist Shameless Hussy Press), oaths of loyalty come under further interrogation; and here Mori's project (the Nikkei "war poem") and Yamamoto's (the representation of Nisei womanhood) conjoin. Unlike Suyemoto, Mori, and Yamamoto, who sought to publish in and to negotiate with literary institutions outside or inside the camps, Yamada kept her poems to herself. Long hidden from view, for years unpublished and unpublishable, *Camp Notes* presents itself as revelation of what was once concealed in domesticity, like the charged material, at once docile and subversive, of Emily Dickinson's fascicles: "My affectionate thanks to Alta and Angel," reads a note on the flyleaf, "who have coaxed *Camp Notes* out of mothballs."[12] The result is a volume of poems far more militant and flagrant than anything by a Nisei woman which found its way into print on the home front or before the war, but also much more clearly marked for and and by silence.

I have so far traced some of the ways in which other Nisei women poets, who are both Yamada's contemporaries and (because of her long-postponed publication) her precursors, struggled with the politics of and constraints upon Nisei language in their attempts to define the "genre" of Nisei selfhood and to "make differences." Yamada's work deals explicitly with those limits of language — what prevents words in and about internment, what encourages and shapes them, what suppresses them. And, in the context of seventies feminism, it insists, among the many silences it contains and contends with, upon what June Jordan calls "silence peculiar to the female."[13]

On the back cover of Yamada's volume, one blurb by Paul Mariah announces, "In all the writings about the Japanese-American detention camps there have been only two by women. No single voice in poetry, until now, with this book." This claim, mystifying on any grounds — since there were at least *three* well-known prose memoirs of internment by women published before 1976, Monica Sone's *Nisei Daughter,* Jeanne Wakatsuki Houston's *Farewell to Manzanar,* and Miné Okubo's *Citizen 13660* — is especially problematic in its erasure of the work of poets like Suyemoto. Moreover, by presenting Yamada's poems as emerging more or less *sui generis,* it prevents recognition of one aspect of the central dynamic in *Camp Notes.*

The text is governed by a principle of recovery, a project at once archival and heuristic which involves reworking in heightened, public, confrontational forms and forums what has previously been consigned to mothballs. That "moth-balled" material includes, of course, Yamada's own old war-period poems, and also, more generally, the legacies of Issei culture. "My Issei parents," reads the dedication, "twice pioneers / now I hear them," and the first poem, transcribed in both Japanese and English, asserts "What your Mother tells you now / in time / you will come to know." But the recovered material in *Camp Notes* also includes the heritage of Nisei camp literature, particularly Nisei women's camp literature, a resource upon which the book draws in the freedom of its late publication, draws upon and also draws *out*, revising Nisei plots and tropes with a new edge of open rage and with newly intensified irony.

Camp Notes's most significant intertextual relation is not to an earlier poetic text but to Miné Okubo's *Citizen 13660*, the earliest of camp memoirs and one of the most influential. In 1946, the artist Okubo, whom we last saw fetching Suyemoto's poems for *Trek* from the barracks door at 3:00 A.M., published her classic collection of drawings of camp life with accompanying prose text, organized as an autobiographical, chronological record from pre–Pearl Harbor days to her departure from Topaz. Commonly praised for its "objectivity" and "humor," *Citizen 13660* in fact repeatedly raises questions about the subjectivity of the Nisei woman artist it self-portrays, and it is remarkable for the range of critique and protestation it inscribes into its documentary record. These projects are mostly carried out beyond words, however, in the artwork which comprises most of the body of the book, and in the dynamic interaction, the blank space for reading into, between the drawings and their far more restrained and cautious textual captions. Okubo's sketches "gaze and call out in silence," like the visual art in an exhibit organized to protest apartheid which Jacques Derrida describes: "And their silence is just. A discourse would once again compel us to reckon with the present state of force and law. It would draw up contracts, dialecticize itself, let itself be reappropriated again. This silence calls out unconditionally. . . ."[14] Beneath the silent drawings, with their strong effect of "doing justice" to the camps in relative artistic and political freedom, the discourse of Okubo's verbal captions is painfully, obviously *guarded*.[15]

The central "Camp Notes" section which gives Yamada's volume its name reduplicates *Citizen 13660*'s chronological documentary structure, beginning with "Evacuation" from Seattle, moving in its representation of Minidoka through "Desert Storm" and "The Question of Loyalty," and concluding with poems recounting relocation to Cincinnati. The design of the book, interspersed as it is with sketches, seems directly to recall Okubo's work, but differs from it in two significant ways. The first difference seems hopeful: the drawings in *Camp Notes* are done by two of Yamada's children, the calligraphy by her husband, and this joint effort underscores a sense of community less noticeable in Okubo's project. The second difference provokes less optimism. Like *Citizen 13660*, *Camp Notes* includes both drawings and text, but it overturns the earlier work's proportions: the discourse of the poems centers on each page, the silent drawings, marginalized, become mere "illustrations." As the first poem, which meditates on the interaction between a picture and its caption, makes very clear, these camp notes *in language* are inescapably caught within the present state of force and law, present both on the home front and in the postwar American culture which remembers internment:

Evacuation

As we boarded the bus
bags on both sides
(I had never packed
two bags before
on a vacation
lasting forever)
the Seattle Times
photographer said
Smile!
so obediently I smiled
and the caption the next day
read:

Note smiling faces
a lesson to Tokyo.

The image at the center of this story, a forced smile, gazes and calls out in silence, but its call is compelled and its silence is unjust. No less than words, it is subject to and manufactured for the insensitive and manipulative readings of a mainstream press which has played a major part in whipping up the hysteria leading to internment. Against the doctrinaire instructions of the caption—"*Note* smiling faces / a lesson to Tokyo"—Yamada's private, autobiographical "notes" (the beginning jottings, not the final closure, of the discourse of the "lesson") oppose a different story. But the obedience of the smile in this poem suggests the difficulty of escaping from the sign-systems and interpretations of the dominant culture, of separating one kind of notes from another.

There is, however, a strong protest both implicit and explicit in "Evacuation": implicit in its narrative movement beyond the smile for the photographer, explicit in the sardonic "I had never packed / two bags before / on a vacation / lasting forever." The heavy play with the word "vacation" here is Yamada's most characteristic poetic strategy. Poem after poem in the "Camp Notes" hinges on a concentrated verbal irony reminiscent of those which structure so many war poems by Owen or Sassoon. Here are a few examples:

> Our father
> stayed behind
> triple locks.
> What was the charge?
> Possible espionage or
> impossible espionage.
> I forgot which.
>
> ("On the Bus")

> A small group
> huddles around a contraband
> radio
> What?
> We
> are losing the war?
> Who is we?
> We are we the enemy
> the enemy is the enemy.
>
> ("Inside News")

> This was not
> im
> prison
> ment.
> This was
> re
> location.
>
> ("Desert Storm")

> Why should I volunteer?
> I'm an American
> I have a right to be
> drafted.
>
> ("Recruiting Team")

In each of these cases, loaded words or phrases — "stay behind," "possible espionage," the national "we," "the enemy," "relocation," "American" — are twisted for reexamination, sometimes literally through enjambment or through a kind of doodling with words in run-on clauses. The catchwords nonetheless cannot be eluded; each joke in the poems turns them around, but only to turn around within them. "Camp Notes" develops a poetics of the gag: punchlines which reveal how language buffets and muffles.

Like the notes Hisaye Yamamoto describes in the following passage, Yamada's long-suppressed, fragmented, minimal "camp notes" question the notion expressed by Ann Nisei which I quoted in the preface to this part of the book, the expectation that experience, "making men and women out of us," would unloose a flood of "authentic Nisei literature." The opening of Yamamoto's elegy to her brother who died fighting in Italy, published in the *Los Angeles Tribune* in November of 1945, uses the inability and the refusal to get past notes as a sign of the enormity of Nikkei silence:

After Johnny died, one kind soul insisted that now I had experienced all a Japanese in America could and that I must put it all down in a book for all the world to read. She even had a title picked out for my chef-d'oeuvre: 'Johnny Got a Zero.' . . . I tucked the notes in my drawer until they grew into a nice pile and chucked them all in the wastebasket. They made a hauntingly lovely thud.[16]

The irony of the "hauntingly lovely thud" is an effect many of Yamada's poems achieve; small, bitter "jokes," they seem barely to emerge out of before falling back into obscurity.

Yamamoto's "After Johnny Died" does not, however, end with the image of the wastebasket. It proceeds with the story of the "Life and Death of a Nisei GI," an account, the author takes pains to point out, which can only now be told and still may not be heard: "I will tell the story of Johnny now, though I doubt that it is the kind patriotic Americans will want to read in the middle of an exciting Victory Loan campaign." This device, deliberately marking a narrative as postponed and endangered revelation, is, of course, a central organizing feature of Yamada's *Camp Notes*, which also moves beyond the story of its own silencing to construct a further plot. But the content of Yamada's halting story differs radically from Yamamoto's. "After Johnny Died" centers on the soldier; Yamada's "notes," though they comprehend a wide variety of Nikkei camp experience, develop a specifically *feminine* poetic narrative which strongly resembles, and equally strongly revises, the masculine plot of conventional modern ironic war literature.

Like many a soldier's story, this narrative begins with separation from the mother and admonitions about honor; then it proceeds to an arena

of conflict and trauma, where bitter ironic truth is revealed. Here, how-
ever, the drama of relocation replaces the drama of combat, the narrative
is a story of coming-to-womanhood, and a distinct, though submerged,
undercurrent of sexual violence may be detected. The plot begins with
an account of very literal "reckoning with the present state of force and
law," a loyalty questionnaire scene unusual in its focus on women's choices,
and then develops the consequences of those choices:

The Question of Loyalty

. . . they said I must
forswear allegiance to the emperor.
for me that was easy
I didn't even know him
but my mother who did cried out
     If I sign this
     What will I be?
     I am doubly loyal
     to my American children
     also to my own people.
     How can double mean nothing?
     I wish no one to lose this war.
     Everyone does.

I was poor
at math.
I signed
my only ticket out.

The Night Before Good-Bye

Mama is mending
my underwear
while my brothers sleep.
Her husband taken away by the FBI
one son lured away by the Army
now another son and daughter
lusting for the free world outside.
She must let go.
The war goes on.
She will take one still small son
and join Papa in internment
to make a family.
Still sewing

squinting in the dim light
in room C barrack 4 block 4
she whispers
Remember
keep your underwear
in good repair
in case of accident
don't bring shame
on us.

Cincinnati

Freedom at last
in this town aimless
I walked against the rush
hour traffic
My first day
in a real city
where

no one knew me.

No one except one
hissing voice that said
dirty jap
warm spittle on my right cheek.
I turned and faced
the shop window
and my spittled face
spilled onto a hill
of books.
Words on display.

In Government Square
people criss-crossed
the street
like the spokes of
a giant wheel.

I lifted my right hand
but it would not obey me.
My other hand fumbled
for a hankie.
My tears would not

wash it. They stopped
and parted.
My hankie brushed
the forked
tears and spittle
together.
I edged toward the curb
loosened my fisthold
and the bleached laced
mother-ironed hankie blossomed in
the gutter atop teeth marked
gum wads and heeled candy wrappers.

Everyone knew me.

Plots in war literature in American culture usually begin with separa-
tions, very often the separation between soldier and mother, that "privi-
leged scenario" of Brooks's "looking," or more generally between soldiers
and civilians—a split, as I have emphasized, which tends to be heavily
gendered, read as identical with a deeply cut gulf between men and women.
Yamada's "The Night Before Goodbye" is founded on a similar structure
of separation, but here, as if the poem operated as a barely functioning
containment vessel, divisions begin to proliferate wildly. The Nikkei family
splits apart in all directions: civilians are segregated from other civil-
ians (a father is in prison); the soldier's departure from his mother is only
one of many choices and coercions exercised by and upon various family
members. Most strikingly of all, this war poem centers on a scene of
mother / *daughter* separation.

The maternal reminder which concludes "Night Before Goodbye"—
"remember / keep your underwear / in good repair / in case of accident /
don't bring shame / on us"—may be read as a woman's version of the
heavy-handed parental admonitions which stoke the ironies of many Great
War soldier poems; compare, for instance, the father's exhortations in
Owen's "S.I.W.": "death sooner than dishonour, that's the style." In one
sense, the words of the two parents which these two very different poems
by Owen and Yamada momentarily parrot are close to identical; both
place stronger emphasis on style than on safety. In other ways, of course,
they differ radically, in an almost direct negative inversion, as masculine
differs from feminine: a man is pushed by his father into blood-and-guts
heroism, a woman by her mother into maintaining properly modest under-
wear; a man is supposed to seek out glory, a woman to render herself per-
fectly invisible, as impervious to notice and comment as possible. And

they differ, too, less markedly, as British differs from Japanese American and potential "victor" from "survivor," with Owen's "father"'s emphasis on "honor" and Yamada's "Mama"'s on "no shame."

Very much as Owen does in numerous poems, Yamada uses a parental admonition to set up the heavy twist of irony which follows in her "Cincinnati" (though the mother in Yamada's "Night Before Goodbye" is far more vulnerable and innocent than Owen's poems' culpable parents). The violence and violation which occur in "Cincinnati" confirm the mother's fears even as they render her injunctions meaningless. The most perfectly mended underwear, the most docile demeanor in the world, provide no defense against the spit and hiss of the racial assault represented here.

The ironies of femininity in "Cincinnati" do not simply supply a distaff version of Owen's soldier poems' ironies of masculinity. They also disrupt some of the basic premises of the tradition of war poetry Owen's work initiated. In conjunction with "Night Before Goodbye," they make the internalization of femininity a dynamic and a question, where in Owen's work and in much masculine war poetry the female is a given; they introduce the politics of race into the war poem; most importantly, they represent violence, and a woman's knowledge of violence, on the home front, that place which in conventionally defined war poetry remains wholly safe and wholly ignorant.

The poem's skeletal ironies are pertinent to the experience of all Nikkei, men and women, especially all those who moved outside the camps during the war years. Representing the impossibility of freedom or safe anonymity for Japanese Americans in the racist war culture of "Government Square," enacting the struggle of an accosted "I" whose self-reflections are inevitably refracted by the dominant fictions of home-front "words on display," "Cincinnati" develops a powerfully condensed paradigm of racial attack. But it also hints, through the final image of the handkerchief, that this racial assault against a woman contains, or is felt to contain, an element of sexual assault, that it differs in particular effect, though not in force and motive, from an attack against a Japanese American man.

> My hankie brushed
> the forked
> tears and spittle
> together.
> I edged toward the curb
> loosened my fisthold
> and the bleached laced
> mother-ironed hankie blossomed in

the gutter atop teeth marked
gum wads and heeled candy wrappers.

Everyone knew me.

Why the handkerchief? In part, to emphasize in graphic terms the filth of the attacker; in part, to establish the figure of a real, molested body here, to call up what spit and tears feel like on a face with as much intensity as language can muster; but also, in part, to recall through the string of adjectives ("bleached laced mother-ironed") and the diminutive ("hankie") the Mama of the previous poem and her inculcations of feminine propriety. The loss of innocence represented by the defiled handkerchief thus entails a specific crisis of femininity: the loss of a sense that the practice of daughterly duty, a certain kind of modest womanhood taught by the mother, could make the world safe for the speaker. Being squeaky-clean, bleached and lacy, does not protect her from the taunt "dirty jap"; and being womanly, simply being a woman, increases the ways in which she is vulnerable to the barely deflected violence represented by "teeth-marks" and "heels." The threat of rape for the young woman relocated by herself, muted but real, haunts the end of this poem.[17]

To be sure, the next and last poem in the "Camp Notes," "Thirty Years Under," emphasizes the general experience of racial oppression shared by all nonwhite men and women in the United States:

I had packed up
my wounds in a cast
iron box

. . . . . .

until one day I heard
a black man . . .
say
there is nothing more
humiliating . . .
than being spat on

like a dog.

But a later poem in the *Camp Notes* volume explicitly recounts the sexual intimidation of "three girls / minding our distance / two thousand miles from home" by a group of violent young men and indifferent policemen, and its title, "Freedom in Manhattan," echoes back to the ironic "freedom" of "Cincinnati"'s first line in a way that supports a reading of veiled sexual threat in "Cincinnati"'s soiled mother-ironed hankie. So does the strong

implicit connection between internment and sexual violence in the climac-
tic poem about the camps in the volume, the Vietnam-era "To the Lady":

> The one in San Francisco who asked:
> Why did the Japanese Americans let
> the government put them in
> those camps without protest?
>
> Come to think of it I
>   should've run off to Canada
>   should've hijacked a plane to Algeria
>   should've pulled myself up from my
>   bra straps
>   and kicked'm in the groin
>   should've bombed a bank
>   should've tried self-immolation
>   should've holed myself up in a
>   woodframe house
>   and let you watch me
>   burn up on the six o'clock news
>   should've run howling down the street
>   naked and assaulted you at breakfast
>   by AP wirephoto
>   should've screamed bloody murder
>   like Kitty Genovese
>
> Then
>
> YOU would've
>   come to my aid in shining armor
>   laid yourself across the railroad track
>   marched on Washington
>   tattooed a Star of David on your arm
>   written six million enraged
>   letters to Congress . . .

In this militant poem, the anguished and accusatory structures of ad-
dress which Wilfred Owen used in his "To a Certain Poetess" persist trans-
formed. But the differences between Yamada's "To the Lady" of the seven-
ties and Owen's poem in its own historical situation are even more striking
than the similarities. Owen's certain poetess's ignorant insistence on sup-
port of government war policy becomes Yamada's lady's ignorant insis-
tence on protest. Yamada's radically destabilizing ironies reach farther
and bounce off no stable center. Their extravagant chronological and

geopolitical sweep both ironically duplicates "the Lady"'s ahistoricism and combatively historicizes the poem in its sixties political context (making, for instance, clear links between the racism and economic exploitation of internment on the one hand and the U.S. war in Vietnam on the other).[18] The innocence of informed sight to which Owen appeals ("If you could see") is unavailable to either speaker or her adversary in a televised culture. And in the figure of Kitty Genovese, Owen's oppositions of gender overturn; screaming "like Kitty Genovese" means crying out to indifferent listeners, but it also means screaming like a woman terrorized by male violence.

Finally, however, in this poem addressed by a *female* speaker to "the lady," the "gulf so deeply cut" across traditional war poetry marks a new divide: ethnic and political divisions *between* women. The concluding lines of "To the Lady" go further. Most of the poem's harsh irony has directed itself pointedly at the "lady"'s aggressively stupid question, but the poem's closing analysis extends from there, describing a mutual responsibility and struggle. Both female speaker and "the lady" reader share two ongoing tasks, extricating themselves from, but also understanding the extent of their connections to, what in street talk gets called "the man":

> But we didn't draw the line
> anywhere
> law and order Executive Order 9066
> social order moral order internal order
>
> YOU let'm
> I let'm
> All are punished.

Yamada's latest volume *Desert Run* (1988) returns to many of the sites delineated in *Camp Notes*: the scene of the camps (a series of desert poems begins the book); the relationship between women; sexual and domestic violence against women (in "The Club," a woman is beaten with one of a man's "overseas treasures," a carved Japanese female figure); and the placement of the Japanese American self in a world mapped out by World War II (the Nikkei speaker in "Guilty on Both Counts" finds herself taking the blame as an "American" for the bombing of Hiroshima and as "Japanese" for the bombing of Pearl Harbor).[19] One additional return interests me here: at several points within this new book, the argument with dominant conventions of American war literature which I have been reading into Yamada's *Camp Notes* poems becomes especially clear and openly polemical.

"Lethe," for instance, describes a teacher's enraged paralysis and silence in the face of the racism of a "veteran student" — presumably a Vietnam veteran. His words begin the poem: "He said / 'With my own eyes / I have seen them . . . '" (82). By its end, the poem defines him as one "who has seen too much / or not enough" (83). "Lethe" denies and charts the cost of the notion of the authority of veteran's experience which has under-pinned much war poetry since World War I.

A more complex example echoes Wilfred Owen directly. "My Cousin" is set in a serenely ambiguous landscape, in which distinctions between Japanese and American territory have collapsed: the cousin, a "failed kami-kaze pilot / who lived to miss only three fingers," sits in a garden of "dwarfed trees" but drinks "California wine," and his "imported chair" sug-gests that trade has lessened distinctions between the two countries once at war. Both he and the landscape are now, perhaps have always been, "pacific." The poem centers on his answer to the speaker's question, "a question I could not / ask for thirty years." Across the gulfs between them — of gender and of nation — comes his reply: "Of course I don't / I don't really believe / 'it is sweet and fitting / to die for one's country'" (73).

What "My Cousin" does with the war poem as it comes down from Owen is open it out. Yamada's poem's most obvious project, one very much in Owen's straightest ironic line, is to correct the American myth (apparently internalized by the Nikkei speaker) of the war-crazed kami-kaze. But its most subtle effect is the introduction of a dialogic principle — a gentle call and response — into the single-minded lecturings of Owen's "Dulce." Cultural inculcations and cultural mysteries multiply; a conver-sation occurs; and the poem ends with figures of myriad voice, in a land-scape at once American as Whitman's and Japanese as Basho's: "It is even-ing and the canary clears its throat. / I leave among cricket sounds in the woods." I would conclude that Yamada, that deliberately uncertain poet (ess), lets her "cousin" answer gently back to Owen, if "answer back" did not imply a more combative and conclusive tone than this poem at least, long after the Second World War, allows.

Part Four

Oblique Places

8

An Oblique Place
Elizabeth Bishop and the
Language of War

War feels to me an oblique place.

Emily Dickinson[1]

Is there a politics of gender (that is, dispute about language, terminology, alloca-
tion of resources, the exercise of power, and the definition of the terms of relation-
ship between the sexes) in the politics of war?

Joan Scott[2]

I

In 1945, Elizabeth Bishop wrote to the publisher of her forthcoming
first book the lines I quoted in chapter 1: "The fact that none of these
poems deal directly with the war, at a time when so much war poetry is
being published, will, I am afraid, leave me open to reproach."[3] Perhaps,
she suggested, Houghton Mifflin could insert a note somewhere in *North
and South* making it clear that "most of the poems had been written, or
begun at least, before 1941."[4] This disclaimer seems strained, particularly
in its isolationist assumption (uncharacteristic of Bishop) that "the war"
placed no demands on poets till after Pearl Harbor. But the letter only
barely conceals a confident assertion which belies its author's demurrals.
After all, *North and South*, as Louise Bogan wrote of "Roosters," one of
the poems within it, "contains all manner of references to war and war-
riors."[5] It is not that these poems do not "deal" with war but that, the
letter lets us know, they do not deal with war "directly." Bishop's first
book might be read, in fact, as a war book *in-directed.* In it the matters
of war literature – naval engagements, border crossings, skirmishes, search
missions, even a monument of sorts – appear, but only as covert opera-
tions. Each takes the form of lyric trope, interiorized, parabolic, skewed.

213

Is there a politics of metaphor in the politics of war? Only Wallace Stevens's lyrics of the period could be said to raise this question as insistently for wartime audiences as Bishop's poems do.[6] But compare the two poets warding off reproaches to which both, as civilians, felt open in the war years; set Bishop's oh-so-delicate disclaimer against Stevens's strutting assertions, in his own blurb on the back of *Notes Toward a Supreme Fiction*, of the virility, equal to the soldier's, of the poet's task: "the two are one . . . the soldier is poor without the poet's lines."[7] In these moments of authorial defense, Bishop's and Stevens's strategies seem caricatures of masculine and feminine approach; and that raises yet a further question.[8] It is one that "Roosters," the longest and most obviously ambitious poem in *North and South*, poses with particular force, but other poems in the volume raise as well: Is there a politics of gender and war in the politics of metaphor?

II

> Even if one were tempted
> to literary interpretations
> such as: life/death, right/wrong, male/female
> — such notions would have resolved, dissolved, straight off
> in that watery, dazzling dialectic.
>
> Elizabeth Bishop, "Santarem," 1978[9]

> In any event, the world as we know it, the world in history, cannot be described in its peculiarities by an idiom of peace. Though we may, ideally, convert the dialectic into a chart of the dialectic (replacing a development by a calculus), we are actually in a world at war — a world at combat. . . .
>
> Kenneth Burke, *A Grammar of Motives*, 1945[10]

In 1948, two poets, a man and a woman, met on a lawn on the Princeton campus. The young woman, Jane Cooper, recorded the encounter soon after — she insists, verbatim and virtually in its entirety — in a poem called "a poem with capital letters" which is written entirely in lowercase:

> john berryman asked me to write a poem about roosters.
> elizabeth bishop, he said, once wrote a poem about roosters.
> *do your poems use capital letters?* he asked. *like god?*
> i said. *god no*, he said, *like princeton!*[11]

Though these lines are not, of course, to be taken too seriously — Cooper's bewilderment and dismay are wry, Berryman's aggression cheerful and his pomposity self-mocking, the whole conversation an arch set piece — we might read this scene, in which a prominent male poet buttonholes a female poet of then more modest stature to offer her instructions, as a parable concerning postwar codes of feminine writing. A woman poet, Berryman's request implies, will write, or should write, may be allowed to write or must be prodded to write a poem about roosters—that is, a poem about male animals. Her example will be, or should be, Elizabeth Bishop's poem "Roosters," written during the Second World War and published in Bishop's first book, *North and South* (1946).

Berryman's demand or advice mocks the woman poet three ways, by insisting that three forces must properly and will inevitably impinge upon her writing: the primacy of the male subject, the narrowness of the domestic, and the paucity of female influence. The message is: look for your poetic foremothers, your sister poets; the tradition they offer you which I endorse, and into which I insist upon placing you, boils down to this—it is about roosters. This is a little like advising a young male artist to paint a picture about a bull, since Picasso in *Guernica* painted a picture about a bull. No wonder the young Cooper resisted defining her poetic identity in relation to Bishop, of whom she writes in an autobiographical essay on why she never published the poems she wrote in this period: "Men's praise of women's poetry didn't seem to go much beyond [Bishop's work, which] I admired, but couldn't then use. The subject I was writing about—war and relations between women and men—seemed also mostly to have remained the property of men."[12]

"Roosters," much-praised, has indeed long functioned as a model of decorum for a woman poet who wishes to make war and the relations between men and women her subject. In 1947 Robert Lowell lauded it, along with "The Fish," as "large and perfect," pronouncing it one of "the best poems that I know of by a woman in this century."[13] Randall Jarrell placed it among "the most calmly beautiful, deeply sympathetic poems of our time."[14] Its measured conclusions might be said to exemplify the qualities of clear elocution and genteel moral fiber admired by Chad Walsh in what is surely the most extreme example of a "right-wing" Bishop criticism, a 1969 review entitled "Never underestimate the power of a lady's voice." Walsh offers Bishop's work as the alternative to bullhorns, tear gas, protests against the Vietnam War, and four-letter words.[15] Critics in the "left-wing" school of Bishop studies have also used the poem as an emblem not only of moderate decencies but of a nonantagonistic feminist vision; Sandra Gilbert and Susan Gubar, for instance, at the end of their response to Frank Lentricchia's attack on their work, invoke "Roosters" as their—and for its—politic gesture of final reconciliation.[16]

But "Roosters" can be cited, too, for opposite effects. After all, one of the poem's first readers, Bishop's mentor Marianne Moore, was irritated and scandalized by the poem precisely on the grounds that it was *unlady-*

like, *im*polite, *in*decorous.[17] What shocked Moore has won over a later generation of feminist readers, for "Roosters" provides a ready fund of barbed indictments of masculine aggression and pretension. When Gilbert and Gubar, at the *beginning* of their answer to Lentricchia, use a line from the poem as one of their epigraphs — "Roosters, what are you projecting?" — the quotation expresses an undeniable, and an undeniably raucous, rage. Berryman may satirically uphold the poem as a ladylike exemplar, but Cooper can, equally satirically, draw on the proof-text to undermine the lesson. Her "poem with capital letters" is, after all, a poem about roosters — and it most resembles Bishop's "Roosters" in its satire on cockiness.

This apparent contradiction — the fact that "Roosters" offers raw material for either ammunition or conciliation — can be easily explained; it depends upon which part of the poem one cites. "Roosters" divides into sections very different in tone, separated in its original publication in the *New Republic* by printer's devices and in later versions by extended white spaces.[18] When Gilbert and Gubar open their answer to Lentricchia with one of "Roosters'" early lines and close with a reference to the poem's conclusion, they work within the long tradition of reading a clear link or segue between the poem's sections. Implicitly, they present this elegant modulation as an argumentative model. When Alicia Ostriker interprets "Roosters" in another recent feminist analysis, she reads the poem, rather, as marred by an abrupt, unwarranted break, and she presents that turn for the worst as a bad example.[19]

My own reading of the whole and parts of "Roosters" is warily dialectical. I aim to counter notions of the text's harmonious largesse by respecting its initial feminist rage, and at the same time to counter overvaluations of that anger by reevaluating the feminist politics of the poem's later, more temperate passages. "Roosters," I argue, not only admits such an interpretation; it also incites it, and then anatomizes it. Dialectic is itself a key self-reflexive subject of the poem, as is the question of women's relation, in a time and state of war, to Western traditions of dialectical thinking (metaphysical and Marxist, philosophical and political). Since "Roosters" (unlike many of the poems I consider in this book) still tends to be read in epideictic terms, either to grant or to deny it status *as model* for current thinking and writing, I am concerned with the question Jane Cooper raises: (How) Can we now use this poem? At the same time, I propose to re-place "Roosters" in its immediate historical context and to trace some of its own compelling models, dialectical and otherwise.

In dialectic proper, Rosamund Tuve advises, "the contrary of a position, later refuted, must be stated with authoritative power, or, in poetry, with utmost vividness."[20] "Roosters" follows this injunction to the utmost, or almost. For all her legendary coolness and apolitical detachment, it is Elizabeth Bishop who wrote, in the first part of the poem, the most fiercely vivid critique of male power and of militarism by an American woman poet during the Second World War. At the same time, her light hand, her wariness of the power of the authoritative which extends beyond the vivid, is apparent from the start.

"Roosters"' situates itself at the moment when, just before the sun rises, the calling of birds begins, not the fluent notes of nightingales or skylarks but a more jarring, antiharmonious figure of voice: "At four o'clock / in the gun-metal blue dark / we hear the first crow of the first cock" (CP, 35–36). The presence of more than one listener at the signal of dawn — "we hear" — invites a reading of the poem as aubade, but these first stanzas do not attend in any obvious ways to the situation of interrupted lovers. Rather, the roosters themselves occupy center stage. Their crows do not function as mere triggers for human love lament, as in the classic alba tradition. Instead, they take over the poem "with horrible insistence." This rude awakening reveals a landscape and a point of view already militarized: a gun-metal blue window through which to investigate a gun-metal blue dark. Outside, the small-town setting of backyard fences and broccoli patches renders this representation of daily outbursts of martial enthusiasm at once both essentially silly and especially ominous, since the chanticleerian homeliness of the scene serves to place the origins of war squarely within the realm of the domestic:

> Cries galore
> come from the water-closet door,
> from the dropping-plastered henhouse floor,
>
> where in the blue blur
> their rustling wives admire,
> the roosters brace their cruel feet and glare
>
> with stupid eyes
> while from their beaks there rise
> the uncontrolled, traditional cries.
>
> Deep from protruding chests
> in green-gold medals dressed,
> planned to command and terrorize the rest,
>
> the many wives
> who lead hens' lives
> of being courted and despised;

> deep from raw throats
> a senseless order floats
> all over town . . .
>   (*CP*, 35)

When Marianne Moore, who read an early draft of "Roosters," objected to the singsong quality of these tercets (going so far as to rewrite them) and also to the presence of bathroom language which violated her standards of feminine propriety (among other things, she wanted Bishop to clean up the poem by substituting for "rooster" the word "cock"!), Bishop defended the poem's crudeness firmly. "I cherish my 'water closet' and other sordities because I want to emphasize the essential baseness of militarism," she wrote to Moore. Tactfully reaffirming her choice of "the rather contemptuous word ROOSTERS" over the "the more classical COCK," she added, "I also had in mind the violent roosters Picasso did in connection with his GUERNICA." Finally, she insisted on retaining the heavy rhythms of her three-line stanzas: "I can't bring myself to sacrifice what (I think) is a very important 'violence' of tone."[21]

If these tercets grate deliberately, they do so in the service of strong criticism not only of militarism but also of traditional constructions of gender. "Roosters"' violence of tone addresses itself first to the coercive force exercised over women in a society of male headship. Implicit in the first part of the poem is a militant analysis of war systems which anticipates and lays the groundwork for contemporary feminist theories of the relation between the military and misogyny, presenting warfare and armed power as both the epitome and the enforcement of patriarchy.[22]

The henhouse culture of "Roosters" is a representation of the consequences of fascist occupation. Bishop wrote Moore that one prototype for her village scene was "those aerial views of dismal little towns in Finland and Norway, when the Germans took over, and their atmosphere of poverty." But she related it as well to a model closer to home, and more chronic—"In the first part I was thinking of Key West, and also of those aerial views . . . "—refusing to limit the repressive familial structure "Roosters" depicts to Nazi social structure only.[23] The poem's critique extends to all forms of territoriality and aggression, linked here specifically to masculine behavior and, perhaps, to masculine nature.

> The crown of red
> set on your little head
> is charged with all your fighting blood.

> Yes, that excresence
> makes a most virile presence,
> plus all that vulgar beauty of iridescence.
>   (*CP,* 37)

    The rooster's crown, compelling and excessive, is a sign of phallic aggression which is naturally attached to a male body (and to which the male is naturally attached). The speaker affectionately grants it some appeal, noting its vulgar beauty, even allowing it that privileged Bishop term "iridescence." Nonetheless, since the crown is an unremovable appendage of the male which swells with "fighting blood," the dominant force of this passage implicates the male animal in an innate aggressive drive. Their bodies inexorably militarized, the roosters proceed to conduct a sunrise war at once primitive and technological which culminates in mass carnage:

> Now in mid-air
> by twos they fight each other.
> Down comes a first flame-feather,
>
> and one is flying,
> with raging heroism defying
> even the sensation of dying.
>
> And one has fallen,
> but still above the town
> his torn-out, bloodied feathers drift down;
>
> and what he sung
> no matter. He is flung
> on the grey ash-heap, lies in dung
>
> with his dead wives
> with open, bloody eyes,
> while those metallic feathers oxidize.
>   (*CP,* 37)

    The male animal, within this system of mechanized destruction, is supposed to act in defense of the female, but in one witty, bitter turn the poem rejects that possibility and provides him with another role only: not protecting but projecting. Converting the alba's traditional complaint at being awakened into a political protest, "Roosters" addresses its roosters with blunt indignation.

Each screaming
"Get up! Stop dreaming!"
Roosters, what are you projecting?

You, whom the Greeks elected
to shoot at on a post, who struggled
when sacrificed, you whom they labeled

"Very combative . . . "
what right have you to give
commands and tell us how to live,

cry "Here!" and "Here!"
and wake us here where are
unwanted love, conceit and war?

                                                   (*CP*, 36)

In a 1977 interview with George Starbuck, Bishop meditated upon the relation of this first half of "Roosters" to one tradition of argument which is distinctly monological, the "tract."

EB: I have an early poem, a long poem, written a long time ago. The Second World War was going on, and it's about that, more or less. "Roosters," I wrote it in Florida, most of it. Some friends asked me to read it a year or so ago, and I suddenly realized it sounded like a feminist tract, which it wasn't meant to sound like at all to begin with. So you never know how things are going to get changed around for you by the times.

GS: But that makes some sense. . . . I'm afraid it's their banner now. You'll never get it away from them.[24]

As Bishop continued, gently, to disclaim, if not to dismiss outright, feminist readings of her poems, Starbuck pressed her further: "Well, which are your feminist tracts?" Her answer was first "I don't think there are any." Then she added, "The first part of 'Roosters,' now, I suppose." This was followed by another demurral: "But I hadn't thought of it that way. Tract poetry . . . " (321).

"Tract poetry . . . ": the voice fades off, elliptically, in amusement and dismay. Is the first part of "Roosters" a feminist tract or isn't it? No one here knows for sure, both because Bishop is too canny to attempt to exert control over the poem's readings and because "knowing for sure" is precisely the operation of tracts she wishes most of all to reject. In a later interview she would state "I've always considered myself a strong feminist"; the problem for Bishop is not feminism as such — whatever feminism

as such might be — but feminism *in poetry,* or for poetry, feminism warp-
ing reading, pushing the poem somehow inappropriately toward the tract.[25]

Bishop poses that problem in the Starbuck interview as one of the rela-
tion between different historical moments of reading: the question of
feminism is one produced by and for the text only in the seventies. "To
begin with," the poem about the Second World War (more or less) "wasn't
meant to sound like that at all." The relation of "Roosters" to any femi-
nism closer to its moments of original inception is thus neatly repressed.
But later in the interview Virginia Woolf's *Three Guineas* surfaces to be
endorsed by Bishop suggestively and I would argue inevitably.[26] For Woolf's
book, published three years before the poem, is undoubtedly "Roosters"'
first obvious intertext, and the controversy over that word "feminism"
which *Three Guineas* both provoked and itself notoriously engaged in
precedes Bishop's poem long before contemporary feminism belatedly
reopened our ears to the sound of that debate.

Three Guineas provides, of course, a model feminist tract on gender
and war, and also a model of elegantly elliptical, intensely ambivalent
relation to both tracts and feminism.[27] In her conversation with Starbuck
as in other remarks made late in her life, Bishop could therefore use Woolf's
name to acknowledge feminist values indirectly while at the same time
affirming an ideal of art's undogmatic triumph over political concerns.
Her prose tribute to Marianne Moore, for instance, invokes Woolf both
to affiliate Moore's work with and to differentiate it from feminist po-
lemic: "one wonders how much of Marianne's poetry the feminist critics
have read. Have they really read 'Marriage,' a poem that says everything
they are saying and everything Virginia Woolf has said?" Moore's "Mar-
riage," Bishop goes on to say, is also "a poem which transforms a justified
sense of injury into a work of art" — a project which in the ambiguous
structures of her argument might either be identified with Woolf's own
work or distinguished from it.[28]

The second part of "Roosters" centers directly upon a figure of art trans-
forming injury; in it Woolf's passionate and enigmatic treatise on patri-
archy and warmaking gives way to a different intertext, another kind of
tract, and the original "violence of tone" modulates into more musical
variations. "When I was writing 'Roosters,'" Bishop once told another in-
terviewer, "I got hopelessly stuck," until, she said, the "rhythms of a Scar-
latti sonata imposed themselves upon me"; from here on in we can begin
to hear the Scarlatti.[29] Across the break between stanzas 26 and 27, the
cockfight is replaced first by religious exhortation and then by more in-
tricate meditations:

St. Peter's sin
was worse than that of Magdalen
whose sin was of the flesh alone;

of spirit, Peter's,
falling, beneath the flares,
among the "servants and officers."

Old holy sculpture
could set it all together
in one small scene, past and future:

Christ stands amazed,
Peter, two fingers raised
to surprised lips, both as if dazed.

But in between
a little cock is seen
carved on a dim column in the travertine,

explained by *gallus canit;*
flet Petrus underneath it.
There is inescapable hope, the pivot . . .
                                    (*CP,* 37–38)

A series of transformations or pivots occurs here in rapid succession.
New Testament crucifixion narrative sharply interrupts the previous de-
scription of backyard carnage. On the one hand, the gospel story suggests
a transcendence of warmaking. On the other, it simply replaces one figure
of slaughter with another, though one which grants to the conflict greater
subjectivity, meaning, and effect of choice. As Moore's Judas and Jarrell's
Pilate have already demonstrated, and as H.D.'s explorations of the Mag-
dalene will later show, Second World War poems often mined the Chris-
tian crucifixion narrative for its lode of images of selfhood in relation to
intolerable betrayal, sacrifice, or murder.[30] Pilate bears the weight of pas-
sive implication in bureaucracies of extermination, and Judas plays a part
in the drama of treachery at its furthest extreme. Bishop chooses Peter,
the most intimate, cowardly, and easily pardoned of this male trio. The
erotics of man-to-man friendship in the Peter/Christ plot underscore an-
other of the poem's conversions: male fighting yields to male bonding. At
the same time, masculinity and sexuality disappear as overt themes, just
as any trace of women vanishes. "Roosters"' version of the crucifixion war
poem further mediates the tradition by pivoting from Christian sermon

and Christian story to more distanced meditation upon Christian art, further still by concentrating finally on the comic allegory of the cock, the other rooster, who proves to "mean"—for his part in crowing three times—not violence but forgiveness.

Alicia Ostriker, analyzing this poem as "a capsule representation of the invisible constraints inhibiting poets who would be ladies," gives the following account of the loaded shift of tone which occurs at the center of "Roosters": Bishop's "strong and brilliant parody of male brutality" is "succeeded not only by Christian moralizing or forgiveness but by a static use of the icon—brute life replaced by sacred and forgiving art." For Ostriker, "'Roosters' is finally a withdrawal of a familiar sort."[31] Other readers from the time of the poem's first publication have, predictably, offered a reverse reading of this sequence, celebrating its progression from a harshness of subject and judgment to a general forgiveness. Willard Spiegelman speaks for that tradition when in a classic article he approvingly describes the poem's action as the "transformation of militancy into humility."[32]

Both Ostriker and Spiegelman share, however, one assumption: a sense of the poem as a development in which a second term conclusively overrides its predecessor. This reading is supported by "Roosters'" own allusions to traditional Western and Christian constructs of events in time. When in the first part of the poem a reference to the Greeks appears, and in the second medieval Christianity is invoked, a Christian theory of historical progress immediately suggests itself. Diachronic readings of the poem, whether approving or disapproving, share the assumption that it stages a movement, like Christian history, toward something momentous: some kind of salvation or, for the resistant reader, final withdrawal.

Yet several aspects of the text challenge interpretations of it which would emphasize the conclusive development of "old" roosters into "new" ones, whether we read that development as an appropriate metaphorical maturation or as an inappropriate accommodation to norms of feminine propriety. When, for example, in the second part of the poem a latent meaning (rooster as forgiveness) displaces the surface meaning established so far (rooster as territorial violence), Ostriker interprets this change in tenor as a flight from nature into culture, from history to aesthetics, and from dynamic narrative to rigid iconography. This reading strongly emphasizes the natural and incontrovertible aggression of the male animal as Bishop represents him in the first section of "Roosters"; it suggests implicitly that a genuine realism in the first half (roosters as roosters, "brute life") gives way to genteel euphemism in the second. But even in the opening section of the poem, several key passages trouble a reading of the roosters as entirely "natural" aggressors. The static icon in the second half, the sacred

Lateran cock, has, in fact, his equally static counterpart in the first, the
profane tin rooster who perches over the churches of the occupied town.
His presence, though brief, is crucial, for it opens up not only the possi-
bility of a paired choice of antithetical icons (tin rooster or carved cock)
but also the possibility of ambiguous signs. The rooster of any given church
might either implicate the religious establishment for its collaboration
with militarism or celebrate the triumph of Christian values over systems
of violence.

What roosters mean, then, is potentially uncertain from early on in the
poem; moreover, as the following lines suggest, at the exact moment
when the poem's critique of male brutality emerges most directly the
meaning of roosters is socially relative and culturally constructed. At one
point in "Roosters'" first half, the roosters are represented as imperiously
mapping out their territories,

> each one an active
> displacement in perspective;
> each screaming, "This is where I live!"
>
> Each screaming
> "Get up! Stop dreaming!"
> Roosters, what are you projecting?
>
> You, whom the Greeks elected
> to shoot at on a post, who struggled
> when sacrificed, you whom they labeled
>
> "Very combative . . . "
> What right have you to give
> commands and tell us how to live . . .
>
> (CP, 36)

Here the final tercet's shift in verb tense to the present, from the active
participles ("dreaming / screaming") and past ("elected / labeled") which
precede it accentuates a radical inversion. To wake into the world of "Roosters"
has up to this point been to enter, under duress, a world badly, exasperat-
ingly, governed by others. Because these others are male, this reluctant
awakening into a "here" where all possibilities are predetermined is figured
(very lightly, very subtly) as a feminine condition. Yet the all-dominant
male leaders who seem to maintain a monopoly over voice turn out them-
selves to be objects defined and subordinated by larger cultural sign-systems:
first that of the Greeks, then, later, that of Christian tradition. The roosters,
heretofore represented as fundamentally, independently violent, are mo-
mentarily revealed to be as much *projected* as *projecting*.

This dazzling "active / displacement of perspective" of the poem's own is the first example of "Roosters'" governing method: dialectics, or, as Kenneth Burke has put it, "the use of symbol-systems to check on symbol-systems."[33] The poem's dialectical models are several. They conflict. And Bishop draws upon each of them, distrustfully, as a symbol-system itself; we might say "Roosters" enacts the use of dialectic to check on dialectic.

One of these traditions is, of course, the dialectical materialism influential in the period of Bishop's poetic apprenticeship. In later interviews Bishop emphasized that she had remained consistently aloof as a poet from all forms of thirties "social consciousness."[34] An eloquent summation of "dialectical thinking" in the Hegelian and Marxist lines by Fredric Jameson, might well, however, be taken as a gloss for the stanzas I have just discussed above:

It is, of course, thought to the second power: an intensification of the normal thought processes such that a renewal of light washes over the object of their exasperation. . . . [T]he mind, in a kind of shifting of gears, now finds itself willing to take what had been a question for an answer . . . understanding the dilemma not as resistance of the object alone, but also as the result of a subject-pole deployed against it in a strategic fashion — in short, as the function of a determinate subject-object relationship.[35]

"You, whom the Greeks elected / to shoot at on a post," "you whom they labeled / 'Very combative'": isn't what happens here exactly the movement away from understanding male aggression solely as "resistant object" and toward defining it as the function of a socially determinate subject-object relation?

"Roosters'" next and major displacement of perspective — the turn from cockfight to the art of the Lateran — derives, however, more clearly from another tradition of dialectic, the metaphysical, which finds all subjects and objects but one impertinent. As Jeredith Merrin shows, Bishop's debt to seventeenth-century poetic models, particularly to George Herbert, was conscious and extensive; in "Roosters" we can trace a clear resemblance to the dialectical moves of those metaphysical poems.[36] Like the dialectic in the seventeenth-century "self-consuming artifacts" Stanley Fish has described, which also involves "breaking out of built-in frames of reference and evidentiary processes," "Roosters'" dominant, structural dialectic is "soul-centered; the response it requires is decisional (in the religious or existential sense) . . . "[37] "There is inescapable hope, the pivot": isn't what happens here exactly an affirmation of spiritual decision over social and material determination?

Perhaps, but "Roosters" in its modernity departs from the spiritual poetics of those precursors in one key—*the* key—respect. Stubbornly skeptical, it will not gesture toward the final self-consumption Fish locates as the goal of dialectic in the experience of seventeenth-century literature. Or rather, it problematizes and ironizes that gesture, inscribing it once more only *inside* dialectic rather than envisioning it at or as dialectic's end. This failure or refusal entirely to transcend is acutely clear, as we might expect, in "Roosters"' final stanzas, which must inevitably bear the weight of the poem's own theory of dialectical conclusions.

In metaphysical dialectic, Fish writes early on in his analysis of seventeenth-century texts, "one moves, or is moved, from the first to the second way, which has various names, the way of the good, the way of the inner light, the way of faith; but whatever the designation, the moment of its full emergence is marked by the transformation of the visible and segmented world into an emblem of its creator's indwelling presence" (3). The turn in "Roosters" toward the figure of Christian forgiveness is a transparent move toward "the way of the inner light"; from there the poem continues precisely toward an emblem which has traditionally functioned as one privileged sign of a creator's presence. Its transactions with that figure are, however, dubious.

In the third and final section, a gentle reduplication of the initial sunrise scene offers a revivified and purified domestic landscape. The broccoli patch, formerly the locus of predawn war cries, turns radiant and silent in the dawn, and the eye moves apparently skyward, away from the "dropping-plastered henhouse floor":

> In the morning
> a low light is floating
> in the backyard, and gilding
>
> from underneath
> the broccoli, leaf by leaf;
> how could the night have come to grief?
>
> gilding the tiny
> floating swallow's belly
> and lines of pink cloud in the sky,
>
> the day's preamble
> like wandering lines in marble.
> The cocks are now almost inaudible.
>
> The sun climbs in,
> following "to see the end,"
> faithful as enemy, or friend.
>
> (*CP,* 39)

It is easy enough to read these lines, bringing to them a range of associations from lyric tradition, from religious proclamation, from political manifesto, as the staging of "the dawning of a new day": a prophet's ecstatic prediction that a new testament will be written, a preamble's dignified promise that a new world will be constituted. The sun rises at the conclusion of the poem, replacing the roosters as object of attention, as if to provide a certain end to the dialectical process and a final limit to relativism. It invites an interpretation which treats the entire movement of the poem as a dramatic progress toward a dawn both literal and ideal.

The last tercet, however, emerges in potential opposition to this reading. No Messiah, this sun, no glorious chariot; rather, linked through a quotation from Matthew, Chapter 26, to St. Peter, who lurked among the servants "to see the end" of Christ's trial, the sun enters belatedly, a follower, traitor, and guilty observer. The last short line packs into its two figurative moves — its simile and its irony, its "as" and its "or" — a final disconcerting oscillation of simultaneous meanings. The sun is "faithful as enemy," a sinister redefinition of faith which assumes that the most unwavering human relationships are those governed by hate. Augmented with "or friend," after the unclear work of a comma,[38] the simile recuperates itself, but not conclusively enough to offer firm reassurance, "particularly," as Lynn Keller notes, "if one recalls that Peter was Christ's friend."[39] The phrase undoes the dualism of ally and antagonist, both by rendering them impossible to tell apart (which is the sun: enemy or friend?) and, more radically, by eradicating those distinctions entirely (the sun's faith may be at once somehow both affectionate and hostile, both familiar and strange).

Undermining these oppositions, "Roosters" does not end, as Ostriker suggests, with a pietistic affirmation of Christian orthodoxy, a neat turning of the other cheek.[40] The poem concludes, reduplicating its original dialectical dynamic in miniature, with a choice of similes, neither of which holds privileged status. The meaning of the sun, like the meaning of roosters before it, is neither naturally transparent nor necessarily, divinely transfigurable. It is determined by human speech: a speech ethically charged and laden with the moral possibility which comes from the conception of alternatives, but always enunciating itself within a material and ideological context which burdens, constrains, and shapes it.

If the dialectical tradition of "self-consuming artifacts" aims, as Fish puts it, to raise "the level of the mind . . . to the point where it becomes indistinguishable from the object of its search, and so disappears" (155); if its spiritual goal is a final "triumph over discursive language" (188) itself, then "Roosters," no matter how emphatically it summons that tradition, lies finally outside it. The end of "Roosters," with its accentuated argumentative simile, highlights the work of discursive language. Its meditative voice does not fade, gesture toward falling silent, in the last line; if anything, it calls renewed attention to its presence. Nothing triumphs over it, though it seems to triumph over nothing. The poem remains in Wallace Stevens's *"pays de la métaphore,"* which here is also, inescapably, the region of irony.[41]

It is also, we might say, the *pays* of New Criticism. A resistance to dialectical resolutions (whether materialist or metaphysical) is by no means Bishop's stance alone; neither is the affirmation of art or language, of the aesthetic medium itself, as the only possible means of synthesis. Rather, both constitute the founding aesthetic principles of a developing literary establishment in the forties.[42] For a full understanding of the context of "Roosters"' dialectical strategies we might also look, however, to the work of another already more maverick critic of the period, Kenneth Burke.

Burke's most explicit analyses of dialectics, his chapters on "Dialectic in General" in *A Grammar of Motives* and his "Four Master Tropes" appendix to that volume, came out in book form in 1945, a year before *North and South*, but four years after "Roosters" was first published. Although limited excerpts from *A Grammar* began appearing in journals as early as 1936, I make no claim that its terms shaped "Roosters" directly. It is likely that Bishop knew Burke's related model of phases in his *Permanence and Change* (1935), since Burke's connection with her mentor Moore was close. Or perhaps her sense of Burke's work came refracted through her reading of Moore's own, since, as Bonnie Costello has demonstrated, Moore's metaphors of combat and Burke's "Anatomy of Purpose" have much in common.[43] Burke probably knew Bishop's poems; but the biographical connections and chains of influence do not much matter. Bishop's "Roosters" and Burke's *Grammar*, read as intertexts, as works of a similar moment, have much to say for and to one another.

Several aspects of the *Grammar*'s forthright principles of dialectical process have implicit parallels in "Roosters" and help clarify the poem's strategies, particularly Burke's equation of dialectics and combat; his model of a secular, humane, anti-Hegelian dialectic which could work toward and exemplify "the purification of war"; and his stress on irony as dialectic's privileged but hard-won mode.[44] To some extent Burke's underlying belief, as Fredric Jameson describes it, "in the harmonizing claims of liberal democracy and in the capacity of the system to reform itself from within" seems "Roosters"' own as well.[45] But if Jameson is correct in his depiction of Burke's modes as "all categories of consciousness, open to the light of day in classical, well-nigh Aristotelian fashion," each "thus always serenely transparent to itself, in lucid blindness to the dark underside of language, to the ruses of history or of desire," then the end of "Roosters" dramatizes the poem's own difference from this kind of Burkean symbolic act.[46] For Bishop's sun — that old emblem of consciousness open to its own full illumination — is a restless "low light" which knows, and knows only, the underneath of things. It gilds the bottom of broccoli leaves, the underbelly of a swallow and the backsides of clouds, but rises no further. "Roosters" converts a classic sign of transcendence to an image of immanence: a sun which lights the nether parts of a world composed of opaque textures. Its low lights glance at dark undersides, hinting of ruses.

Language, history, desire. To these factors which impede and complicate figures of rational or spiritual transcendence at the end of "Roosters" we can add a fourth, the ruses of gender. The first half of "Roosters" has explored strutting roosters and exploited hens, and thus has made gender difference, no matter how submerged it seems in the poem's later turns, an unavoidable issue; Bishop's dialectic, unlike Burke's, is explicitly a dialectic of sex. It is also, by Burke's lights, a dialectic foreign to her sex. In a 1942 review of Moore's poems, Burke would note that Moore showed a "feminine preference" for "refuting by silence" rather than employing "the dialectician's morality of eristic."[47] It is, perhaps, not surprising that Bishop's own morality of eristic turns so squarely upon the questions of preferences feminine and masculine.

There is one moment in *Grammar of Motives* when Burke, objecting to idioms in which "the admonition against the threat of absolute warlike substance is replaced by the exhortation to the promise of an absolute peacelike substance," illustrates the problem with a chart. On the left side ranges a series of assertions, each beginning with the phrase "Men are essentially" and concluding with some accusatory and pessimistic term: Men are essentially fools, crooks, automata, fighters, or, the last line reads, "suit yourself." On the right side hangs the ineffectual assertion "But let's have peace" (333).

The two halves of "Roosters" might seem to replicate that unfortunate structure: "Men are essentially cruel, territorial, combative, cocks; still — think of Peter — let's have peace." But the radical ambiguity of the figures of roosters and sun in Bishop's poem subverts assumptions of essential or literal substance, melding a metaphor which implies that "Men are essentially fighters" in tight coincidence with one which implies "Men are estially forgiven and forgivers." A further complication arises along with Bishop's sun: who is included in the category "men," the invitation "let's"? "Men" for Burke means simply "human beings," and at the same time his chart illustrates the errors a male subject might fall into when

he examines himself. But "men" in "Roosters" means in the beginning, une-
quivocally, "male," though it slides in the poem's second part toward some-
thing universal; a potential gender gap is opened between the object under
scrutiny and the subject who surveys. What if the chart reads "Men are
essentially roosters, but let's us hens have peace"? If the question of sexual
difference is raised, does anything change?

What do women say next, after saying "men are essentially"? And what
do women say then about ourselves? "Roosters" offers, I would argue, a
sexual dialectics still useful for feminists thinking about these questions.
The poem enacts not the "familiar withdrawal" Ostriker finds but a pro-
vocative advance. "Roosters" begins by representing militarism as a quality
embedded in the very essence of maleness. The feminist anger which in-
forms such a conception is valuable, for it forces attention to the problem
of men's sanctioned violence and men's legitimated dominance "in the
home" and to the connections between that violence and dominance and
the larger war culture.[48] But such an approach can also be "demoralizing
and even paralyzing," as the military sociologist Cynthia Enloe warns,
"for it implies that only transformation so basic as to alter the very char-
acter of men as men can effectively curtail the military invasion of ordin-
ary women's lives."[49] Enloe goes on to propose an alternative feminist pro-
ject, one less concerned with discovering the origin and more concerned
with elucidating repeated patterns of warmaking. "What are the *processes*
that reproduce the kind of social relations that enhance militarism," she
asks, and do they "never falter"? To focus on process, Enloe argues, is to
put "*power* back into the picture," since such an emphasis assumes that
"there were and still are *choices*."[50]

The concluding line of "Roosters," replicating the dialectic which through-
out the poem directs attention to how things repeat and how they may
be altered, focuses finally, intently, on the *process* of meaning, the process
of poetic figuration itself. "Faithful as enemy, or friend": the indetermi-
nacy here stems from an uncertainty about the givens (has the sun acted
as an enemy or not?), but it also emerges as a staging of potential ethical
and imaginative options (will I, or will you, objectify the sun as enemy
or not?). The selection of trope becomes, then, a metaphor for all par-
ticipation in the social order and all making of social change. There were
and still are choices: the last words of the poem depend upon and insist
upon this presumption.

What is enacted here is, in part, an ethics of relation to others. The en-
tities outside the self in "Roosters" (the cocks, the sun) retain a strangeness
and complexity which cannot wholly be subdued and contained by any
of the varying figurative uses of them; the poem thus offers an alternative

to the aggressively objectifying, rigid symbolic structures of the roosters who, in the first part of the poem, mark up the world with pins as if it were all their map. "Each one an active / displacement of perspective," the speaker describes those imperious mapmakers, disapprovingly; but who displaces perspective more actively, or more positively, than this woman's voice itself?[51]

Such a positive account of "Roosters'" conclusion must, however, be qualified, and a feminist model less sanguine than Enloe's about the powers of thought and intention may be seen equally to apply. The poem's final similes lie as much in the region of ruse as in the region of choice. And the dark undersides of language, the ruses of history and desire, which show up faintly but distinctly here must finally be referred back to the speaker herself, not to any Other.[52] Except, perhaps, the one "other" whose particularly oblique, almost entirely buried presence further displaces the perspectives of this war poem: the speaker's lover.

At a few key points, as I have already suggested, "Roosters" recalls an aubade. "We hear the first crow": at least two people are present at this dawn, presumably in the same room and the same bed.[53] The story of the alba, the scene of lovers waking — particularly if we read it, knowing what little we now know of Bishop's life, as potentially a lesbian alba — might provide a redemptive counterplot, an antipatriarchal alternative, to the war poem (not least because it unsettles both the absolute rooster-hen sexual dualism of the barnyard and the henless rooster culture of the Vatican).[54]

This is, though, an anxious alba. Compared to one of its obvious precursors, Donne's "The Sunne Rising," it seems doubly decentered and jarred: first by forces of exclusion (the relationship is barely voiced here, unlike the cock-and-hen pairing gleefully self-proclaimed by Donne's lover), but second, by some motivating disconcertion of its own. "What right have you," the roosters are upbraided, "to . . . / wake us here where are / *unwanted love*, conceit and war?" (emphasis mine). Later, lines like "how could the night have come to grief," or the last tercet's fear of an enemy yet to be revealed and a crucifixion only now about to begin, suggest as well some kind of private pain which underlies and coincides with the more traditionally "political" topics of the poem.[55]

In "Roosters," a poem which has by and large presented itself in resolutely public mode (invoking the grand discourses of metaphysics, gospel, *Guernica*, war narrative, theories of history), the latent private strain serves several purposes. Drawing the Peter/crucifixion analogy *inward* — into the bedroom, that sphere of the private, the domestic, the feminine, the sexual, the dream — it implicates the woman speaker in psychic structures of conflict, violence, and betrayal formerly reserved for specifically

male or vaguely generalized others. Burke could read this as the culmina-
tion of a mature dialectic, which should demonstrate, he wrote, "true irony,
humble irony, based upon a sense of fundamental kinship with the enemy,
as one . . . is not merely outside him as an observer but contains him
within" (514). (Moore, we have seen, strives for such an irony.) But the
true and humble ironies of this early war poem by Elizabeth Bishop do not
produce the ideal, unconflicted, "dazzling, watery dialectic" beyond all
dualisms which Bishop imaged in her very late "Santarem." Disavow your
difference from your enemy, "Roosters" seems to say, and discover, like
Peter, how treacherous and unreliable all your disavowals are; find kin-
ship with your enemy, and in the process feel all your own recalcitrant
unkindness. We might say, invoking Kristeva, that "Roosters" finally mutes
and muddles the drama of "'fight to the death' between rival groups and
thus between the sexes . . . not in the name of some reconciliation—
feminism has at least the merit of showing what is irreducible and even
deadly in the social contract—but in order to show that the struggle, the
implacable difference, the violence be conceived in the very place where
it operates with the maximum intransigence, in personal and sexual iden-
tity itself. . . ."[56]

Compared to the later poems by, say, Plath or Sharon Olds exploring
what Kristeva calls "the potentialities of *victim/executioner* which char-
acterize each identity, each subject, each sex" (52), "Roosters'" links of
conflicts, public and private, seem oblique and cautious.[57] Compared,
however, to those strategic, noble, inward wars which Moore and Stevens
urged poets in the forties to wage, Bishop's skirmishes which never end
seem bold in their uncontrollable violence, and in the unchecked eros of
that violence. (By "Stevens" I mean the Stevens of overtly war-related
statement, not the Stevens of lyric, whose boldness matches and counters
Bishop's own.) If "Roosters" offers an example of dialectics-well-done, it
also hints more radically and scandalously at a crisis which disables dialec-
tics itself.[58]

That founding model of Western dialectic, the *Phaedrus*, as Stanley
Fish has argued, implicitly equates "the dialectician and the good lover,
on the one hand, and the rhetorician-writer and the bad lover on the
other" (17). "Roosters" demonstrates the good dialectic; but it does so in
the voice of one who may in fact be a bad lover. Even if not, she lives,
at any rate, in the region of the badly loved, where rhetoric keeps insinuat-
ing itself. (Think of how easily the tone of the line "How could the night
have come to grief?" slides from meditation to melodrama.) Dialectics,
with its processes and intent choices, may salvage this scene. "Roosters"
implies so, but it gestures also in its buried aubade toward an irrationality

which the self's mediating arguments can neither confront nor evade, and toward differences that are not dialectical.[59]

These conflicts are not only part of the poem's themes or content. "Roosters"' scheme itself, its formal ordering, figures in them (and figures them *in*).[60] Bishop teasingly apologized to Moore for the poem's relentlessly patterned triplet stanzas, calling them "a bad case of threes"; she also, as I have noted, defended them as part of the poem's necessary "violence of tone," a violence she linked to the "essential baseness of militarism." There is a model for these "violent" tercets, one Bishop certainly knew, but it is not a war poem. Richard Crashaw's love poem "Wishes. To his (supposed) ₊Mistresse" uses the same unusual stanzaic pattern—one line with two stresses, one with three and one with four—to imagine and to specify the ideal object of desire.[61]

Crashaw's "not impossible shee" has a "face thats best / By its owne beauty drest, / And can alone commend [var. "command"] the rest."[62] A "Divine / *Idea*," she takes on a bodily "shrine / Of Chrystall flesh, through which to shine" (195). Repeatedly compared to the sun, she promises "Days, that need borrow, / No part of their good Morrow, / From a fore spent night of sorrow" (197). Bishop's roosters have "chests / in green-gold medals dressed, / planned to command and terrorize the rest." They occupy an opaque world in which enlightenment may not occur. In that world nights seem to "come to grief."

Charles Sanders reads these links as ironic reversals, in which Crashaw's perfect supposed mistress contrasts with the "here-and-now master," the "all too 'possible he'": "'Roosters,' ostensibly about world war, locates the war . . . in the psychological relations (among many others) between the sexes" (56–57). Heather Weidemann suggests that Bishop invokes Crashaw's idealizing blazon in order to expose and disavow it as another form of masculine territoriality and conquest, a rhetorical violence.[63] These are both illuminating readings; they open up still another possibility. It is plausible that the echoes of "Wishes" in "Roosters" are not critical but themselves wishful; that in addition to indicting heterosexual relations they encode lesbian desire, loss, and betrayal; that there is a "(not?) impossible she" both longed and mourned for in Bishop's poem; and that the stanzaic reference and verbal allusions to Crashaw work to signal her existence. Either way, the formal allusion to Crashaw's own bad case of threes suggests that the violences of tone which are necessary here are due not only to the "essential baseness of militarism" but also to the inessential slidings of desire. Not only but also: it is not that "Roosters" is ostensibly a war poem but actually a love poem; it is that the two here are impossible to tell apart.

Jane Cooper has said of her own late forties "war poems from a woman's point of view" that the war, she now recognizes, had begun to function for her as "a mask, something to write *through* in order to express a desolation more personal."[64] (Bishop was, perhaps, a closer, wiser precursor for Cooper than Cooper could have recognized at the moment of John Berryman's harassments.)[65] "Roosters" works here within a distinct tradition of women's lyrics which use war as metaphor for conflicts in the home or bedroom or psyche (looking backward to Dickinson, forward to Cooper and Plath); but here, as elsewhere in that tradition, the war is also more than metaphor, not only mask.[66] There is no difference between war and not-war, public and private, for metaphor to fuse into identity. The war inheres; there is no writing through it.

III

Wars are everywhere in *North and South*. Tracking them, we could turn to the "nature poems"—"Florida," "Little Exercise," "The Fish"—for their landscapes, creatures, and crises marked by natural aggressions and subsiding into natural reconciliations. Or we could look to the dreamy Paris-related poems in which violence surfaces where the civil meets the surreal. "Sleeping Standing Up," for instance, explores, in a wittily literalized figure, the state of those for whom war feels an oblique place (the speaker includes herself among the group). "War," we might claim—it is a common claim in the twentieth-century United States, perhaps especially for women—seems mystified, opaque, and far away in others' hands; but in dreams, the poem implies, our bluff gets called and our own bents revealed as the most violent of inclinations:

> As we lie down to sleep the world turns half away
>   through ninety dark degrees;
>   the bureau lies on the wall
> and thoughts that were recumbent in the day
>   rise as the others fall,
>   stand up and make a forest of thick-set trees.
>
> The armored cars of dreams, contrived to let us do
>   so many a dangerous thing,
>   are chugging at its edge
> all camouflaged . . .
>
>   (*CP*, 30)

All this ugly military apparatus of the dream is mobilized ridiculously, futilely, to search for crumbs or pebbles like those scattered by Hansel and Gretel after they are forced out of their childhood home in the fairy tale ("sometimes we went too fast," the speaker reports, "and ground them underneath. How stupidly we steered"). The poem does to family romance what "Roosters" does to aubade, tying war to personal trauma and, in this case, to the most primal and interior of damages in early childhood. (These lines are the closest we come in *North and South* to an autobiographical register of Bishop's own losses of both her parents – her father to death, her mother to madness – before the age of five. But orphanhood here, too, is an oblique place. And the poem on the whole refuses sentiment; the self is a dense tank, dangerous or ludicrous, working both for and against any bereft missing children out there in the dream's erected forest.)[67]

The poems in *North and South* which seem to me, however, to be most interestingly related to "Roosters"' project are neither the exterior landscapes nor the interior dreamscapes but two lyrics which spotlight the operations of poetic language. "Spotlight" here is meant to invoke the theater; both "Wading at Wellfleet" and "Casabianca" are openly *stagy* and rhetorical, poems treading the boards. Both are also poems on the open sea. They are part of a series of lyrics in the volume in which two images of the ocean alternate. One kind of sea is pliant or recessive and one is stiff as a platform, "hard as diamonds." One gives naturally; the other threatens theatrically, "less subtile, as when driftwood pieces make up a proscenium to set off the dazzling white of seafoam."

Those last words are the artist Joseph Cornell's, in a 1948 exhibition statement on the references to water in his shadow boxes.[68] Bishop paid her respects to Cornell – in characteristically oblique fashion – through her late translation of Octavio Paz's tribute to the artist.[69] These early poems make no direct allusions to Cornell's work and in no way seem occasioned or overtly prompted by it. All the same, their peculiar forms of linguistic shadowboxing are suggestively Cornell-like. Just as Cornell's boxes assemble and disarrange Victorian bibelots and ephemera, placing them into austerely formalized structures which turn them somehow into surreal riddles, so the stagy, watery set pieces "Wading in Wellfleet" and "Casabianca" repeat and mysteriously disperse bits of verbal cliché.

"Casabianca"'s allusion is obvious; its title duplicates that of Mrs. Hemans's famous clunker "The boy stood on the burning deck" (still memorized, so I'm told, in certain obscure schoolrooms). Willard Spiegelman has hinted that "Wading" contains a "whispered reminder" of Byron's "The Destruction of Semnacherib."[70] I would argue that the reference is more than glancing, and that in fact "Wading at Wellfleet" and "Casabianca" are companion pieces of sorts, each designed to do odd things with a bit of nineteenth-century poesy.

The two poems Bishop takes as pre-texts here have several things in common. Each is the kind of poem one might be made to recite in the kind of school where fishing-town children learn (as Bishop did in Nova Scotia) to write on slates. They stand for long traditions of old-fashioned inculcation, for force-fed rhetoric, and, of course, for sheer *corn*. Importantly, both "Destruction of Semnacherib" (allegorically) and Hemans's "Casabianca" (topically) have served as declamations on the Napoleonic wars.[71] Reworking them, Bishop's poems thus comment not only on the language of war but, in exaggerated fashion, on poetry's promotional and disciplinary functions in modern Western war systems.

In "Wading at Wellfleet" the sea as proscenium relaxes into water more in-giving; in "Casabianca" the loss of the platform means not wading but drowning. "Wading" averts war, finally; "Casabianca" reveals violence as inadvertent. "Wading," by its close, diminishes aggression and terror; "Casabianca" rapidly accentuates it. These distinctions are partly impelled by gender, in ways connected to the workings of "Roosters." "Wading at Wellfleet" reforms one tradition of masculine action and desire epitomized by Lord Byron's poem. "Casabianca" exposes through Mrs. Hemans an equally but differently pernicious feminine line of action and desire. The poems of the Lord and the Mrs. represent two separate but dependent martial languages and stances, conventionally gendered, which Bishop's poems in turn refract and in some antididactic manner correct.

"Wading at Wellfleet" revolves around an analogy (between water and weapons, or more generally between elemental and cultural strife) which by its close the poem undoes; in the end it is figural revolving itself which is negated. The poem begins with an account of an ancient, victorious Assyrian chariot which had wheel blades designed to cut warriors' heels and pull them under. The chariot is then compared to the glinting Wellfleet sea in the early morning, which rolls even more ominously, with a metallic sheen, toward the shins of the water. "The war rests wholly with the waves," the final stanza starts; "they try revolving, but the wheels / give way; they will not bear the weight." The sea which originally bore the weight of heroic trope now admits the presence of a simple, "actual" wading figure, and in the process becomes once again only water. Here where there turn out to be no Achilles's heels, epic tradition is casually annulled, and that cancellation constitutes the poem's action.

"Wading"'s Byronic pre-text has enacted a similar movement, but for different ends. Byron's Assyrian Semnacherib, in keeping with his story in the biblical books of Kings and Isaiah, comes down with infamous flourish "like the wolf on the fold," onto the cities of Judah with his cohorts: "And the sheen of their spears was like stars on the sea, / When the blue wave rolls nightly on deep Galilee."[72] It is the poem's pleasure and duty to demolish this initial warrior/sea analogy. In the morning, after their silent conquest by the Angel of Death, the Assyrian forces lie dead in the literal surf, their might "unsmote by the sword" but "melted like snow in the glance of the Lord." Here we can trace the structure which Bishop's "Wading" mimics but diverts; for Byron and for the Bible, false might "gave way" long before Wellfleet, but it did so through the force of God which the light of day revealed. At Wellfleet, the morning sun creates rather than dispels the sensation of threat, and a human heel, not God's hand, parts the waters to chasten and lighten heroic simile.

Bishop's thematic revisions of Byron are matched by even more playful rhythmic hints of "Destruction of Semnacherib." If the stanzas of Bishop's poem are stretched out two at a time into single long sentences paired as couplets, as their matching end-rhymes tease us to do, they turn singsong in a manner somewhat reminiscent of Byron's verse's awful gallop. In their form on the page, however, their varied tetrameter and enjambment deflect the rousing oratory of schoolroom verse.[73]

But "Wading at Wellfleet" does more than undo the hackneyed; a more moving example of vehicle and tenor is also disassembled. Byron is not the only precursor lurking at Wellfleet. In fact, Bishop's poem's only direct quotation is from "Affliction IV" by George Herbert: "This morning's glitterings reveal / the sea is 'all a case of knives.'" In Herbert's text, it is "my thoughts" which are "all a case of knives, / Wounding my heart / With scatter'd smart."[74] "Affliction IV" interiorizes the conflict which "Destruction at Semnacherib" historicizes; it also places both writer and reader on the battle's other side. Voice in Byron's poem allies itself smugly, even sadistically, with God. Herbert's speaker is in a position far less secure; the poem begins with voice begging, "Broken in pieces all asunder, / Lord, hunt me not," and describes a tortured, violent world in which the very "elements are let loose to fight, / and while I live, trie out their right." Herbert's "I" pleads finally with God to "dissolve the knot" of inherent strife, "As the sunne scatters by his light / All the rebellions of the night."

In Bishop's poem the psychological structures of Herbert's are brought forward, I would argue, remedially; they check and reform Byron's pseudo-epic (here again, as in "Roosters," masculine tradition is not monolithic). "Affliction" acts as a reminder of conflicts and threatening forces less easily eradicable than enemy "Assyrians," because internal. Its image of the self asunder, as much at odds with peace as inclined toward it, emends the glib "Destruction of Semnacherib." But "Wading"'s glittering morning proves Herbert's model no less false than Byron's, since in Wellfleet's glare, as in the daybreak in "Roosters," the sun unknots and scatters nothing.

("Seeing the light," in fact, is associated in Bishop's poem only with the appearance of aggression.) Byron's "Destruction" and Herbert's "Affliction" are alike in one key respect: both demand and depend upon an overriding authority, appeal to the virile might of God. "Wading" accomplishes its unknotting without reference to any Lord, martial or otherwise, and with only the most minimal and ironic of conquests—a foot's harmless pressure on the medium that surrounds it.

In "Wading at Wellfleet," what breaks down heroic simile and narrative is just that, the breakdown of simile and narrative. Here, as in "Roosters," what makes war and what routs it, what distinguishes the glaring scene from the serenely luminous one, is human language, human image-making, only. The war rests wholly, we might say, with the words. It "rests" there in the two senses which form the hub of the poem's wit: is contingent upon, and ceases.[75]

"Wading at Wellfleet" mocks and deconstructs a fantasy of dominance. "Casabianca" less happily exposes the reverse desire, submission. Lord Byron's despotic scenario—we might say it represents one bad line of masculine martial tradition—is dispelled with ease on the shores of Wellfleet; but Mrs. Hemans's tactics, which represent in turn the worst bequests of nineteenth-century "female poetry," persist exaggerated at the structural core of Bishop's "Casabianca."[76] Here, as in "Roosters," the epic realm of public male heroics is more easily reformed than the lyric regions of private female eros. "Wading'"s strategy is revision by dissolution; "Casabianca'"s, confrontation by accentuation. From its first word, the joke title "Casabianca" which parrots its predecessor compulsively and histrionically, Bishop's revision of Hemans enters an unresolvable fray of figuration.[77] I quote it here in full:

> Love's the boy stood on the burning deck
> trying to recite "The boy stood on
> the burning deck." Love's the son
>   stood stammering elocution
>   while the poor ship in flames went down.
>
> Love's the obstinate boy, the ship,
> even the swimming sailors, who
> would like a schoolroom platform, too,
>   or an excuse to stay
>   on deck. And love's the burning boy.
>   (CP, 5)

The poem commences with the most artless and standard of poetic formulations: "Love is . . . " As it rapidly disturbs the order of simple metaphor with its odd confusions of tense and syntax, the opening line most resembles Emily Dickinson's disorientations of definition;[78] it also constitutes, already, a wry critique of the maternal pre-text which it gamely quotes. Cora Kaplan has suggested that in martial scenes like that of "Casabianca" Felicia Hemans unconsciously invested the personal "emotions of loss and feelings of betrayal" which feminine propriety prevented her from otherwise expressing.[79] Mrs. Hemans's poems might function, then, as worst cases of the very technique which *North and South* itself seeks to exploit; they might be said to exemplify the ultimate ersatz use of war as metaphor. Bishop's "Casabianca," as if to expose these vicarious operations, begins by deliberately flaunting them, definitively linking private loss and masochism to martial myth. The blatant, offhand copula— "Love *is* the boy stood"—enacts metaphor's baldest connection; the effect, though, is mystifying rather than clarifying.

Let us put aside for a moment questions referring the definition of love to the content of Hemans's poem; Bishop's riddles entice us to reread "Casabianca," but they also deter us. Love is, the poem first announces, rhetorical, and nothing more. Bad rhetoric comprises love; here there will be no reassuring dialectic such as that which Wellfleet offered.[80] The rhetoric is, worse yet, self-reflexive ("the boy stood on the burning deck / trying to recite 'The boy stood on'"); worse still, coerced through the most humiliating and banal forms of tutelage ("stood" in the sense of "made to stand," rather than in the active past tense); worst of all, incapable—it cannot even work by rote. Love combines stolid obedience to the rules with aphasia, and its only situation is disaster.

For readers who cannot recite "Casabianca" on cue, a quick summary is in order here. Hemans's poem concerns a boy who, during the Napoleonic wars, goes loyally down with the ship along with his French Captain father. "Casabianca" is the name of the dead father (or the senseless father, since Hemans takes great pains to emphasize the unconsciousness which prevents him from giving his son permission not to commit suicide). The boy, through several verses, shouts things like "Speak, Father! If I may yet be gone!" and "My Father! must I stay?" Finally the ship blows up, with the "gallant child" still on deck, and then, gruesomely, aberrantly, comes the question and answer which clinch this howler:

> The boy!—oh! where was he?
> Ask of the winds that far around
> With fragments strew'd the sea!—

> With mast and helm, and pennon fair,
> That well had bore their part—
> But the noblest thing which perish'd there
> Was that young faithful heart![81]

Semnacherib the Assyrian got into military trouble because he thought he was in charge. This boy gets into trouble because he thinks somebody else is. Hemans's plot suggests a further "translation" of Bishop's epigram. If love "is" "Casabianca," then love, that ill-fated disciplining of eros, emerges out of loyalty to law which is inapplicable or dead; unconsciousness makes the martial law of patriarchy untenable, but unconsciousness *of* unconsciousness prevents its revocation. Put simply: Love is being violently abandoned, yet still refusing to abandon.[82]

The violence of abandonment intensifies as Bishop's poem widens from ironic replication of Hemans's final terms (in which the ship and "obstinate boy" are one) to a broader scene at once more literal and more fantastic. Realistic "swimming sailors" mark the edge of the platform where declamation stops and real drowning starts. (This poem was first published in 1936; in 1945, when it came out in book form, those sailors may well have recalled for readers actual sea battles.) But the sailors' envy of the boy orator, as if they swam around the schoolroom, forces the poem more toward the surreal than the real.

"And love's the burning boy." This final plain sentence enacts not so much rhetoric's collapse as its epitome. On the one hand, it seems to establish for the first time a literal body, a sheer register of pain and feverish desire, beyond rhetoric's convolutions. On the other hand the burning boy—who else is he but Cupid imploded?—exemplifies for the first time the power of poetry and of love's traditional figurations. Who else is he? Christ, perhaps, the sacred "burning Babe" of Robert Southwell's poem who proves "Love is the fire."[83] But he is also Hemans's profane boy—a figure in Bishop's hands at once exposed as horrific and rendered fiercely ironic, embodying in his burning both the death of bad rhetoric and its obscene apotheosis.

There is a moment in Bishop's later, great poem "At the Fishhouses" when the speaker, placed at the sea's edge, describes a seal as "like me a believer in total immersion." The clichéd phrase "total immersion"—a Baptist practice, a pedagogical method (for learning language, among other things), and of course a physical state—might be said to be the central *matrix* of "At the Fishhouses" in Riffaterre's sense of that word: "The poem results from the transformation of the *matrix*, a minimal and literal sentence, into a longer, complex, and non-literal periphrasis."[84] Across the range of Bishop's career, "total immersion" works as a kind of matrix of matrixes: the sign of what is literal, minimal, essential, of the origin and the solution (identified, too, in "At the Fishhouses," with that other *matrix* the mother). Around it complex, leisurely periphrasis sometimes develops.[85]

Is there a politics of gender and war in the matrix of "total immersion"? Consider Klaus Theweleit's visionary invocation of Elaine Morgan's *The Descent of Woman* in the midst of his provocative analysis of male fascists' dread of flux and flow. Summoning Morgan's controversial thesis that human evolution went through an aqueous stage which was led by the female of the species, Theweleit continues with an imaginative description of the human return to land:

Here the hunter enters and temporarily dominates the scene, bringing with him male bonding and warfare (which she [Morgan] agrees with Lionel Tiger, is a function of male bonding). Her book ends with the words: "All we need to do is hold out loving arms to him and say "Come on in. The water's lovely." She doesn't mean that women should once again be confined to their sexual functions; instead, she is voicing a desire for a life lived under the sign of a female pleasure principle that will hold out *water* against male aggression.[86]

At moments, Bishop's poems voice the sign of a water principle—a "come on in"—which may be read as political, or which may be politicized. Listening recently as Carol Cohn described a man in the American intellectual defense establishment who spoke of the vulnerability of peninsulas dangling unprotected from large land masses, I thought of the peninsulas in the first poem of *North and South*, "The Map," which "take the water between thumb and finger / like women feeling for the smoothness of yard-goods," unthreatening and unthreatened.[87]

But Bishop finds herself—this is crucial—as much invited (or not invited) as unthreatened inviter; in her poems the female self stands on the water's edge more often than not, unembraced. "Casabianca"'s *matrix* is, after all, the cliché of cliché itself, the cliché of the bad foremother who is addicted to victimization, who vicariously identifies with the suffering of (male) others, who in her own way glorifies war, and whose water is not lovely. This poem's tight knot of "non-literal periphrasis" will not unwind. "Wading at Wellfleet" comes closer; wading is, after all, partial immersion. But in *North and South*, that book of poems at war, what we get, as in so much of Bishop's work, are figures not immersed in "dazzling, watery" synthesis but perilously hovering in opposition, as in the image of the poet's task in an essay Bishop published in 1934: "I have heard that dropping shells from an airplane onto a speeding battleship below, in an uncertain sea, demands the most perfect and delicate sense of timing imaginable."[88] This passage well anticipates *North and South*'s dialectical maneuvers in the fields of gender, war, and language: those perfectly delicate, uncertain, violent poems, each as indirect as the angle of a targeted missile.

9

Myrrh to Myrrh

H.D., War, and Biblical Narrative

> Describing circle after circle
> a wheeling vulture scans a field
> lying desolate. In her hovel
> a mother's wailing to her child:
> "Come, take my breast, boy, feed on this,
> grow, know your place, shoulder the cross."
>
> Centuries pass, villages flame,
> are stunned by war and civil war.
> My country, you are still the same,
> tragic, as beautiful as before.
> How long must the mother wail?
> How long must the vulture wheel?
>
> Alexander Blok, "The Vulture," 1916[1]

> . . . but you repeat your foolish circling—again, again,
> again;
>
> again, the steel sharpened on the stone;
> again, the pyramid of skulls
>
> . . . .
>
> Yet resurrection is a sense of direction,
> resurrection is a bee-line,
>
> straight to the horde and plunder,
> the treasure, the store-room,
>
> the honeycomb;
> resurrection is remuneration,
>
> food, shelter, fragrance
> of myrrh and balm.
>
> H.D., "The Flowering of the Rod," 1944[2]

> Like Kaspar she brought myrrh to myrrh.
>
> Norman Holmes Pearson on H.D.[3]

242

I

In 1950, in Switzerland, H.D. sent out an unusual kind of Christmas card: a war poem. The poetic greeting, a privately printed slim volume titled *What Do I Love?*, conveyed several messages. Although H.D. was American by birth, she had stayed in London throughout the Second World War years. "The background to this war," Stephen Spender had written in 1943, "corresponding to the Western Front in the last war, is the bombed city."[4] *What Do I Love?*, written during the war, reminded its British readers of what they and the poet with them had endured, exploring what it meant to live in one of those bombed cities.

Marshaling the classic forms and phrases of dominant wartime British rhetoric, the first poem of *What Do I Love?*, "May 1943," contrasts the struggles of H.D.'s chosen compatriates with the sheltered ignorance of Americans. It develops a revisionary eulogy for a female hero (a young woman killed in the line of duty during an air raid), and in general it valorizes a specifically civilian war heroism.[5] Though not a single one of the many wartime anthologies of war poetry circulated in London included an example of H.D.'s work, *What Do I Love?* asserts her place as a war poet.[6] During the war years she had signally, as Robert Duncan puts it, "moved as a poet to the battlefront."[7]

At the same time, this 1950 missive settled a more anxious, and anxiously gendered, score. Surely it suggested to her friends that she had recovered from the serious, war-related breakdown which had brought her in 1946 to Switzerland's Kusnacht Klinic. But it also implied a stubborn refusal to relinquish the "dangerous symptom" associated with that collapse, and an insistence on redefining that symptom as valid inspiration.[8]

During the Second World War H.D. had begun an increasingly troubled relationship with the famous Air Chief Marshal Lord Dowding, architect of the Battle of Britain, whose name, Churchill said, would "ever be linked with" the "splendid event" of that battle, and who, after his son died in combat, had become heavily involved in spiritualist efforts to contact dead R.A.F. pilots through mediums. When H.D. told Dowding she was receiving messages of her own from dead pilots which seemed to link her own name to the splendid event, visitations in which she said the spirits warned of the dangers of the atomic age, Dowding's rejection of her claims as "frivolous," "uninspiring," and of a "lower order" than his own psychic dealings precipitated the breakdown which sent her to Kusnacht. "Dowding's brush-off," Rachel Blau DuPlessis comments dryly, "was a revelation that conventional sexual politics operate even in the spiritual realm, which H.D. had thought was exempt."[9]

The second poem in *What Do I Love?*, "R.A.F.," records an episode resistant to that revelation. It describes a series of mystical encounters with a dead pilot and represents them as undeniable signs of authentic divination. Still, not surprisingly, symptoms of gendered stress pervade this middle poem, as if its voice, marked as feminine and civilian, could barely counter, or legitimate itself near, either the power of the male familiar or the power of the disapproving male Commander — as if, despite the hardship and the bombing H.D. had passed through, and no matter how finely tuned her spiritual insight, hers would always be only a voice on the sidelines.

But *What Do I Love?*, by its close, stages a resolution of all the conflicts of the war and all the conflicts of the war poem, including gender anxieties, and it does so in the classic manner of the Christmas card — through a manger scene. The final poem of the three in the volume, "Christmas 1944," explores bombed London to consider what can be salvaged from its ruins, what loved objects it is most important to save. It concludes with a verbal offering of these objects of desire to an infant Christ. "Christmas 1944" seems to have been written coterminously, in December of 1944, with the third part of *Trilogy*, "The Flowering of the Rod"; if this dating is correct, then both texts were written in a burst of intense creativity leading up to Christmas of that year.[10] Sending out her "Christmas 1944" in 1950, H.D. heralded a mode and body of epiphanic writing which she had salvaged from the wreckage of her second war and could now offer as a gift; she marked the anniversary not only of the birth of Christ but also of the culmination of her *Trilogy*.

With surprising frequency in H.D.'s cluster of work of the Second World War period, plots of war give way disconcertingly or are transformed openly to scenarios which have something to do with Christmas. It happens, obviously, when *What Do I Love*, which starts out as an elegy for war dead, ends as "Christmas 1944." It happens, memorably, in the roman à clef H.D. began in 1939 concerning the traumatic events of her experience of the First World War, *Bid Me To Live*, which opens as a war novel and shifts genre midstream, ending in yet another complex, laden nativity scene. In *The Gift*, H.D.'s autobiography written from 1941 to 1943 from a London under attack, figures of bombing and Christmas interweave in a tense logic of dream association. The most striking example occurs, of course, in "Flowering of the Rod," which moves *Trilogy* conclusively away from its map of the bombed city into a disruptive and disrupted New Testament narrative. Though that plot refers insistently to other inseparably related biblical passages, particularly crucifixion and Revelation, it also has something to do with the Christmas story — something of association, something of transformation.[11]

"War" and "Christmas" may seem at first glance an improbable pairing, and at second glance a banal one. The combination is commonplace in the war narratives of Anglo-American popular cultures, even obsessive in Second World War London. It could be put to bitterly ironic use, or (more often) function plaintively and reassuringly in a city under severe threat. It could take wistful and/or patriotic form: "the conservative hegemony of Christmas as a unified emblem of national nostalgia," as Cora Kaplan has sharply described this latter mode, " . . . the wooden nativities, those familial idols."[12]

H.D.'s negotiations with nativities and idols in the context of the war were in general neither escapist nor politically naive.[13] Like the Christmas celebrations she recalled from her Moravian childhood, her biblical plotting sought, in her words, "a ferocity not to be imagined."[14] She tapped the Christmas narrative, like many of her Christian contemporaries, for its powerful, sanctioned lode of antimilitarist sentiment. But she also used Christmas, like some of her contemporaries, in an attempt to explore and dislodge the limiting structures of traditional forms of Anglo-American antimilitarism. These included the potential "conservative hegemony" of Christianity itself. In a war against Nazism, in the context of the Holocaust, the risk of anti-Semitism in any turn to the New Testament, however well meant, was great; H.D. struggled, too, to free other non–Judeo-Christian belief systems from Christmas's overriding dominion. In addition, *Trilogy*'s Christmas tale — especially its exploration of that gift of the magi, myrrh — exposes and counteracts the "conservative hegemony" of the familial and erotic arrangements of sexual difference encoded in canonical renditions of the story.

I hope to demonstrate the power of *Trilogy*'s engagement with its New Testament master plots not by trying to extricate it from but by deliberately reembedding it within the mass of cultural artifacts in wartime London, and specifically the war poems, which deployed Christmas and other biblical narratives. "The Flowering of the Rod" has been well illuminated by critics examining it in a variety of contexts crucial for an understanding of the poem, especially in its connections to psychoanalytic theory, modernism, occult lore, and generalized conceptions of "women's" or "feminine" writing.[15] But this "tale of a jar or jars" needs to be read, as well, in relation to one of its most narrow and historically specific "horizons,"[16] as a "war poem" talking with and back to other forties war poems and other forms of war rhetoric and representation. It bears distinct and as yet unacknowledged resemblance, for instance, to the poetic work of other women publishing in London in the war years such as Anne Ridler and Kathleen Raine. And it is part of larger conflicts over the rights to and significance of biblical narrative, conflicts which exerted stress upon and shaped Anglo-American war poetry throughout this century, from Owen's crucified soldiers to the uses of biblical figures in the work of H.D.'s fellow modernists Eliot and Lawrence (and in poems we have already seen by Jarrell, by Bishop, by H.D.'s friend and contemporary Marianne Moore).

Trilogy's version of Christmas legend takes part in a complex and broad intertextual conversation which I will be tracing in some detail here. For a start, I would argue that the poem cannot be entirely extricated from, and may be fairly read within, the immediate context of the booming production of Christmas mythologies in the British war culture of the early forties. "This year England celebrates Christmas underground. The stable in Bethlehem was a shelter too," the voice-over of one 1941 Ministry of Information Blitz newsreel proclaims.[17] In the following lines on the aftermath of bombing from H.D.'s "Christmas 1944," we can read an obvious relation to this kind of popular wartime rhetoric of national Christianity: "we think and feel and speak / like children lost, / for one Child too, was cast / at Christmas, from a house . . . " (CP, 504). These proliferating Christmases, as I said earlier, often took solacing or exhortatory forms. Like the lines above, they imaged shelter warding off danger, or an innocence deprived of cover but only seemingly unguarded. Or they celebrated hardship redeemed, as in a 1943 propaganda film: "We won't be cooking a turkey this year, but we will be cooking Hitler's goose." Trilogy's much more subtle Christmas scene of comfort and of closure performs some rhetorical functions not entirely unlike these reassurances.

But "Christmas Under Fire," as another newsreel put it, could only at best be "a Christmas of contrasts — holly and barbed wire, guns and tinsel," and those contrasts could as easily provoke grief and horror as offer hope, especially for those whose families, friends, and lovers were taken away by the war. Even Christmas, that celebration of "peace on earth, goodwill to men," might be inseparable from or even an incentive to the war effort, a fact accepted with more than stalwart resignation in this notice from an English wartime women's magazine: "Did You Realize that eight old Christmas Cards will provide our Commandos with a demolition carton to contain 1 1/4 lb of TNT?"[18] Even Christmas might be inseparable from violence itself, a fact inscribed more cynically, if graphically, in the popular use by Londoners of the adjective "Christmas" or the coined verb "Christmassing" for the incandescent visual effects of bomb attacks. (Or inscribed today, for that matter, in the Department of Defense's coded references to nuclear weapons as "Christmas trees.")[19] In 1933, walking to an appointment with Freud in Vienna, H.D. had stooped down to pick up a handful of confetti "like the ones we pulled out of our Christmas bonbons" and found it consisted of gilded paper swastikas and Nazi mottos (*TF,* 58).

When the very young Denise Levertov, then still living in England and as yet unaware of H.D.'s work, wrote a poem entitled "Christmas 1944," including the lines "every carol / bears a burden of exile, a song of slaves"; when, in a very different mode, Dylan Thomas concluded his "Ceremony After a Fire Raid" with "The masses of the infant-bearing sea / Erupt, fountain, and enter to utter forever / Glory glory glory"; when numerous poets published their versions of the Christmas war poem in most of the major London wartime journals that H.D. would have been reading, they were using the Christmas myth, in a variety of ways, to explore the issue which for H.D. too was paramount: the uneasy relation of cultural ceremonies of peace to cultural systems of violence.[20]

II. Imagery/Done to Death: Crucifixions

One verse of a Moravian Christmas hymn which H.D. included in her notes to "The Gift" ran

> Not Jerusalem,
> Rather Bethlehem,
> Gave us that which
> Maketh life rich;
> Not Jerusalem.[21]

Some key lines from "The Flowering of the Rod" repeat the "Not Jerusalem" motif: "let us leave / The-place-of-a-skull / to those who have fashioned it" (F 2). The place-of-a-skull is Golgotha, where Christ was crucified. *Trilogy's* third part is taken up with leaving it behind — with imagining a Bethlehem which could be extricated from the Jerusalem of violence and betrayal. "The Flowering of the Rod" introduces into *Trilogy* a plot which seems unmoored in any historical particulars, as artless as fairy tale and as profound as parable or gospel; the poem which began with a scene of war's destruction ends as a — or the — Christmas story. Still, that Christmas tale remains bound up with an altered Jerusalem narrative, as the stories of three women at the start and near the end of the life of Christ — Mary the Mother, Mary of Bethany and Mary Magdalene — blur and merge, and the familiar New Testament plots are disarranged at moments to the point of derangement.

I want to read these threads of biblical narrative not only in relation to the modernist texts among which *Trilogy* is usually placed but also in relation to the tradition of openly declared "war poems." (These two traditions are not, of course, unrelated or necessarily distinguishable; H.D.'s work in particular has a way of revealing the modernist canon *as* war literature.)²² "Flowering of the Rod" begins with a voice placed in a field it would disclaim, a textual ground defined as neither the poet's nor the reader's own making:

> . . . this is not our field,
>
> we have not sown this;
> pitiless, pitiless, let us leave
>
> The-place-of-a-skull
> to those who have fashioned it
>   (F 2)

What and where is this place-of-a-skull, this Golgotha, from which the poem must dramatize its own departure? That field, I would argue, is not only the site of modern warfare but also, specifically, one site of dominant Anglo-American war poetry, which, from the Great War soldier poets onward, had frequently located "the poetry" of war in "the pity" and insisted, correspondingly, on the proper centrality in the war poem of the sacrificial Passion. The turn to Christmas narrative in "Flowering of the Rod," as well as other aspects of *Trilogy*, may be read, then, in part as a calculated resistance to the fashion of the crucifixion in the fashioning of masculinist war poems — and therefore, as H.D. saw it, in the fashioning of wars.

When George Barker, in a 1939 eulogy on García Lorca, wrote that from Lorca and Wilfred Owen "we can learn that the act of war is a violation and a coldblooded crucifixion of the imagination," he was employing a by then firmly conventionalized but still powerfully effective rhetorical strategy.²³ As Paul Fussell and Judith Rosen have shown, a wide variety of both patriotic and oppositional, blasphemous and orthodox, Great War discourses exploited the figure of the soldier (or, in rare cases, notably D. H. Lawrence's Great War work, the war resister) as a type of crucified Christ.²⁴ H.D.'s soldier husband during that war, Richard Aldington, was one of many others to compare himself to a Christ slaughtered by an indifferent father, in his ironic "Vicarious Atonement," and John Cournos lampoons both Aldington and an entire discursive tradition when the Aldington character in Cournos's *roman à clef Miranda Masters* invokes Golgotha to describe the horrors of having to do K.P.²⁵ The "war crucifixion" in its most potent cultural images and forms was not, however, easily dismissed. Wilfred Owen's famous, anguished 1918 letter to Osbert Sitwell summons and exemplifies the compelling rhetorical powers of the combat/crucifixion equation. (And H.D.'s remote personal connection through her close friends the Sitwells to Owen is worth noting in preface to his lines.) "For fourteen hours yesterday I was at work," Owen writes of his training of new troops,

— teaching Christ to lift his cross by numbers, and how to adjust his crown; and not to imagine he thirst till after the last halt. I attended his Supper to see that there were no complaints; and inspected his feet that they should be worthy of the nails. I see to it that he is dumb, and stands at attention before his accusers. With a piece of silver I buy him every day, and with maps make him familiar with the topography of Golgotha.[26]

The clear-cut literalizing ironies of Great War images of futile sacrifice of the innocent soldier gave way later to even more painfully compromised, ambiguous, self-suspicious, and antireferential uses of crucifixion mythology, in David Jones's war epics, for instance, and in numerous Second World War poems such as Robert Lowell's "The Soldier" or F. T. Prince's important "Soldiers Bathing." Second War poems return to the image of Christ on the cross in order to revise it for a new war poetry, in a variety of ways: by applying the type of Christ to others besides the soldier, by tracing civilian familiarity with the map of suffering emblematized by Golgotha, or by blurring distinctions between the crucifier and the crucified. Many of them — we have already seen examples written by Bishop, Moore, and Jarrell — place newly intensified emphasis on the position of the guilty observer of the crucifixion scene which Owen's letter already had begun to anticipate, as in David Gascoyne's lines from his 1943 war poem "Ecce Homo," "And we are onlookers at the crime, / Callous contemporaries of the slow / Torture of God." Within these variations, the "new" war poetry shared with the old a central focus on the "place-of-a-skull" and what went on there.[27]

So many memorable texts or passages within texts in the war poetry tradition took for their ground the topography of Golgotha that the site of the Passion might be said to be *the* crucial plot — if one single battle-and-burial ground, one sheer type, had to be demarcated — of the modern Anglo-American war poem. It was, by the forties, not only masculine ground; numerous Second War poems had extended the boundaries of its suffering, its cross, to include women, children, noncombatants generally. But, like the ambiguous body of Christ in Christian tradition, it retained, as much as it denied, tenacious specific links to masculinity (and therefore, in the sexual logic of war poetry, to combat) which were difficult to banish wholly. Sandra Gilbert's survey of gendered conflicts in Great War literature opens with a paradigmatic masculine war poem by that paradigmatically combative noncombatant Lawrence; it is not surprising that the text cited takes for its title a cry of the dying Christ. "Eloi, Eloi, Lama Sabachthani" might stand as a metonym for the dominant voice of twentieth-century antiwar poetry in English, both in its "soldier poem" and in its variant modes.[28] H.D. herself, early on, had summed up this developing tradition with a related cry. Her first historical novel, *Pilate's Wife*, centered on the crucifixion; there she treated the words "crucify him" as the quintessential "cry to war, having nothing to do with any set of voices, or peoples." Crucifixion, *Pilate's Wife* made clear, had by 1924 already become established for H.D. and her culture as the figurative equivalent and the literal epitome of "war-madness, war-hysteria."[29]

Why, at the beginning of "Flowering of the Rod," is the imperative to abandon the field punishments and field positions of all these eloquent Golgothas so urgent? Why testify so vehemently against, and attempt to move so assertively past, the reproduction of the crucifixion in war poetry? Of course, getting past the crucifixion to resurrection is the oldest and most significant plot twist in the Christian book. "London certainly supplied the *Inferno* of my *Commedia*," H.D. wrote in notes looking back to her writing of the Second War years, and *Trilogy* clearly reduplicates the pattern of that powerful, desirable, requisite comedy, moving from the terror and Apocryphal fire of the early pages of "Walls Do Not Fall" to a serene "Flowering of the Rod" which is both annunciation and Easter.[30] But the structures of the *Commedia* plot, this resurrection myth, however strong, do not fully account for all the intensities and peculiarities of *Trilogy*'s arguments with the wartime poetics of crucifixion.

One reason for resistance to crucifixion narrative suggests itself obliquely in a passage from the journal H.D. kept during her psychoanalysis in the thirties with Freud. She begins by meditating on a text she feels she cannot discuss with Freud, Lawrence's revision of the story of Christ's death and resurrection, *The Man Who Died*; this leads to the record of an unspeakable memory of watching a form of torture as a small child. She recalls herself doll-like and inarticulate ("Perhaps I cannot really talk yet . . . I can scream, I can cry"), staring "at one remove" while an unspecified "they" put salt on a caterpillar, "and it writhes, huge like an object seen under a microscope, or looming up it is a later film-abstraction." Then:

No, how can I talk about the crucified Worm? I have been leafing over papers in the cafe, there are fresh atrocity stories. I cannot talk about the thing that actually concerns me, I cannot talk to Sigmund Freud in Vienna, 1933, about Jewish atrocities in Berlin. (*TF*, 134–35)

The powerlessness and wordlessness of the child onlooker to torture in this memory becomes the even more painful silence of the adult in Vienna

mature enough to remember herself. The image of the "crucified Worm" is un-
speakable because it registers, with too much intensity, atrocities too close to
a Jew in Vienna in 1933. It is unspeakable, too, however, because historically
the crucifixion narrative has functioned not only as a figure for atrocity but,
in anti-Semitic practice, as an excuse for it.[31] This is why, in the lines I quoted
earlier from H.D.'s own fictional version of the crucifixion, *Pilate's Wife*, care
is taken to specify that the cry to crucify Christ has "nothing to do with any
set of voices, or peoples," for historically the dominant Christian crucifixion
plot has almost inevitably put Jewish voices, Jewish peoples, in danger of mis-
representation if not in far worse danger. Recurring analogies throughout
Tribute to Freud between Freud and Christ work in part to counteract this
danger, as well as performing a complex set of other rhetorical functions—
defamiliarizing and psychologizing Christianity, authorizing and Christianiz-
ing psychoanalysis and emphatically Judaizing both (*TF*, 104, 141).

The primary concern of H.D.'s diary entry above is not with the politics of
unspeakability and the representation of ethnic or religious difference but—as
the magnification of the caterpillar as if under a microscope or on a film screen
signals—with the problem of the seen, the question of seeing, and the cor-
responding construction of sexual difference in the crucifixion plot.[32] The field
of "the crucified worm," of Golgotha, is revealed as a visual space, or, in Jac-
queline Rose's resonant phrase, as a field of vision.[33] And in that field, as I
have suggested throughout this book, looking on "at one remove," in distress,
is the position and the function of the feminine. For H.D., the most acute
problem with the tradition of war poems as Golgothas is their placement—
and their simultaneous effacement and judgment—of women. That means,
further, the problem of where they place the gaze: how they invite, impel, and
situate the view of the suffering, sacrificed male body which traditionally oc-
cupies their center stage.

Not surprisingly, H.D.'s most strenuous and open criticism of the struc-
tures of visual representation in the war/crucifixion/Passion sequence
comes in the form of a film review, one published long before the writing
of *Trilogy*. In a 1928 essay on Carl Dreyer's film about Jeanne D'Arc, "The
Passion and Death of a Saint," and in a follow-up piece called "An Apprecia-
tion," she spelled out clearly her reasons for refusing to stay put, as artist
or audience, in a textual "place of a skull." The sacrificed hero in this par-
ticular representation is, of course, not Christ but Jeanne; but the
problems of the sacrificial Passion are not dispelled by her sexual difference.

H.D.'s critique of Dreyer's *Jeanne D'Arc* focused on the film's emphasis
on pain, a stress she described not only as thematic but also as techni-
cal and physical: "Do I *have* to be cut into slices by this inevitable pan-
movement of the camera, these suave lines to left, up, to the right, back,

all rhythmical with the remorseless rhythm of a scimitar?" Such strategies, she maintained, were "calculated to drive in the pitiable truth like the very nails on the spread hands of Christ" on "skull-hill."[34] The audience viewing Jeanne's torture — cruelty which H.D., following the film's repeated images of "soldier iron-heeled great boots," linked to war and militarism — was, she argued, "left pinned like some senseless animal, impaled as she is impaled by agony" (J, 20). The refusal to be so impaled might, she acknowledged, be "cowardice," or "phobia that I myself, so un-Jeanne-like, was unwilling to face openly" (J, 20). But even worse than that refusal was the willing gaze at agony. The problem as H.D. saw it was not only in how filmic or textual violence affected, but also in how it constituted, an afflicted but helpless viewer: "I do not mind crying (though I do mind crying) when I see a puppy kicked into a corner but I do mind standing aside and watching. . . . I can NOT watch this thing impartially" (J, 20).

Here again, as in the "crucified worm" passage, the role of the viewer was figured as a particularly feminine one. Crying and watching, bullied into pity, Jeanne D'Arc's spectators were compelled to occupy a position quintessentially women's own in war narrative. The position of the weeping woman was, for H.D., an intolerable one to be put into by a text (and by structures of power which the text represents) and an untenable one to aim to enforce as authorial agent. Dreyer's Jeanne might be a technical masterpiece, endorsed by the great filmmaker Pabst,[35] but H.D.'s final reference to it, in her later essay "An Appreciation," associated the Dreyer film with Pabst's Great War experiences in order to disassociate herself from both: "We must leave that, we must leave dead bodies of heroes achieving no names on tablets set at the base of statues nor on gold-wreathed slabs set ornate and respectable above bank-presidents' mahogany roll-top desks."[36] Let us leave the place of a skull to those who have fashioned it.

"An Appreciation" contrasted Dreyer's Jeanne with Pabst's Joyless Street (which H.D. also read as a war film), praising Pabst for deflecting rather than focusing attention on the tortured body of the victim (here, again, a female victim). In Joyless Street, she wrote, a corpse goes almost unnoticed by a viewer; this is because, in Pabst's words, "I did not mean you to see the body of the murdered woman on the floor" (A, 68). The medium which fully discloses but nevertheless does not "mean you to see" the acts and results of individual and institutional violence, which does not hold its readers inexorably in place within systems of victimization and aggression, becomes H.D.'s desired model.

Her ideal method was, then, "not meaning you to"; in addition, these reviews insisted upon a different system of meaning which would be "not meant." Criticizing Dreyer for his materialism and nihilism, his unwillingness to affirm the spiritual by representing Jeanne's visions of angels, H.D. returned to the question of the textual medium: "Such psychic manifestation, I need hardly say, need be in no way indicated by any outside innovation of cross lights or of superimposed shadows. It is something in something, something behind something" (J, 22). These final lines, written in 1929, point directly toward *Trilogy*, which takes as the vital first principle of its spiritual poetics the search for and demonstration of psychic manifestation, of things, in the midst of Second World War London, behind and within.[37]

What next, then, after such absolute dismissal of "the place of a skull"? Where to? Still within the field of biblical narrative, *Trilogy* explores several alternatives. The first of these is the most obvious, and the most common in modernist transpositions of New Testament plots into war stories: not to leave Golgotha but to read it over, redefining its usual central figure, Christ. This project begins in *Trilogy* long before "The Flowering of the Rod." The search for a transformative and transformed "masculine initiator" commences very soon after the opening of "The Walls Do Not Fall," with the announcement of the discovery of the footprints of "a new Master" who is "Mage, / bringing myrrh." A crucial initial step in *Trilogy*'s quest, this tracking of the male mediator is not, however, by itself sufficient; by the end of the three parts of the poem the master's traces are misleading enough to need to be erased from the text.

For the traditional Christ sacrificed at the Golgotha of numerous modern war poems, *Trilogy* would substitute four other "Christos-images." The first is a jubilant Christ, disentangled from the "art-craft junk-shop / paint and plaster medieval jumble / of pain-worship and death-symbol" (W, 18). Velasquez's master representation of Christ crucified is recalled but rejected; in its place comes an unbidden dream image, not Christ the victim but Christ victorious. *Trilogy* also pursues the pagan or at any rate "non-Christian" Christ (that is, a Christ symbol which evades establishment as figurehead for a Christian culture at once parochial and imperial), challenging the hegemony of Golgotha as the primary or conclusive location of cultural crisis. At the same time, as many critics have noted, *Trilogy*'s Christos becomes feminine, or at any rate differently masculine; in this he resembles H.D.'s earlier representations of a Christ who not only responds to but also contains and embodies the feminine.[38] Finally, the poem seeks an even more radically defamiliarized Christ, both by decentering the figure and by positively removing his, or its, relation to the *human* body. By "Flowering," section 11, Christ is a wild goose, the leader of a swarm.[39]

In *Trilogy*'s most direct visit to the site of Golgotha, "Flowering," section 11, a crucifixion which hardly registers as such is also, at the same

instant, a flight: "He was the first to wing / from that sad Tree. . . . " This
Christ is no objectified, isolated sacrificial object; rather, his flight is a
spiral of desire in which both personal and collective needs conjoin. With
its late bird figures, *Trilogy* attempts to position itself entirely beyond
what Julia Kristeva has called "the deeper workings represented by the
Cross: that of caesura, discontinuity, depression"; and it attempts to posi-
tion a self entirely beyond what Andrew Ross has called "the implication
of the body as object" in the structures of martyrdom."[40] This means
specifically rejecting the implication of the martyred *male* body, convert-
ing it figuratively to a birdlike being which is barely gendered, barely em-
bodied, or not at all.

What happens immediately after this juncture, this erasure of gender,
is precisely, however, the development of a plot which strongly under-
scores the problem of sexual differences in the place-of-a-skull. The gener-
alized sacred ecstasy of "Flowering," section 11, is replaced by the more
blasphemous and contentious story of the Marys and the Arab, with its
stress on the politics of "negligibility"[41] in general and of feminine margin-
ality in particular. In this plot, the mature Christ, however transfigured,
turns out to pose as many problems as he solves. The rest of *Trilogy* will
infantilize him, displace him, avoid him, resist him, and even go so far
as to surgically remove him, in its urgent focus instead on the situation
of the women at Golgotha.

Out of the first draft of "Flowering," four sections were, as H.D. noted
carefully, "Deleted from: / The Rod" and preserved but pushed into the
realm of apocryphal marginalia.[42] They came originally at a forceful mo-
ment of revelation in section 27. Between the symbolic crucifixion in sec-
tion 11 and here, two gospel-like "tales of a jar or jars" have emerged and
begun, delicately, intricately, to merge; their narrative configurations will
conclude the *Trilogy*. Both move in reverse trajectory, with highly unstable,
oscillating chronologies, away from the crisis of crucifixion, even as they
shadow that scene and are shadowed by it. One involves the "other Mary"
and one the "mother Mary"; one, the Magdelene's intimacies with Christ —
her gestures of adoration which are read, crudely, by Judas and Simon,
as transgression — in the period immediately before his death, and the
other, reaching back even earlier, the Adoration of the Magi and the fixed,
primal, approved relation of the infant Christ to Mary in Bethlehem. Both
plots (which are the same plot, or circular) concern an erotic economy,
a visionary exchange, in which a "gift of myrrh" is transferred from the
Arab Mage Kaspar to the two Marys. To "the mother Mary" the gift is
given by the Wise Man freely and formally, according to the script(ures),
and the exchange must be in some sense resisted or disrupted in the text

as well as accepted; to "the other Mary," who wants myrrh-salve to anoint
the body of Christ shortly before he dies, "sanctioned" myrrh is at first
denied, and it must be obtained, hard won, as well as offered. In section
27, at the height of the power struggle between Kaspar and the Magda-
lene, the Mage has a moment of recognition when Mary's veil drops and
the sight of her hair brings on a vision. (Not incidentally, this passage
gives Mary Magdalene, for perhaps the first time in her textual history,
something else to do with her hair than wipe feet.)

   In the four following sections of the poem which H.D. excised, Kaspar's
"original" vision is organized around a heightened return to the import of
the crucifixion, and it is fully centered on the presence and voice of the
self-sacrificing Christ. The deleted version of Kaspar's trance reveals Christ
shortly before his death, sitting alone with an otherwise unspecified woman
named Mary. To her "shrill cry" – "woe, woe – aie,aie/ wail for Adonis" –
he responds "peace – I say – / peace – be still" (CP, 622–23), at once solac-
ing and silencing her. What follows in the next sections is novel for Trilogy.
An extended monologue in Christ's voice, it begins: "True I must die, but
wail no more . . . "

> true I must suffer for alas, they know
>
> not yet My Father; true I must pass the gate
> of death, of Hell, but wail no more,
>
> I come to comfort you (O, soon I come),
> there I will save all beauty that has been,
>
> there I shall create all beauty that shall be,
> peace Spirit of Beauty that has been,
>
> Peace, Aphrodite, peace Astarte, peace Cyprus,
> peace, be still:
>
> peace Cybele whose worship on the hills,
> brought many from their weary toil,
>
> from the stale air of teeming cities;
> I who have loved the mountains, can I fail to see
>
> that mountain-worship is allied to Beauty?
> peace, Cybele, the hills have known me and shall know:
>
> peace Maia, Gaia, Kore – you have known
> peace more than many, many that shall come;

your orgies were not of the sword
your hedges border paradise,

the blood you shed was of the bull and ram,
not of your fellow-man . . .   (CP, 623)

This is not, of course, the first time the "Master"'s voice has appeared
in the text of *Trilogy*—a poem composed, as we know from the surviving
notebook for "Flowering" at least, with biblical citations arranged, pre-
sumably as mnemonic and organizational guides, in its margins. Before
this point, however, the Christian word in the poem is not, like these lines,
a matter of dramatic improvisation but rather the material of actual scrip-
tural quotation, familiar gospel wording like *"In the beginning was the
Word"* (W 10) or *"Be ye wise as serpents"* (W 35). The words of scripture
heretofore have been not only orthodox in origin but also set off carefully
through the text's typography, italicized to indicate both that they are
other words imported into the text from an outside source and that they
are master words, discourses of authority. (In much the same manner of
these italics, the words of Christ in some Christian Bibles are heightened
and isolated by being printed in red.)

From the start, of course, the text has been not only traversed by or
interspersed with these scriptural maxims but also in contention with
them, either actively resistant (as in the argument with John's taboo against
adding at the end of Revelation) or quietly revisionary (as in the several
places where epithets applied in scripture to its Judeo-Christian male au-
thorities, the apostles, Christ or God, are unobtrusively transferred over
to one of the Maries or to Osiris). Moreover, *Trilogy* is willing to italicize
its *own* words, to cite itself, using graphics identical with those that mark
its biblical quotations, the same slant emphasis, to set off words of H.D.'s
own as kinds of antiscripture or alternative gospel. Often this occurs pre-
cisely in those passages where meaning is most in question or most pro-
vocatively daemonic; it is as if some modernist red-letter bible were being
published with the honor of marked print reserved not just for Christ but
for all lines spoken by obsessive doubters and insurrectionary demons.
Still, despite its free play with the politics of italics throughout, the vi-
sionary *Trilogy* never wholly subverts, only disruptively supplements, the
authority of Christian scripture, and in particular it never challenges the
authority of the words of Christ himself.[43] Up to this "wail no more"
speech in the excised section 30, it quotes Jesus but stops short of writing
new speeches for him. Here, however, words are put freely into the mouth
of a ventriloquized Christ.

There was, in England in the early forties, a law on the books prohibiting the dramatic representation of any person of the Holy Trinity – and not a dead law, either; Dorothy Sayers, for instance, ran famously afoul of it with her quite traditional radio play-cycle on the life of Christ which was broadcast by the BBC in 1941–1942, a version of the gospel which I suspect, from intertextual echoes, H.D. may have heard or read and attended to with some real interest.[44] The deletion of this speech of Christ's from "The Rod" may be due in part to surprisingly traditional anxieties arising from the intensity of that taboo against "impersonation." The apology immediately following, in the last excised section, suggests as much: "This was never the word of the Master, / nor can we by any process of imagination / or inspiration ever re-capture his thought . . . " (CP, 623–24). But we can speculate on several other equally likely and more blasphemous reasons why this Christ himself must be "stilled" in Trilogy, and why Kaspar's vision finally must take substantially different form. H.D. may well have excised this passage simply because she felt the quality of the verse was weak; still, she completely changed the text, rather than revising to improve it.

First, let us consider what the deleted vision passage seeks to accomplish. It may be read as a paradoxical attempt to invoke Christ and Christianity as bodies of authority in order to divest them of some of that singular power. Even as Christ offers himself here as the central future savior, he lends his imprimatur to the fertility goddesses who preceded him – Aphrodite, Astarte, Cybele, Kore, and so on.

Clearly at stake in both the new standard and the earlier discarded representation of Kaspar's vision is the relation of the Christian belief system to these earlier divinities and their rituals. This is, after all, what the journey and gaze of the Magi has worked to signify through centuries of Christian narrative: the cusp or crisis at which ancient, pagan authority confronts the new mysteries of Christ, a moment which is often taken in modernity as a metonym for all cataclysmic ideological transition.[45] Both the retained and the rejected versions of Kaspar's revelation in "Flowering" work in ardent opposition to this tradition. Trilogy imagines this cusp, the moment of the Mage's gaze, not to register how Christianity supercedes barbarity but to reread, reinscribe, and praise the pagan (feminine) in the Christian. The vision does not deplete the "technically heathen" Kaspar but fills him, momentarily, in its final authorized version, with an ecstasy like "labour" (F 28). And it is provoked, of course, not even at the sight of the meek Virgin Mother and Holy Child but at the sight of a dishevelled Mary Magdalene who has never wanted or needed to get rid of her connection to anterior demons. The discarded version mediates, and therefore mutes, this vision through the homily of Christ.

The final version, with greater visionary efficacy, lets its pagan feminine daemons utter themselves, announce their own meanings, in an unsanctioned eruption into Golgotha's boundaries of the pre-Christian, prehistoric, and prenatal.

By relying on its Christ, the Son of the Father, the Word of the Law, for a verbal endorsement of the pagan, the excised version of Kaspar's vision deprives its ancient mother-goddesses of their own multiple epiphanic and signifying powers. The retained version, in contrast, brooks no hierarchical distinction between the Revelation of Saint John and the revelations of its daemon cultures. The daemons are, we are told in section 26, "now unalterably part of the picture"; it is Christ, in fact, who is here exorcised, "cast out" of the definitive canon of texts which will comprise the official book of *Trilogy*.

The problem with the deleted text has, however, as much to do with its representation of the cusps of gender as with its representation of the meeting between Christian and pagan. And in particular it has to do with women's relation to slaughter. The daemons revealed to Kaspar in the two alternative versions differ not only in how they are transmitted but in what they seem to mean. In the abandoned section 30, Christ is called upon to recuperate the ancient protean Goddess in surprising and provocative terms: "the blood you shed," he tells her approvingly, "was of the bull and ram, / not of your fellow-man." At this astonishing moment, the text through its Christ sanctions a form — an orgy — of sacred female violence. Such violence gains approval because it is ritual and relatively harmless, but it is violence nonetheless; and behind the sacrifice of "bull and ram" lie traces of the threatening women's blood-rites which might constitute a feminine and anarchic equivalent of, rather than alternative to, war — Bacchic frenzies, the dismemberments of Acteon, Pentheus, and Orpheus. *Trilogy* in its final form cuts this impulse, shying away from this momentary release of or relapse into a licit, archaic violence and sacrificial desire for women, and pursuing instead, in the oceanic imagery of Kaspar's authorized Atlantean revelation, hints of a femininity essentially pacific. (This is not, however, *Trilogy*'s final word on the question of women's distinctive peacefulness, as I will later show; and as early on as "Walls Do Not Fall," section 34, where a scorpion goddess is invoked, female figures have been granted a power potentially violent.)

But the woman who sheds blood of rams presents less of a problem here, I think, than the woman who stands on the edge of the vicious circle keening while men kill each other. First writing this scene between heroic Christ and wailing Mary, then writing it off in December 1944, H.D.

enacts *upon* her text the dynamic I have been tracing within it: that re-
peated, difficult attempt to move this war poem beyond the usual place
of women in the place-of-a-skull. One reaction is expected from and ob-
liged for women who watch from the periphery: weeping. "The regularity
with which . . . women's tears are mentioned in every variety of war narra-
tive is both impressive and frightening," writes Nancy Huston.[46] *The Iliad*,
for instance, Huston argues, "culminates in non-language, the inarticulate
cries of women, deformed and distorted echoes of the *faits accomplis* of
men"; and real women have cooperated, down through "thirty centuries
after the *Iliad*, in playing the roles handed out to them, the same old roles:
weep for your dead men; moan; suffer; scream so as to consecrate their
hero status; these women said yes" (279).

As H.D.'s earlier poem "Magician" puts it, "too long have we slain,
too long have we wept" (*CP*, 434). *Trilogy* finally banishes its wailing ver-
sion of Mary, retainingly only a Mary of Magdala who comments sternly,
self-reflexively, perhaps even sardonically on her role as weeper, all the
while with her "voice steady" and her eyes dry (F 17). "Flowering" substi-
tutes for the "deformed and distorted echoes" of women's grieving the
"echo / of an echo in a shell" (F 32) which means—whatever it means—a
register not defined by, provoked by, or responsive to men's wars. We can
read these deletions, then, in part, as an attempt to find a way within the
master plot of Western male sacrifice for a woman in a narrative of vio-
lence, for a narrative itself, to say no.

Aside from their characteristic helpless lamentation, the other aspect
which distinguishes the women in biblical accounts of Golgotha, and in
some strands of war-related literature which follow those accounts, is the
women's curious indistinguishability. They all seem to be named Mary,
and are told apart only with some difficulty—Mary Magdalene the peni-
tent follower, Mary the mother of Jesus, Mary the mother of James the
less, Mary the wife of Cleophos and sister of Mary, Mary of Bethany. In
sacred or heroic versions, this blurring or reduplication of women's names
and women's functions lends a severe generic quality to these women,
who become through their barely differentiated roles the abstract keepers
of perfect sorrow. In profane and ironic versions, their identical names
suggest either a kind of banal sameness, the multiplying maudlin, or a
sinister reproduction, hysterical proliferation. We have seen them the world
over. In Yeats's *Calvary*, three unspecified Marys act on identical cue, cast-
ing themselves on the ground before the cross to clean Christ's feet with
their hair, and then immediately disappear, clearing the stage for Judas's
individual confrontation with Jesus. In Lawrence's *The Man Who Died*,

a jumble of trivial, undifferentiated Marys is casually dismissed: "the Marys do not know it, none of the four Marys. For they never found the lost male due to their risen man, their risen God."[47]

Trilogy's gospel tale decenters that risen God, and in his stead dramatizes and reflects upon the terms of Marian knowledge: What does each Mary know in this story? How have they been and are they now to be construed? Exploring these questions, H.D. exploits — with a difference — the conventional multiplication of the Marys. On the one hand, the strategic superimposition or fusing of one Mary and another in this singular/ plural "tale of a jar or jars" is a way of refusing splitting. It refutes externally imposed divisions of women into fixed, separate, and hierarchically opposed roles. In dominant Christian tradition, after all, the Madonna and the Whore do more than occupy two set poles of femininity; they *are* those poles. *Trilogy* collapses them, with some precedent from H.D.'s Moravian heritage, for in the history of Moravianism the two women are traditionally seen as one.[48] On the other hand, however, the text's "more-than-one" Mary, its shifting and swift displacement from one Mary to another, is a way of insisting on splitting. It emphasizes the inward variance and instability in any feminine identity, in an identity at all. Marys-a-plenty: both overflowing with a plentitude of identity and dispersed, divided.

Leaving behind the place of a skull, *Trilogy*, in its final sections moves back toward Bethany/Bethlehem — that is, moves back toward places marked off as feminine terrain. This is not, however, a simple turn "back to basics." Rather, it constitutes a series of multiple entrances into further arenas where essences — like the myrrh of the Marys — are mercurial, insecured and subject to contest and question.

III. Christmases

You got into the wrong pig stye, ma chère.
    But not too late to climb out.
                        (Ezra Pound in a letter to H.D., 1954)[49]

We have the old and the elderly, who were never exposed to the guns, still fatuously maintaining that man is the Christ-child and woman the infallible safeguard from all evil and all danger. It is fatuous, because it absolutely didn't work. Then we have the men of middle age, who were all tortured and virtually put to death by the war. They accept Christ crucified as their image, are essentially womanless, and take the great cry: *Consummatum est! — It is finished —* as their last word. Thirdly, we have the young, who never went through the war. They have no illusions about it, however, and the death cry of their elder generation: It is finished! rings cold in their blood.
                        (D. H. Lawrence, 1929)[50]

From Golgotha, then, to Bethlehem: "She is the single one among the Moderns," Alicia Ostriker writes of H.D., "who begins poems with death and ends them with birth."[51] Perhaps, but among the moderns with a small "m" the sequence is not at all unusual. In fact, collections of British war poetry written during the Second World War abound with examples of texts which, starting from the intolerable image of crucifixion, close by appealing to a transfigured and blessed or slouching toward a disfigured and cursed mother-and-child. The final turn to the manger is a familiar one in certain Anglo-American discourses of war, so familiar that D. H. Lawrence's impatient account of New Testament paradigms in post–Great War thinking treats it as the fatuous mythology of an entire generation and an entire gender. The birth scene often displaces the masculine-centered allegorical Golgothas of war poetry. But the aftermath of that substitution is not necessarily a release of feminine *jouissance*, beatitude, or insurrection. In place of the cross the son's stable might lodge as an equally familiar structure, one we have also "seen the world over." And the woman war poet, climbing into that wrong(ed) pig stye, might find herself vulnerable to charges of fatuousness, or might find, as Laura Riding put it, that Christmas still confounded her mouth.[52]

Nonetheless, the manger scene inspired women war poets as much as it stymied them. Not only *Trilogy* but a number of other war poems by women published in London in the early forties mapped the topography of Bethlehem, that scene of motherhood where a temporary shelter is erected in war-occupied territory. They are part of a larger body of Second War poems, a few of which I have considered in my earlier chapters, which take up the key question of motherist rhetoric. Is there an essential, or essentially different, feminine nature which derives from or is grounded in a peaceful, nurturing maternity?[53] Or is such an idea "fatuous," or any feminine practice proceeding from that "nature" unworkable? This was not, of course, a question only or necessarily "for" women. Indeed, it often functioned as an interrogation *of* and *against* women, like Freud's "Was will das Weib," rather than as a query *by* them. Still, for many women writers thinking about the war it was a pressing subject of inquiry. In poems which, like H.D.'s, organize an exploration of the question of the mother in war around a Bethlehem narrative, extra emphasis falls on how mothers are *told* maternity as a doctrinal tale in Western war culture, just as in other modern war poems the narrative of Golgotha works to foreground the power of the story of masculine sacrifice to impel men into combat.

Among the forties Bethlehem/war poems with which H.D.'s telling of the Marys might be said to be conversing, two general thematic complexes emerge. One group of poems represents a maternity at war. In these texts warfare violates the powerless precepts of maternal love, pathetically deprives the vulnerable of maternal protection, or, with a harshness which seeks to expel all pathos, reveals motherhood as the source and prop, as well as the subject, of atrocity. The poems represent cruel parturitions, infanticide or child abandonment, dead mothers, sinister lullabies, a mangled nest of Bethlehem in which the boy child dandles on the knee of a woman who already knows herself as Pietà. When the war-mother speaks, she has some version of Blok's mother's wail in the opening epigraph to this chapter: "Come, take my breast boy, feed on this, / grow, know your place."

The voice here is curiously divided, suffering and resigned but also, somehow, secretly and strangely jubilant in its urging; this mother is already, in Adrienne Rich's resonant phrase, "working for the army."[54] Julia Kristeva glosses this duplicity in her "Stabat Mater" as a "'coded' perversity" of maternal self-denial and masochism.[55] This *"pere-version"* or "father-version" as Kristeva describes it is a psychic structure exploited by totalitarian regimes in which the mother, "assured of a place in an order that surpasses human will," experiences both suffering and "a reward of pleasure" as she socializes her child into the violent structures of her culture. "The feminine *père-version*," Kristeva writes, "lies coiled in the desire of the law as desire of reproduction and continuity" (116). There is a chilling passage in Lawrence's essay on Revelation (a text H.D.'s exploration of that final biblical book in *Trilogy* both recalls and revises) which offers an accusatory version of Kristeva's image of the *pere-verse*: "no-one is coiled more bitterly in the folds of the old Logos than woman. It is always so . . . a fixed and evil *form*, which coils around like mummy clothes. . . . All women today have a large streak of the police-woman in them."[56] Come, take my breast, boy, shoulder the cross.

In forties London, the most outrageous poetic uncoilings of this "pereversion" unleash, as in a grand backlash, in Edith Sitwell's intensely theological, macabre versions of wartime maternity. These are the poems of "great symbolic force" that Henry Reed cited in his 1944 assessment of Sitwell as a major war poet.[57] In Sitwell's astonishing "Lullaby," for instance, a Babioun — a baboon — dances out as surrogate mother to nurse an infant abandoned in the carnage, chanting, in a "fouled nest" under a "judas-colored sun," a far more aggressive and depressing version of Blok's Pietà's masochistic maternal urging:

> . . . steel wings fan thee to thy rest,
> And wingless truth and larvae lie
> And eyeless hope and handless fear—
> All these for thee as toys are spread . . .
> And with the Ape thou art alone—
> Do, Do.[58]

"Do, do": this is the baby talk of a mother tongue which reassures only to compel. Other forties pietàs enact the weak desire to sing lullabies, rather, of "don't, don't," as in Kathleen Raine's "Christmas Poem," which considers the Christ child: "Lovely He will grow—oh women hide him / Where men find shelter, in her apparent breast. . . . "[59] The irony of such lines rests, of course, in the impossibility of such shielding, for the martial Pietà poem invokes the inexorable plot line which will induct the boy from the Madonna's bosom into the grand agon of the "Stabat Mater" or the Gold-star mother, and in which "taking the breast" of acculturation and "shouldering the cross" or machine gun prove identical moves.[60]

Another very different group of biblical war poems represents a maternity and a birth scenario before, beyond, and outside war. These texts replace the man who bears the cross and the woman who "cannot bear it" with the woman who safely bears the child. In such poems motherhood carries what Rachel Blau DuPlessis calls "the authority of 'Otherness,'" and a "feminism of difference" organizes itself around the mother-child dyad as well as around a female-centered and/or child-centered community.[61] Sitwell provides a notable example of this type, too. It is her "Still Falls the Rain," another poem also among the Moderns which begins with death and ends with birth. The painful complex of crucifixion/war conceits which structure "Still Falls the Rain" throughout gives way, at the end of the poem, to the dawning closure of Bethlehem: "Then sounds the voice of One who like the heart of man / was once a child who among beasts has lain— / 'Still do I love, still shed my innocent light, my Blood, for thee.'"[62] If the poem can end its wars only by appealing to the transcendant voice of male Logos, it also, however, through its simile "like the heart of man," invokes an experience of infancy represented as natively innocent because archaic and animal, because it lies among beasts; and behind that infant lie the traces of a maternal body and the productive bloodshed of labor.

An even more overt version of a Bethlehem of feminine difference occurs in Anne Ridler's verse play *The Shadow Factory*, published by Faber and Faber in 1945 and produced on the stage in that December of 1944 which saw the drafting of "The Flowering of the Rod." The play is set in a factory, "a year or two after the war."[63] It looks forward, therefore, to the social changes of the new postwar order, and does so with anxiety. The factory is run by an exploitive, deadened Director, the schedules of its largely female work force punctuated by the blaring of totalitarian maxims out of loudspeakers. Ridler's conservative critique of the unfettered capitalist/bureaucratic/industrialist ethos, which the play represents as shadow production, reads it as a form of spiritual error, and seeks an orthodox corrective: to reform the factory, to return to the church and the family as the proper sites of external and internalized authority. In this protest against the "hypertrophy of the motive of Profit"[64] and this projection of an "Idea of a Christian Society," *The Shadow Factory* bears strong resemblance to Eliot's late work, and it comes as no surprise to find in the note on the author of the play that "Anne Ridler before her marriage was secretary to Mr. T. S. Eliot." But *The Shadow Factory* does not only transmit an Eliot-like vision in the manner of a good amanuensis or of the well-married-off-disciple who has left the work force. Its central crisis restages the scene of Eliot's "The Journey of the Magi," but does so in ways which differ critically, though not categorically, from Ridler's former boss, and which to some extent run parallel to H.D.'s project in *Trilogy*. I want to consider Ridler's nativity scenes at some length here, in order to contrast *Trilogy*'s strategies.

The most ominous aspect of Ridler's negative setting, the Shadow Factory, is its Director's desire to interfere with the reproductive process. He dreams of a rationalist, technological, masculine takeover of birth itself: "Soon perhaps we shall have solved the mystery of birth, and learned to prevent the great catastrophe of death. . . . I only ask of you that you should become modern citizens, with all that those words connote: I only ask that you should assist at this new birth"(40–41). Two worrisome postwar prospects lurk in this dystopian projection. One, I think, is Ridler's fear of the ameliorist schemes and rhetoric of a postwar Labour government; the other, more important for my purposes, is the fear of the government of labor — the fear that men and industry will coopt the distinctive female, traditionally domestic sphere of childbirth. Here the production of shadows (the military/industrial/bureaucratic complex which is the domain of the Director) and the reproduction of the species (that matrix which is the domain of the mother) threaten to merge, and it is this indifferentiation that the play's Bethlehem scene must challenge.[65]

The salvation of the factory comes through an influx of different values, feminine and familial values, via its women laborers, and it comes in the form of a mother-and-child-centered crèche. I am not referring here to an in-house daycare center; the play's intense pronatalism stops short of offering such a concrete reform. Rather, this crèche is part of an office Christmas party Nativity pageant which is represented as both naive and profound. The workers have no trouble casting the main roles in the Nativity scene which, when enacted, will begin the process of spiritual conversion for the Director and others in the plot. Women, for instance, play the three lowly shepherds. But they run into difficulties when they try to find male players for the more elevated roles of the Magi, and are saved only when the Director himself steps in to play Melchior.

At the epiphanic moment of each Mage's gift giving—a moment we have already seen as highly charged for H.D.—a strong and surprising line of rhetoric, not only pronatalist but also feminist, emerges. The men's speeches as they lay down their "gold," "frankincense," and "myrrh" are represented as authentic counters to the Director's earlier bureaucratese. Both in impulse and in content, these addresses to the Child offer pointed cases against masculinist values and utopian examples of the transfiguration of masculinity. Each Mage's gift involves a rejection of the normative gendering of men. The Education Officer who plays Balthazar discovers in his gift of myrrh a suicidal form of masculinity passed on from father to son:

> Bitter myrrh is because of your manhood, princeling.
> Men have a deep wish to die; I know it;
> My life was ruled by it, and here I offer it.
> Bear my gift, and taking it from me, give
> O give me a better, make me desire to live.
>   (he kneels)
>
>   (54)

The Parson, playing a Caspar not unlike H.D.'s Kaspar in some respects, breaks down his dependence on the rationalist hegemony of past authoritative texts, learning the irrational and visionary:[66]

> Caspar brought incense to the baby.
> Incense — knowledge of mysteries
> Beyond the rational, beyond the personal.
> He must offer the inherited wisdom he clings to,
> Learning to see with his own sight . . .
>
>   (54-55)

And finally, the Director puts his gold before his employee's infant, a gesture interpreted as a laying down of his power and of his fear of losing power.

The Shadow Factory's crèche scene develops a probing analysis both of the production and motivation of manhood in wartime and of the production and motivation of wars by men. Unconscious desires for death, overweening rationalism and materialism, and the defensive-aggressive need for power are implicated as world-threatening problems stemming from the social construction of masculinity and of patriarchy—problems subject to change through a kind of deprogramming-by-Nativity. Femininity in Ridler's text, by contrast, comes naturally to its nativities. Here, as in the "Bethlehem" conclusion of "Still Falls the Rain," the affirmation of natural (animal) feminine and maternal values collides or colludes with the affirmation of the transcendent Logos. In Ridler's drama, the part of Mary devolves automatically, gracefully, upon the woman who is already pregnant, already named Maria. And the focus of the drama is above all on the boy Christ child, "who among beasts has lain" but whose light alone—the sign of his Father and his selfhood, not of his mother—is the source, for Ridler, of true social transformation.[67]

In its protest against masculinist values and power structures, Ridler's *Shadow Factory* thus resorts to what Denise Riley, in her study of child-care policy in wartime England, calls the "deeply conventional" and "overinsistent naming of the mother",[68] and to an equally conventional and insistent naming of her Son. H.D.'s own Mage/Mary scene conspires to an extent in this litany of naming, and for some of the same purposes as Ridler's: first, to locate a mother who might stand, at least potentially, in reverse, not perverse, relation to systems of violence; second, to affirm the conventional maternal values of nurture and empathy. But in *Trilogy* we can read as well moments of interruption and disavowal which disrupt the mechanisms of the conventional appeal to the sanctified mother-minded crèche.[69]

After all, the alternative sign whose presence suspends and supercedes *Trilogy*'s crucifixion plot in the final pages of "Flowering" is not the Christ child on his mother's lap, not exactly. It is certainly not the sturdy boy god who, as Sylvia Plath puts it in one of her own versions of the war/ Bethlehem matrix, "solid the spaces lean on, envious / . . . the baby in the barn."[70] *Trilogy*'s stable is, we might say, unstable, and the story it contains concerns not solid Logos but dissembling metaphor, not birth— exactly—but *myrrh*.

Compare the final invocation in "Still Falls the Rain" to the One who "was once a Child who among beasts has lain" with *Trilogy*'s last section. Here, too, the closure of the war poem seems destined to take the form of orthodox Christian consolation in the name of the Christ child. The Magi come to behold Mary; at this point a healed spectatorship resolves the problem of looking which the crucifixion narrative has raised. They give their gifts to her, Kaspar's myrrh last:

> she said, Sir, it is a most beautiful fragrance,
> as of all flowering things together;
>
> but Kaspar knew the seal of the jar was unbroken.
> he did not know whether she knew
>
> the fragrance came from the bundle of myrrh
> she held in her arms.
>
> (F 43)

This is an elusive, even a devious scenario, with a number of obvious detours from the usual circuit of the Magi's gift giving. For one thing, Mary already possesses myrrh (in some unprocessed vegetable form) before the wise man brings her any; what's more, the infant Christ, traditional center of this adoration, is either absent entirely or else mildly decentered through a trope which submits him to the transfers of language rather than exempting him from them; and in place of the canonical certitude which the arrival at the manger usually represents, in place of the sight of that "only nonsign"[71] Himself, we are offered instead a distinct thematics of uncertainty: "he did not know whether she knew." This moment is rather more like Riffaterre's "epiphany of the semiosis" arrived at by a reader struggling with linguistic disarrangement and with disorienting metaphor than like the Christian epiphany predicated on the discovery of the literal ground of the Bethlehem manger.[72]

The myrrh *Trilogy*'s last Mary holds disconcertingly in her arms both signifies and produces a complex series of dislocations and substitutions of meaning. In fulfillment of the prophecy of "Flowering"'s section 10, it is, first of all, *the* counter-sign to Golgotha. It declaratively breaks through, and stands for all that breaks through, the history of violence, usurpation, and destruction: "a flower-cone, / not a heap of skulls," which grows out of a grain like the mustard seed of Christian parable and offers "balm," "heal-all," "greatest among herbs." But the herb at *Trilogy*'s close is transplanted even further, for the crucifixion scene in section 11 has already troped upon the image of the flowering tree in its symbol of the cross bursting into vine and flower. So once again at *Trilogy*'s conclusion myrrh undergoes and signifies a transfer or eclipse: from Golgotha's ground to Bethlehem's; from "grave-edge" to "birthright" (F 35); and from metonymy (the flowering rood associated with Christ) to metaphor (the flowering rod as Mary's, and as her infant's, body).[73]

Most obviously, myrrh stands properly for, and/or improperly in the way of, the infant who should by all rights own and solely occupy the space between the Madonna's arms. Read as a reverent poetic sign for Christ, as a way of making new Him who makes all things new, the stalk of myrrh signifies the organic cycles that Christ, in his incarnated and resurrected forms, both exemplifies and transcends. Read more irreverently (as far as the Christian fathers would be concerned), but still as a clear figurative manifestation of a male god, the sheaf of myrrh "carries over" surviving ancient, esoteric fertility rites, as in Yeats's description in *A Vision* of the link between the birth of Christ and the death and resurrection of Dionysus:

Near that transition the women wailed him, and night showed the full moon separating from the constellation Virgo, with the star in the wheatsheaf, or in the child, for in the old maps she is represented carrying now one now the other.[74]

Carrying now one now the other: when *Trilogy*'s Mary/Virgo is charted onto this easygoing old map, her myrrh in no way signifies repudiation of the infant male god; rather, it simply manifests another version, a ritual and figurative transformation, of the body of the Holy Child.

But *Trilogy*'s Mary seems, almost certainly, to be stepping as well into or out of an unwritten map of the new, "not / the tome of ancient wisdom" (T 38). And her myrrh must be read also as a potential alternative to, not a signifier of, her usually requisite sacred and to-be-sacrificed son. *Trilogy*'s earlier dream vision in "Tribute to the Angels" of a Sophia/Madonna–like lady makes the case explicit—"the Lamb was not with her, / either as Bridegroom or Child"—as does the later *Sagesse*'s revision of this scene:

> but *Dieu Saveur* last night was manifest,
> the attribute of Seket and her hour,
>
> 1.20 while we sleep;
> no infant in the straw,
>
> but simply Mary's flower,
> "Marah" the *Grande Mer*, patron and protectress,
>
> sword-lilies on their stalks,
> Creatrice de la Foi . . .
>
>   (73)

In all these passages we find images of fertility without maternity, nativities opposed to pronatalism. Mary holds nothing but a sign of herself, since she herself, in "Flowering," section 16, gives her name as "Mary-myrrh." Displacing the child, uncoiling, the flowering myrrh signifies the plenitude, sufficiency, and power of a feminine identity which coincides with but does not consist solely or necessarily of maternity.[75] Nor is it an identity which consists necessarily of *virginity*, that other prerequisite of the Mother Mary's constitution; if the myrrh-jar, with its seal "unbroken," seems to signify chastity or freedom from violation, the nonetheless escaping scent and myrrh-in-full-bloom this Mary carries suggest a free state less intact and infolded. The jar is, as Duncan puts it, "a-jar somehow."[76] Not only an identity is figured here but also an erotics; the "bundle of myrrh" recalls the beloved of Song of Solomon: "a bundle of myrrh is my beloved to me." And not only an erotics but also a nonviolent, life-affirming, body-affirming *ethics*, something like the feminine and heretical *herethics* of Kristeva's vision, which Jacqueline Rose has eloquently summarized:

. . . while this may seem to come close to a history of oppressive discourses which have given to women as mothers the privilege of the ethical (and not a great deal else), for Kristeva *ethics* has nothing whatsoever to do with *duty* or the idea that women should people the race. No ethics *without* maternity, but not mothering as ethical *duty* or *role*: "The ethical which aims for a negativity is opposed to ethics understood as the observation of laws."[77]

H.D.'s Madonna-and-(not child) sequences, each an affirmation of conventional nurturing values hedged with qualifications, rebuttals, and uncertainties, each marked by a polysemous lily or myrrh sheaf that spills away from the famous mother's embrace, signal an ethics of maternity for a modern destructive world: a nativity meaningful only insofar as it is also a *negativity*.[78]

IV. Words Men Can Say for Us, or The Traffic in Myrrh

It is especially in the domain of war that we, the bearers of men's bodies, who supply its most valuable munition, who, not amid the clamour and ardour of battle, but singly, and alone, with a three-in-the-morning courage, shed our blood and face death that the battlefield may have its food, a food more precious to us than our heart's blood; it is we especially, who in the domain of war, have our word to say, a word that no man can say for us.

Olive Schreiner, *Women and Labour*[79]

Trilogy's myrrh signifies, of course, positively and assertively as well as negatively and by inversion. Certainly the "raw" myrrh which H.D.'s Mary gathers already prior to Kaspar's gift of his "cooked" salve represents, though in displaced form, some fresh, natural female force not only of childbirth but more generally of a feminine eros. A paean to Winifred Bryher written over a decade earlier, "Let Zeus Record," is suggestive here. That poem celebrates Bryher's 1919 rescue of H.D., who was abandoned, seriously ill, and close to the delivery of her daughter; it marks the crossing over of the threshold of their long relationship:

> yet when Love fell
>
> struck down with plague and war,
> you lay white myrrh-buds
> on the darkened lintel;
>
> you fastened blossom
> to the smitten sill;
> let Zeus record this,
> daring Death to mar.
>
> (*CP,* 284)

Whether in this earlier poem H.D. was imaginatively transforming Bryher's generosities into versions of the present of the Mage or whether Bryher actually performed this particular offering of the lover and the midwife is unclear. Either way, H.D.'s later scene of Kaspar's myrrh-tribute at the end of *Trilogy* rewrites this prior type as the New Testament rewrites the old, as the Magi recalled Sheba and before her the gift-bearing nymphs. Like Bryher, H.D. brought myrrh to myrrh.

But at the same time myrrh in *Trilogy* is emphatically a substance *made,* not born or simply gathered and garlanded. It is first and most importantly a word, a name, which the Magdalene applies to herself in her interview with Kaspar:

> I am Mary, she said, of Magdala,
> I am Mary, a great tower;
>
> through my will and my power,
> Mary shall be myrrh . . .
>
> (F 16)

Mary herself, through her will and her power, effects this metamorphosis into myrrh, not a higher god. Her self-baptism recalls in turn the dramatized high *poein* of "Tribute to the Angels"'s earlier incantatory exhibition of verbal alchemy:

> Now polish the crucible
> and in the bowl distill
>
> a word most bitter, *marah*,
> a word bitterer still, *mar*,
>
> sea, brine, breaker, seducer,
> giver of life, giver of tears;
>
> now polish the crucible
> and set the jet of flame
>
> under, till *marah-mar*
> are melted, fuse and join
>
> and change and alter . . .
>   (T 8)

If *myrrh*, then, arrives like the natural sign of the flowering tree in "Tribute," section 19 — "visible and actual, / beauty incarnate, / as no high-priest of Astoreth / could compel her" — it comes, too, compelled and coaxed along by the elaborate making of the woman-poet-as-alchemist.

At the same time, if *myrrh* seems to fulfill Olive Schreiner's desire for a sign or language which women alone would "have to say" about war, for a word-made-flesh from the crucible of the childbed which "no man can say for us," it also is a word men *can* say and all too often have. Kaspar's myrrh in "Flowering" is, after all, a product whose formula has passed down by hereditary right from one generation of male artisans to another.[80] (Traditionally, the historian of spices Marcel Detienne tells us, myrrh-makers were forbidden contact with women while they harvested the crop.[81]) When a woman poet goes after those patriarchal goods, she may find herself trading, like Julia translating Greek in *Bid Me To Live*, in "the myrrh of the dead spirit," taking "the old manner of approach . . . as toward hoarded treasure, but treasure that passed through too many hands" (*BML*, 162).[82] It would be difficult to overemphasize the extent to which the particular word "myrrh" itself exemplified for H.D. this kind of depreciated, too extensively disseminated currency. It signified a common coinage generally "bruited about" in the modernist marketplace. But it also functioned specifically as a counter all too often handed over in what must have felt like direct exchange, in literature, much of it overtly war related, written by famous male modernists — texts which she could hardly fail to read as addressed to her or as transactions which concerned her personally.

To interpret this modernist trafficking in the sign "myrrh" as exclusively masculine, or H.D.'s part in it solely as autobiographical response, would be to perpetuate a wrongful misreading of her work. "The Flowering of the Rod" asks us to read myrrh as in its best manifestation the token in a gift economy which Christmas is meant to exemplify, one which abandons "purse and script" (F 12), changes the marketplace, and includes women in its circuits as both givers and receivers, not just interchangeable givens. The myrrh scene seeks a strong revision, therefore, of systems of exchange which make up wars, transforming the usual martial exchanges of information, of fire (it takes heat to make myrrh), and of women as no more than property or symbols.[83] *Trilogy* is deliberately ambiguous about whether these valid interchanges are part of the lost past, or have always been actual and possible, or are now in the process of reforming, or are future ideals. One thing is clear, however: the Magdalene herself barters and makes offers within these systems. And H.D. herself, as some of her diaries show, read the particular invocations of myrrh by male modernists which I will now discuss as reciprocal exchanges, seeing them as written *after* her as well as written *at* her, in a complex web of appropriations and affiliations.

Pound

Take, for instance, her representation in her late memoir *End to Torment* (1958) of herself as woman reader, reading modernism, fascism, war, Ezra Pound. Beginning "I have only lately dared to try to read through the *Cantos*," the passage initially portrays reading as a painful process of sorting through a "rubble heap." This debris consists at once of Pound's uneven, difficult verse lines, of the intricate postwar legal briefs against him, and of the wreckage left behind by his fascism, by "my actual war experience," and by her long ago broken engagements with "Ezra." When the task becomes overwhelming and the reader "dazed and dizzy," suddenly "some of my own lines came to me and laid the ghost, as it were." Which lines these were is unspecified, but a clue comes further down the page, at the moment in which the salvage of the *Cantos* for and by this reader is enacted. Seeing, as for the viewer of Dreyer's *Jeanne D'Arc*, is difficult, but the *sound* of the words allows a breakthrough.

I could not see clearly but I could *hear* clearly, as I read, "M'elevasti/ out of Erebus." I could at last accept the intoxication of "Kuthera sempiterna" and the healing of "Myrrh and olibanum on the altar stone / giving perfume."[84]

In this generous and at the same time rapacious passage H.D. recuperates Pound by reading his *Cantos*, in effect, as if they were in the end a tale of a jar or jars, as if they were at this moment in the line of, were themselves, her *Trilogy*.

A later moment in *End to Torment* spells out the complexities of this exchange of myrrh in more detail. It starts with a meditation on "writing down" as a way of "putting up all your defenses against" what Erich Heydt, her current analyst, calls "impopery, impropery or improperty" and H.D., the native English speaker, names "impropriety." From there the passage moves into consideration of writing's violations of property and propriety:

The *Chronicle* spoke of Ezra collecting, appropriating, stealing lines and phrases . . . and building a nest like a magpie. It asserted, however, that the effect was astonishing and "make it new" had vitalized a host of lesser satellites. I tell this to Erich but I explain that I feel the process is that of a Phoenix, rather than that of a magpie. There is fragrance. What did he write? "Myrrh and olibanum"? I said, "You catch fire or you don't catch fire." (*ET*, 46)

Here again hide teasing allusions to *Trilogy* and behind it to entire systems of esoteric mythology. The phoenix is a Greek transposition of the *bennu* bird of Egyptian myth and "The Walls Do Not Fall," section 25. "Bird of the sun as well as of spices," writes Marcel Detienne, the phoenix "always possesses myrrh and frankincense, using them to build its nest . . . and finally being consumed on the pyre that it has built by heaping together perfumed substances of all kinds" (*ET*, 30). The phoenix solves the problem of the magpie, theft, through metamorphosis and miracle, and therefore offers a model of a poetic genius which is more than propriety, a poetic jubilation.

This jubilation prompts a different kind of jubilate: the open fantasy of figuratively having Ezra's baby, "Christo Re, Dio Sole." Simultaneously, the figure of the magpie — transgressive, indebted, inappropriate — rises once more from the ashes of the phoenix to confront this woman poet. Frankly examining the constellation of anxieties and desires which attends the female disciple placed in the position of "lesser satellite," she queries, "What am I hiding? . . . Am I stealing, have I stolen?" The final question in this diary entry, however, once again slyly asserts the possibility of a proper, unappropriated, central female authority at Bethlehem: "Is my own magpie nest a manger?" The manger, too, is a place where myrrh is brought, phoenixlike, to bearing. Perhaps it is the place where the desire to have the master's offspring may be fulfilled. But the male mentor himself might also be the one who stands at the margins of the poetic miracle, excluded and protesting — as H.D. writes that Pound objected at her daughter's birth — "My only real criticism is that this is not my child" (*ET*, 30).

Of course, suspecting the self and others of the magpie's crime, plagiarism or unoriginality, is an activity by no means limited to H.D. or women writers. Keeping within the bounds of Bethlehem mythology, we might, for instance, cite the argument Charles Olson made to Pound against Eliot in 1947, over who properly owns a Madonna. On a postcard of the Gloucester Notre Dame, Olson accuses Eliot of stealing in his "The Dry Salvages" from Olson himself: "Here is my Lady that Possum stole. Best dead Madonna this side Atlantic." Or we might rephrase: "My only real criticism is that this is *my* mother." Robert Duncan, interestingly, suggests that Eliot's sea-Madonna reworks H.D.'s in her early poem "The Shrine," in which case her "Lady" might be read as the *Grand Mer* of them all.[85]

Phoenix or magpie, theft or transformation, spice-kindling or war-rubble: the question of which modern poetry, hers in particular, will comprise and whose shrine it will be was a live one centered on myrrh for H.D. reading Pound in 1958, but not much more so than it must have been for her reading Pound in 1905. In the very early "Hilda's Book" written, hand-bound, and sewn in vellum for H.D. by Pound in 1907, the dedicatory poem "I strove a little book to make for her" expresses the hope that "all . . . wold smells subtle as far-wandered myrrh / Should be as burden to my own heart's song" (*ET*, 69). In one poem among these many others that address an iconic "Saint Hilda," she is even called upon to act as a kind of Mage-in-the-house in order to bring her poet lover into line:

> Thou that spellest ever gold from out my dross
> Mage powerful and subtly sweet
> Gathering fragments that there be no loss
> Behold the brighter gains lie at my feet.
>
> (*ET*, 71)

In this context, "myrrh" might well have operated across the decades of the twentieth century for H.D. as a quintessential sign of the bittersweet gifts of a modernism she helped, with Pound, to make. On the one hand, this Mage gathering and integrating fragments prophetically presages the verbal alchemies of H.D.'s own *Trilogy*. On the other, "Hilda's Book" as gift of myrrh firmly places its recipient in the role of the passive and specularized lady, the best dead Madonna, who proves where the gains lie first and properly: at the male poet's own feet.[86]

Aldington

Pound was not the only male figure whom H.D. had watched bringing offerings of poetic myrrh in her early years. In the roman à clef *Bid Me To Live*, the H.D. character's husband Rafe/Richard Aldington is said to be writing "hyacinth / myrrh poetry . . . a love-and-war sequence" (*BML*, 95) for Bella, his mistress, when he comes home on leave from the trenches. These poems have their actual counterparts in Aldington's work. In texts written by H.D.'s husband during or shortly after the Great War (and during the breakup of their marriage), "war" and "myrrh" merge and diverge in ways which after twenty years still bear directly on the plots of *Trilogy*.

Aldington organized his early poems along a thematic divide which he demonstrated structurally in 1919, sorting his poems into two separate volumes to indicate a cleft at the heart of imagism: *Images of War, Images of Desire*. Myrrh abounds in these texts, as do Marys, but not side by side. Since, as I have already pointed out, Aldington's "images of war" frequently involve heavily ironized crucifixion scenes and place their soldiers on the site of Golgotha, it is not surprising that amidst the skull-heaps scorn heaps upon the four Maries. In a typical example, "An Old Song," a Mary we will recognize is rebuffed and in her stead the poem praises another unnamed lady, who is "not clothed in sad / Raiment like Mary" and whose eyes are "not tear-rimmed / Like those of Mary." The other woman's eyes dim "only with love . . . / When she kisses me," and the poem's action consists of the dramatized choice of her eros over the Christian model of maternal grief: "By God, though she be God's mother, / I care not for Mary, / Only to serve this other."[87] Within the thematic schema of Aldington's early work, it is not farfetched to read the poem as an exorcism of the credulous Pietà-as-image-of-war in favor of a rebellious woman-as-image-of-desire outside the law (with a corresponding repudiation of the maternal in favor of the "other" erotic). Biblical mythology's "other," non-maternal Mary fares no better. The high-pitched "Blood of The Young Men," for instance, includes this stanza:

> O these pools and ponds of blood . . .
> Blood of the young men, blood of their bodies . . .
> Poured out to cover the lips of Magdalen,
> Magdalen who loves not, whose sins are loveless.
> O this steady drain of the weary bodies . . .
> The exquisite indifference of women.[88]

At best hysterical, at worst ghoulish and vampirish, indifferent, one Mary in Aldington's book of war is as much to blame as the other.

In sharp relief against the discourse of war in which Mary's name is always implicated, however, stands Aldington's discourse of desire, the way of that "other lady," whose name, when it is said at all, means *myrrh* or "not-Mary." A hetaera of spices, she represents a system of relationships and allocations of power which could pull a man away from war, from history, and from a compulsively destructive masculinity rather than impelling him inexorably toward them. In Aldington's book of prose poems *The Love of Myrrhine and Konallis* (1926), *Myrrh*ine is so entirely removed from heterosexual and "heterosocial" power relations that she exists in a separate lesbian space, but one which abuts always on the war poems which lurk across the border of her lyrics. As a Sapphic-stylized heroine, Myrrhine proffers what Susan Gubar, in a related context, has called "the flagrant fragrance of Continental eroticism . . . the lexicon of scents, the syntax of flowers, the sign language of fingers on the flesh."[89]

Gubar contrasts these "voluptuous" Sapphic lyrics of Aldington's with those many written by H.D. at around the same time which, she argues, more combatively and anxiously address "the contradiction for the woman poet between artistic vocation and female socialization."[90] But I would emphasize that Aldington uses his own "sapphistries" to address an intensive contradiction of his own — the conflict for the male poet between artistic vocation and masculine military socialization. It is a contradiction emblematized by the two poles of relation to Mary (in the Judeo-Christian role of manly sacrificing soldier) or to Myrrhine (in the Hellenic role of feminized voyeur or of the sensual girl himself). And it is a contradiction emblematized by myrrh and its opposites. On the one hand, we find the langorous myrrh-posing of Aldington's "Reaction" in *Myrrhine* (written, significantly, in an "Officer's Camp, Fressin, 1918): "Ah! To retain this fragrance, to make permanent this most precious of essences, this mingling of suave and acrid perfumes — something wild and tender and perverse and immortal! . . . I will make for myself . . . an Aphrodite . . . and in her hand shall be a perfume ball sweet with this divine fragrance." On the other hand we find, in the immediately following pages, a representation of an attack of phosgene gas.[91]

When the fantasized anti-Mary, the myrrh-bearing woman, turns her erotic attentions to the man in Aldington's Great War poems, a catastrophic disruption of the homosocial phosgene-circuits of war occurs, as in "Prayer":

> She touches me with her hands
> And I am faint with beauty.
> Therefore I am not willing to die
> Since she needs me.
> For her sake I would betray my comrades . . .
>
> (*C*, 138)

She touches me with her hands. If we let myrrh lead us back to Golgotha rather than, as Aldington wants, away from it (and back, eventually, to

Trilogy in turn), this phrase might suggest to us two critical and poten-
tially opposed passages in Biblical narrative: Mary's anointing of Christ's
feet (in H.D.'s version, with myrrh) in the house of Simon the leper or
Simon the Pharisee, touching him with her hands, and the countermo-
ment when Christ, whom she has witnessed risen from the tomb, warns
her now decisively *not* to touch him.

Owen

That warning is a common command in modern war/Golgotha poetry,
far more frequent than reversals of it like Aldington's. In Wilfred Owen's
brilliant "Greater Love" (1917), for instance, the mechanisms that Alding-
ton's lyrics of desire dream of sabotaging remain in full coercive gear; the
love of military comrades is the only remaining good; and Christ's *Noli
me tangere* is brandished as the motto of exclusion, warning and admoni-
tion to the Magdalene who is Everywoman. This particular *Noli me tangere*
might be said to define the voice of the dominant modern soldier's antiwar
poem in much the same way as Golgotha marks its site, for voice here
manages, powerfully and remarkably, to erode the doctrine of Christian
Passion with a fierce graphic irony at the same time as it capitalizes upon
it for all its eulogistic force:

Greater Love

Red lips are not so red
    As the stained stones kissed by the English dead.
Kindness of wooed and wooer
Seems shame to their love pure.
O Love, your eyes lose lure
    When I behold eyes blinded in my stead!

Your slender attitude
    Trembles not exquisite like limbs knife-skewed . . .

Your dear voice is not dear . . .
    As theirs whom none now hear,
    Now earth has stopped their piteous mouths that coughed . . .

And though your hand be pale,
Paler are all which trail
Your cross through flame and hail:
    Weep, you may weep, for you may touch them not.[92]

What this voice does to biblical narrative in its final lines — at once un-
doing and unleashing it — is prepared for by its earlier manipulation of the
blazon. Nothing like "My mistress' eyes are nothing like . . . ," this cata-

logue repeats in every stanza its flight from any matrix of heterosexual praise and into a homosocial milieu—a scene then further, compulsively, "knife-skewed" and twisted into the no-man's-land of death in war. More than any hope of masculine rebirth, the last lines resurrect in that compact, sinister phrase "your cross" an absolute accusation of female guilt. "In John's Gospel," writes Marguerite Waller, "Christ says *Noli me tangere* not to signify that he is . . . not available or accessible to Mary Magdalene, but to warn her that the situation is one of ambiguity and transience."[93] In Owen's "gospel," which is followed by no Revelation, no qualifications modify the final refusal of the woman's touch. Punitive, fastidious, remote, this Christ/not-Christ turns John's gentle inquiry—"Woman, why weepest thou? Who seekest thou?"—into coercive permission, even to a demand, for women's tears, words as enraged and alienated as the prohibition against touching.[94] In its gleeful anguish at the rules it enforces, it might be read as a voice of masculine *père-version*. Let me make very clear that this *"père-version"* as I invoke it here has nothing to do with the category "sexual perversion," nor with the poem's homoerotic strain; it lies not in "desire for men" but in what Kristeva calls "the desire of the law as desire of reproduction and continuity." No transience here, except the most continuous, unmitigated, and agonized of masculine crossings away from, and on account of, women; and no ambiguity here that is not impasse.

In a poem written in 1915, before he joined the army in active service, Owen had contrasted two kinds of women. Most women, the poem argued, "Live this difficult life / Merely in order not to die the death / . . . Accepting backyards, travail, crusts, all naif; / And nothing greatly love. . . . " A few women, though, "seemingly"—but only seemingly—"forget / That men build walls to shelter from the wet." These women live in a world not of crusts and travail but of glamour and embellishment; they "dress to show their lace; suppose the earth for gardens; hands for nard." The sonnet ends: "Now which you hold as higher than the other / Depends, in fine, on whether you regard / The poetess as nobler than the Mother."[95] The tone and stance here are unclear, but one thing seems certain: from the trenches both feminine positions as the poem defines them would appear equally problematic for Owen. Neither the mother incapable of greater love (a kind of "mother Mary") nor the poetess who sought a sheltered garden and who offered a nard which was just one more frill (a kind of "other" Mary) could claim nobility in any way in which that term might matter.

Lawrence

Tracking these Marys and myrrhs, these intertextual "treasures that passed through too many hands" toward *Trilogy*, we need to attend to one other prior *Noli me tangere* of the corpus of modernism which, the records show, H.D. took personally. The text is Lawrence's fictional version of Golgotha and its aftermaths, *The Man Who Died* (1928, 1931). Like Aldington's constellation of Mary/Myrrhine poems and Owen's address to the Magdalene, *The Man Who Died* is structured around a rhetorical pattern which by now will begin to seem constant, a schema we might call the "Greater Love" plot. In each of these works there is, in the explicit or implicit context of a war, a *y* love and an *x* love. One term is privileged, one degraded, so that *y* is greater than *x*. The weeping "Mary" of Golgotha invariably occupies the denigrated position. But her figurative blandishments and seductions, frequently encapsulated in her jar of nard or myrrh-ointment, can separate from her and circulate to either side of the equation, depending on whether the text's designs are to recuperate some other version of an exciting feminine-outside-war or to repudiate an inciting feminine-in-war categorically. In Aldington's verses the opposing terms are linked to two different archeologies or cultural traditions, Sapphic lyric and biblical narrative, and all the avenues of transience and ambiguity in Lawrence's novel, too, depend on the difference between two civilizations, the Judeo-Christian and the Egyptian. In Lawrence's version, to put it simply, greater love hath no Mary than the priestess and courtesan of Isis.

Earlier in this chapter I quoted Lawrence's objections to both the "fatuous" appeals to a safe Bethlehem and the "womanless" obsession with a past crucifixion which he saw as the two schools which dominated the post–Great War thinking of his (and H. D.'s) generation. *The Man Who Died* presents the third obvious alternative in biblical war narrative, resurrection. Its plot begins with a wounded Christ, taken down from the cross too soon, who escapes from the tomb in which he is buried alive. When he encounters the Magdalene, here called Madeleine, in a rehearsal of the canonical scene in the garden, his insistence that she not touch him is represented as a perversity within a system of perversities and therefore as both harmful and imperative. Something sickens him — a "flicker of triumph" in Madeleine's eyes, her "greed of giving" and need to cast him, inexorably, as her savior — and warns him to look "on the world with repulsion, dreading its mean contacts" (26, 34).

If this shuddering nausea is a danger symptom of what we might now call post-traumatic stress disorder, it is also the crucial survival strategy of a soldier still in hand-to-hand combat, who at all costs must prevent himself from being captured by the enemy. In order to be cured, he must be touched — but not by the hands and ointment of the adversary Magdalene. Lawrence's Christ-no-more finds his way to a different woman, a priestess of Isis; and in her temple, with "all his flesh . . . still woven with pain and the wild commandment: *Noli me tangere!* . . . Oh, don't touch me," he learns to overcome his fear: "Shall I give myself into this touch? Men have tortured me to death with their touch. Yet this girl of Isis has a tender flame of healing" (46).

The priestess has been saving herself, as Lawrence tells us "rare women" do, for a "re-born man," not throwing herself away on a common man "in the Roman spell, assertive, manly, splendid apparently, but of an inward meanness, an inadequacy" (39). She anoints the returned antihero with oil in a scene whose center of mystery and revelation lies in its own difference from that earlier biblical application of "spikenard." He realizes that the Magdalene had washed his feet with tears, wiped them with her hair, and poured precious ointment upon him *prior* to any injury to him, as if to encourage and ensure his future crucifixion, to induce him to Golgotha; that she did not love him but only, still in the terms of a prostitute, wanted to serve him; and that he in turn had participated in this system of suicidal prostitution, offering them "only the corpse of my love . . . They murdered me, but I lent myself to murder" (56).

Madeleine, that is, comes to bury the Christ, but the Priestess of Isis comes to raise him; and because, as a Priestess of Isis, she knows a great deal about the importance of reconstructing the missing phallus, and because this is a novel by D. H. Lawrence, that rebirth takes the form, as Janice Robinson neatly puts it, of "an erection in the Resurrection (or, conversely, a resurrection in the erection)," [96] and results in the Priestess's pregnancy. To the extent — and I would argue that the extent is broad — that this fable invites reading as a Great War novel, the resurrection might be said to signify the possibility of a masculinity demilitarized through the spiritually sensuous touch of a woman who knows that real men didn't need to lend themselves to the war.

"This is Isis lore," Lawrence wrote in a draft of the second part of the novel, "which Isis women forever understand and only they . . . the Marys do not know it, none of the four Marys . . . But Isis knew, long ago, and Isis women know today" (125). "I read myself into the story," H.D. wrote in 1955 of *The Man Who Died*.[97] But onto which side of the Isis/Magdalene divide, then, into which half of this split feminine figure, did she read herself?

In a series of emphatic *readings-into* written at various stages, and particularly in dairy entries which record her conflicted responses to her old relationship with Lawrence during her psychoanalysis with Freud in 1933, she repeatedly cites the authority of her friend Stephen Guest to locate herself categorically in the position of the greater lover, the Isis priestess who is antiMagdalene.

"I wasn't fair but I could hardly cope with his enormous novels," she begins her discussion of Lawrence in a passage which like her myrrh-reading of Pound establishes her initially as a burdened, inadequate, and angry reader. Here, too, a breakthrough occurs:

. . . *The Man Who Died?*
I don't remember it, I don't think of it . . . it came too late.
I don't mean that.
I have carefully avoided coming to terms with Lawrence . . .
But there was this last Lawrence . . .
I don't want to think of Lawrence . . . (*TF*, 134)

Stephen Guest brought me a copy of *The Man Who Died*. He said, "Did you know that you are the priestess of Isis in this book?" (TF, 141)

Whether or not he meant me as the priestess of Isis in that book does not alter the fact that his last book reconciled me to him. (TF, 149–50)

Stephen Guest insisted that H.D. was this Isis. I read myself into the story. [98]

Stephen Guest's interpretation, one H.D. desired (in the context of the barrage against the Marys I have been tracing, who would not?), rapidly establishes itself in certain circles as a privileged and canonical biographical gloss of *The Man Who Died* and the text of the Lawrence/H.D. relationship. Janice Robinson, for instance, footnotes her assertion that "Lawrence's references to Isis in his writing were veiled references to H.D." with a chain of scribal authorities leading inevitably back to Guest: Robinson states that Professor Kenneth Fields states that Professor Irwin Swerdlow says that Stephen Guest's report is "very likely true."[99]

We know, however, that in Vienna in 1933 H.D. was also reading, with much excitement and disturbance, Aldous Huxley's edition of Lawrence's letters, and that one of those letters, addressed in 1917 to Cecil Gray (who would shortly thereafter become H.D.'s lover) at the height of Lawrence's involvement with H.D., writes her into the position of a Magdalene. Gray and Lawrence were apparently immersed in a debate about the interpretation of myrrh:

You are only half right about the disciples and the alabaster box. If Jesus had paid more attention to Magdalene, and less to his disciples, it would have been better.

It was not the ointment-pouring which was so devastating, but the discipleship of the twelve. . . .

Take away the subservience and feet-washing, and the pure understanding between Magdalene and Jesus went deeper than that between the disciples and Jesus. . . . But Jesus himself was frightened of the knowledge which subsisted between the Magdalene and him, knowledge deeper than the knowledge of Christianity and "good," deeper than love, anyhow. . . .

As for spikenard, if I chance to luxuriate in it, it is by the way; not so very Phillippically filthy either. Not that it matters. . . .

And my "women," Esther Andrews, Hilda Aldington, etc. represent, in an impure and unproud, subservient, cringing, bad fashion, I admit—but represent none the less the threshold of a new world, or underworld, of knowledge and being. . . . my "women" want an ecstatic subtly-intellectual underworld, like the Greeks—Orphicism—like Magdalene at her feet-washing—and there you are.[100]

Here the media of the Magdalene—an ointment, alabaster box, foot-washing—slide in meaning, at some points into Isis-like signs of deep knowledge, ecstacy, subtlety, and sexy intellect, at others into the denigrated place they will occupy in the later *Man Who Died* (impure, unproud, subservient, cringing, bad). The slipperiness of this ointment might permit, for H.D. as the later reader of this letter, a potential closing of the gap between the figural work of the Magdalene and that of Isis. The explicit naming of H.D. ("Hilda Aldington") as Magdalene, however, must to some extent have countered those gains for her as reader, threatening to fix her too firmly on the wrong side of the binary scheme to which *The Man Who Died*'s last repudiating word adhered.[101] I suspect, therefore, that she read herself into, and, much more importantly, read the category *woman* into, both poles of Lawrence's logic at once.[102]

H.D.'s Marys respond in direct and obvious, and to a certain extent autobiographically charged, ways to *The Man Who Died* and Aldington's early war poems, and they enter argumentatively into the discursive field of Golgotha in war poetry which Owen's stringent *Noli me tangere* guards and represents. But *Trilogy* does not simply react to the configurations of a prior masculine modernism and canon of war poetry. H.D., in the earlier stages of her career, had worked to create and shape both those traditions. She read *The Man Who Died*, for instance, as at least a joint project with and perhaps influenced by, if not even scandalously indebted to, her own early version of biblical narrative, *Pilate's Wife*, and she understood both texts to be part of a larger context than a reductively autobiographical one, citing an important earlier precursor novel with the same plot by George Moore.[103]

Trafficking in myrrh, she revised a canon composed, as much as by anything else, by previous texts she herself had written. *Trilogy's* myrrh, which originated, Kaspar speculates, in a year when the trees from which it is culled were "mortally torn, / when the sudden frost came," recalls the lyric flower catalogues and herb ceremonies, at once ecstatic and painful, in her earlier poems and, back further, the bruised and marred sea flowers of the earliest poems in *Sea Garden*. And behind those flowers, as Aldington's Lesbos-lyrics have already suggested, lies a tradition of female lyric work. It is, after all, Sappho who first polished the crucible of this myth, naming the Myrrha of later Ovidian mythology for the first time *Myrrha* and giving her name to myrrh.[104]

V. The Double Code of Myrrh

For H.D. terms are either duplicit or complicit, the warp and woof of a loom.
Robert Duncan, from the *H.D. Book*[105]

Joseph. He has stretched out his little hand and grasped the bundle of myrrh . . .

Mary. Do they not embalm the dead with myrrh? See now, you sorrowful king, my son has taken your sorrows for his own.

Joseph. Myrrh is for love also; as Solomon writes in his song: A bundle of myrrh is my beloved unto me.
(Dorothy Sayers, from the nativity scene in
The Man Born To Be King, 1941)[106]

I rose to open to my beloved; and my hands dropped with
myrrh, and my fingers with sweet-smelling myrrh, upon
the handles of the lock.
I opened to my beloved; but my beloved had withdrawn
himself, and was gone: my soul failed when he spake:
I sought him, but I could not find him; I called him,
but he gave me no answer.
The watchmen that went about the city found me, they
smote me, they wounded me; the keepers of the walls
took away my veil from me.
Song of Sol. 5: 5–7

We must take as our starting point the myrrh tree whose
form its namesake, Myrrha, adopts, and whose excep-
tional fruit bears the name Adonis . . . the status of spices,
the function of perfumes: these are the problems and ques-
tions by means of which the botanical code that il-
luminates the whole of this mythology can be deciphered.
Marcel Detienne, *Gardens of Adonis*[107]

Let us come back to the place-of-a-skull and to all those who fashion
it. What does it mean to name a feminine self "Mary-myrrh" on or near
this ground? It means first of all to cross, and to cross out, the "greater
love" divide. As the dialogue between Sayers's Joseph and Mary suggests,
the sign *myrrh* fuses death and birth, sorrow and eros, war and peace,
sacrifice and redemptive love, in one grand providential cycle.[108] More-
over, myrrh fuses classical, Hebraic, Christian, and Egyptian mythology.
Gathered traditionally at the rising of Sirius — the star form of Isis, "whose
rising in the East just before dawn heralded the annual inundation and
the rebirth of vegetation"[109] — myrrh correlates faith with faith, recovers
that secret of Isis in "Walls Do Not Fall" (section 40):

> there was One
>
> in the beginning, Creator,
> Fosterer, Begetter, the Same-Forever
>
> in the papyrus-swamp
> in the Judean meadow.

Trilogy foregrounds the Marys denigrated in the other versions of the
"Greater Love" plot I have traced. But at the same time the text is shot
through with myriad, intricate strands of Isis imagery, sometimes sub-
merged, sometimes ecstatically revealed, right to the end where the myrrh
which Mary has already gathered at Bethlehem hints of Isis's star. It is
not coincidental that the interpretation of myrrh plays a significant part
in Edmund Leach's recent structuralist reading of the New Testament, and
behind it the Moses story, as two "complicated transformations" of the
Isis-Osiris-Horus legend. Leach traces the connections between "Mary
(Miriam) the Virgin Mother of Jesus," the composite figure of Mary of
Magdala/Bethany, "Miriam, the Virgin Sister of Moses," Astoroth and
"the archetypal figure of Isis who manages to be mother, sister, wife,
daughter all at once."[110] Myrrh was brought to Bethlehem as the original
Christening or primal coronation gift, carried to the tomb in Jerusalem
to wrap into Jesus' shroud, but used traditionally, as the Canticles suggest,
as an aphrodisiac and in bridal ceremonies. It thus becomes for Leach,
and for H.D. in the tradition of interpretation before him, the emblem of
this "all-at-onceness," linking the reduplicating figures and structures of
a variety of cultural narratives and belief systems in a single complex Isis-
centered whole.

At the same time as she rejects the opposition and division of myths,
"Mary-myrrh" rejects the binary partition of women in the "greater love"

scenario. Naming herself, she challenges the hierarchy of value which elects one (Aldington's dream-woman Myrrhine, Lawrence's priestess of Isis) as the greater lover, and scapegoats an other. The doubling hyphen in her name enacts H.D.'s Mary's self-conscious crossing, her refusing, of that breach.[111]

But if the suffix myrrh seals rifts between, it also exposes rifts within cultures and women. Who is this Mary, on her way to anointing Christ just before his crucifixion? Her namesakes suggest a conflicting heritage and a conflicted present social practice. On the one hand, the text tells us specifically, she calls herself after the Ovidian Myrrha:

> I am Mary — O, there are Marys a-plenty,
> (though I am Mara, bitter) I shall be Mary-myrrh;
>
> I am that myrrh-tree of the gentiles,
> the heathen; there are idolaters,
>
> even in Phrygia and Cappadocia,
> who kneel before mutilated images
>
> to burn incense to the Mother of Mutilations,
> to Attis-Adonis-Tammuz and his mother who was myrrh;
>
> she was a stricken woman,
> having borne a son in unhallowed fashion;
>
> she wept bitterly till some heathen god
> changed her to a myrrh-tree;
>
> I am Mary, I will weep bitterly,
> bitterly . . . bitterly.
>
> (F 16)

To be Mary-Myrrha is to be Mary still, with a vengeance. It is to baptize oneself into tears, as the tearful one: Mary of Sorrows and Mutilations. Consider the Ovidian account of Myrrha, the mother of Adonis. Myrrha falls desperately in love with her royal father Cinryas; she arranges to sleep with him repeatedly, each time hiding her identity from him. Soon she becomes pregnant. When Cinryas discovers that his lover is his own daughter, she flees from his murderous rage and, after praying to the gods, is rescued by metamorphosing into a myrrh tree — a pregnant myrrh tree. In labor, the bark of the tree strains, cracks, and finally splits to release the infant Adonis, who is washed in his mother's tears. "Yet still she weeps, and warm drops flow from the tree," the drops of the essence myrrh. Adonis grows up to be lover of Venus, but dies (an antitype of Christ) when he is wounded in the groin by a boar; hence Myrrha is "Mother of Mutilations," as if she gives unhallowed birth not only to the son who will be mutilated but to the structure of mutilation itself.[112]

The powerfully explanatory formulation which comes down from Ovid, myrrh = tears (with H.D.'s additional parsing, Mary = myrrh = tears), suggests one disturbing reading of the substance the Magdalene carries to the banquet; it is a kind of lachrymatory agent, like tear gas. Anointing Christ with it, Mary-Myrrha might be said to prepare him, and herself, for their parts in the agony to come: him for mutilation and burial, herself for grieving. She embalms him in advance, makes him a premature mummy. In this way she is not unlike the Great War women H.D. described in her early novel *Asphodel*, who make bandages and talk "as if they were enjoying it . . . O God, don't they see what they're making them for?"[113] Mary-Myrrha, rather than escaping from the place-of-a-skull, makes it up, as a mother or a lover makes a bed. She answers Lawrence's and Aldington's briefs against encrypting, voyeuristic, necrophiliac Marys not by denying them but by exploring in her own voice the partial truth in the allegations, meditating on women's substantial role in encouraging and sustaining war as sacrificial practice.

As a mythological antitype of Mary the mother, however, Myrrha also lays bare structures of violence *against* women and in women's own lives not in evidence in Aldington's or Lawrence's or Owen's representations of Mary's part in the blood sacrifice. To read the Virgin Mary as a version of Myrrha is to expose currents not only of incestuous desires (the virgin daughter *wants* to coil up with her Father and bear his child) but also of patriarchal rage. There is nothing beatific about the birth of Adonis; he emerges wrackingly, violently, like myrrh itself, which was traditionally gathered by men who slashed the trees with axes as Detienne, in *Gardens of Adonis* tells us, "at the places where the bark, being very thin and distended, seemed to be most swollen with sap" (6). To be *Myrrha* is to uncover, then, a violent feminine desire for the patriarchal law (represented by that ultimate form of *père*-version, father-daughter incest) and a sadistic punishment of women by and under the law.[114]

But Mary-myrrh hides within her name another matronymic, one which uncovers, rather, women's potential active freedom from and resistance to the law of war. Aldington has already given us her name, *Myrrhine*. Where she shows up in classical literature, scholars sometimes link her to another aspect of Myrrha — the effective seductress who gives birth to Adonis, to Venus's archetypal lover and the charmed antithesis of the warrior hero. To be Mary of this myrrh is to have a name "as ointment poured forth," as in the Song of Solomon. It is to claim myrrh not as tears or as the incense of sacrifice but as the spice of erotic rite, the perfume of choice in the Canticles, in Sappho's garden of Aphrodite, and in every liminal "place of seclusion," as Eileen Gregory puts it, "where intense desire is felt."[115] To be Mary-myrrh(ine) is to be Mary-Isis, or, simply, to affirm the "sensuous principle of Mary Magdalene"[116] herself. Applying myrrh, this Mary suspends the lure of war, orchestrating a festive ritual whose design, either through transforming or entirely resisting sacrifice, is rebirth, resurrection.[117]

The naming of Myrrh(ine) in Mary resists all versions in war literature of the *Noli me tangere*. It does not do so by suggesting naively that all that is needed to heal men's wounds, to quell wars attributed solely to men, is woman's touch (the violences of Myrrha, still tightly and emphatically encoded in the name, ward this off). Rather, it exposes the misogyny of any myth of war which renders womens' relations with male combatants as categorically malignant; and it underscores the futility of any antiwar myth which reinforces the social segregation of genders structurally enforced in most versions of militarist ideology. Both Mary plots in *Trilogy* move toward the same matrix, a moment in which some version of Christ's body is touched, must be touched, by a woman's hands.

I have already shown how this moment is both valorized and disrupted when the central Mary is maternal. But what about the Magdalene, the figure for whom the erotic "Myrrhine" is antitype? We might expect, in the place of the *Noli me tangere*, a reactionary heterosexual economy. We might expect, for instance, that the Magdalene's myrrh anointment of Christ would embody, in its high value, the "relations between the sexes" Lévi-Strauss so infamously rhapsodized as surviving forms of "that affective richness, ardour and mystery which doubtless originally permeated the entire universe of human communications."[118] But this is not exactly what we get in *Trilogy*, which pays scant explicit attention to the actual scene—and none at all to the actual event—of the anointment. If *Trilogy* gestures toward this "affective richness," it also strongly ironizes such conceptions (think of Mary Magdalene's struggles in Kaspar's marketplace), much along the lines of Gayle Rubin's reply to Lévi-Strauss, in which she accuses him of presenting "one of the greatest rip-offs of all time as the root of romance."[119]

The "original" Myrrhine knows quite a bit about this rip-off, and carries, along with her eros, a fund of critical skepticism about and outrageous, balmy mockery of the systems of exchange which Lévi-Strauss describes. Her text is the great male-authored master text of feminine pacifism in Western culture, Aristophanes' *Lysistrata*. Early on in *Lysistrata*, the question of women's power in war systems is phrased as a question about ointments and scents — "What good can we poor women do. . . . We who sit indoors, perfumed" — to which Lysistrata replies, "These are the very things . . . the paints and perfumes — which I hope are going to save us . . . So that never again in our lifetime will man lift up a hostile spear against a fellow man, put on a shield or draw a sword."[120] This aromatic agency is illustrated when the Athenian women's program for stopping the Peloponnesian war, withholding their sexual favors from men, refusing their usual role as wives till it ends, produces a scene between one military man, Kinesias, and his wife, one Myrrhine. Myrrhine's comic strategy of war resistance involves sexually arousing her husband in order to make her final refusal of him all the more effective, and her most frustrating form of teasing takes the form of rubbing him with a perfumed ointment — presumably, as her name implies, with myrrh. (Unlike Lawrence's priestess of Isis, this woman calls up the phallus in order to rebuff and debunk it.) Myrrh stands in *Lysistrata*, then, for an eroticized exchange between a woman and a man which undoes war, by temporarily undoing, first, conventional patriarchal structures of heterosexual and marital relations, through a series of woman's touches alternating with a woman's *Noli me tangere* — signifying, as surely as Owen's "You may touch them not": End this violence.

H.D.'s Mary-myrrh contains all the oppositional possibility of this Myrrhine. But Myrrhine's name leads, also, back to war, as Dale Davis's research into "the matter of Myrrhine" has shown. When manuscripts of Aldington's Myrrhine poems showed up in the Beinecke Library's H.D. archives and were originally thought to have been composed by H.D., Davis's detective work tentatively tracked the name Myrrhine to a further, different classical source. "Myrine" is a Libyan Amazon, a woman warrior and military commander. She founds the city Mitylene in Lesbos, naming it after a fellow Amazon fighter.[121] Her root "Myr" suggests, therefore, a female community which not only refuses to demur from war-making but even actively admires and conspires in a military cause — perhaps somewhat like Bryher, whose strong antifascist activities in the thirties prompted Freud to suggest to H.D., uneasily, that she might influence Bryher to become "less warlike."[122]

Bryher's part in prewar and wartime "refugee work" helping Jews escape from Europe brings us back to the forties, and reminds us that H.D.'s is finally a very different war from any Myrrhine's. Writing from Second World War London, H.D. felt the present impossibility of simply organizing by fiat a departure from the place-of-a-skull, simply leaving it to those who fashioned it. It was impossible first of all because the place-of-a-skull was not only some abstract masculine battleground. It was Auschwitz, where, as Primo Levi writes, the prisoners told each other their stories, each "simple and incomprehensible like the stories in the Bible. But are they not themselves stories of a new Bible?"[123] The place-of-a-skull was the place of fascism. It was bombed London where H.D. lived; in the air war, it was the skies over her head. And it was impossible to leave it, too, because as the active supporter of the war effort who eulogized the R.A.F. and girl driver in *What Do I Love?*, she could not and would not entirely relinquish her own part in fashioning a war she saw not only as abhorrent but also as imperative.

Wallace Stevens, as if writing directly to H.D., advised a "madanna" in his "Late Hymn from the Myrrh Mountain" to "unsnack your snood . . . / Take the diamonds from your hair and lay them down. / The deer grass is thin. The timothy is brown. / The shadow of an external world comes near."[124] H.D. knew the shadow of that external world. In 1955, after listening to tapes of herself reading her next major poem which returned to her "'war' complex or compulsion," *Helen in Egypt*, she wrote, quoting Ellen Glasgow's recently published autobiography: "as *The Woman Within* asks, 'Is it true, I wonder, that the only way to escape a war is to be in it?'"[125] Her tightly intertwined crucifixion and Christmas myths in *Trilogy* suggest that in the Second World War the answer for her was finally "yes." "For it seems," she wrote in *The Gift*, "we are not able to stabilize our purpose, to affirm in positive and concrete terms . . . until we are forced to face up to the final realities, in a ship-wreck or . . . massed air attack, in the small hours of the morning."[126]

"The fragrance came from the bundle of myrrh / she held in her arms": in this context of contradictions, the bundle of myrrh, an image of both war and desire, is a figure of the proverbial "bundle of contradiction." But those contradictions are not only thematized in the myrrh exchanges in "The Flowering of the Rod." They are exemplified by the function of the poem itself. *Trilogy* gestures repeatedly, eloquently, toward a utopian pacifism sealed in its final lyric Bethlehem. But a more explicitly historically grounded text like *What Do I Love?*, written around the same time, reveals that utopian idea as at that moment unsustainable.[127] H.D.'s myrrh (Myrrha/Myrrhine), her Bethlehem which cannot wrest itself from Jerusalem, encodes what Christa Wolf, in her *Cassandra*, has called "the double code of Western Christian Civilization,"

which must perform a prodigious mental feat of increasingly subtle and ingenious demagoguery in order to acknowledge the commandment *Thou shalt not kill* as the ethical foundation of its life and, without suffering a moral breakdown, simultaneously rescind it for its practical action . . . And literature, by describing this double code, has helped to structure it.[128]

It is H.D.'s *Helen in Egypt*, that precursor of *Cassandra* written in the following Cold War years, in the nuclear age, which of all H.D.'s work explores with the most painstaking self-consciousness the implications of this double code.[129] In one Bethlehem story among a mass of Bethlehem stories produced in the middle of the most heated of wars, employing its culture's most ready, dominant, and duplicitous myth of peace, *Trilogy* both helped to shore up this eloquent structure and helped, with equal subtlety, to demystify it – in particular to demystify women's parts within it. H.D.'s own "moral breakdown" came a year later. *Trilogy*'s double code of myrrh both anticipates its cure and at the same time, irrevocably, necessarily, inscribes its causes.

Conclusion

In 1946, Lorine Niedecker wrote to Louis Zukofsky from the isolated region of Wisconsin where she lived most of her life. Describing her response to William Carlos Williams's praise of her poems, she used terms which called the war just ended to mind: "Ten years ago, such a letter would have sent me higher than the great blue heron. Guess now I've got my feet on bombed ground."[1] I invoke this woman with her feet on bombed ground to underscore three final points.

First, to recall the bombings of Hiroshima and Nagasaki, events which in one real sense have eradicated all the meaningful distinctions between front and home, and between (male) protector and (female) protected, that I have been tracing in poems throughout this book: now we all stand on (potentially) bombed ground. Niedecker's "In the great snowfall before the bomb," written around 1950, looks back from a post-Hiroshima vantage point to the last months of the war, during which Niedecker worked as a proofreader in the local Hoard's Dairyman print shop; it confronts American poetry's and more generally American language's implications in the making of atomic culture. This is Niedecker's version of the Christmas/war poem, in which a local blizzard and the hint of coming atomic fallout, gentle lights and muffled darkness, and poetry and military technology cheerfully, chillingly, intertwine:[2]

> In the great snowfall before the bomb
> colored yule tree lights
> windows, the only glow for contemplation
> along this road
>
> I worked the print shop
> right down among em
> the folk from whom all poetry flows
> and dreadfully much else.[3]

This poem recalls something else as well: women's work, other than poetic work, on the home front. And it recalls the subject of social class. Once I asked a working-class writer who had begun her authorial and political career in the 1930s what she had read during the Second World War. Did she read much poetry? "I didn't read anything," she responded incredulously. "I didn't have time." Niedecker's "In the great snowfall" represents the situation of a woman with little time. The print shop in which she works is a harassing and a wearing environment, much like the shop which Niedecker described in an untitled prose work from the same period: "this organization, as good an avenue for plunder as any business is, protects and is protected by that other and still more expensive organiza-tion, war. . . . Grime, guts, gloom, the crash and roar of the big presses, speed, overtime speed, reason jarred."[4] In the poem, in characteristic Niedecker fashion, this workplace provokes an exuberant proliferation of slangy metaphor to counter the "rehashings" of the dominant home-front culture:

> I was Blondie
> I carried my bundles of hog feeder price lists
> down by Larry the Lug,
> I'd never get anywhere
> because I'd never had suction,
> pull, you know, favor, drag,
> well-oiled protection.
> I heard their rehashed radio barbs —
> more barbarous among hirelings
> as higher-ups grow more corrupt.

Still, "In the great snowfall" celebrates as much as it satirizes the lives of "hirelings" — as long as they are women. Against violence and imposed labor, the poem juxtaposes, moving into the present tense, a vivid com-munal identity:

> But what vitality! The women hold jobs —
> clean house, cook, raise children, bowl
> and go to church.

Here the lives of working and working-class women managing their double shifts, women who barely make their appearance in the canon of war poetry (including my own gathering in this book), can begin to be discerned.[5]

The last lines of the poem, however, represent the woman poet not in solidarity with but in estrangement from these vital women in their sphere of material labor, recalling the question of poetry's difference from other forms of home-front making. "What would they say," the speaker wonders about the women she has just described:

> What would they say if they knew
> I sit for two months on six lines
> of poetry?

Throughout, this poem has conducted a critique of notions of aesthetic transcendence: the poet "Blondie," lugging loads of print, remains "right down among em," and her barbed poem flows from "the folk," along with radio jokes and bombs. The poem's conclusion does not waver from this stance. But it does suggest one way in which poetry might differ or might distance itself from war culture, while still "right down among em." Not a proclamation but a question, "What would they say if they knew?" estranges the poet pleasurably from her violent and banal society even as it includes her in it, directing her and our attention to it. In this gentle, muted, dialogic ending, the hint of art's distanciation from society embeds itself in a political, economic, and gendered community.[6] Does the poet "sit for two months on six lines / of poetry" for lack of time, like the writer/worker I spoke to of her war years, or does she do it because she has all the time in the world, the expansive privilege of radical lyric privacy? Both, I think. For here the gulf between the production by the woman of her poem and the production by her culture of the bowling alley, the Christmas decoration, the nuclear family, and the nuclear bomb is represented with a double-edged irony: in this text, it is both deeply and not so deeply cut.

Niedecker's especially nuanced ambiguities may be usefully juxtaposed with a recent comment by Paul Fussell on gender, subtlety, and irony in war poetry. In his 1984 review of Jon Stallworthy's *Oxford Book of War Poetry*, Paul Fussell criticizes Stallworthy for padding the anthology "with things like Edith Sitwell's preposterous, theologically pretentious 'Still Falls the Rain,' that implausible theatrical farrago which seems now the very *locus classicus* of 1940s empty portentousness."

That Sitwellian disaster prompts this question: why haven't more women written good "war poems"? From Homer's Andromache to Vera Brittain . . . bereaved women, next to the permanently disabled, are the main victims in war, their dead having been removed beyond suffering and memory. . . . Yet the elegies are written by men, and it's not women who seem the custodians of the subtlest sorts of antiwar irony. That seems odd, and it awaits interpretation.[7]

By now the systematic suppression of women's poetry at work in this representative passage will, I hope, seem to my readers both "odd" and very familiar. I have tried to show how the developing canon of twentieth-century Anglo-American war poetry has served a tautological function ("Yet the elegies are written by men." Why? *Because* the elegies are written by men.) I have tried to show, too, how this tautology has worked both to deter and to mark women's war writing. If women's absence from the ranks of "good war poets," so firmly asserted here by Fussell, nonetheless "seems odd," that apparent aberration has everything to do with the structural "seeming oddities" of femininity in wartime society, and with the formal principles or "grids of concordance," in Genette's and Nancy Miller's terms, which have defined what constitutes "implausibility" or notable irony in war literature.[8] I have tried to offer a different set of grids, ones in which both Niedecker's muted "plausibilities" and Sitwell's theatrical voice might be given a sympathetic reading.

What subtleties of women's ironies have been lost on the male custodians of modern (anti)war poetry, and what laws of gender govern these custody suits? Consider, for instance, how often the women's poems I have analyzed here have, with a great deal of subtlety, refused the position of sheer grieving given to women in classic war narrative. It is, ironically, the only position Fussell grants to women in the above passage. His discussion of women's victimization in war recognizes no dead or disabled women, and it allows for no female participation in war except bereavement. If these are the terms in which irony is discerned, then it is not surprising that so many women's poems are found lacking.

Part of my purpose here has been to question the privileged status of irony, especially insofar as it has been linked to masculinity, in modern war poetry. Another part has been to make interpretable the subtle ironies, many of them centered on questions of gender, in the women's Second World War poems I have presented. Another part has been to read the poems in contexts other than the canon of modern war poetry — in the context, for instance, of feminist theory. These poems played, as I have shown, an early and significant part in the development of contemporary feminist theories of war and gender, even as the workings of poetic language within them complicate any reading of them as forensic exercises, and even as their historical otherness troubles any simple contemporary identification with them.

I have offered in these pages some women's war poems that I consider worth the reading. But far more women have written more good war poems, across this century and in other poetic traditions, than I have included here (not all of them subtle, "antiwar," or ironic). I eagerly await their interpretation.

Notes

Acknowledgments

Index

Notes

Introduction

1 Louise Bogan, "Verses," *New Yorker*, 21 October 1944, 91. Hereafter cited in the text. The most complex and useful feminist study of Bogan's complicated relation to the category "woman poet" is Gloria Bowles's *Louise Bogan's Aesthetic of Limitation* (Bloomington: Indiana Univ. Press, 1987); I am indebted to Gloria Bowles for first sending me to look at this review.

2 Jane Cooper, "Nothing Has Been Used in the Manufacture of This Poetry That Could Have Been Used in the Manufacture of Bread," *Scaffolding: New and Selected Poems* (London: Anvil, 1984), 23. Hereafter cited in the text.

3 Jane Marcus has eloquently warned feminists about the political dangers of reconfirming and revalorizing "the male canon of war literature from Lawrence to Hemingway to Wilfred Owen" and thereby "contributing to that pile of skulls, the patriarchal 'civilization' of Antaeus." I find this an important admonition. But Owen's poems and those by other Great War soldier poets were, I will argue, an undeniable, energizing and agitating influence on many – though by no means all – of the female-authored poems I consider here. See Marcus, "The Asylums of Antaeus," in *Feminism and Critical Theory: The Differences Within*, ed. Elizabeth Meese and Alice Parker (Philadelphia: Benjamins North Am., 1988), 54, 61.

4 Margaret Mead, "The Women in the War," in Jack Goodman, ed., *While You Were Gone* (New York: Simon & Schuster, 1946), 274.

5 Roland Barthes, *A Lover's Discourse: Fragments*, trans. Richard Howard (New York: Hill & Wang, 1978), 14.

6 Virginia Woolf, *Three Guineas* (New York: Harcourt Brace Jovanovich, 1938), 4. Hereafter cited in the text.

7 Louise Bogan, "To My Brother Killed: Haumont Wood: October, 1918," *The Blue Estuaries: Poems 1923-1968* (New York: Farrar, Straus & Giroux, 1968), 77. Poems in this edition are hereafter cited in the text.

8 Margaret Randolph Higgonet et al., eds., *Behind the Lines: Gender and the Two World Wars* (New Haven: Yale Univ. Press, 1987), 4.

9 Page duBois, *Sowing the Body: Psychoanalysis and Ancient Representations of Women* (Chicago: Univ. of Chicago Press, 1988), 67, 65. Hereafter cited in the text.

10 Ezra Pound, "Envoi," *Personae: Collected Shorter Poems* (New York: New Directions, 1971), 194.

11 I am indebted to Ramsay Bell Breslin for her suggestion of this reading of the second and third stanzas. My use of "making" and "unmaking" here has been influenced by Elaine Scarry's deployment of those terms in her *The Body in Pain: The Making and Unmaking of the World* (New York: Oxford Univ. Press, 1985).

12 Ruth Limmer, ed., *What the Woman Lived: Selected Letters of Louise Bogan 1920–1970* (New York: Harcourt Brace Jovanovich, 1973), 239.
13 This reading supports Gilbert and Gubar's claim that in the aftermath of the war, the "modernist woman of letters . . . felt, though at times quite guiltily, that she could speak because she *must* speak; there were not so many men left to do the verbal work of no man's land." Sandra M. Gilbert and Susan Gubar, "Soldier's Heart: Literary Men, Literary Women, and the Great War," *No Man's Land 2: Sexchanges* (New Haven, Yale Univ. Press, 1989), 309. "Soldier's Heart" appeared in essay form in several publications under Gilbert's name alone; the lines I quote here appeared only in the jointly authored book.
14 Jan Montefiore, *Feminism and Poetry: Language, Experience, Identity in Women's Writing* (New York: Pandora, 1987), 65, 69.
15 To what extent destruction and historical crisis could or should be represented as universal, or as beyond or before ideology, has been, from the start of the modern history of the subgenre "war poetry," a matter of sharp debate, some of which I trace in this book. We have seen Bogan enter that debate already.
16 H.D.'s use of the phrase "iron-ring" is in *Helen in Egypt* (New York: New Directions, 1961).
17 See Maureen Honey, *Creating Rosie the Riveter: Class, Gender and Propaganda During World War II* (Amherst: Univ. of Massachusetts Press, 1984), and also Leila Rupp, *Mobilizing Women for War: German and American Propaganda, 1939–1945* (Princeton: Princeton Univ. Press, 1978) and Susan Hartmann, "Prescriptions for Penelope: Literature on Women's Obligations to Returning World War II Veterans," *Women's Studies* 5 (1978): 273–39.
18 "The question of value must always be posed historically," writes Francis Mulhern in his "Marxism in Literary Criticism," *New Left Review* 108 (March/April 1979): 86. See also Michael André Bernstein's assessment of the problem of discussing the evaluation of political poetry: "Because *all* of the terms of the question are themselves historical in nature, functioning quite differently in the context and rhetoric of different eras, a series of individual studies is likely to prove far more profitable than any global claims." Bernstein, "'O Totiens Servus': Saturnalia and Servitude in Augustan Rome," in *Politics and Poetic Value*, ed. Robert von Hallberg (Chicago: Univ. of Chicago Press, 1987), 39.
19 I have learned from Barbara Herrnstein Smith's important essays on literary value to think of evaluation as something that begins as early as the stage of composition; see, for instance, her "Fixed Marks and Variable Constancies: A Parable of Literary Value," *Poetics Today* 1.1–2 (Autumn 1979): 18.
20 Montefiore, *Feminism and Poetry*, 188.
21 Tony Bennett, "Marxism and Popular Fiction," *Literature and History* 7.2 (Autumn 1981): 145.
22 Herrnstein Smith questions the notion of "constant" and Terry Eagleton, the notion of "immanent" value. See Herrnstein Smith, "Fixed Marks," and her "Contingencies of Value" in *Canons*, ed. Robert von Hallberg (Chicago: Univ. of Chicago Press, 1984), and Eagleton, *Criticism and Ideology: A Study in Marxist Literary Theory* (London: Humanities, 1976).
23 Cary Nelson, *Our Last First Poets: Vision and History in Contemporary American Poetry* (Urbana: Univ. of Illinois Press, 1981).
24 The first phrase is from Paul Fussell, "The War in Black and White," *The Boy*

Scout Handbook and Other Observations (New York: Oxford Univ. Press, 1982), 237; the second, from Geoffrey Perrett, quoted in Fussell on the same page.

25 On the judgment of literature not by its "message" but by the way in which it "borrows materials from the world only in order to designate itself," see Jean Ricardou, *Problèmes du nouveau roman* (Paris: Seuil, 1967), 202, quoted and translated in Susan Suleiman, *Authoritarian Fictions: The Ideological Novel as Literary Genre* (New York: Columbia Univ. Press, 1983), 18.

26 James Longenbach, *Stone Cottage: Pound, Yeats and Modernism* (New York: Oxford Univ. Press, 1988), 113. Elsewhere Longenbach has played an important part in the development of a feminist analysis of writing and the Great War, one alert to women's presence and to how the writing of (literary) history has constructed that presence. See his "The Women and Men of 1914," in *Arms and the Woman*, ed. Helen Cooper, Adrienne Munich, and Susan Squier (Chapel Hill: Univ. of North Carolina Press, 1989), 97–123.

27 See, for instance, the accounts of the war poetry issue in A. Walton Litz, *Introspective Voyager: The Poetic Development of Wallace Stevens* (New York: Oxford Univ. Press, 1972) and in Glen Macleod, *Wallace Stevens and Co.: The Harmonium Years, 1913–1923* (Ann Arbor: UMI Research Press, 1983).

28 Louise Driscoll, "The Metal Checks," *Poetry* 5.11 (November 1914): 49. Hereafter cited in the text.

29 In addition to the works by Mulhern, Herrnstein Smith, Eagleton, and Bennett cited above, I am indebted to Anne McClintock for her "'Azikwelwa' (We Will Not Ride): Politics and Value in Black South African Poetry," in von Hallberg, ed., *Politics and Poetic Value*, 225–51. "Transitive" is Eagleton's term, in Terry Eagleton and Peter Fuller, "The Question of Value: A Discussion," *New Left Review* 142 (November/December 1983): 77. Cary Nelson's important analysis of poetic evaluation, *Repression and Recovery: Modern American Poetry and the Politics of Cultural Memory, 1910–1945* (Madison: Univ. of Wisconsin Press, 1989), appeared too late for me to make full use of it in the writing of this book, but the relation of my project to Nelson's will, I hope, be clear.

30 I am indebted here to Francis Mulhern for his summary of Eagleton's work on value; Mulhern insists that the question of value must always be put in the form "valuable *to whom* and *in what conditions*?" (Mulhern, "Marxism," 86).

31 Higgonet et al., eds., *Behind the Lines*, 15.

32 Ada Jackson, *Behold the Jew* (New York: Macmillan, 1944), 1. Hereafter cited in the text.

33 Authorial biography of Ada Jackson in the English printing of *Behold the Jew* (London: Journal of the Poetry Society, 1944). According to Catherine Reilly's bibliography of Second World War literature, "E. V. Lucas named her [Jackson] 'the English Emily Dickinson' while in America she was called 'the Elizabeth Barrett Browning of Our Time.'" Reilly, *English Poetry of the Second World War: A Bibliography* (New York: Mansell, 1986), 179.

34 Marianne Moore, "Who Has Rescued Whom," *New Republic*, 16 October 1944, 449–500. Reprinted in *The Complete Prose of Marianne Moore*, ed. Patricia Willis (New York: Penguin, 1986), 402–3.

35 Benjamin Harshav and Barbara Harshav, *American Yiddish Poetry: A Bilingual Anthology* (Berkeley: Univ. of California Press, 1986), 803–4.

36 On Glatshteyn's work, see ibid., 204–385 (*Exegyddish* is their translation); Irving

Howe, Ruth R. Wisse, and Khone Shmeruk, *The Penguin Book of Modern Yiddish Verse* (New York: Penguin, 1987); Richard J. Fein, "Yankev Glatshteyn, *Yankev Glatshteyn*: Ambivalent Modernist," *Yiddish* 6.1 (Spring 1985): 55–66; Janet Hadda, *Yankev Glatshteyn* (Boston: Twayne, 1980); and Irving Howe, "Journey of a Poet," *Commentary* 53.1 (January 1972): 75–77.

37 Jacob Glatshteyn, "Ada Jackson," *In Tokh Genumen* (New York: Farlag Matones, 1947), 416–22. The translation I am using was done by Daniel Marlin, Berkeley, California, 1989. My thanks to him for his help with this project, including translations of two other essays by Glatshteyn from this volume, on Marianne Moore and on Kadia Molodowsky. The Moore review has been translated by Doris Vidaver and appears in *Yiddish* 6.1 (Spring 1985): 67–73. Glatshteyn's essay on Ada Jackson, like the other essays in *In Tokh Genumen*, was originally printed as a column in the New York–based socialist weekly *Yiddisher Kemfer*.

38 Herrnstein Smith, "Contingencies of Value," 13.

39 Among the general books to which I am broadly indebted are: Shari Benstock, *Women of the Left Bank* (Austin: Univ. of Texas Press, 1986); Rachel Blau DuPlessis, *Writing Beyond the Ending: Narrative Strategies of Twentieth-Century Women Writers* (Bloomington: Indiana Univ. Press, 1985); Sandra Gilbert and Susan Gubar, eds., *Shakespeare's Sisters: Feminist Essays on Women Poets* (Bloomington: Indiana Univ. Press, 1979); Margaret Homans, *Women Writers and Poetic Identity: Dorothy Wordsworth, Emily Bronte and Emily Dickinson* (Princeton: Princeton Univ. Press, 1980); Suzanne Juhasz, *Naked and Fiery Forms: Modern American Poetry by Women, A New Tradition* (New York: Harper & Row, 1976); Cora Kaplan, *Salt and Bitter and Good* (New York: Paddington, 1975) and *Sea Changes: Essays on Culture and Feminism* (London: Verso, 1986); Montefiore, *Feminism and Poetry*; Alicia Suskin Ostriker, *Stealing the Language: The Emergence of Women's Poetry in America* (Boston: Beacon Press, 1986); Diane W. Middlebrook and Marilyn Yalom, eds., *Coming to Light: American Women Poets in the Twentieth Century* (Ann Arbor: Univ. of Michigan Press, 1985); Cheryl Walker, *The Nightingale's Burden* (Bloomington: Indiana Univ. Press, 1982); Emily Stipes Watts, *The Poetry of American Women from 1632 to 1945* (Austin: Univ. of Texas Press, 1977). For works on individual authors, see the chapters on specific authors which follow.

40 Crucial general works on gender and war include: Cynthia Enloe, *Does Khaki Become You? The Militarization of Women's Lives* (London: Pluto, 1983); Jean Bethke Elshtain, *Women and War* (New York: Basic, 1987); Higgonet et al., *Behind the Lines* (the two important essays by Sandra Gilbert and Susan Gubar on gender and war literature in World War I and World War II are included here); Sharon Macdonald, Pat Holden, and Shirley Basingstoke, *Images of Women in Peace and War* (Madison: Univ. of Wisconsin Press, 1988); Judith Hicks Stiehm, ed., *Women's Studies Int. Forum*, 1982, no. 5.3–4 (this issue is on women and men's wars); Carol Berkin and Clara M. Lovett, eds., *Women, War and Revolution* (New York: Holmes & Meier, 1980); Cynthia Enloe, "Feminists Thinking About War, Militarism and Peace," in *Analyzing Gender: A Handbook of Social Science Research*, ed. Beth B. Hess and Myra Marx Ferree (London: Sage, 1987), 526–47; Bell Hooks, "Feminism and Militarism," in her *Talking Back: Thinking Feminist, Thinking Black* (Boston: South End Press, 1989); Micaela Di Leonardo, "Morals, Mothers, and Militarism: Antimilitarism and Feminist Theory," *Feminist Studies* 11.3 (1985):

598–617; Nancy Huston, "The Matrix of War: Mothers and Heroes," in *The Female Body in Western Culture*, ed. Susan Rubin Suleiman (Cambridge: Harvard Univ. Press, 1986), 119–38; Sara Ruddick, *Maternal Thinking: Towards a Politics of Peace* (Boston: Beacon Press, 1989); Carol Cohn, "Sex and Death in the Rational World of Defense Intellectuals," *Signs* 12:4 (1987): 687–718; Nosheen Khan, *Women's Poetry of the First World War* (Brighton: Harvester, 1988); Marcus, "Asylums of Antaeus"; the anthology of essays on gender and war literature *Arms and the Woman* edited by Cooper, Munich, and Squier (Chapel Hill: Univ. of North Carolina Press, 1989); and Catherine Reilly's two anthologies *Scars Upon My Heart: Women's Poetry and Verse of the First World War* (London: Virago, 1982) and *Chaos of the Night: Women's Poetry and Verse of the Second World War* (London: Virago, 1984). Claire M. Tylee's *The Great War and Women's Consciousness: Images of Militarism and Womanhood in Women's Writings, 1914–64* (Iowa City: Univ. of Iowa Press, 1990) came out, unfortunately, too late to be of use in the writing of this book. On World War II specifically, I have learned much from the feminist work of Susan M. Hartmann, *The Home Front and Beyond: American Women in the 1940's* (Boston: Twayne, 1982); of Karen Anderson, *Wartime Women: Sex Roles, Family Relations, and the Status of Women during World War II* (Westport, Conn.: Greenwood, 1981); and of D'Ann Campbell, *Women at War With America: Private Lives in a Patriotic Era* (Cambridge: Harvard Univ. Press, 1984). I am also indebted to other work on the World Wars – to John Morton Blum's *V Was For Victory: Politics and American Culture During World War II* (New York: Harcourt Brace Jovanovich, 1976), for instance, and to Paul Fussell's important *The Great War and Modern Memory* (New York: Oxford Univ. Press, 1975).

41 Stipes Watts's *Poetry of American Women*, for instance, includes a quick reminder near its close that "interest in social or political causes has, as we have seen, always been at least a peripheral concern of American women poets" (174). In Cheryl Walker's *Nightingale's Burden*, similarly, one of the final footnotes qualifies the author's emphasis on the themes of private love and erotic sorrow in American women's lyrics: "I am well aware that there were other women poets . . . who departed from the thrust of this tradition and directed their poetry to social and political concerns" (172).

42 Ostriker, *Stealing the Language*, 55.

43 Barbara Guest, *Herself Defined: The Poet H.D. and Her World* (New York: Doubleday, 1984), 235.

44 W. H. Auden, "The Shield of Achilles," *Collected Poems*, ed. Edward Mendelson (New York: Random, 1976), 454–55.

45 Marianne Moore, "A Draft of XXX Cantos" (322) and "The Cantos" (272), *The Complete Poems of Marianne Moore* (New York: Macmillan, 1967). Carolyn Burke discusses Moore's critique of Pound in her instructive "Getting Spliced: Modernism and Sexual Difference," *American Quarterly* 39.1 (Spring 1987): 116.

Chapter 1. Writing War Poetry "Like a Woman": Moore (and Jarrell)

1 W. H. Auden, review of *Nevertheless*, by Marianne Moore, *New York Times*, 15 October 1944, 20.

2 Randall Jarrell, "Poetry in War and Peace," *Partisan Review* (Winter 1945): 120; reprinted in Jarrell, *Kipling, Auden and Co.: Essays and Reviews, 1935–1964* (New York: Farrar, Straus & Giroux, 1980), 127. Hereafter abbreviated "PWP" and cited in the text.

3   Robert Graves, "The Poets of World War II," *The Common Asphodel: Collected Essays on Poetry 1922–1949* (London: Hamish Hamilton, 1949), 308.

4   See Siegfried Sassoon, introduction, *Poems*, by Wilfred Owen (London: Chatto & Windus, 1920). For a recent appeal to the authority of the veteran's experience, see Paul Fussell, "Thank God for the Atom Bomb," *Thank God for the Atom Bomb and Other Essays* (New York: Summit Books, 1988), 13–27.

5   Graves, "Poets of World War II," 310.

6   Richard Eberhart, "Preface: Attitudes to War," in *War and the Poet: An Anthology of Poetry Expressing Man's Attitude to War from Ancient Times to the Present*, ed. Eberhart and Selden Rodman (New York: Devin-Adair, 1945), xv, xiii. Hereafter cited in the text.

7   I am indebted to Frederick C. Stern's emphasis, in a letter to me, on Stevens's function as representative of the philosophical and the aesthetic here. Stern goes on to caution against my sexualizing reading of the "peignoir," arguing that 'Sunday Morning' is in no way "a poem involving coquetry, or, in any sexual sense, desire." Whether the offhand reference to the "peignoir," and the implicit image of the woman in dishabille, can be so thoroughly desexualized is a question I leave open to my readers.

8   Compare Jacob Glatshteyn's review of the Yiddish woman poet Kadia Molodowsky, in which he writes that after the holocaust she "drew a sackcloth over her shoulders and became a mourner. And as a mourner who neither washes nor looks in the mirror, she gave up her whole unique poetic toilette, with its alluring, coquettish preening. She cut her lines to the bone and let them out in the street, where they joined the common funeral procession of the Yiddish poem." Glatshteyn, "Kadia Molodowsky's New Book of Poetry," *In Tokh Genumen*, 86. Translated by Daniel Marlin, Berkeley, California.

9   Oscar Williams, ed., *The War Poets: An Anthology of the War Poetry of the Twentieth Century* (New York: John Day, 1945), 6.

10 Bonnie Costello, *Marianne Moore: Imaginary Possessions* (Cambridge: Harvard Univ. Press, 1981), 110. "The pressure of news" is a phrase from Wallace Stevens, "The Noble Rider and the Sound of Words," *The Necessary Angel: Essays on Reality and the Imagination* (New York: Vintage, 1951), 20. John Slatin argues that Moore's war work is evidence of a poetic decline, linked to Moore's "urgent imperative to keep things as they are, or rather to keep them *as they were before the war.*" Slatin, *The Savage's Romance: The Poetry of Marianne Moore* (University Park: Pennsylvania State Univ. Press, 1986), 14. And Harold Bloom writes: "When her wildness or freedom subsided, she produced an occasional poetic disaster like the patriotic war poems. . . ." Bloom, "Introduction," *Marianne Moore* (New York: Chelsea House, 1987), 3. But see, for recent significant and positive readings of the poem, Grace Schulman, *Marianne Moore: The Poetry of Engagement* (Urbana: Univ. of Illinois Press, 1986), 70–75, and especially Margaret Holley, *The Poetry of Marianne Moore: A Study in Voice and Value* (New York: Cambridge Univ. Press, 1987), 119–21. Holley's analysis, which I read only after completing this chapter, takes up several points related to my own reading. On the history of the "polarization of art and improvisation, poetic and non-poetic language, the Book and the Newspaper" and of key moments when that opposition has been broken down, see Marjorie Perloff, "The Supreme Fiction and the Impasse of Modernist Lyric," in *Wallace Stevens: The Poetics of Modernism*, ed. Albert Gelpi (New York: Cambridge Univ. Press, 1985), 50–51.

11 John Slatin has argued that "In Distrust of Merits" is a worse poem than Moore's 1919 version of "The Fish," which he reads persuasively as a Great War poem. He praises "The Fish" for deriving "much of its considerable force from the tension created by its effort to abstain from any overt reference either to the war or to the men who are, like those in the later poem, 'lost at sea' before they reach the battlefront" (*Savage's Romance*, 76). What I would emphasize here is that "The Fish," however delightfully recoverable as war poem, has been read for decades without any reference to combat, and that this degree of indirection was undesirable to Moore and many others in the midst of the Second World War.

12 Elizabeth Bishop to Houghton Mifflin, 22 January 1945, in *Elizabeth Bishop: A Bibliography, 1927–1979*, ed. Candace W. MacMahon (Charlottesville, Va.: Univ. Press of Virginia, 1980), 8.

13 Marianne Moore, "Interview with Donald Hall," *A Marianne Moore Reader* (New York: Viking, 1961), 261.

14 See Laurence Stapleton, *Marianne Moore: The Poet's Advance* (Princeton: Princeton Univ. Press, 1978), 134. It may well be that the "pressure" of guilt and knowledge under which this poem was forged came not only from images of combat — scenes, incidentally, only then very recently allowed to get past the censor — but also from a growing sense of what was happening to the Jews overseas; Moore's campaign for Ada Jackson was roughly concurrent with the drafting of this poem. My thanks to Frederick Stern for reminding me to look beyond the image of the soldier which, here as so often, tends to dominate the terrain of the American war poem. On the politics of censorship and images of combat in the war years, see Susan D. Moeller, *Shooting War: Photography and the American Experience of Combat* (New York: Basic, 1989).

15 Moore, "In Distrust of Merits," *The Complete Poems of Marianne Moore* (New York: Macmillan, 1967), 136–38; all further quotations of "In Distrust of Merits" are from these pages. The collection is hereafter abbreviated *CP* and cited in the text.

16 Costello describes extensively how the emblems in Moore's poems of "a world already represented" draw "descriptions of the world into a private setting where the world might be brought under imaginary control," epitomizing Moore's method of "imaginary possession" (Costello, *Imaginary Possessions*, 6).

17 Ibid., 38.

18 Moore had been a war poet from the start; see her early poems "To the Soul of 'Progress,'" *Egoist* 2 (April 1915): 62, and "Reinforcements," *Egoist* 5 (June–July 1918): 83. Her 1923 review of H. D. praised H. D.'s poetics as oppositional to war ("Hymen," *Broom* 4 [January 1923]: 133–35), as H. D. before her had praised Moore ("Marianne Moore," *The Egoist* 3 [May 1916]: 118).

19 Quoted in Stapleton, *Marianne Moore*, 130.

20 The quotations from Moore's unpublished material which follow are taken from conversation and reading notebooks in the Moore collection of the Rosenbach Museum and Library, Philadelphia, Pennsylvania. Excerpts are cited hereafter as "Rosenbach," followed by their file numbers. This entry is from Rosenbach 1251/1 (conversation notes 1935–69), dated 10 June 1938, VII:04:03.

21 Rosenbach 1251/12 (poetry notebook 1933–1940), three entries: 23 July 1942; 22 March, 1943; undated.

22 For an excellent discussion of "images of sweetened combat" in Moore's work, see Costello, *Imaginary Possessions*, 108–32.

23 Moore, "There is a War that Never Ends," *Predilections* (New York: Viking, 1955), 41.

24 Both entries are taken from Rosenbach 1251/1. On the Christian tradition of spiritual warfare narrative, see Sue Mansfield, *The Gestalts of War: An Inquiry into Its Origins and Meanings as a Social Institution* (New York: Dial, 1982), 127–33.

25 Rosenbach 1251/1, dated 9 August 1937; 1251/1, dated 23 September 1940; 1251/12, undated.

26 Rosenbach 1251/12, dated 22 March 1943.

27 John Ellis, "Victory of the Voice?" *Screen* 22.2 (1981): 69.

28 Rosenbach 1251/12, dated 23 July 1942.

29 Rosenbach 1251/12, undated.

30 Rosenbach 1250/6 (reading notebook 1930–1943), undated. Source not verified.

31 The feminist historian Susan M. Hartmann notes, "The global scope of American involvement, the increasing complexity of modern war, and the development of military technology had reduced the proportion of military personnel directly engaged in battle. During World War II 25 percent of military personnel never left the United States, and only about one in eight actually saw combat." Hartmann, *Home Front*, 34.

32 Enloe, *Does Khaki Become You?*, 15.

33 Geoffrey Hartman, "Six Women Poets," *Easy Pieces* (New York: Columbia Univ. Press, 1985), 111.

34 Nelson, *Last First Poets*, 17.

35 Jonathan Culler, "Apostrophe," *Diacritics* 7 (Winter 1977): 60.

36 Jane Tompkins, *Sensational Designs: The Cultural Work of American Fiction 1790–1860* (New York: Oxford Univ. Press, 1985), xvii, 151. Paul Fussell discusses the metrical shift at the end of the poem in *Poetic Meter and Poetic Form* (New York: Random, 1965), 8–9.

37 Compare Grace Schulman's account of a conversation with Moore about the Vietnam War, in which Moore veered from the statement that American soldiers in Vietnam were "learning better why they are fighting" to a principle of nonviolence (via a maternal love she represented by citing her "The Paper Nautilus"), and in which she emphasized her difficulty in seeing war directly: "I don't dare face it, actually." Schulman, *Marianne Moore*, 68.

38 Moore, "Interview," 261.

39 Elie Wiesel, *A Jew Today*, trans. Marion Wiesel (New York: Random, 1978), cited in Annette Insdorf, *Indelible Shadows: Film and the Holocaust* (New York: Vintage, 1983), xi.

40 Perhaps the most famous text in the long tradition in which an overprotected, feminine *hortus conclusus* is opposed to masculine engagement in historical crisis is Ruskin's "Of Queen's Gardens," *Sesame and Lilies: Three Lectures* (Leipzig: Bernhard Tauchnitz, 1906), 172–75. In the Second World War period, see Arthur Koestler's Sylvia in "The Artist and Politics," *Saturday Review of Literature* 25 (31 January 1942): 3–4, 14–15; the attack on American women for failing to prevent war in Philip Wylie's *Generation of Vipers* (New York: Farrar & Rhinehart, 1942); Pearl Buck's chapter on women, domesticity, and war in *Of Men and Women* (New York: John Day, 1941); and Oscar Williams's image of American civilians protected by a wall of flesh, quoted earlier in this chapter.

41 Bonnie Costello argues persuasively, in her discussion of Jarrell's review, that Moore's work not only is part of a tradition of domestic "feminine realism . . . which links observation to ethical generalization" in American women's poetry but also constitutes a transformation of that tradition: "All the poems follow a dictum of resistance even while they move through an apparent structure of observation-moral, for they continually propose definitions only to unravel them." Costello, "The 'Feminine' Language of Marianne Moore," in *Women and Language in Literature and Society,* ed. Sally McConnell-Ginet, Ruth Borker, and Nelly Furman (New York: Praeger, 1980), 235. Costello follows Emily Stipes Watts's work in *Poetry of American Women.*

42 Jarrell, "Ernie Pyle," *Kipling, Auden and Co.,* 112. Hereafter abbreviated "EP" and cited in the text.

43 See, for instance, Jarrell's repeated quotations from Whitman in "These Are Not Psalms," *Kipling, Auden and Co.,* 122–26.

44 I owe to conversation with Catherine Gallagher my formulation of this point.

45 Gertrude Stein, *Wars I Have Seen* (New York: Random, 1945), 9.

46 A similarly complex conflation of "real" and "imaginary" occurs in Jarrell's description of Owen as "a poet in the true sense of the word, someone who has shown to us one of those worlds which, after we have been shown it, we call the real world." Jarrell, "The Profession of Poetry," *Kipling, Auden and Co.,* 169. Ernest Hemingway's introduction to his anthology of writing about war, *Men at War,* reveals the same ambivalence. On the one hand, Hemingway, paying tribute to Stephen Crane's *Red Badge of Courage,* argues that the writer's imagination "should produce a truer account than anything factual can be. For facts can be observed badly." On the other hand, he praises Crane's depiction of a boy "facing *that thing which no one knows about who has not done it.*" Hemingway, introduction, *Men at War: The Best War Stories of All Time* (New York: Crown, 1942), xv, xviii; my italics). See also the strained arguments about experience in Williams's collection of prose statements by poets on poetry and war, part of his *War Poets.* Williams's anthology displays in its very structure a paradigmatic self-consciousness and anxiety about what constitutes experience, who has it and why it matters; it segregates "Poems by the Men in the Armed Forces" from "War Poems by Civilian Poets," but this clear-cut split poses problems of categorization Williams addresses in the introduction: "it might have been fairer to the English civilian poets to have included them in the services' section since they have endured as much danger and engaged in almost as much defensive battle action as the military, but some kind of arbitrary division was necessary" (9).

47 William James, "The Moral Equivalent of War," *Memories and Studies* (Westport, Conn.: Greenwood, 1941), 291–92.

48 Ibid., 292.

49 Costello, "The 'Feminine' Language," 234; see Sara Ruddick, "Pacifying the Forces: Drafting Women in the Interests of Peace," *Signs* 8 (Spring 1983): 479.

50 J. Hillis Miller, "Mr. Carmichael and Lily Briscoe: The Rhythm of Creativity in *To the Lighthouse,*" in *Modernism Reconsidered,* ed. Robert Kiely (Cambridge: Harvard Univ. Press, 1983), 188.

51 Ruddick, "Pacifying the Forces," 472.

52 Jarrell's cross-gender identifications were perhaps unusually complex, and they occurred throughout his career; he went on, for instance, to write sensitive dramatic

monologues in female voice. I do not posit him, then, as some kind of generic Every Soldier Poet; nor, however, do I posit him as unique in his perspective and his strategies here. My thanks to Paul Alpers for reminding me of Jarrell's continuing strong identification with women in poems like "The Woman at the Washington Zoo."

53 Margaret Homans, *Bearing the Word: Language and Female Experience in Nineteenth-Century Women's Writing* (Chicago: Univ. of Chicago Press, 1986), 5, 88. My argument simplifies and to some extent skews Homans's model, in which women writers are presented as distinctively rooted by Western culture in the "literal" side of the opposition of literal to figurative, and in which that opposition—and that rooting—are understood in psychoanalytic terms. I am, as Carolyn Porter has suggested to me, using Homans's literal/figurative paradigm as a "cultural code," and treating it as rather more flexible and manipulatable at the surface level of polemical discourse than Homans's argument suggests.

54 Ibid., 26.

55 See Wilfrid Owen, "Dulce et Decorum Est," *Collected Poems*, ed. C. Day Lewis (New York: New Directions, 1964), 55. Unless otherwise stated, all further citations to Owen's work are to this edition. For the Jessie Pope connection, see Day Lewis's notes on the manuscript variations on the same page. On the persistent analogy in Western culture between war making and childbearing, see Huston, "Matrix of War."

56 Many of the essays in the "American Representations of Vietnam" issue of *Cultural Critique* 3 (Spring 1986) explore American culture's continuing myths of the special value of the soldier/veteran's experience. See especially Michael Clark, "Remembering Vietnam," 46–78; Rick Berg, "Losing Vietnam: Covering the War in an Age of Technology," 92–125; John Carlos Rowe, "Eye-Witness: Documentary Styles in the American Representation of Vietnam," 126–50; Philip Francis Kuberski, "Genres of Vietnam," 168–88.

57 Nor do I mean to imply that women in American culture cannot and do not employ strategies of literalization in their representations of war. Parts of Elaine Scarry's recent, powerful treatment of "injury and the structure of war" in *The Body in Pain* are, for instance, very much within the tradition advocated and represented by Jarrell here.

58 Tompkins discusses related problems in the evaluation of popular nineteenth-century works with "designs upon their audiences" in her introduction and throughout *Sensational Designs*.

59 Homans notes this danger in myths of female experience (see *Bearing the Word*, 15), citing Jane Gallop on the inherently conservative nature of a "politics of experience." In her discussion of Irigaray's work on the female body, Gallop goes on, however, to warn at the same time against unproblematic *denials* of experience; "the gesture of a troubled but nonetheless insistent referentiality is essential" if one's aim is "a *poiesis* of experience, that attempts to reconstruct experience itself, to produce a remetaphorization . . . a salutary jolt out of the compulsive repetition of the same." Gallop, "Quand nos lèvres s'écrivent: Irigaray's Body Politic," *Romanic Review* 74 (January 1983): 83. The most powerful "soldier poems" in the present canon of war poetry—Owen's "Dulce," for instance, or Jarrell's "Death of the Ball Turret Gunner"—certainly attempt to produce such salutary jolts, strongly revising the metaphors which formerly applied to the male body in war.

60   Randall Jarrell, "Eighth Air Force," *The Complete Poems* (New York: Farrar, Straus & Giroux, 1969), 143.
61   Grace Schulman makes a parallel point; see Schulman, *Marianne Moore*, 5.
62   It is possible that Jarrell's "Pilate" also directly responds to Ada Jackson's *Behold the Jew*:

> Behold the Jew, in whom I find
> no more of fault than lies within
> the soul of any other man.
> Thus do I cry; thus, sharp and thin,
> half wavering before the mob,
> spake Pilate in another day
> of Christ the Jew—and left it there;
> and washed his hands, and turned away.
> But I can never leave it there
>   (20–21)

Jarrell's speaker is far less capable of definitively saying or knowing that he "can never leave it there" or what "leaving it there" means. The connection to Ada Jackson seems even more likely in the light of another parallel; Jarrell's reference to Maidanek in his review of Moore — "At Maidanek the mice had holes, but a million and a half people had none" — recalls Jackson's opening of *Behold the Jew*, in which the speaker asserts that she prays most for Jews of "all the hunted things," since Jews alone have no place to hide (1).

63   David Bromwich, "Comment: Without Admonition," in von Hallberg, ed., *Politics and Poetic Value*, 328.
64   W. B. Yeats famously refused to include Great War poetry in his *Oxford Book of Modern Verse* on the grounds that "passive suffering" was no material for the poem. Yeats, *The Oxford Book of Modern Verse 1892–1935* (New York: Oxford Univ. Press, 1977), xxxiv–xxxv. "Pity" is, of course, Owen's own word, claimed in the preface he drafted for his book of poems: "My subject is War, and the pity of War. The Poetry is in the pity." The preface is reprinted in manuscript facsimile as the frontispiece for Wilfred Owen, *The Complete Poems and Fragments*, ed. Jon Stallworthy (London: Hogarth, 1985). This edition of Owen's poems hereafter cited as Stallworthy, ed., *Complete Poems and Fragments*. On Owen's admiration of Barrett Browning, see Sven Bäckman, "Wilfred Owen and Elizabeth Barrett Browning," *Studia Neophilologica* 49 (1977): 29–214; the connection, if accepted, is especially intriguing, since it suggests that Barrett Browning's late Risorgimento poems such as her antiwar "Mother and Poet" may have offered Owen female-authored precursors for the ironic war poem. On Owen as antipatriarchal poet, see Caryn McTighe Musil's feminist reading "Wilfred Owen and Abram," *Women's Studies* 13 (1986): 49–61.
65   Seamus Heaney, "The progress of a soul," *Times Literary Supplement* (8–14 April 1988): 381.
66   Wallace Stevens, "Life on a Battleship," *Opus Posthumous: Poems, Plays, Prose*, ed. Samuel French Morse (New York: Vintage, 1982), 79. All further citations to this poem are from this version of the text.
67   I am echoing the title of Susan Gubar's well-known essay, "The Echoing Spell of H.D.'s *Trilogy*," *Shakespeare's Sisters*, 200–218.

68 For accounts of Sitwell's association with Owen and her responsibility for the first appearance of his poetry in *Wheels*, see John Pearson, *The Sitwells: A Family's Biography* (New York: Harcourt Brace Jovanovich, 1978), 160–61; Victoria Glendinning, *Edith Sitwell: A Unicorn Among Lions* (London: Wiedenfeld and Nicolson, 1981), 61–62. The most interesting version of the story is Sitwell's own, in her letters to Susan Owen: Edith Sitwell, *Selected Letters*, ed. John Lehmann and Derek Parker (New York: Macmillan, 1970), 13–25.

69 Edith Sitwell to Susan Owen, 21 June 1919, in Sitwell, *Selected Letters*, 17.

70 Edith Sitwell to Mrs. Owen, 3 October 1919, in ibid., 20. The letter continues: "I feel doing so more than I can express. I have only one comfort; at least some of his wonderful work is coming out in *Wheels*, and I *have* worked heart and soul at getting his work ready for publication."

71 Edith Sitwell, "Three Eras of Modern Poetry (Second Lecture)," in Edith, Osbert, and Sacheverall Sitwell, *Trio: Dissertations on Some Aspects of National Genius* (London: Macmillan, 1938), 114.

72 Edmund Blunden, "Memoir," in *The Poems of Wilfred Owen*, ed. Blunden (London: Chatto and Windus, 1931), 3.

73 Dominic Hibbard, *Owen the Poet* (London: Macmillan, 1988), 154, 184.

74 Cecil Bowra, *Edith Sitwell* (Monaco: Ladybird Press, 1947), 29.

75 For an account of Sitwell's wartime poetry reading, see Robert Hewison, *Under Siege: Literary Life in London 1939–1945* (London: Weidenfeld and Nicolson, 1977), 170. On the Entretiens de Pontigny incident, see John Peale Bishop, "Entretiens de Pontigny: 1943. Introduction," *Sewanee Review* 53 (1944): 492–98.

Chapter 2. Writing Propaganda "Like a Man": Millay (and MacLeish)

1 Edmund Wilson, "Epilogue, 1952: Edna St. Vincent Millay," *The Shores of Light: A Literary Chronicle of the Twenties and Thirties* (New York: Farrar, Straus and Young, 1952), 779–80.

2 Alice Duer Miller, *The White Cliffs* (New York: Coward-McCann, 1940); Muriel Rukeyser, *Wake Island* (Garden City: Doubleday, Doran, 1942); Kay Boyle, *American Citizen, Naturalized in Leadville, Colorado* (New York: Simon & Schuster, 1944).

3 On the distinction between propagandas of "agitation" and "integration," see A. P. Foulkes, *Literature and Propaganda* (New York: Methuen, 1983), 71. On agonistic vs. antagonistic narrative structures, see Suleiman, *Authoritarian Fictions*, 102–3.

4 Eleanor Wheeler, *Lidice* (Prague: Orbis, 1962), 12–13.

5 These figures are taken from Wheeler, who provides a sobering account of both the destruction of Lidice and the Nazi record of that destruction.

6 Writers' War Board, foreword, *The Murder of Lidice*, by Edna St. Vincent Millay (New York: Harper & Brothers, 1942), v. This version of Millay's play and the foreword are hereafter cited in the text. On the Writers' War Board, see Maureen Honey, "Recruiting Women for War Work: OWI and the Magazine Industry During World War II," *Journal of American Culture* 3.1 (1980): 47–51. The Writers' War Board was not a governmental agency, though as Honey points out it was often mistaken for one; it did, however, receive government funding. On broader governmental supervision of wartime publishing, see Alan Winkler, *The Politics*

of Propaganda: The Office of War Information 1942–1945 (New Haven: Yale Univ. Press, 1978). Paul Fussell discusses the "OWI generation" of American writers in "Writing in Wartime: The Uses of Innocence," *Thank God for the Atom Bomb,* 74–80.

7   See, for instance, William Rose Benét, "Salute, Czechoslovakia!" 18 July 1942, 5, and Norman Cousins, "Remember Lidice," 11 July 1942, 10, both in the *Saturday Review of Literature;* Ernst Waldinger, "Lidice," *War Poems of the United Nations,* ed. Joy Davidman (New York: Dial, 1943): 21; and Cecil Day Lewis, "Lidice," *Collected Poems* (London: Jonathan Cape, 1954), 230. Hans Jelinek's woodcuts are included in Ellen Landau, ed., *Artists for Victory: An Exhibition Catalog* (Washington: Library of Congress, 1983). For accounts of commemorative activities, the "Lidice Shall Live" campaigns, and the name-changing of towns, see Wheeler, *Lidice,* and also Geoffrey Perrett, *Days of Sadness, Years of Triumph: The American People, 1939–1945* (New York: Coward, McCann & Geoghegan, 1973), 235.

8   "The World and the Theatre: The Radio, The Poet and the News—The Moon is Down Once Again," *Theatre Arts* 26.12 (December 1942): 733.

9   Winkler, *Politics of Propaganda,* 54.

10 "Edna Makes the Supreme Sacrifice," *Vice Versa* 1.1 (November/December 1940): 27; *Time* 36 (9 December 1940). *Vice Versa* was particularly snide. Its second issue includes a review of Millay's *Make Bright the Arrows:* "She [Millay] has changed from the jaded creature who had forgotten how much necking she had done . . . to a regular old tartar of a drummer girl. Right now she should be called the Boadicea of Austerlitz. According to her new book she's awfully mad at someone—I think it's the Germans but, as always with Miss Millay, one is never quite sure. It may be merely something she ate." *Vice Versa* 1.2 (January/February 1941): 31. Not only Millay, and not only women, were ridiculed in reviews like these as the question of evaluating political poetry heated up in the late thirties and early forties. Robert Sherwood, another prominent literary figure turned wartime government official, was criticized for his interventionist "There Shall Be No Night" (1940); see, for a relatively measured critique, "Hello to Arms," *New Yorker,* 11 May 1940, 28. And MacLeish shares the blame in this review from the first issue of *Vice Versa:* "We don't, however, see why political manifestations, which have their own somewhat crude methods of solving themselves, should excuse Miss Millay's writing more stupidly than usual, or permit Mr. MacLeish, rolling up and down the Library of Congress steps in his sack-cloth and ashes, another, shall we say, about-face." *Vice Versa* 1.1 (November/December 1940). But negative reviews of Millay and other women were frequently phrased in misogynist terms, adding another dimension of attack.

11 Williams, *War Poets,* 6.

12 Frederik Prokosch, "Regarding War Poetry," in Williams, *War Poets,* 22.

13 On Millay's FBI file, see Natalie Robins, "Hoover and American Literature: The Defiling of Writers," *Nation,* 10 October 1987, 368. For examples of Millay's earlier political poetry, see "Hangman's Oak" and "Justice Denied in Massachusetts," *The Buck in the Snow* (New York: Harper, 1928). The latter poem was famously criticized by Allen Tate in "Tension in Poetry," *Reason in Madness: Critical Essays* (New York: Putnam, 1941), 63–64. See also Millay's early antiwar play *Aria Da Capo* (New York: Mitchell Kennerley, 1921).

14 Edna St. Vincent Millay to George Dillon, 29 November 1940, in *Letters,* ed.

Allan Ross Macdougall (New York: Harper & Brothers, 1952), 309 ("not poems" and "impassioned propaganda"). Wilson, "Epilogue," 785 ("issued in the same format").

15 Edmund Wilson, "Visit to Edna Millay," *The Forties: From Notebooks and Diaries of the Period*, ed. Leon Edel (New York: Farrar, Straus & Giroux, 1983), 290. Hereafter abbreviated as "Visit" and cited in the text.

16 Edna St. Vincent Millay to Mrs. Charlotte Babcock Sills 2 January 1941, in Macdougall, ed., *Letters*, 310–12, letter 228.

17 Wilson, "Epilogue," 781.

18 On Benét's death and his work as a propagandist, see the eulogies in *Saturday Review of Literature*, 27 March 1943, and "Stephen Benét: The Ultimate Objectives of Free Men Are To Be Discovered in Their Acts and Letters," *Life*, 5 April 1943, 22.

19 Wynn Wright, "Production Note" to "The Murder of Lidice," in Margaret Cuthbert, *Adventure in Radio* (New York: Howell, Soskin, 1945), 237. Both the radioscript version of Millay's play and Wright's note are hereafter cited in the text.

20 On rape and propaganda, see Susan Brownmiller, *Against Our Will: Men, Women and Rape* (New York: Simon & Schuster, 1975). Ezra Pound, incidentally, offers a classic example of the use of rape propaganda in poetry in his Italian Canto 73, in which an Italian peasant girl takes revenge on a group of Canadian soldiers who raped her: see Massimo Bacigalupe, "The Poet at War: Ezra Pound's Suppressed Italian Cantos," *South Atlantic Quarterly* 83.1 (Winter 1984): 69–79. The comparison between Millay's activities and Pound's during the war is worth bearing in mind throughout this chapter, especially in regard to their uses of the radio. The association of propaganda and prostitution so infiltrates the antipropaganda rhetoric of the period that no example seems needed; but see, for instance, Hemingway's discussion of writing and chastity in his *Men at War*, xv. The "poster girl" as a figure for propaganda created by admen crops up in home-front debates over the OWI's methods of "selling" the war; see William Rose Benét's poem "Try our delicious, health-building war" in *Saturday Review of Literature*, 8 May 1943, 22. On the association of indirect "black propaganda" with feminine wiles, see, for example, Elizabeth Macdonald, *Undercover Girl* (New York: Macmillan, 1947), 31–32. Mansfield, in *Gestalts of War*, discusses "the parallels between indirect [military] strategy and traditional female gender roles" (211–12). A paradigmatic case history of the association between hysteria and propaganda is provided in the history of reception of Rudyard Kipling's Great War stories "Mary Postgate" and "Mrs. Bathhurst," particularly "Mary Postgate," in which the question of propaganda-induced female hysteria has become an interpretive crux; see John Bayley, *The Short Story: Henry Jones to Elizabeth Bowen* (Brighton: Harvester, 1988), 84–93, for an account of the debate. Much of MacLeish's writing of the war period, some of it cited later, develops an association between reading or being influenced by propaganda and emasculation.

21 R. S. P., "Grandeur and Misery of a Poster Girl," *Partisan Review* 10.5 (1943): 471–73. On this incident, see Louise Kertesz, *The Poetic Vision of Muriel Rukeyser* (Baton Rouge: Louisiana State Univ. Press, 1980), 179–81. For counter-defenses of Rukeyser by Rebecca Pitts, Babette Deutsch, and Thomas Mabry, see "The Rukeyser Imbroglio," *Partisan Review* 11.1 (Winter 1944): 125–27, and F. O. Matthiessen, *Partisan Review* 11.2 (Spring 1944): 218. Rukeyser had quit the Graphics

Division of the OWI in late 1943, one of many well-publicized resignations by writers and artists who felt that the organization was being taken over by "high pressure promoters who prefer slick salesmanship to honest information." See "Miss Rukeyser Quitting," *New York Herald Tribune*, 12 May 1943. For overviews of the larger controversy of which the "Rukeyser Imbroglio" was a part, see Rupp, *Mobilizing Women*, 91–92; Sydney Weinberg, "What to Tell America," *Journal of American History* 55 (June 1968): 73–89; Richard Polenberg, *War and Society: The United States 1941–1945* (New York: Lippincott, 1972), 51–53; and Winkler, *Politics of Propaganda*.

22   Prokosch, "Regarding War Poetry," 22.

23   Nancy Miller, *Subject to Change: Reading Feminist Writing* (New York: Columbia Univ. Press, 1988), 126.

24   The narrative of the massacre which Millay would have been given probably included little more than is sketched out in the Writers' War Board summary in *The Murder of Lidice*, v. For an example of stock rape atrocity narrative, see Anita Chartres's famous Great War novel *The Outrage* (New York: Knopf, 1918).

25   Quoted in Norman A. Brittin, *Edna St. Vincent Millay* (Boston: Twayne, 1982), 110.

26   Stephen Spender, "Warnings from the Grave," *New Republic,* 18 June 1966, 26. Hereafter cited in the text.

27   "If, in our culture, the woman is by definition associated with madness, her problem is how to break out of this (cultural) imposition of madness *without* taking up the critical and therapeutic positions of reason: how to avoid speaking both as *mad* and as *not mad*." Shoshana Felman, "Women and Madness: The Critical Phallacy," *Diacritics* 5.4 (Winter 1975): 10. Note that the story by Balzac whose reception as "realistic" (at the expense of rendering the woman unreadable) which Felman analyzes is a *war* story.

28   Gertrude Stein, "Patriarchal Poetry," *The Yale Gertrude Stein*, ed. Richard Kostelanetz (New Haven: Yale Univ. Press, 1980), 116.

29   Archibald MacLeish, preface, "The Fall of the City," *Six Plays* (Boston: Houghton Mifflin, 1980), 68. All further quotations from the play are from this edition and are hereafter cited in the text. The preface is hereafter cited as "Preface."

30   Archibald MacLeish, foreword, *The Fall of the City: A Verse Play for Radio* (New York: Farrar and Rhinehart, 1937), ix. Hereafter referred to as "Foreword" and cited in the text.

31   MacLeish had written before about Aztec culture, in his *Conquistador* (New York: Houghton Mifflin, 1932). Randall Jarrell's brilliantly scathing review of *The Fall of the City* is particularly acute about the political implications of MacLeish's projection of fascism and isolationism onto the primitivized Aztec Other (and equation of contemporary conditions with ancient ones); see "The Fall of the City," in Jarrell, *Kipling, Auden and Co.*, 101–11.

32   Jacqueline Rose has challenged the equation of fascism and the irrational in her "Sylvia Plath and the Obscenity of Literary Criticism," Oxford English Limited Conference, May 1987, and in "Getting Away With Murder," *New Statesman and Society*, 22 July 1988, 34–37.

33   MacLeish, preface, "Air Raid," *Six Plays*, 97. All further quotations from the play are from this edition and are hereafter cited in the text.

34   Susan Gubar, "'This Is My Rifle, This Is My Gun': World War II and the Blitz on Women" in Higgonet et al., eds., *Behind the Lines*, 227–59.

35 On male modernists' appropriations and repudiations of the feminine, see Gilbert and Gubar, *No Man's Land 2*, especially 324–76.

36 MacLeish's lines resemble Lacan's: "There is woman only as excluded by the nature of things which is the nature of words, and it has to be said that if there is one thing they themselves are complaining about enough at the moment, it is well and truly that—only they don't know what they are saying, which is all the difference between them and me." *Feminine Sexuality: Jacques Lacan and the école freudienne*, ed. Juliet Mitchell and Jacqueline Rose (New York: Norton, 1982), 144. This is also much like MacLeish's comment on why he never showed his wife his poems, in words which sound almost like parodic proof of Margaret Homans's argument (in *Bearing the Word*): "She has a wonderful, literal-minded, womanly approach to the experience of life. . . . literal-mindedness is very, very close to literality, to what is *truly true*. And women are really close to what is truly true most of the time." Quoted in Helen E. Ellis, "MacLeish and the Nature of Woman," *The Proceedings of the Archibald MacLeish Symposium*, ed. Bernard A. Drabeck, Helen Ellis, and Seymour Rudin (Lanham, Md.: Univ. Press of America, 1988), 88.

37 Archibald MacLeish, "Prophets of Disaster," in *A Time to Act* (Boston: Houghton Mifflin, 1943), 89.

38 Ibid.

39 Archibald MacLeish, "Public Speech and Private Speech in Poetry," *A Time to Speak* (Boston: Houghton Mifflin, 1951), 64. Compare his preface, "The War is Ours," *New Masses*, 22 June 1937, in which he implies that anti-interventionist liberals are like prudish and overly timid women: "To my mind there is something unpleasantly squeamish and virginal about this fear of being used, this phobia of being maneuvered—something almost indecently coy. The danger of rape has always existed in this world, but only the tenderest spirits let it keep them in at night."

40 Millay works here in ways much like those employed in the tradition Paula Rabinowitz has analyzed, maternal imagery used by the bourgeoise woman activist "who can use her class position to aid her radical politics," for whom "maternity appears linked to revolutionary action." Charlotte Nekola and Paula Rabinowitz, eds., *Writing Red: An Anthology of American Women Writers, 1930–1940* (New York: Feminist Press, 1987), 27.

41 See, for example, Stephen Vincent Benét's "Letter from a Housewife" in "Dear Adolf," *We Stand United and Other Radio Scripts* (New York: Farrar and Rhinehart, 1942).

42 On the "moral mother" and her opposite, the "Woman Warrior," see Di Leonardo, "Morals, Mothers, and Militarism." Millay's "moral mother" is also, of course, a "woman warrior."

43 Thomas Hardy, *The Dynasts: A Drama* (New York: Macmillan, 1931), viii.

44 See Wheeler, *Lidice*, 20–30.

45 On "high-mindedness" in home-front culture, see Paul Fussell's eloquent critique in *Wartime: Understanding and Behavior in the Second World War* (New York: Oxford Univ. Press, 1989), 164–80.

46 Cary Nelson's brief but forceful discussion of *Murder of Lidice* and the political function of poetry "in periods of historical crisis" came out in print after I completed this manuscript. See Nelson, *Repression and Recovery*, 41–43.

Chapter 3. The Masculine V-Letter

1 Woolf, *Three Guineas*, 38.
2 Deena Metzgar, *The Woman Who Slept with Men to Take the War Out of Them* (Culver City, Cal.: Peace Press, 1978), 14.
3 The phrase "inherited myth" is Paul Fussell's, from his *Great War and Modern Memory*, ix.
4 "Recognition scene" is another of Fussell's phrases (ibid., 335).
5 Cooper, "Nothing Has Been Used," 36.
6 Paul Fussell, introduction, *Reviewing the Forties*, by Diana Trilling (New York: Harcourt Brace Jovanovich, 1978), vi–vii.
7 Ibid., vi.
8 Laura Mulvey, "Visual Pleasure and Narrative Cinema," *Screen* 16 (Autumn 1975): 7. By quoting only this line, I have, of course, omitted reference to Mulvey's complex psychoanalytic anatomy of visual pleasure. What counts here for my purposes is simply her emphasis on the immobility and passivity of the female figure who is gazed at.
9 For a more complex analysis of the workings of advertising, see Judith Williamson, *Decoding Advertisements: Ideology and Meaning in Advertising* (Boston: Marion Boyars, 1978).
10 See, e.g., Stanley Kunitz, "Night Letter," Karl Shapiro, "V-Letter," James Forsyth, "To My Wife," Roy Fuller, "Spring 1945," William Meredith, "Love Letter from an Impossible Land," Keidrych Rhys, "Letter to My Wife," Seldon Rodman, "V-Letter to Karl Shapiro in Australia," Randall Swingler's letter series, Julian Symon's "For My Wife," and Dunstan Thomas, "This Loneliness for You Is Like a Wound," all poems by British or American male poets collected in Oscar Williams's anthology *War Poets*. Lest it seem that this penchant for letter form is Williams's alone, see also Peter Viereck, "By V-Mail to Ellen," *New Yorker*, 13 November 1943, 32; Horace Gregory, "If You See My Face You Will Know I Am At Home," *Saturday Review of Literature* 27.2 (8 January 1944):10; Thomas McGrath, "A Letter for Marian," *Poetry* 64.3 (1944): 130–31; Trevor Middleton, "The Solitary Soldier," in *Poets Now in the Services* (London: Favil Press, 1943), 11; Louis Coxe, "For M. E. S. Before D-Day," *Poetry* 66.6 (1945): 313; Joseph Rogers, "To Another Lucasta," in *Reveille*, ed. Daniel Henderson *et al.* (New York: A. S. Barnes, 1943); Gavin Ewart, "Sonnet," and G. S. Fraser, "Christmas Letter Home" in *More Poems from the Forces*, ed. Keidrych Rhys (London: George Routledge and Sons, 1943); John Ciardi, "Poem for my Twenty-Ninth Birthday" in his *Other Skies* (Boston: Little, Brown, 1947). Related poems which make use of the image of the letter include Randall Jarrell's "Mail Call" in *Little Friend, Little Friend* (New York: Dial, 1945) and Rolphe Humphries' translation of Louis Aragon's "I Wait for Her Letter in the Twilight," *Poetry* 63.6 (1944): 306. Finally, see Edward Fenton's poem on the uses of "the rhetorical [female] You" in *Poetry* 65.1 (1944): 28–29.
11 Sassoon, "Introduction."
12 Paul Fussell, "The War in Black and White," 231. As recently as 1982, Ian Hamilton used the phrase "letter home" to mean something like "humble reportage," in his review of Dan Davin's anthology *Short Stories from the Second World War*: "Missing from all those decent, genuinely suffered letters home was, quite simply, the flicker of an individual talent. . . ." See Ian Hamilton, "Among the Muckers,"

Times Literary Supplement, 12 November 1987, 1243. Compare A. T. Tolley who writes in his *The Poetry of the Forties* (Manchester: Manchester Univ. Press, 1985) of a "typical" British Second War poem by Geoffrey Parsons, "Airgraph I": "The poem assumes the most modest of forms, the epistle, in the guise of the wartime microfilmed letter, the 'airgraph,' which the poet is writing in his tent in Burma. . . . The poet turns his back on the war to find consolation in the sensed presence of the woman he loves" (208). Bernard Spencer's poem "Letters," in Williams, ed., *War Poets*, also uses the image of the letter to explore distinctions between public and private discourse.

13 Karl Shapiro, "V-Letter," in Williams, ed., *War Poets*, 227. Hereafter in chapter 3 cited in the text. William Meredith, "Love Letter from an Impossible Land," in Williams, ed., *War Poets*, 199.

14 Karl Shapiro, "Since the War Began," in Williams, ed., *War Poets*, 27. The technical meaning of "V-Letter," to which Shapiro refers in his simile, is explained by this blurb from the *Saturday Evening Post*: "What's the secret of V-mail? By photography on microfilm, your hand-written letter shrinks from page to postage-stamp size. Now a miniature — it crosses the ocean. Enlarged overseas, the letter becomes readable V-mail." Quoted in *American Speech* (October 1944): 226.

15 Oscar Williams, introduction, in Williams, ed., *War Poets*, 5.

16 W. H. Auden, "Sept. 1, 1939," *The English Auden*, ed. Edward Mendelson (New York: Random, 1977), 247.

17 Ann Rosalind Jones, "Assimilation with a Difference: Renaissance Women Poets and Literary Influence," *Yale French Studies* 62 (1981): 136. For two excellent analyses of the function of the *blason* in Renaissance love poetry, see Jones, "Assimilation with a Difference," 147–52, and Nancy J. Vickers, "Diana Described: Scattered Women and Scattered Rhyme," in Elizabeth Abel, ed., *Writing and Sexual Difference* (Chicago: Univ. of Chicago Press, 1982), 95–110.

18 Mary Ann Doane makes a related point in her analysis of the function of letters in forties film love stories (where they show up frequently). See her *The Desire to Desire: The Women's Film of the 1940's* (Bloomington: Indiana Univ. Press, 1987), 113–14. Hereafter cited in the text. On the place of the heroine in forties war films, Barbara Deming's early study remains provocative and useful: Barbara Deming, *Running Away from Myself: A Dream Portrait of America Drawn from the Films of the Forties* (New York: Grossman, 1969).

19 Earle Birney, "On Going to the Wars," in Williams, ed., *War Poets*, 91–93.

20 Richard Lovelace, "To Lucasta, Going to the Warres," *The Poems of Richard Lovelace*, ed. C. H. Wilkinson (Oxford: Clarendon, 1925), 2:16. Hereafter cited in the text. Compare Rupert Brooke's Great War version of this leave-taking scene, "Safety," *The Poetical Works of Rupert Brooke*, ed. Geoffrey Keynes (London: Faber & Faber, 1946), 20.

21 Seldon Rodman, "V-Letter to Karl Shapiro in Australia," in Williams, ed., *War Poets*, 219–20.

22 See Eric Leed's discussion of Great War participants' sense that they were immersed in a war which was an authorless "text": "The Event as Text," *No Man's Land: Combat and Identity in World War I* (Cambridge: Cambridge Univ. Press, 1979), 33–38.

23 Owen, *Collected Poems*, 74.

24 The class-marked voice in the lines from "The Letter" which follow is not "Owen's own" (its jingling Cockney rhymes contrast sharply, for instance, with the reso-

nant, melancholic pararhymes and iambic measure of his "Strange Meeting"), but this man nonetheless speaks for Owen as Owen speaks for him.

25 In one draft of "S.I.W." which Jon Stallworthy's edition prints in facsimile, Mother is given a line which at first glance might appear to grant her some effective knowledge and agency: "'Get yourself wounded cushy,' Mother said." At second glance, however, even this—like the mother's wish for a "nice safe wound" for her boy in the later version of the poem—is ironized at her expense, for she seems in part to plant in her son the idea of self-mutilation. In the same earlier draft, the father appears as a potential final addressee: "Some day I mean to tell his noble dad / Those splendid words of his that killed his lad, / And what it was that kept his features smiling." These lines are clearly excised in favor of a version which focuses on the mother and emphasizes her ignorance. See Stallworthy, ed., *Complete Poems and Fragments*, 327–31.

26 The drafts of "The Send-Off" are reprinted in ibid., 346–49.

27 Jessie Pope, or her publishers, apparently found it necessary to bolster her literary authority by reprinting a facsimile of a soldier's letter from the front on the inside cover of her *War Poems* (London: Grant Richards, 1915), endorsing that volume. The letter goes in part: "The Verses were much admired by us all out here, and I want you to send them to my wife for me, as . . . bucking up means so much to those at home as well as for us."

28 Fred D. Crawford, *British Poets of the Great War* (Selinsgrove, Pa.: Susquehanna Univ. Press, 1988), 59–60.

29 Robert Graves, *Goodbye to All That: An Autobiography* (New York: Jonathan Cape and Harrison Smith, 1930), 271–76; Sassoon's "In the Pink" (25), "The Hero" (20), "Their Frailty" (58), "Return of the Heroes" (67), "Reconciliation" (87), in *The War Poems of Siegfried Sassoon* (London: William Heinemann, 1919). Sandra Gilbert's "Soldier's Heart" is still the most important analysis of Great War misogyny and antifeminism: "Soldier's Heart: Literary Men, Literary Women and the Great War," in Higgonet et al., eds., *Behind the Lines*, 197–226.

30 Nina Baym, "Melodramas of Beset Manhood: How Theories of American Fiction Exclude Women Authors," *American Quarterly* 33.2 (1981): 129–30, 133.

31 Horace, "Ode III. ii," *The Odes and Epodes*, ed. and trans. C. E. Bennett (Cambridge: Harvard Univ. Press, 1947), 175.

32 The equation of warmongering literature with the representation of the female spectator is by no means Owen's alone. In his *Inter Arma: Being Essays Written in Time of War* (New York: Scribner, 1916), for instance, Edmund Gosse included two examples of what he called "the conventional battle-composition": Erasmus Darwin's "Battle of Minden," in which Eliza is a "spectatress of the fight," and *Marmion*, whose heroine Gosse ridicules as well: "[This] tradition affected every writer who attempted to picture warfare long after the romantic method had displaced the classic. It was supposed to be romantic, and we have only to turn to *Marmion* to see that Clara at Flodden is the younger and somewhat less maniacal sister of Eliza of the red and rolling eye" (111–12). Virginia Woolf offers a feminist and antimilitarist critique of the "spectatress" of war, and attempts to devise alternatives for instigating spectatorship for women, throughout *Three Guineas*.

33 Dominic Hibbard, *Owen the Poet* (London: Macmillan, 1986), 59.

34 For this letter and reproductions of the various drafts of the "Kings and Christs / women and slain" poem, see Stallworthy, ed., *Complete Poems and Fragments*, 503 and 500–509 generally.

35 Ibid., 503.
36 In addition to Gilbert's pioneering essay "Soldier's Heart," see the answers to Gilbert by Marcus, "Asylums of Antaeus," and Claire M. Tylee, "'Maleness Run Riot'—The Great War and Women's Resistance to Militarism," *Women's Studies Int. Forum* 11.3 (1988), 199–210. See also Khan's very thorough summary in *Women's Poetry of the First World War.*
37 Amy Lowell, "Patterns," in *Men, Women and Ghosts* (New York: Houghton Mifflin, 1916), 3–9. The reader taught first by "Patterns" to make one kind of analogy, between the patterns of dress and garden and the stifling of sexual and imaginative energy in women, is only then compelled by the revelation of the letter to make another kind of analogy, between pattern and violence men do to men in war. The links Lowell makes are tentative, however; the handwriting on the letter signals its distance from the world of the telegram. The deliberate archaism of "Patterns" is a highly effective screen, a displacing device which allowed Lowell to retain the scene of female reading and still resolve some of the problems posed by Great War conventions of guilty female spectatorship, but which also prevented her poem from becoming a strong model for modern war poetry by women.
38 Eleanor Farjeon, "Easter Monday: In Memorium E. T.," in Reilly, ed., *Scars Upon My Heart*, 36. See Jan Montefiore's discussion of this poem in *Feminism*, 66–68. Farjeon's poem echoes one of Thomas's own, "In Memoriam (Easter, 1915)." See Robert Giddings, *The War Poets: The Lives and Writings of the 1914–1918 War Poets* (London: Bloomsbury, 1988), 63.
39 Alys Eyre Macklin, *Lyceum Book of War Verses* (London: Erskine Macdonald, 1918). Lilian Rowland Brown, "War Poetry of Women," *Nineteenth Century* 81 (February 1917): 452. There is a chance that Lilian Rowland Brown is the pen name of a man; her name is followed by the unexplained parenthetical reference "Rowland Grey."
40 Virginia Woolf, quoted in Giddings, *War Poets*, 110.
41 On Shapiro's and others' votes against rewarding the Bollingen to Pound, see *Partisan Review* (May 1949), 512–22.
42 Quoted in John Crowe Ransom, "Artists, Soldiers, Positivists," *Kenyon Review* 6 (1944): 276–77.
43 Hugh Kenner, *The Pound Era* (Berkeley: Univ. of California Press, 1971), 202. On Pound's early poetry and the Great War, see also Longenbach, *Stone Cottage*, 105–27.
44 Longenbach vividly traces Pound's complicated and vexed relation to the Great War and the newly developing category "war poetry" in his *Stone Cottage*. It is important to note here that Pound did try to enlist in 1915, despite his bitter objections to the war at its outset, but was turned down because the British army was not accepting American citizens. See Longenbach *Stone Cottage*, 123.
45 Pound, "The River Merchant's Wife: A Letter," *Personae*, 130–31. Kenner, *Pound Era*, 202.
46 Lawrence Lipking asserts that Li Po himself "gave the 'river-merchant's' wife a voice, according to scholars, in order to express his own loneliness; decorum required that the weakness of the man be projected onto the woman." Lipking, *Abandoned Women and Poetic Tradition* (Chicago: Univ. of Chicago Press, 1988), 132. Lipking cites Ronald Bush, "Pound and Li Po: What Becomes a Man," in *Ezra Pound Among the Poets*, ed. George Bornstein (Chicago: Univ. of Chicago Press, 1985), 40–42.

47 Pound's ambiguous relation to the combatants' "we" is illustrated also in the progressive publications of his "Poem: Abbreviated from the Conversation of Mr. T. E. H.," a representation of the trenches which was first published in Pound's *Catholic Anthology* under Hulme's name and then later signed by Pound in *Umbra*. See Longenbach, *Stone Cottage*, 125.

48 I take the phrase "poetic manhood" from Frank Lentricchia, in his *Ariel and the Police: Michel Foucault, William James, Wallace Stevens* (Madison: Univ. of Wisconsin Press, 1988), 162. In general, Lentricchia's explorations of Stevens's desires for and fears of femininization are pertinent throughout this discussion. Unlike Lentricchia, however, I see those desires and fears as in no way a threat to the concept of or the workings of patriarchy; the "man's hand," as I argued in chapter 1, retains its power. See Sandra M. Gilbert and Susan Gubar's analysis of "virilization" in their response to Lentricchia, "The Man on the Dump vs. the United Dames of America, or, What Does Frank Lentricchia Want?" *Critical Inquiry* 14 (Winter 1988): 406.

49 See "Exile's Letter," one of Pound's Chinese poems which speaks from the position of a waiting *male* correspondent, for examples both of the fetishization of women's bodies in response to loss and powerlessness (note the emphasis on the women's green eyebrows in the second reunion scene) and of muted homoeroticism.

50 "Lyric privacy" is Herbert Tucker's phrase, in his "Dramatic Monologue and the Overhearing of Lyric," in *Lyric Poetry: Beyond New Criticism*, ed. Chaviva Hosek and Patricia Parker (Ithaca: Cornell Univ. Press, 1985), 230.

51 A. Walton Litz notes that the final poem in the manuscript sequence is numbered "XVII," suggesting that there may at one time have been more poems. See Litz, *Introspective Voyager*, 309.

52 Stevens recommended the American translation to Harriet Monroe in his letter to her concerning the "Lettres"; see Letter 212, in *Letters of Wallace Stevens*, ed. Holly Stevens (New York: Knopf, 1966), 202.

53 See Litz, *Introspective Voyager*, 71–73, and Macleod, *Wallace Stevens and Co.* on the history of the sequence.

54 Macleod, *Wallace Stevens and Co.*, 58.

55 Compare the soldiers quoted in Leed, *No Man's Land*, 91, on "becoming a common man."

56 In this way Lemercier's function for Stevens resembles Gaudier-Brzeska's function for Pound; on the resonant lyric qualities in Gaudier-Brzeska's letters from the front, see Longenbach, *Stone Cottage*, 121.

57 On the breakdown in the pastiche of credence in a single speaker or single voice, see David Bromwich, "Parody, Pastiche and Allusion," in Hosek and Parker, eds., *Lyric Poetry*, 337. Critics have frequently suggested that the relation between Stevens's poems and Lemercier's letters is combative and ironized, but I agree with Glen Macleod's assessment that "the overall relation of the series to its source is . . . uncharacteristically straightforward" and that "the attitudes expressed are generally in perfect harmony with Lemercier's book" (*Wallace Stevens and Co.*, 57).

58 Theodor Adorno, "Lyric Poetry and Society," *Telos* 20 (Summer 1974): 59.

59 Macleod, *Wallace Stevens and Co.*, 59.

60 Wallace Stevens, "Lettres d'un Soldat," in Litz, *Introspective Voyager*, app. B, 309–15. All further quotations are from this version of Stevens's poem, hereafter cited in the text.

61 A. Clutton-Brock, preface, *Letters of a Soldier 1914-1915*, by Eugene Lemercier, trans. V. M. and with a preface by André Chevrillon (London: Constable, 1917). This edition of Lemercier's letters and both prefaces are hereafter cited in the text.

62 On the "semiotic" see Julia Kristeva, *Desire in Language: A Semiotic Approach to Literature and Art*, ed. Leon S. Roudiez, trans. Thomas Gora, Alice Jardine, and Leon S. Roudiez (New York: Columbia Univ. Press, 1980).

63 Even the recovery of an enveloping, redeeming (we might say pre-Oedipal) maternal presence at the end of the poem, which begins and concludes "The moon is the mother of pathos and pity," is already compromised, outdated, only nostalgic: "over the houses, a golden illusion / Brings back an earlier season of quiet / And quieting dreams in the sleepers in darkness. . . ."

64 Marina Warner, *Monuments and Maidens: The Allegory of the Female Form* (New York: Atheneum, 1985), 332-33.

65 See Lemercier, *Letters of a Soldier*, 41-42.

66 Wallace Stevens, "The Figure of the Youth as Virile Poet," *The Necessary Angel*, 66.

67 Stevens, "Figure of the Youth," 52. Susan Gubar discusses at length representations of the threat of emasculation in Second War literature by men; see her "This is My Rifle, This is My Gun," in Higgonet et al., eds., *Behind the Lines*, 227-59.

Chapter 4. (Not) Playing with Mimesis: Gwendolyn Brooks and the Stuff of Letters

1 On "transferred voice" in war poetry, see Judith Kazantzis, preface, in Reilly, ed., *Scars Upon My Heart*, xvii, and Reilly, *English Poetry of the Second World War*, 12. Reilly's research suggests that women poets in the Second World War often used the "transferred voice," but I would emphasize that American women poets already publishing in the well-known literary journals, an especially self-conscious group, almost never did.

2 Gwendolyn Brooks, *Report from Part One* (Detroit: Broadside Press, 1972), 156.

3 Margaret Walker, "New Poets," *Phylon* 11 (1950): 352.

4 Luce Irigaray, "The Power of Discourse and the Subordination of the Feminine," *This Sex Which Is Not One*, trans. Catherine Porter (Ithaca: Cornell Univ. Press, 1985) 76. Hereafter cited in the text.

5 Playing with mimesis, as Irigaray formulates it, means the deliberate choice of *not* "demanding to speak as a (masculine) subject," of *not* coveting a position of power from which one could appropriate, exploit, and resist the feminine. Instead, the expert player of the game of mimesis would practice a fluid and playful mimicry of feminine language only, speaking as a woman in order to enact her critical distance from the language she so perfectly parrots. (Within the literature of the forties in the United States, perhaps the best example of this rhetorical strategy is the body of fiction by Dorothy Parker, with its expert, arch, and implicitly sharply critical representations of the conventional language of women.) The challenge and the power of this tactic lies in its ironic overturning of the gender assumptions which attach to the traditional definition of the rhetorical term invoked: if mimesis means "a figure of speech whereby the supposed words or actions of another are imitated," then the joke of the play with mimesis is that the woman player takes the *feminine*, not the masculine, as the alien behavior of another, which she can deftly imitate but which she does not come by "naturally." By this definition, Brooks's imitations of the soldier-as-subject, of the masculine

"other," would precisely *not* qualify as play with mimesis. I find this distinction slippery, however, when it comes to analysis of literary texts, and am unwilling to assume that Brooks's fictive acting out of a male persona — perhaps particularly the fragmented, vulnerable Black veteran persona of this war poem — necessarily constitutes a "demand" to speak as a "(masculine) subject." What I wish to take from Irigaray is the large concept of repeating symbolic structures which subordinate the feminine (or some other "other") but repeating them with a difference, of critical miming. American feminist critics have interpreted the concept of mimesis both broadly and narrowly. At times, as in Mary Jacobus's influential discussion of this passage, which reads it in line with Irigaray's most radical conception of all discourse and all systems of representation as masculine, any entrance into language whatsoever by a woman writer may be interpreted as an act of mimesis, subversive if undertaken deliberately and playfully. Mary Jacobus, "Men of Maxims and the Mill on the Floss," *Reading Woman: Essays in Feminist Criticism* (New York: Columbia Univ. Press, 1986), 64–67. For other feminist critics, the game of mimesis seems to come to mean, more specifically, freestyle femininity, the tongue-in-cheek flaunting of feminine language and manner, as in this discussion of Irigaray's related concept of masquerade by Mary Russo: "For a woman to dress, act, or position herself in discourse as a man is easily understandable and culturally compelling. To 'act like a woman' beyond narcissism and masochism is . . . trickier. That is the critical and hopeful power of the masquerade. . . . To put on femininity with a vengeance suggests the power of taking it off." Mary Russo, "Female Grotesques: Carnival and Theory," *Feminist Studies/ Critical Studies*, ed. Teresa de Lauritis (Bloomington: Indiana Univ. Press, 1986), 224. See also Mary Ann Doane's eloquent advocacy of "an active differentiation between gesture and 'essence,' a play with the signs previously anchored by a set notion of sexual difference," in her *Desire to Desire*, 183. Other feminist discussions, often focused on specific literary readings, and concerned, as I am, with the ways in which in a text — not only *language* but also *image, form*, and other aspects of *genre* — might be open to subversive mimicry, take a middle line. This position is described in Tania Modleski's association of "playing with mimesis" with the general notion that "a female 'speaker' (or reader) may be articulating a different meaning when she repeats a male text," whether she repeats it in a voice openly marked as feminine or not. Tania Modleski, "Feminism and the Power of Interpretation," in Teresa de Lauretis, ed., *Feminist Studies/Critical Studies*, 128–29. Louis A. Renza sceptically outlines such an application of the term in his own mimicry of a "radical feminist" reading of Sarah Orne Jewett's "A White Heron"; see his *"A White Heron" and the Question of Minor Literature* (Madison: Univ. of Wisconsin Press, 1984), 80–94. For a useful summary of the numerous influential feminist analyses which in some way draw on the concept of mimeticism or related formulations, see Naomi Schor, "Dreaming Dissymmetry: Barthes, Foucault, and Sexual Difference," *Men in Feminism*, ed. Alice Jardine and Paul Smith (New York: Methuen, 1987), 110; and on the uses of the term in work on psychoanalysis and cinema (where the notion has been most widespread), see Stephen Heath, "Joan Riviere and the Masquerade," *Formations of Fantasy*, ed. Victor Burgin, James Donald, and Cora Kaplan (New York: Methuen, 1986), 45–61. "Masquerade" is, of course, in some sense a central defining feature of all dramatic monologue, which is governed by what Alan Sinfield calls "the concept of the feint" (25), a "double perception" (33), and a "teasing self-awareness" on the part of the reader (33–34). Sinfield, *Dramatic Monologue* (New York: Barnes & Noble Books, 1977). To call it "play with mimesis" in Irigaray's sense or "mimicry" in Homi Bhabha's (see note 6 below) is to politicize that feint, and to foreground the politics of gender and race within these monologues. If, however, "feint" is the *norm* in this type of poem, then those politics may be muted by regular generic conventions and the poems may come to seem less than subversive. This possibility will, in a variety of ways, be a recurrent suspicion throughout the pages of chapter 4.

6   "The ambivalence of mimicry" is Homi Bhabha's phrase: "the discourse of mimicry is constructed around an *ambivalence*: in order to be effective, mimicry must continually produce its slippage, its excess, its difference." Bhabha, "Of Mimicry and Man: The Ambivalence of Colonial Discourse," *Politics and Ideology*, ed. James Donald and Stuart Hall (Philadelphia: Open Univ. Press, 1986), 199.

7   Henry Louis Gates, Jr., describes this double-voicedness as a common feature of the Black canon: "in the case of the writer of African descent, her or his texts occupy spaces in at least two traditions: a European or American literary tradition, and one of the several related but distinct black traditions." "Criticism in the Jungle," *Black Literature and Literary Theory*, ed. Gates (New York: Methuen, 1984), 4.

8   Brooks did not capitalize the separate titles of the poems within the "Gay Chaps" series; I have followed her example. I refer, then, to the series as a whole as "Gay Chaps at the Bar," but to the first poem in the sequence as "gay chaps."

9   Gwendolyn Brooks, "Gay Chaps at the Bar," *Blacks* (Chicago: The David Company, 1988), 64. All further citations to Brooks's work are to this volume, unless otherwise specified, and are given in the text.

10 Owen Dodson, "Open Letter" (103), "The Signifying Darkness" (13), "Samuel Chapman Armstrong" (23–27), and "Conversation on V" (91), in his wartime collection, *Powerful Long Ladder* (New York: Farrar, Straus, 1946); Melvin Tolson's title poem (8), his "The Unknown Soldier," (34), and "Dark Symphony," (40), in his *Rendezvous with America* (New York: Dodd, Mead, 1944); Langston Hughes, "Southern Negro Speaks," *Opportunity* 23 (April-June 1945): 65, "Private Jim Crow," *Negro Story* (March/April 1945):2, and "Beaumont to Detroit: 1943," *Common Ground* (August 1943): 104.

"Remember Pearl Harbor, and Sikeston too" is a ubiquitous slogan in the radical Black newspapers of 1942 — see, for instance, any issue of the *Chicago Defender* in the winter issues of that year. On the lynching of Cleo Wright at Sikeston, and for a contemporary overview of racial tensions during the war, see Cary McWilliams, "What We Did About Racial Minorities," in Goodman, ed., *While You Were Gone*, 89–112. Black Second War rhetoric often juxtaposed Sikeston and a more publically recognized atrocity of the war, as in this example from "An Open Letter to President Roosevelt," *Crisis* (January 1943): "[Black soldiers] fight because they wish to aid in wiping out the Sikeston lynchings, as well as the Lidice horrors" (8). Patrick Washburn's *A Question of Sedition: The Federal Government's Investigation of the Black Press During World War II* (New York: Oxford Univ. Press, 1986), 55, gives a good account of the "Double V" campaign of the *Pittsburgh Courier*, which began in February of 1942. The "Half American" slogan occurs also in the *Pittsburgh Courier*, on January 31, 1942 (quoted in Washburn, *A Question of Sedition*, 55).

For literary representations by American Black authors praising the Black soldier and/or staging his alienation from a culture at war which was riddled with racism, see, for example, the many war poems in Beatrice M. Murphy, ed., *Ebony Rhythm* (New York: Exposition, 1948); Countee Cullen, "Apostrophe to the Land," *Phylon* 3.4 (1942): 396–397; Cara Ball Moten, "Negro Mother to her Soldier Son," *Opportunity* 21 (1943): 76; Frank Marshall Davis, "War Quiz for America," *Crisis* (April 1944): 113–114, 122; Binga Desmond, "We Who Would Die" in his book by the same name (New York: Associated Authors, 1945); Ruth Albert Cook, "Blackout," *Opportunity* 20 (March 1942): 82; Lucia Mae Pitts, "A Wac Speaks to a Soldier," *Negro Story* (December/January 1945): 63; Grace Tompkins, "The Smell of Death," *Negro Story* (August/September 1945): 50; Nick Aaron Ford, "The Negro Soldier Speaks," *Negro Story* (May/June 1944): 60.

Washburn's *A Question of Sedition* and Abby Arthur Johnson and Ronald Maberry Johnson's *Propaganda and Aesthetics: The Literary Politics of Afro-American Magazines in the Twentieth Century* (Amherst: Univ. of Massachusetts Press, 1979) provide broad surveys and incisive analyses of Black publishing in the forties. See, in addition, Neil Wynn, *The Afro-American and the Second World War* (London: Paul Elek, 1976) and Lee Finkle, *Forum for Protest* (Cranbury, N.J.: Associated University Presses, 1975).

11 For an earlier discussion of a concept with some resemblance to "playing with mimesis" in the context of race relations, see Zora Neale Hurston's version of the Negro's "art of mimicry" in her "Characteristics of Negro Expression," *Negro: An Anthology*, ed. Nancy Cunard (1933; reprint, New York: Frederick Ungar, 1970).

Homi Bhabha's work on colonial mimicry—in which, as he puts it in "Of Mimicry and Man," "the look of surveillance returns as the displacing gaze of the disciplined"—employs in the context of colonial power structures a concept of critical miming similar to Irigaray's. See also Bhabha, "Signs Taken for Wonders: Questions of Ambivalence and Authority under a Tree Outside Delhi, May 1817," *'Race,' Writing, and Difference*, ed. Henry Louis Gates, Jr. (Chicago: Univ. of Chicago Press, 1986), 163–84. Also pertinent here is the discussion by Houston A. Baker, Jr., of Afro-American modernism's transformation of the minstrel mask "and its sounds into discursive currency," and his conception of the "mastery of form"; see Baker, *Modernism and the Harlem Renaissance* (Chicago: Univ. of Chicago Press, 1987), especially 24 and 49–50.

12 This point about conceptual structures which, by separating the issue of racial oppression from feminist concerns, ignore the existence and the particular struggles of nonwhite women is made with eloquent clarity in the title of and throughout the important volume edited by Gloria T. Hull, Patricia Bell Scott, and Barbara Smith, *All the Women are White, All the Blacks are Men, But Some of Us Are Brave: Black Women's Studies* (Old Westbury, New York: Feminist Press, 1982). See also, among many other Black feminist works which consider this issue, Bell Hooks, *Ain't I A Woman* (Boston: South End Press, 1981); Hortense Spillers, "Gwendolyn the Terrible: Propositions on Eleven Poems," (233–44) and Gloria T. Hull, "Afro-American Women Poets: A Bio-Critical Survey," (165–82) both in Gilbert and Gubar, eds., *Shakespeare's Sisters*. Other work specifically on Brooks which treats the intersections of race and gender is contained in *A Life Distilled: Gwendolyn Brooks, Her Poetry and Fiction*, ed. Maria K. Mootry and Gary Smith (Urbana: Univ. of Illinois Press, 1987).

13 "My boy is going to be a man! A real man, doing the kind of work he wants – not what they jim-crow him into doing," exclaims the Black mother in Press Hawkins's "Living Like a Half Man," *The Crisis* (July 1942): 234. If her son is killed in combat, she goes on, "Then he'll have died like a man, which is better than living like a half man, a second rate human" (235). The "proof of Black manhood" motif is so common in the rhetoric of the forties Black press that it needs no formal citation; for an especially impassioned example, see the full-page public service advertisement on page 24 of the March 28, 1942, issue of the *Chicago Defender*. Higonnet et al., in their introduction to *Behind the Lines* (2–3), provide an insightful analysis of recent scholarship on the general and compelling issue of crises of masculinity in twentieth-century war systems, and Susan Gubar treats the question of masculinity in the context of Second World War literature specifically in her essay in that volume ("This Is My Rifle").

14 Jane Morrison, my research assistant in 1986, not only discovered these texts for me but also analyzed them brilliantly. My discussion of them in this paragraph draws directly on her thinking. "Amidst white America's return to domesticity," Morrison speculates, "these articles may represent some tension and uncertainty among Black intellectuals about the proper definition of gender roles in postwar America." See Roi Ottley, "What's Wrong With Negro Women," *Negro Digest* (December 1950): 71–75, and the two essays cited in notes 15 and 16 below.

15 St. Clair Drake, "Why Men Leave Home," *Negro Digest* (April 1950): 26.

16 Gwendolyn Brooks, "Why Negro Women Leave Home," *Negro Digest* (March 1951): 28.

17 Note appended to Brooks's "Negro Hero – To Suggest Dorie Miller," *Common Ground* (Summer 1945): 45.

18 Alice Browning, "Letter to Our Readers," *Negro Story* (May/June 1944): 1.

19 The term "homosocial" has come into wide use in the time since the publication of Eve Kosofsky Sedgwick's pioneering *Between Men*, which defined it for and played a crucial role in introducing it to literary studies. Sedgwick, *Between Men: English Literature and Male Homosocial Desire* (New York: Columbia Univ. Press, 1985).

20 Washburn (*A Question of Sedition*, 15) uses the phrase "combined criticism-and-support approach" in his preliminary discussion of Black newspapers in World War I.

21 Harry B. Shaw, "Perceptions of Men in the Early Works of Gwendolyn Brooks," in *Black American Poets Between Worlds*, ed. R. Baxter Miller (Knoxville: Univ. of Tennessee Press, 1986), 138.

22 I wish to raise, too, the possibility that Harry Shaw and I do not disagree coincidentally. Perhaps we stand for, or stand in for, the "two bodies" whose shapes Susan Winnett has tentatively traced: "[If men and women] do read differently, is it not necessary to figure out how and where we do so? To what extent is the 'body of scholarship' on any given author really *two* bodies?" Our divergences over the body of the Negro Hero may be understood as symptomatic and instructive, a parable of what Winnett calls "reading and sexual difference." To say this is *not* to say that all men, left to themselves, will inevitably read "Negro Hero" as Shaw does and all women as I do; I prefer what I take to be the poem's own model of reading, which presents a man engaged in interpretation in such a way as to imply that men may read their masculinity self-critically and variously. Win-

nett is quoted in Nancy K. Miller, "Rereading as a Woman: The Body in Practice," *The Female Body in Western Culture*, ed. Susan Rubin Suleiman (Cambridge: Harvard Univ. Press, 1986), 354.

23 Peter Schwenger, *Phallic Critiques: Masculinity and Twentieth-Century Literature* (London: Routledge & Kegan Paul, 1984), 69. Cited in Elaine Showalter, "Rivers and Sassoon: The Inscription of Male Gender Anxieties," in Higgonet et al., eds., *Behind the Lines*, 69.

24 The boldness of the "boy itch" passage in "Negro Hero" should be read in the context of a number of equally skeptical representations of masculine aggression in Second War literature by women — including, among the texts represented in this volume, Elizabeth Bishop's "Roosters" and H. D.'s *Helen in Egypt*. For a remarkable example of open feminist sarcasm about notions of manhood which was published in the Black press of the period, see the weekly columns of Rebecca Stiles Taylor in the *Chicago Defender* (those on 1942 January 3 and March 28, and on 1943 January 2 and April 10, all on page 17, are of special interest). One notable example of an ironic analogy between the war and boy's games in a male-authored Second War text occurs in Owen Dodson's "Poems for My Brother Kenneth: II," *Powerful Long Ladder*, 66; another, in Robert Lowell's "Christmas Eve Under Hooker's Statue," *Poems 1938–49* (London: Faber & Faber, 1950), 27.

25 Perhaps the most direct and obvious analogues to these lines from "Negro Hero" in their day were the openly rhetorical representations of democracy and the Black man in the editorial cartoons of the Black press. One typical example from 1942 shows a Black man, bound and tied, struggling to free himself in order to save a blonde, scantily clad "America" who is being molested by "War": "Still Not Too Late to Cut His Bonds," the caption reads. Another, titled "He Never Dies Alone," depicts the body of a lynched Black man hanging next to the corpse of a white female "Democracy." See, for example, the *Chicago Defender*, 1942 January 10 and February 14, and 1943 March 13.

26 Melvin Tolson's well-respected *Rendezvous with America*, for instance, offers multiple versions of a democracy or nation allegorized as feminine but not marked as white: an America capable of becoming either a madonna or a harlot in the title poem's section 6 (8), a France who "was a virgin till . . . [a traitor's] deception led / Her to the harlotry of Vichy's bed" ("The Traitor to France," 64). Walter Arnold's "Interrogation," in the anthology of popular verse *Ebony Rhythm*, enacts a scene similar to the "white-gowned democracy" stanza in "Negro Hero" without explicitly representing as fair the lady of whom the soldier asks "no more . . . / Than that she treat him not as worthless dust / But like a man in a democracy. . ." (Murphy, ed. *Ebony Rhythm*, 3).

27 William Couch, "To a Soldier," *Negro Story* (May/June 1944): 60.

28 Wilfred Owen, "Insensibility," *Collected Poems*, 38.

29 "Bar" and "order" might be read as "hypograms" in Michael Riffaterre's sense; see his *Semiotics of Poetry* (Bloomington: Indiana Univ. Press, 1978).

30 Alfred Lord Tennyson, "Crossing the Bar," *The Poems of Tennyson*, ed. Christopher Ricks (Harlow: Longmans, 1969), 1458–59.

31 Just as "gay chaps at the bar" bears a direct relation to William Couch's "To a Soldier," so "still do I keep my look, my identity" may be read as an argument with another war poem published a few months earlier in *Negro Story*: Elsie Mills Holton's "Renunciation," which includes the lines "Our men are running as rapidly

into death as other men, / And death leaves one without identity." *Negro Story* (July/August 1944): 21.

32 Owen, "Disabled," *Collected Poems*, 68. Also compare to Brooks's poem, in the Afro-American tradition of protest poetry, Owen Dodson's representation of a sinister female spectator in his Samson and Delilah poem, "The Watching" (*Powerful Long Ladder*, 98); and, in the female tradition of war poetry, Patricia Ledward's "Air-Raid Casualties: Ashridge Hospital" (*Chaos of the Night*, 77–78), which directly revises Owen's "Disabled" to prove a woman's empathy for a wounded soldier.

33 No feminist critic working on gender and war literature could use the word "glee" in this context without citing Sandra Gilbert's resonant use of the term in her discussion of the "release of female libidinal energies" and "liberation of female anger" in the First World War. Gilbert, "Soldier's Heart," in Higgonet et al., eds., *Behind the Lines*.

34 Hartmann, "Prescriptions for Penelope."

35 Barbara Johnson, "Apostrophe, Animation and Abortion," *A World of Difference* (Baltimore: Johns Hopkins Univ. Press, 1987), 189.

36 Brooks, *Report from Part One*, 184.

37 Huston, "Matrix of War," 134.

38 John Berger's by now classic passage in his *Ways of Seeing* is pertinent here: "A woman. . . . is almost continually accompanied by her own image of herself. Whilst she is walking across a room or whilst she is weeping at the death of her father, she can scarcely avoid envisaging herself walking or weeping . . . men *act* and women *appear*. Men look at women. Women watch themselves being looked at. . . . The surveyor of woman in herself is male: the surveyed female. Thus she turns herself into an object—and most particularly an object of vision: a sight." Berger, *Ways of Seeing* (New York: Penguin, 1977), 46–47.

39 Compare Owen Dodson's representation of fully present, confident, naturally powerful Black motherhood and Black maternal language in his "Black Mother Praying in the Summer 1943"; even here, this eloquent mother pauses to ask in the face of war and racism, "How can I pray again when my tongue / Is near cleavin to the roof of my mouth?," but she concludes with "I ain't never gonna hush my mouth or lay down this heavy, black, weary, terrible load / Until I fights ta stamp my feet with my black sons / On a freedom solid rock and stand there peaceful. . . .,"*Powerful Long Ladder*, 10. Gwendolyn Williams's "Heart Against the Wind," a war story published in 1944 in the NAACP's journal *The Crisis*, presents a more complex version of maternal silencing, one with closer connections to "looking." A young Black wife sits down to announce her pregnancy in a letter to her soldier husband overseas. She is first bitter and enraged: "'Stephen, why are you fighting? It boils down to the fact that you are on a foreign soil to free the enslaved peoples of a foreign land while at home they step in the faces of your brothers. . . . I would rather destroy this child and go to hell than to deliver it into a world like this. . .'" (18). Then, flooded with light and "a fresh point of view, Stephen's point of view," she tears up her first letter and writes: "We are going to be the proud parents, within this year, of a very special citizen. Don't worry about me, everything is going swell" (26). Gwendolyn Williams, "Heart Against the Wind," *Crisis* (January 1944), 18, 26.

40 See Jeffrey Walsh, *American War Literature, 1914 to Vietnam* (New York: St. Martin 1982), 173–84, for a discussion of the relation of aesthetics to war in Second

War poetry; compare J. Glenn Gray's discussion of war and "the lust of the eye" in *The Warriors: Reflections of Men in Battle* (New York: Harper & Row, 1970), 25–39.

41 Ernest Hemingway, "Soldier's Home," *The Short Stories* (New York: Scribner, 1953), 147.

42 Ernest Hemingway, interview, *Paris Review* 5 (Spring 1958): 84.

43 Stacy Carson Hubbard, "'A Splintery Box': Race and Gender in the Sonnets of Gwendolyn Brooks" (Unpublished essay, Cornell University), 11.

44 Gloria T. Hull, *Color, Sex and Poetry: Three Women Writers of the Harlem Renaissance* (Bloomington: Indiana Univ. Press, 1987), 213, 217.

45 Barbara Christian, *Black Feminist Criticism: Perspectives on Black Women Writers* (New York: Pergamon, 1985), 13.

46 Brooks's readers frequently contend with a doubleness or disjunction, usually understood in the context of notions of racial, not sexual, difference, which they perceive in some of her pre-1967 poems. (Her work underwent a self-declared and evident transformation in the late sixties; the 1967 turning point is taken from her own accounts.) One of the most common moves in criticism of her work is, in fact, the admission of a disjunction followed by the denial of it. Here is Houston Baker (*Singers of Daybreak: Studies in Black American Literature* [Washington, D.C.: Howard Univ. Press, 1983]), for instance, on Brooks's work: "What one seems to have is 'white' style and 'black' content — two warring ideals in one dark body" (43). Baker then follows up the promise of his "seems" by dispelling the myth of "this apparent dichotomy" (44). Brooks herself, too, has taken pains to deny the apparent dichotomy. "In 1945 I was saying what many of the young folks said in the sixties," she said in a 1983 interview, defending her second war work. "But it's crowded back into language like this," she continued, quoting a poem from *Street in Bronzeville*. In that interview, Brooks broadens the scope of subjects "crowded back into language" to include gender as well as race: "My works express rage and focus on *rage*. . . . I don't know whether you want to include woman rage in this discussion or not. But I hope you sense some real rage in 'The Ballad of Pearl May Lee.' The speaker is a very enraged person. I know because I consulted myself on how I felt" (in *Black Women Writers at Work*, ed. Claudia Tate [New York: Continuum, 1983], 42–43). Brooks's argument here suggests that any consideration of the recurrent tension between style and content, or between technique and essence, in her early work should include woman rage in the discussion.

47 See, for instance, Harry Shaw, "Perceptions of Men," 139, and D. H. Melhem, *Gwendolyn Brooks: Poetry and the Heroic Voice* (Lexington: Univ. of Kentucky Press, 1987), 47–48.

48 Nancy Vickers, "'This Heraldry in Lucrece' Face'," in Suleiman, ed., *Female Body in Western Culture*, 213–14, 220.

49 Elizabeth Young, in a class seminar at the University of California-Berkeley, Spring 1989. As Susan Gubar puts it, "Although such black women writers as Gwendolyn Brooks and Ann Petry record the suffering of black soldiers in an army as fascist in its racism as are Germany's services, they also present the ways in which even these victimized men treat their women as whores" (Gubar, "This is My Rifle," 257). The "love notes" may be read as part of the body of texts by Second War women authors who expose what Gubar calls "the elaborate images . . . men construct as a compensation for and a retaliation against the sex they are presumably fighting to preserve — but that they are really preserving themselves

to fight" (ibid.). But the "love notes" do so primarily in order to expose *racial* retaliations *against* Black men, and Black relations to the "elaborate images" of democracy in U.S. culture.

50 The condition represented here resembles the dangerous situation described by Luce Irigaray in her address to another woman in "When Our Lips Speak Together": "Listen: all round us, men and women sound just the same. . . . Absent from ourselves: we'll be spoken machines, speaking machines. . . . Outside, you try to conform to an alien order. . . . as you allow yourself to be abused, you become an impassive travesty" ("When Our Lips Speak Together," *This Sex Which Is Not One,* 205, 210). Both Mary Jacobus's and Louis Renza's treatments of the strategy of playing with mimesis (see note 5 above) come round to a chastened view of its powers, though to quite different ends: Renza, to emphasize the dangers for the feminist theorist of privileging this tactic; Jacobus, to reassert finally "the necessary utopianism of feminist criticism" (*Reading Woman,* 77). Each of these texts focuses specifically on female desire. "Gay Chaps at the Bar" 's representation of the powers and limits of mimeticism as a strategy of survival, expression, and critique in wartime invites consideration of masculinity as well as femininity as they are defined and imposed by an "alien order."

51 Hubbard, "'A Splintery Box,'" 20.

52 Gwendolyn Brooks, "Revision of the Invocation (The Negro: His Pleas Against Intolerance)," *Negro Story* (May/June 1945): 77. In several of his essays on mimicry Homi Bhabha invokes Lacan, quoting the following lines: "Mimicry reveals something in so far as it is distinct from what might be called an *itself* that is behind. The effect of mimicry is camouflage, in the strictly technical sense. It is not a question of harmonizing with the background but, against a mottled background, of being mottled — exactly like the technique of camouflage practiced in human warfare." Bhabha continues at one point after this quotation, "to the extent to which discourse is a form of defensive warfare, mimicry marks those moments of civil disobedience within the discipline of civility: signs of spectacular resistance." Bhabha, "Signs Taken for Wonders," 181. The exhilarating praise of mimesis as resistance in these concluding pages of Bhabha's essay provides a useful historical and cultural contrast and an important corrective to the pessimism of my conclusions following Brooks's conclusions about playing with mimicry. At the same time, Brooks's grim explorations in the Second World War period of what industrialized, mass "human warfare" entails suggest that the image of camouflage — a form of mottling designed for male soldiers by military experts — as a figure of liberating resistance might be a questionable one. Still, Bhabha's invocation of the camouflage of guerila warfare points toward Brooks's later militance. Her first book of poems after *A Street in Bronzeville, Annie Allen* (1949), ends with the "Revision of the Invocation" and its exhortation to Black people: "Rise. / Let us combine." "Gay Chaps" is not Brooks's last word on war, and "war" means more for the Black woman poet than the official U.S. fight against external enemies. Brooks's later poems, more and more, confront political conflicts and violence *within* U.S. culture, and they confront too a Black struggle, engaged in by both men and women, increasingly defined (and provisionally embraced) as revolutionary.

Chapter 5. The Letter and the Body: Rukeyser's "Letter to the Front"

1 Muriel Rukeyser, "Gift-Poem," *Beast in View* (Garden City: Doubleday, Doran, 1944), 33. Hereafter poems in this collection, abbreviated *BV*, are cited in the text.

2 Muriel Rukeyser, "Many Keys" (Unpublished talk, in the Muriel Rukeyser Papers held by William Rukeyser. Davis, California), 4–5. The talk was probably given sometime in the sixties. My thanks to William and Alison Rukeyser for allowing me to look through the papers. And my thanks to Martha Evans at the University of California-Davis, who is currently at work on a biography of Rukeyser, for introducing me to this talk and to the papers in Davis in general, and for her very helpful reading of this chapter. The papers in William Rukeyser's possession are hereafter cited as Muriel Rukeyser Papers, with additional citations of their box numbers.

3 Bob Ray, "'Middle of the Air' Premiere," *Daily Iowan* (Iowa City, Iowa), Muriel Rukeyser Papers, Box 3.

4 Margaret Buell Wilder, *Since You Went Away . . . Letters to a Soldier from His Wife* (New York: McGraw-Hill, 1943). The presence of models of women's war letters in no way guaranteed encouragement and validation of women's writing during the war years. Fictional renditions by women authors of the scene of a woman's wartime letter writing to an absent soldier are common, but they are notable for their consistently anxious representations of the possibilities of expression and communication through the letter. Challenging the dominant ironic representation of the woman-back-home as flighty and indifferent, these scenes suggest that women censor themselves under the pressure of trauma in wartime much as Wilfred Owen's letter-writing soldiers did. See, for instance, Dorothy Parker's "The Lovely Leave," *Woman's Home Companion* 70 (December 1943): 22–25, 85, 88–90, which includes this passage on the decorum of female letter writing: "You must know the rules and abide by them. She could do that. . . . Never say to him what you want him to say to you. Never tell him how sadly you miss him, how it grows no better. . . . Set down for him the gay happenings about you, bright little anecdotes. . . . Do not bedevil him with the pinings of your faithful heart because he is your husband, your man, your love. For you are writing to none of these. You are writing to a soldier" (24–25). See also the remarkable Great War letter-writing scene in H. D.'s *Bid Me To Live (A Madrigal)* (New York: Grove, 1960), 42–44, and Gwendolyn Williams's "Heart Against the Wind." Even Wilder's sanitized view of the woman letter writer and the war which surrounds her focuses in part on women's self-censorship, and on the contradictions within homefront domestic ideology; at one point, the heroine breaks off her account of her new war job as a journalist: "But I won't talk about it any longer now — promise. In fact, I'll try never to sound like a lady executive or be anything but helpless and white organdy even if I'm ink and enthusiasm to my elbows. Because if I did you might stop loving me — and that, my Pudding, is more important than all the pages in the world" (*Since You Went Away*, 18).

5 Linda S. Kauffman, *Discourse of Desire: Gender, Genre, and Epistolary Fictions* (Ithaca: Cornell Univ. Press, 1986), 56. Hereafter cited in the text. I am indebted to Kauffman's definition and discussion of amorous epistolary discourse throughout this chapter. "Letter to the Front" and the other love poems in *Beast in View* exhibit all or most of the characteristics Kauffman describes as central to the genre of the literary feminine love letter: "the genre . . . is epistolary; the mood is amor-

ous and elegiac; the situation is the aftermath of abandonment. The heroine . . .
utters her desire in the absence of her beloved. . . . the heroine's writing reenacts
seduction, confession, persuasion, and these constitute what 'happens' in the text.
She . . . transform[s] herself in the process from victim to artist" (26). See espe-
cially Kauffman's final chapter on *The Three Marias: New Portuguese Letters* (by
Maria Isabel Barreno, Maria Teresa Horta, and Maria Velho daCosta), a text which
she takes to be both a culmination and a radical revision of amorous epistolary
discourse, and which Rukeyser's "Letter" in some ways resembles and anticipates.

6 Kauffman develops this pun on "abandonment" at length; see 305–6. For a perti-
   nent debate on the frequency and meaning of the "abandoned woman" motif in
   literature by and about women, see Lawrence Lipking, "Aristotle's Sister: A Poet-
   ics of Abandonment," in von Hallberg, ed., *Canons* 85–103 (the discussion is ex-
   tended in Lipking's *Abandoned Women*), and Joan DeJean, "Fictions of Sappho,"
   Critical Inquiry 13 (Summer 1987): 787–805. Lipking refers to Rukeyser explicit-
   ly, describing her (I think wrongly) as a woman poet who attempts to deny her
   descent from Sappho (*Abandoned Women*, 107).

7 Edna St. Vincent Millay, for instance, in her sardonic "An Ancient Gesture,"
   treats the tears of an abandoned Penelope as the single archetypal gesture of
   women; it constitutes feminine formula. "An Ancient Gesture," *Collected Poems*
   (New York: Harper & Row, 1967), 501.

8 Louise Kertesz's indispensable book on Rukeyser provides an account of Rukey-
   ser's relationship to Boch. Kertesz, *Poetic Vision of Muriel Rukeyser*, 121,
   200, 308. Rukeyser continued throughout her life to address poems to Boch; see,
   for instance, her "Endless" in *The Speed of Darkness* (New York: Random, 1968).
   Martha Evans suggests, however, that lesbian relationships were important to
   Rukeyser during the war period; the heterosexual romance with the soldier dis-
   played in these poems might function, then, in part as a screen. (Personal conver-
   sation with Martha Evans.)

9 Muriel Rukeyser, "Poem Out of Childhood," *The Collected Poems* (New York:
   McGraw-Hill, 1978), 3. Poems in this collection, abbreviated *CP*, are hereafter
   cited in the text. Note, however, that despite the dismissal of Sappho here, Rukey-
   ser's versions of amorous epistolary poetry begin very early; a poem published in
   1935, entitled "Letter, Unposted," starts with an epigraph from Joyce: "My love,
   my love, my love, / Why have you left me alone?" (*CP*, 14). Rukeyser claimed
   Sappho as a model in her "Many Keys." Muriel Rukeyser Papers, 2.

10 See Muriel Rukeyser, "The Lynchings of Jesus" (1935), *CP*, 24–30; "The Book of
   the Dead" (1938), *CP*, 71–102; and the many poems of protest in *The Speed of
   Darkness* (1968) and *Breaking Open* (1973), also reprinted in *CP*.

11 R. P. Blackmur noted, and criticized, the centrality of sexuality in *Beast in View*
   in his review of that volume: "Miss Rukeyser is confused about sex. . . . It may
   be thrown out for what it is worth that sex seems to be the source of what organiza-
   tion there is in Miss Rukeyser's poems, but that until she decides whether sex
   is predominantly a force or a sentiment, her poems and her readers' response to
   them will be left at a loss." Blackmur, *Kenyon Review* 7 (1945): 339. As Louise
   Kertesz notes, Blackmur's distinction between force and sentiment refers to a pas-
   sage in chapter 25 of *The Education of Henry Adams*, in which Adams claims
   that of American artists, only Whitman "had ever insisted on the power of sex . . .
   All the rest had used sex for sentiment, never for force" (Kertesz, *Poetic Vision*

of Muriel Rukeyser, 206). The distinction between force and sentiment is not sexually neutral; it has an obviously gendered valence: masculine force, feminine sentiment. In terms which comprehend and extend beyond sexuality, the struggle of women for access to and acknowledgement of female force as well as feminine sentiment is a major subject of Rukeyser's poetry in general and "Letter to the Front" in particular.

12   Robin Ruth Linden et al., eds., *Against Sadomasochism: A Radical Feminist Analysis* (East Palo Alto: Frog in Well, 1982). Andrea Dworkin defines her written work as *Letters from a War Zone* in a text which begins with a reference to Rukeyser (London: Secker & Warburg, 1988).

13   On the mythology of "front" and "frontier" in left-wing thinking in the Spanish Civil War years, see Benstock, *Women of the Left Bank*, 405–6.

14   Compare another example of radical American women's writing, Joy Davidman's "Letter to a Comrade" in her book of the same title (New Haven: Yale Univ. Press, 1938), 13–19.

15   Margaret R. and Patrice L. R. Higgonet, "The Double Helix," in Higgonet et al., eds., *Behind the Lines*, 46. See also Enloe, "Feminists Thinking About War," 390.

16   On the "structures of permutation" in poems which use refrain lines or words, see John Hollander, "Breaking into Song: Some Notes on Refrain," in Hosek and Parkers, eds., *Lyric Poetry*, 75.

17   Ernest Hemingway, "The Butterfly and the Tank," *The Fifth Column and the First Forty-Nine Stories* (New York: Scribner, 1938); Dorothy Parker, "Who Might Be Interested," in *Voices Against Tyranny: Writing of the Spanish Civil War*, ed. John Miller (New York: Scribner, 1986), 192–97; W. H. Auden, "Spain," *Selected Poems*, ed. Edward Mendelson (New York: Vintage, 1979), 51. For significant exceptions to these gendered formulations, see Nancy Cunard's body of antifascist war poems, such as *Relevé into Maquis* (Derby: Grasshopper, 1944), and the women's writing in Nekola and Rabinowitz, eds., *Writing Red*. See also Barbara Brothers, "Writing Against the Grain: Sylvia Townsend Warner and the Spanish Civil War," in Mary Lynn Broe and Angela Ingram, eds., *Women's Writing in Exile* (Chapel Hill: Univ. of North Carolina Press, 1989), 349–68.

18   For a full account of the male domination of the Popular Front and thirties proletarian culture (and, at the same time, of women's participation in them), see Paula Rabinowitz, "Women and U.S. Literary Radicalism," in Nekola and Rabinowitz, eds., *Writing Red*.

19   Rukeyser, "War and Poetry," in Williams, ed., *The War Poets*, 25. Another version of this argument occurs in Rukeyser's wartime book *Willard Gibbs* (Garden City: Country Life, 1942): "Such foreboding is not the dark gaze, but the creation of images which speak for the future *as it arrives*, with the speed of the poet, and not the attendance on the fact of the reporter" (435).

20   Oscar Williams, *New Poems 1943: An Anthology of British and American Verse* (New York: Howell, Soskin, 1943), vi. See, for another representative example, the "Editor's Statement" in *Twice A Year: A Book of Literature, the Arts and Civil Liberties* 8/9 (1942): "It was the artist who first warned, understood, about the war. And now during the war the constantly sharp vision of the artist will continue to foresee the subtle issues that must be faced in the future and that *war itself cannot resolve*" (12). For a powerful contemporary version of this argument which is also a critique of claims to poetic prophecy, see Czeslaw Milosz's discus-

sion of twentieth-century poetry's apocalyptic visions and premonitions, and of "the limitations to any prophesying": Milosz, *The Witness of Poetry* (Cambridge: Harvard Univ. Press, 1983), 103-16.

21 Claudia Koonz, *Mothers in the Fatherland: Women, Family Life and Nazi Ideology 1919-1945* (New York: St. Martin, 1986).

22 Whitman figures his book as "a lone bark cleaving the ether, purpos'd I know not whither, yet ever full of faith" in "In Cabin'd Ships at Sea," *Leaves of Grass*, ed. Harold W. Blodgett and Scully Bradley (New York: W. W. Norton, 1971), 3. Peter Revell discusses Whitman's visionary ship imagery in his *Quest in Modern American Poetry* (New York: Barnes & Noble Books, 1981), 39-40.

23 Muriel Rukeyser, "Introduction," *The Life of Poetry* (New York: Current Books, 1949). Hereafter abbreviated *LP* and cited in the text.

24 Janet Gurkin Altman, in her detailed study of the use of the formal properties of letters to create meaning in literary texts, devotes a chapter to "The Weight of the Reader," whose presence, as she notes, "alone distinguishes the letter from other first-person forms. . . . In no other genre do readers figure so prominently within the world of the narrative and in the generation of the text. . . . The epistolary form is unique in making the reader (narratee) almost as important an agent in the narrative as the writer (narrator). . . . In epistolary writing the reader is called upon to respond as a writer and to contribute as such to the narrative." Altman, *Epistolarity: Approaches to a Form* (Columbus: Ohio State Univ. Press, 1982), 87, 88, 89. Mikhail Bahktin emphasizes that a "characteristic feature of the letter is an acute awareness of the interlocutor" and that the letter has "a second meaning — an intentional orientation toward someone else's word." Bahktin, *Problems of Dostoevsky's Poetics*, ed. and trans. Caryl Emerson; introduction by Wayne C. Booth (Minneapolis: Univ. of Minnesota Press, 1984), 205.

25 Henry James, *The Portrait of a Lady* (New York: Scribner, 1908), 45-46.

26 On the feminine reader, see for instance Nancy K. Miller's discussion of the masculinity of letter writing in a scene from Choderlos de Laclos's *Les liaisons dangereuses* as a "sexualization that . . . dangerously privileges the letter writer over the letter reader; and conflates predictably, virility and authority." Miller argues that "the dominant trope of the act of novel-reading in the eighteenth century is the figure, or allegory, perhaps even the fact, of the *lectrice*, the woman reader reading." Miller, "Rereading as a Woman," 358. In a discussion more directly pertinent to the Second World War period, Mary Ann Doane analyzes the cultural position of women as "perfect spectators" in her book on forties films, drawing on the concept of a female reading public; see her *Desire to Desire*, 2.

27 Klaus Mann, "Editorial," *Decision* 1.4 (April 1941): 6. For Rukeyser's involvement with *Decision*, see Kertesz, *Poetic Vision of Muriel Rukeyser*, 171-72.

28 Altman, *Epistolarity*, 43.

29 Shapiro, "V-Letter," in Williams, ed., *War Poets*, 228. Louise Kertesz compares "V-Letter" to the poems in *Beast in View* periodically throughout her chapter on Rukeyser's work in the forties; see her *Poetic Vision of Muriel Rukeyser*, 199, 201 and 216.

30 Franz Werfel, *The Song of Bernadette*, trans. Ludwig Lewisohn (New York: Viking, 1942). Werfel published in *Decision* — see, for instance, his essay on American poetry in the first issue, January 1941; he may have known Rukeyser through that connection.

31 Audre Lorde, "Poems are no Luxuries," *Chrysalis* 3 (1977): 7–8.

32 Ezra Pound, "Hugh Selwyn Mauberley," *Personae*, 185.

33 Olive Schreiner, *Women and Labour* (1911; rpt. London: Virago, 1978), 178. Charlotte Perkins Gilman, *The Man-Made World, or Our Androcentric Culture* (1911; reprint, New York: Johnson Repr., 1971), 99. The coined, half tongue-in-cheek term "motherist" is finding currency among feminist historians of women's social movements which appeal to motherhood; several panels and gatherings at the 1987 Berkshire Conference of Women Historians used the word in their titles.

34 Some of the negative consequences for the woman poet of a "motherist" stance are apparent in a 1945 review of *Beast in View* by Heinz Politzer, who portrays Rukeyser as "Niobe, the mother bent over the corpses of her slaughtered children. . . . Now that she has discovered the mythical qualities of motherhood she does not need to mythologize herself any longer." Politzer, "A Contemporary American Poet," *Forum-Jerusalem Radio*, 21 December 1945. See also Politzer's description of Rukeyser's "combatant motherhood" in his "Poems of Torment," *Palestine Post* 5 July 1946. On the regressive celebration of motherhood in the Popular Front, see Rabinowitz, "Women and U.S. Literary Radicalism," 9–13.

35 Rukeyser, *Willard Gibbs*, 355. As Louise Kertesz notes (*Poetic Vision of Muriel Rukeyser*, 225), Rukeyser wrote many poems celebrating childbirth and motherhood; see, for instance, "Speech of the Mother" (*CP*, 275), and "All the Little Animals" (*CP*, 506). In a review in the late forties, she criticized the lack of adequate and powerful representations of birth: "A Simple Theme," *Poetry* 74 (July 1949): 236–39.

36 DeJean, "Fictions of Sappho," 789.

37 Compare the prose piece "I Help at the War Service Club" by Dorothy Norman, the editor of another left-wing journal with which Rukeyser was associated. A woman in Norman's essay goes to work at a club "to help ease the lives of the men who are fighting. Fighting for what I believe in; fighting for *me*." But after a confrontation with an anti-Semitic soldier, she realizes: "This man . . . is my enemy." She addresses the man: "What has the field of battle to do with what I wish to make clear to you? What has the field of battle to do with what this war is supposed to be about?" Norman, *Twice A Year* 10/11 (1943): 231–37.

38 Muriel Rukeyser, "Over the Cradle / The Only Child," unfinished draft in the Berg collection, reprinted in Kertesz, *Poetic Vision of Muriel Rukeyser*, 229. Kertesz eloquently discusses the "Nine Poems" (224–29).

39 The biddy's miniature "women's lyric" embedded within the larger, looser poem resembles the "blues song" Adrienne Rich took as the negative, admonitory capsulation of female tradition at the end of her original version of "When We Dead Awaken": "I dreamed I was asked to read my poetry at a mass women's meeting, but when I began to read, what came out were the lyrics of a blues song. . . . Much of women's poetry has been of the nature of the blues song: a cry of pain, of victimization, or a lyric of seduction." In a later, added footnote Rich corrects this harsh judgment of the blues: "When I dreamed that dream, was I wholly ignorant of the tradition of Bessie Smith and other women's blues lyrics which transcended victimization to sing of resistance and independence?" Like the blues in Rich's essay, the biddy's song may—and the larger poem around it certainly does—sing of resistance. Rich, "When We Dead Awaken: Writing as Re-Vision," *On Lies, Secrets, and Silence: Selected Prose 1966–1978* (New York: Norton, 1979), 48.

40 Nancy Vickers, "Diana Described," *Writing and Sexual Difference*, 103. Hereafter cited in the text.

41 Mary Jacobus, "Apostrophe and Lyric Voice in *The Prelude*," in Hosek and Parker, eds., *Lyric Poetry*, 176.

42 Samuel Richardson, *Clarissa* (New York: Dutton), 2: 431.

43 Shapiro, "V-Letter," in Williams, ed., *War Poets*, 229.

44 An analogue, if not a direct source, for the following lines from "Letter" is the opening of an editorial by Klaus Mann for an issue of *Decision* for which Rukeyser was associate editor: "In 1919, the peoples actually *wanted* 'a better world.' . . . It is the fault . . . of the responsible leaders that the majority of men keep thinking in the categories of nationalism: 'I want *my* country to be strong and prosperous.' . . . What trash! There is no such thing as 'the interest of *my* country.' To imagine that one part of this planet could be kept in a state of slavery and starvation while another prospers, is not only immoral but unrealistic to boot." Mann, "Free World," *Decision* 2.3 (September 1941): 3–4.

45 Leed, *No Man's Land*, 74.

46 Erich Auerbach, *Mimesis: The Representation of Reality in Western Literature*, trans. Willard R. Trask (Princeton: Princeton Univ. Press, 1953), 552.

47 Altman, *Epistolarity*, 122, 163.

48 Rukeyser was interested in 1944 in editing a book on Jewish life underground in Europe. See the letter to Rukeyser from Solomon Grayzel (30 October 1944), Muriel Rukeyser Papers, Box 3.

49 Kenneth Rexroth, foreword, in Kertesz, *Poetic Vision of Muriel Rukeyser*, xii.

Preface to Part Three

1 John L. DeWitt, commander of the Western Defense Command, was the military leader designated by Secretary of War Henry L. Stimson to carry out the "evacuation" of Japanese Americans. He appears to have made several slightly varied public versions of this statement; the one printed here, taken from his testimony on April 13, 1943, to a House Naval Affairs Subcommittee on Housing, is quoted in Yoshiko Uchida, *Desert Exile: The Uprooting of a Japanese-American Family* (Seattle: Univ. of Washington Press, 1982), 56–57. See also Carey McWilliams, *Prejudice: Japanese-Americans: Symbol of Racial Intolerance* (New York: Little, Brown, 1944), 116. Compare also the famous moment in Frank Capra's *Know Your Enemy—Japan* (1945) in which the point is made that the Japanese people are all "photographic prints off the same negative"; for a discussion of Capra's film and for the larger context of what John Dower calls "blood-will-tell racism" (80) in American home-front culture see Dower, *War Without Mercy: Race and Power in the Pacific War* (New York: Pantheon, 1986).

2 Mitsuye Yamada, "Invisibility is an Unnatural Disaster: Reflections of an Asian American Woman," in *This Bridge Called My Back: Writings by Radical Women of Color*, ed. Gloria Anzaldua and Cherrie Moraga (Watertown, Mass.: Persephone Press, 1981), 36.

3 Ann Nisei, "On Nisei Writing: Experiences of Evacuation Provide Material of Literature," *Pacific Citizen*, 7 January 1943, 5. Hereafter cited in the text. Ann Nisei's columns ranged over topics from the problems of child-raising in the camps to "Slip Covers Do Wonders for that Barracks Apartment." Nisei, *Pacific Citizen*,

18 March 1943. Similar women's columns appeared in many of the internal camp newspapers; the Minedoka *Irrigator*, for instance, ran a column called "Feminidoka."

4 On the history of the *Pacific Citizen* and other Nikkei newspapers during the war years, see Harry H. L. Kitano, "The Japanese-American Press," in *The Ethnic Press in the United States: A Historical Analysis and Handbook*, ed. Sally M. Miller (New York: Greenwood Press, 1987), 192–202. Though it was allowed to remain in operation, the paper was forced during the war to relocate its offices to Salt Lake City.

5 Lawson Fusao Inada, "Tribute to Toshio," in *Ayumi: A Japanese American Anthology*, ed. The Japanese American Anthology Committee (San Francisco: Japanese American Anthology Committee, 1980), 189.

6 Histories of internment and relocation and related issues include Roger Daniels, *Concentration Camps USA: Japanese Americans and World War II* (New York: Holt, Rhinehart & Winston, 1971); Roger Daniels, Sandra Taylor, and Harry H. L. Kitano, *Japanese Americans: From Relocation to Redress* (Salt Lake City: Univ. of Utah Press, 1986); Peter Irons, *Justice at War: The Story of the Japanese American Internment Cases* (New York: Oxford Univ. Press, 1983); Michi Weglyn, *Years of Infamy: The Untold Story of America's Concentration Camps* (New York: Morrow Quill, 1976); Eric J. Sundquist, "The Japanese-American Internment: A Reappraisal," *American Scholar* (Autumn 1978): 529–47; and the books produced by the University of California's wartime sociological studies of internment. These include the "canonical"—Dorothy Swaine Thomas and Richard S. Nishimoto, *The Spoilage* (Berkeley: University of California Press, 1946) and Dorothy Swaine Thomas, with the assistance of Charles Kikuchi, *The Salvage: Japanese American Evacuation and Resettlement* (Berkeley: Univ. of California Press, 1952)—and the "apocryphal"—Morton Grodzins, *Americans Betrayed: Politics and the Japanese Evacuation* (Chicago: Univ. of Chicago Press, 1949).

For a Nisei wartime debate on problems of representation of the experience of internment and relocation, see the controversy surrounding Jobo Nakamura's representation in several short sketches of the relocated Nisei Masao: "Masao Pro" and "Masao Con," *Pacific Citizen*, 11 August 1945, 5, and Larry Tajiri, "A Character Named Masao," *Pacific Citizen*, 25 August 1945, 4.

Chapter 6. Toyo Suyemoto and the "Pre-Poetics" of Internment

I have been greatly helped in my work on this chapter by Julie Chang and Rob Kaufmann; my thanks, too, to James D. Houston and Grant Din for their passing on of materials. I am heavily indebted throughout to the important work of two historians, Valerie Matsumoto and Sandra Uyeunten, for my understanding of the history of Issei and Nisei women's lives in the forties, and also to Elaine Kim's scholarly work on Asian American literature. Finally, I thank Toyo Suyemoto for her generous responses to my inquiries, and Stan Yogi for his guidance, great funds of knowledge, and inspiration.

1 Toyo Suyemoto, "Writing of Poetry," *Amerasia Journal* 10.1 (1983): 75.

2 My question echoes Jones's own: "How, then, do we now read a woman who could be condemned in 1550 as unworthy of hearing precisely because she wanted to be heard? Pre-poetically, by necessity." Ann Rosalind Jones, "Surprising Fame: Renaissance Gender Ideologies and Women's Lyric," in *The Poetics of Gender*, ed. Nancy K. Miller (New York: Columbia Univ. Press, 1986), 93.

3   Ibid., 74, 93.

4   Ibid., 92.

5   Monica Sone, *Nisei Daughter* (New York: Atlantic-Little, 1953), 156. Hereafter cited in the text.

6   Uchida, *Desert Exile*, 63.

7   Suyemoto, quoted in Tim Doulin, "Woman Recalls Pain of Internment Camps," *Columbus Dispatch*, 22 April 1987, 2E. Sometimes, though — in Topaz, for instance — public Japanese libraries were patched together; for a pro-WRA account of one, see Allen H. Eaton, *Beauty Behind Barbed Wire: The Arts of the Japanese in Our Relocation Camps* (New York: Harper & Brothers, 1952).

8   Miné Okubo, in *Beyond Words: Images from America's Concentration Camps*, ed. Deborah Gesensway and Mindy Roseman (Ithaca: Cornell Univ. Press, 1987), 69.

9   Jiro Nakano and Kay Nakano, *Poets Behind Barbed Wire* (Honolulu: Bamboo Ridge Press, 1984), vii.

10 The experience of the poet Muin (Otokichi Ozaki) is described in Nakano and Nakano, *Poets Behind Barbed Wire*, 5.

11 Charles Kikuchi, *The Kikuchi Diary: Chronicle from an American Concentration Camp — the Tanforan Journals* (Urbana: Univ. of Illinois Press, 1973), 158. "Like all other newspapers," the WRA Program Guide stated, "relocation center papers will enjoy full freedom of editorial expression. The Project Director, however, may suspend publication of the newspaper at any time if this seems necessary in the interest of public peace and community security." Quoted in Gesensway and Roseman, eds., *Beyond Words*, 77. A few other examples from the *Kikuchi Diary*: "It's [the newspaper is] probably about the most censored thing in camp. This morning Greene went through the dummy with a fine tooth comb and made us eliminate Kotex from the drug store items carried, because it 'was not in good taste.' Then he makes the classic statement that there is absolutely no censorship around here!" (100) Another narrative describes the confiscation of an issue of the paper which contained an article written by Kikuchi the administration wanted to suppress; see 160–61.

12 On the publishing history of Mori's important work, see Elaine Kim, *Asian American Literature: An Introduction to the Writings and Their Social Context* (Philadelphia: Temple Univ. Press, 1982), 168. Mori's writing was buried in more ways than one during the war; at the time of forced evacuation, he left almost two hundred stories stored in a barn, and returned to find them destroyed by bookworms.

13 Okubo, quoted in Gesensway and Roseman, eds., *Beyond Words*, 74.

14 *Trek*, the literary journal published by internees in Topaz (officially known as the Central Utah Relocation Center), for instance, literally stopped publication during the registration period for the stated reason that the WRA required its personnel and facilities for the loyalty questionnaire procedure. "To Our Readers," *Trek* (dated as February 1943 but published sometime later): 1. A succinct account of the crisis of the loyalty oaths and the WRA's subsequent segregation policy is provided in Gesensway and Roseman, eds., *Beyond Words*, 80. Given these conditions, it is not surprising that the woman poet in Hisaye Yamamoto's one story of the camps, "The Legend of Miss Sasagawara," *Kenyon Review* 12.1 (1950): 99–115 — a figure whom Stan Yogi has recently linked to an actual Nisei woman poet, Teru Izumida, who was at Poston — goes crazy.

15 Globularius Schraubi, "Yule Greetings, Friends!" *Trek* (December 1942): 13. The part of H. L. Mencken's *The American Language* to which "Schraubi" seems to be referring occurs in its first supplement, in the section called "The Two Streams of English," 148–50. H. L. Mencken, *The American Language: An Inquiry into the Development of English in the United States, Supplement 1* (1919; reprint, New York: Knopf, 1960). On "Schraubi"'s identity, see Jim Yamada, "Falderol," *Trek* (February 1943): 42.

16 Grant Din, "An Interview with Toyo Suyemoto – A Lifetime of Writing," 15 June 1983, 4–5 (unpublished). Parts of this interview were published by Din under the title "Soft Silver Interwoven with Quick Fire" in *East Wind* 3.1 (1984): 8–9.

17 Sandra Uyeunten, "Hatsugen-ken: The Right to Speak One's Mind" (Paper delivered to the Berkshire Conference on Women's History, Wellesley, Mass. June 1987).

18 On Issei women in the earlier part of the century, see Yuji Ichioka, "Amerika Nadeshiko: Japanese Immigrant Women in the United States, 1900–1924," *Pacific Historical Review* 49 (1980): 339–57.

19 Gesensway and Roseman, eds., *Beyond Words*, 104.

20 Ibid., 106.

21 Eaton's *Beauty Behind Barbed Wire* includes frequent references to poetry, including this description of one artifact: "Every War Relocation Center had its poetry societies with contests sometimes extending to other camps. The decorated wooden panel shown here was made for a prize winner from Minedoka, Idaho, where it was photographed. . . . The poem may be in the handwriting of the verse maker, but is more likely to have been done by a camp calligrapher, as his contribution to the poetry award" (110). Eaton's presentation of camp arts, from the moment he introduces them as "a part of the distinguished record of the War Relocation Authority," clubs them to death in a number of ways which typify the uses of creative projects as a means of social control by the WRA. He holds them up as proof of the humane conditions and generous spirit of a model camp administration and government policy; he Japanizes them heavily, making little or no distinction between Japanese and Japanese American culture; perhaps most importantly, he finds – or publishes – only examples of art which testify to patient endurance, and censors, for instance, any example of a poem in Japanese which comments in any way on internment. The spirit of the volume is typified in its foreword by Eleanor Roosevelt justifying internment on the grounds that it protected Japanese Americans, and arguing that Eaton's collection "shows how well the War Relocation Authority did its work, one of the achievements of government administration of which every American citizen can be proud" (xi). Eaton's book does, to do it justice, include a protest against internment strong for its time. But although it remains valuable as a record of artistic achievement, its mystification and justification of the camps as cozy and aesthetically pleasing places provides a negative, admonitory example for any project, including my own, in danger of simply celebrating "beauty behind barbed wire." Both Gesensway and Roseman's *Beyond Words* and *Ayumi* offer strong examples of visual art done in the camps, with much more useful political analysis.

22 On tanka, senryu, and hokku writing in the camps, see Nakano and Nakano, *Poets Behind Barbed Wire*; Wakako Yamauchi, "The Poetry of the Issei on the American Relocation Experience," in *Calafia: The California Poetry*, ed. Ishmael Reed (Berkeley: Yardbird Publ. Co., 1979), lxxi–lxxviii; "Footprints: Poetry of the

American Relocation Camp Experience," ed. and trans. Constance Hayashi and Keiho Yamanaka, *Amerasia Journal* 3.2 (1976): 115–17 (a particularly powerful collection); Constance Hayashi and Keiho Yamanaka, "Senryu and Tanka of the American Relocation Camp Experience," in *Ayumi*, 87; Shizue Iwatsuki, "A Cycle of Poems from World War II," trans. Stephen Kohl, in *Turning Shadows into Light: Art and Culture of the Northwest's Early Asian/Pacific Community*, ed. Mayumi Tsutakawa and Alan Chung (Seattle: Young Pine Press, 1982), 62–64; Peter Suzuki, "Wartime Tanka," *Literature East and West* 21 (1977): 242–54.

23 Valerie Matsumoto, "Japanese American Women During World War II," *Frontiers* 8.1 (1984): 160–67.

24 Kim, *Asian American Literature*, 142.

25 See Suyemoto's description of Nisei literary culture in this period in her "Writing of Poetry," 74; Hisaye Yamamoto's account in "Writing," *Amerasia Journal* 3.2 (1976): 127–29; and Larry Tajiri, "Nisei U.S.A.: Notes on Nisei Writing," *Pacific Citizen*, 9 April 1949.

26 Kenny Murase, "Who's Who in the Nisei Literary World," *Current Life* (October 1940): 8–9.

27 On the majority of female editors at the *Free Press*, see James Oda, *Heroic Struggles of Japanese Americans: Partisan Fighters from America's Concentration Camps* (Los Angeles: KNI, 1980), 21. Hisaye Yamamoto provides another good example of a woman publishing regularly in camp outlets. She was feature editor of the *Poston Chronicle*, in which she wrote a column called "Small Talk." Her general tone of levity sometimes gave way to not-so-small talk, as in the subtle commentary on the situation of internment through a meditation on the meanings of the Blue Willow china pattern, in the column which ran on 16 May 1943. Yamamoto's publications in the paper included a serialized murder mystery called "Death Rides the Rails to Poston," in which a Nisei man condemned as a collaborator by his fellow "evacuee" passengers is murdered on a train en route to the internment camp (*Poston Chronicle*, 9 January to 26 February 1943). Cherry Obayashi was another Nisei writer who used the publishing arena and journalistic formula to good advantage; see, for instance, her camp version of true romance centered on the problem of obtaining permission to relocate, "Love Needs No Permit," *Poston Chronicle*, 30 May 1943. One powerful collection of a woman's camp writing comes from Canada: Muriel Kitagawa, *This Is My Own: Letters to Wes and Other Writings On Japanese Canadians, 1941–1948*, ed. Roy Miki (Vancouver: Talonbooks, 1985).

28 Wakako Yamauchi describes her friendship in the camps with Hisaye Yamamoto, and its later development, in Frank Chin et al., eds., *AIIIEEEEE!: An Anthology of Asian-American Writers* (Washington, D.C.: Howard Univ. Press, 1974), 192. See also Dorothy Ritsuko McDonald and Katharine Newman, "Relocation and Dislocation: The Writings of Hisaye Yamamoto and Wakako Yamauchi," *Melus* 7.3 (1980). Yamamoto gives an eloquent retrospective account of Nisei writers in the camps in her "I Still Carry It Around," *Rikka* 3.4 (1976): 11–13, an account which insists, I should add to counterbalance any overly optimistic and cheerful reading of the situation of Nisei women writers as I describe it here, on "remembering primarily the attrition of the spirit in camp" (13).

29 Uyeunten, "Hatsugen-ken."

30 This account is based on the work of Valerie Matsumoto and Sandra Uyeunten.

On Nisei women's lives during this period, see also Mei Nakano, *Japanese American Women: Three Generations, 1890–1990* (Berkeley: Mina Press, 1990), 135–56.

31 Ann Nisei, "Mental, Moral Stamina Shown by Nisei in Relocation," *Pacific Citizen* 25 December 1943, 20.

32 See, for instance, Larry Tajiri, "The Nisei in Literature," 4 September 1943; "The Literature of Evacuation," 31 July 1943; and "The Evacuees and the Arts," 27 October 1945; Tomoye Takahashi's call for camp literature in "Women's Mirror," *Topaz Times* 1 January 1944, 11; and also the articles by William Saroyan in *Current Life* and Woody Guthrie in *Pacific Citizen* (both men were often taken as models for Nisei authors) encouraging a new Nisei voice: "William Saroyan Salutes Current Life," *Current Life* (May 1941): 8–9; Woody Guthrie, "Take it Easy — But Take It!" *Pacific Citizen*, 12 January 1946.

33 Yamamoto, "Writing," 129. See also her description of Nisei literary culture in her short story "Epithalamium," *Carleton Miscellany* 1.4 (1960): 63.

34 Suyemoto, in Din, "Interview with Toyo Suyemoto," 2, 5–6, 9. Suyemoto, "Writing of Poetry," 76. Yamamoto, "Writing," 133. In Uchida's *Desert Exile*, see for example 25, 83.

35 My thanks to Stan Yogi for his analysis of this point. Yogi discusses the representation of Issei women in "Legacies Revealed: Uncovering Buried Plots in the Stories of Hisaye Yamamoto and Wakako Yamauchi" (Unpublished M.A. thesis, University of California at Berkeley, 1988).

36 The relative prevalence of poetic activity and its association with women in the culture of the Japanese mainland and/or in Issei culture often prompts non-Japanese American critics writing on the subject into uncomfortable formulations about poetry and gender. Allen Eaton, for instance, asserts that "it is difficult for us Westerners to understand how deeply ingrained poetry is in the lives of the Japanese," and adds, "there was nothing effeminate about the practice; at one time, poetry writing and football were the two highest achievements that Japanese noblemen could aspire to . . . " (*Beauty Behind Barbed Wire*, 110). Donald Keene writes of "a characteristically feminine poetry that . . . became the dominant tone of Japanese poetry as a whole" (26), and then devotes extended pages to qualifications such as "but the Manyoshu is prevailingly masculine in tone" and explanations such as noting the frequency of poems about "the decline of beauty, in itself a feminine preoccupation" (30). Keene, *Landscapes and Portraits: Appreciations of Japanese Culture* (London: Secker & Warburg, 1972).

37 Several recent books by Japanese American women might be said to be organized around the general principle of recognition/recovery of the mother; see for instance Janice Mirikitani's powerful *Shedding Silence* (Berkeley: Celestial Arts, 1987), especially "Generations of Women" (10–16) and the extraordinary poem "Breaking Silence," (33–36) which incorporates Mirikitani's mother's testimony before the Commission on Wartime Relocation and Internment of Japanese American Civilians; the Japanese Canadian Joy Kogawa's classic novel *Obasan* (New York: Penguin, 1981); Jeanne Wakatsuki Houston's "Beyond Manzanar," and elsewhere in her *Beyond Manzanar: Views of Asian-American Womanhood* (Santa Barbara, Cal.: Capra Press, 1985); and Mitsuye Yamada's *Camp Notes and Other Poems* (San Lorenzo, Cal.: Shameless Hussy, 1976). See also Toyo Suyemoto's moving sequence of poems to her mother at the end of her "Writing of Poetry," 77–79. Lengthier representations of writing in Nisei women's prose include the writing

mother in Hisaye Yamamoto's "Seventeen Syllables" *Seventeen Syllables: Five Stories of Japanese American Life*, ed. Robert Rolf and Norimitsu Ayuzawa (Kirihara Shoten, 1985) and Monica Sone's account of her attempt to console her mother by composing tanka upon their arrival at Puyallup Fairgrounds (*Nisei Daughter*, 175). These tributes contrast sharply with the version of the smothering, crazed Issei mother in John Okada's famous earlier novel of internment, *No-No Boy* rev. ed. (Seattle: Combined Asian American Resources Project, 1976; 1st ed., Rutherford, Vt., and Tokyo, Japan: Charles E. Tuttle, 1957). One very different visual representation by a man of a mother in the camps, Henry Sugimoto's "Longing," exhibited in 1942 at the Hendrix College museum in Arkansas, inspired John Gould Fletcher's poetic tribute to maternal care, "For the Picture 'Longing' of Henry Sugimoto": " . . .what rests above the present terror of this flood; / Mother love, sad with presage, yet accepting all. / Lacking this, we would be nothing. . . ." (reprinted, along with Sugimoto's painting and a broad selection of Sugimoto's work, in Gesenway and Roseman, eds., *Beyond Words*, 39–40). The maternal representations in Mirikitani's, Kogawa's, Wakatsuki Houston's, and Yamada's recent work (see note 37 above) are at odds both with the fear of the Issei mother in *No-No Boy* and the totalizing idealization of Fletcher's response. But compare also the lovingly, complexly represented, and culturally specific figure of the Issei mother in numerous stories by the important male author Toshio Mori; see, for instance, Mori's "Tomorrow is Coming, Children," *Trek* (February 1943): 13–17, and "Homecoming," in *Ayumi*, 137–45.

38   Hisaye Yamamoto was also making serious inroads into mainstream American literary publications at around the same time, but with short fiction, publishing several short stories in the *Partisan Review* and the *Kenyon Review* in the years immediately following the war.

39   For Suyemoto's personal and publishing history, see the interview with Grant Din and her "Writing of Poetry."

40   Walker, *Nightingale's Burden*, 140. At times, Suyemoto's early poems provide textbook illustrations of motifs discussed by Walker; her "Shelter" (*Ayumi*, 157), for instance, is usefully read as part of the tradition of women's sanctuary poems Walker describes (*Nightingale's Burden*, 145). Lillian Faderman and Barbara Bradshaw, in their study questions accompanying two of Suyemoto's poems, link her work to Emily Dickinson's: See Faderman and Bradshaw *Speaking for Ourselves* (Glenview, Ill.: Scott, Foresman, 1969), 223. See also Eric Mendelsohn, "Toyo Suyemoto," in *Longman Anthology of World Literature by Women 1875–1975*, ed. Marian Arkin and Barbara Sholler (New York: Longman, 1989), 574–75.

41   Toyo Suyemoto, "Retrospect," *Yale Review* (Winter 1946): 251.

42   Toyo Suyemoto, "Japonica," *Current Life* (March 1941): 4.

43   *Trek's* first issue, December 1942, was edited by Jim Yamada; for its second, February 1943, issue, Yamada was joined by Taro Katayama and Marii Kyoguku on the editorial board. Both issues note that "*Trek* is a special publication of the Project Reports Division, Central Utah Relocation Center."

44   Taro Katayama, "State of the City," *Trek* (December 1942): 2–11 (Suyemoto's poem interrupts this text on 7); Frank Beckwith, Sr., "Escalante in Millard County," *Trek* (February 1943): 17–20 (Suyemoto's poem is on 20).

45   For compact accounts of U.S. governmental policies about Japanese Americans' relation to land and agriculture long before, immediately before, and during internment, see Weglyn, *Years of Infamy*, 37, 77, 84, 97–100.

46   See, for example, Cherry Obayashi, "Poston," *Pacific Citizen* 23 July 1942, 6; Toyo Kazato, "Golden Poplar," in *Ayumi*, 23; "The Dandelion in the Letter," *Topaz Times* 1 April 1944; Taro Suzuki, "Japanese Dirt Farmer," *Rafu Shimpo*, 21 December 1941, 15; Ruth Tanaka, "Saga of a People," *Poston Chronicle* 9 June 1945; Miko Tamura, "Evacuee," *Pacific Citizen* 22 December 1945, 37; and Tamura's "Issei," *Pacific Citizen* 16 February 1946, 5.
47   Toyo Suyemoto, "Hokku" (17) and "Tanka" (45), in *All Aboard* (Spring 1944).
48   Toyo Suyemoto, "Gift of Quince," *Yale Review* (Winter 1946): 251.
49   Taro Katayama, "Agronomy," *Trek* (February 1943): 34.
50   Taro Katayama, "Nightmare," *Trek* (December 1942): 25; "The Volunteer," *Trek* (February 1943): 28.

Chapter 7. Identity and Contestation in Nisei Women's War Poetry

1   "The conflict [of registration] was much greater for Nisei males than females," wrote two historians of internment in 1956.

The expectations of both peer group and family were less demanding for females. The male Nisei's actions were decisive for the family because he was the major resource upon which the Issei depended. . . . The acculturated peer group viewed the Nisei [male's] compliance [to some parental demands to answer loyalty questions negatively] as disloyalty and cowardice. Females did not have these problems, and submission to parental demands coincided with their role expectations.

Leonard Broom and John Kitsuse, *The Managed Casualty: The Japanese-American Family in World War II* (Berkeley: Univ. of California Press, 1956), 47–48.

2   Chiye Mori, later interned at Manzanar, went on to become the feature and news editor of the camp's *Free Press* for a time, and at one point she planned to edit a camp literary magazine as well. Some information about her early life is given in the biographical notes at the end of *Reimei* — see 1.1 (July 1932): 33; 1.2 (November 1932): 32; and 1.3 (Spring 1933): 33, in which her first marriage, to Issei poet Bunichi Kagawa, is celebrated. I am grateful to Stan Yogi and *Nikkei Review* for information about Mori.
3   "Preface," *Reimei* 1.2 (November 1932): 3. The editor of this issue was Yasuo Sasaki. Names listed on the editorial board for other issues include Katayama, Iwao Kawakami, and Hoshina Airan.
4   Yasuo Sasaki and Hoshina Airan, "War and Youth," *Reimei* 1.2 (November 1932): 27. Hereafter cited in the text. Stan Yogi informs me that "Hoshina Airan" means "Star of Ireland" in Japanese.
5   Chiye Mori, "Vain," *Reimei* 1.1 (July 1932): 12.
6   Chiye Mori, "Japanese-American," *Reimei* 1.2 (November 1932): 30.
7   Typical examples of poems published to illustrate Japanese American patriotism include A. Okasaki, "America (My Home Sweet Home)," *Rafu Shimpo* 10 December 1941, 4; Private Kuni Nakao, "Nisei Americans," *Rafu Shimpo* 29 December 1941, 7; and, before Pearl Harbor, Iwao Kawakami, "The Memory of an Eagle," *Current Life* 1.1 (October 1940): 15. But see also Ayoko Noguchi's poetic call for U.S. nonintervention, "A Plea for Peace," *Current Life* (February 1941): 13 (a poem which a year later would not have been published, and probably not written) and Mary Oyama's foreboding "War Play," *Current Life* (July 1941): 10.

8   Hisaye Yamamoto, "Et Ego in America Vixi," *Current Life* (June 1941): 13.
9   We might compare this self-representation with another example on the same page
    of the journal in which this poem appeared, Chiduyo Imoto's chatty cosmetology
    piece "The June Bride." Advising the bride to "wear makeup which harmonizes
    with the pigmentation of the skin," Imoto suggests: "If you have the darker skin
    and bolder features of the brunette type, don't indulge in makeup that is too light
    for you." Yamamoto's text resembles Imoto's in its girlish self-regard, but differs
    from it in a more overt acceptance of and pride in Japanese appearance than
    Imoto's anxiously self-scrutinizing characterization of the "brunette type" allows.
10 Patricia Parker, "Rhetorics of Property: Exploration, Inventory, Blazon," *Literary
    Fat Ladies: Rhetoric, Gender, Property* (New York: Methuen, 1987), 132, 154.
11 Compare Janice Mirikitani's blazon of rebellion and revenge in her "Slaying Dra-
    gon Ladies" (Shedding Silence, 44).

> You don't know me.
> Geisha girl.
> China Doll.
> Slant cunt whore.
> Objects dangled
> in the glare
> . . . .
> You cannot see me.
> my breasts are Manzanar's desert
> my thighs an Arkansas swamp
> my veins are California's railroads
> my feet a Chicago postwar ghetto . . .

12 Yamada, *Camp Notes*. *Camp Notes* is unpaginated; all further quotations of
    Yamada's poems are from this volume.
13 June Jordan, "Case in Point," *Passion* (Boston: Beacon Press, 1980), 13.
14 Jacques Derrida, "Racism's Last Word," trans. Peggy Kamuf, in Gates, ed., *"Race,"
    Writing, and Difference*, 338.
15 As the anonymous review of Okubo's book in the *New Yorker* (12 October 1946)
    put it: "The captions are written with restraint and humor and seem to depreciate
    the inconveniences of the camps; the drawings themselves do not minimize them
    at all" (104). With a subtle form of racism, the reviewer comments on this disjunc-
    tion: "there is a certain Oriental subtlety in the illustrations." One might better at-
    tribute this subtlety to the effects of a specifically American act of oppression, the
    internment itself. On Okubo, see Betty LaDuke, "Miné Okubo: An American Ex-
    perience," *The Forbidden Stitch*, ed. Shirley Geok-lin Lim, Mayumi Tsutakawa,
    and Margarita Donnelly (Corvallis, Ore.: Calyx Books, 1989), 189–206.
16 Hisaye Yamamoto, "After Johnny Died," *The Los Angeles Tribune*, 26 November
    1945, rpt. in *Pacific Citizen*, 1 December 1945, 5. The essay is especially poignant
    in the light of Yamamoto's earlier writing on her brother in her Poston "Small Talk";
    see, for instance, her column on his leaving the camp in the 23 May 1943 issue
    of the *Poston Chronicle*.
17 Compare the treatment of sexual violence in Janice Mirikitani's internment story
    "Tomatoes" (with its own strong intertextual connections, like Yamada's work,
    to earlier literature by Nisei women, particularly, in the case of "Tomatoes," to
    Yamamoto's "Seventeen Syllables"). "Tomatoes" begins with an epigraph, a "dialogue

with my daughter," explicitly signaling its relation to and swerve from canonical war narrative: "'We have to read *The Red Badge of Courage.*' 'We all had to read it.' 'But all heroes are not men.'" It goes on to recount the response of a mother, recently returned from the camps, to a sexual threat to her daughter. Mirikitani, *Shedding Silence*, 37–40. Joy Kogawa's contemporary internment novel *Obasan*, like "Tomatoes," takes up the subject of sexual molestation. Both these texts, like Yamada's *Camp Notes*, develop narratives of war, internment, and their consequences which focus at some point on potential sexual violence that threatens a mother-daughter dyad.

On sexual violence or the fear of it in the camps, see Uchida, *Desert Exile*, 58, and Thomas and Nishimoto, *The Spoilage*, 111.

18   Other contemporary Japanese American works which link internment and Vietnam (and/or more generally U.S. policy toward and action in the Third World) include Mirikitani's "Spoils of War," (57–62) and "Who is Singing this Song?" (102–108) in *Shedding Silence*, and in *Ayumi*, Y. J. Suzuki, "Poems from East of the Rockies," (80) and Doug Yamamoto, "Matsutake Hunting" (250–52). Often, too, postwar literature of internment connects the imprisonment and exile of Japanese Americans or Japanese Canadians to the atomic bombing of Hiroshima and Nagasaki, and in Nisei and Sansei women's writing that connection also prompts meditation on gender roles in wartime and the problem of masculinity and femininity in the nuclear age. See, for instance, Kogawa's *Obasan* and Hisaye Yamamoto's "The Streaming Tears," *Rafu Shimpo*, 20 December 1951, 22, 24.

19   Mitsuye Yamada, *Desert Run: Poems and Stories* (Latham, N.Y.: Kitchen Table, 1988). Hereafter cited in the text.

Chapter 8. An Oblique Place: Elizabeth Bishop and the Language of War

1   Emily Dickinson to Thomas W. Higginson, in *The Letters of Emily Dickinson*, ed. Thomas Johnson (Cambridge: Harvard Univ. Press, 1958), 280.

2   Joan W. Scott, "Rewriting History," in Higgonet et al., eds., *Behind the Lines*, 26.

3   Elizabeth Bishop to Houghton Mifflin, 22 January 1945, in MacMahon, ed., *Elizabeth Bishop: A Bibliography*, 8.

4   The statement actually published in the book read, "Most of these poems were written, or partly written, before 1942." Diana Wyllie's list of the publication dates of the individual poems in *North and South* shows that almost all of them were published in some form before the volume. Many, beginning with "The Map" and "The Imaginary Iceberg" in 1935, were in print before the forties. Diana Wyllie, *Elizabeth Bishop and Howard Nemerov: A Reference Guide* (Boston: G. K. Hall, 1983). In general, with the exception of "Late Air," which was published first as early as 1938, the poems in the latter part of the book, from "Roosters" on, were published in the years immediately around the war. It is worth noting that none came out at the war's height, in 1942 or 1943, and only one in 1944. Bishop did not have an easy war. Lynn Keller summarizes her problems of the war years, which included difficulty in finding work (at one point she was employed briefly in a Key West naval yard) and her upset at the disruption of Key West's formerly quiet daily life by war industry. "These upheavals interfered with her writing," Keller writes, and adds, quoting one of Bishop's letters, "as did wartime's 'terrible *generalizing* of every emotion.'" Keller, "Words Worth a Thousand

Postcards: The Bishop/Moore Correspondence," *American Literature* 55.3 (October 1983): 425.

Interestingly, Oscar Williams misread the intentions of Bishop's disclaimer, taking it as an apology "to the academic powers" intended to prove that Bishop took a long time polishing her poems. "Since the world's greatest literature was written before 1942," he commented, "she should know she is on the right side of the fence." Williams, "North but South," *New Republic* (21 October 1946): 525; rpt. in Lloyd Schwartz and Sybil P. Estess, eds., *Elizabeth Bishop and her Art* (Ann Arbor: Univ. of Michigan Press, 1983), 185.

5   Louise Bogan, "On North and South," in Louise Bogan, *A Poet's Alphabet* (New York: McGraw-Hill, 1970), 219; originally published in *New Yorker*, 5 October 1946, 113.

6   Several recent analyses of the politics of lyricism in Stevens's work are provocative in relation to Bishop's. See for instance Marjorie Perloff's suspicious reading, "Resolving in Crystal," which criticizes the *Notes* as "a kind of antimeditation, fearful and evasive," and problematizes Stevens's patriarchal invocation of the "major man." (Bishop, of course, offers no such figure except ironically in "Roosters," one way in which her model of "antimeditation," if that is what her poems are, deviates clearly from Stevens's.) Perloff, "Resolving in Crystal: The Supreme Fiction and the Impasse of Modernist Lyric," in Albert Gelpi, ed., *Wallace Stevens: The Poetics of Modernism* (New York: Cambridge Univ. Press, 1985), 41–64. Charles Berger's analysis of Stevens, in contrast, is not only uncritical but celebratory; his elegiac reading in *Forms of Farewell: The Late Poetry of Wallace Stevens* (Madison: Univ. of Wisconsin Press, 1985) of slant, obliquely topical war poems suggests obvious comparisons between Stevens's and Bishop's projects of the forties, though it systematically avoids reference to gender. Frank Lentricchia (*Ariel and the Police*) conducts an extended and at its most Stevens-focused points insightful analysis of Stevens's "politics of lyricism" and its relation to the poet's fears of and desires for "feminization"; as Gilbert and Gubar suggest when they draw upon "Roosters" in their response to Lentricchia, setting Bishop's work next to Stevens's in the context of Lentricchia's argument is a useful way to begin to explore the limits and implications for women of that argument (or the differences between the effects of patriarchies on women and on men). Gilbert and Gubar, "The Man on the Dump vs. the United Dames of America."

7   "It might be nice," Stevens wrote to Cummington Press before their edition of *Notes* appeared, "to have on the back outside cover of the book a border consisting of a line or two of the poem beginning 'Soldier, there is a war' etc.: enough to state the idea." Wallace Stevens to Katherine Frazier, 1 June 1942, in *Letters of Wallace Stevens*, ed. Holly Stevens (New York: Knopf, 1966), 408. Stevens, *Notes Toward a Supreme Fiction* (Cummington, Mass.: Cummington, 1942).

8   Feminist critics have frequently considered the kind of "indirection" Bishop practices here as a particular mode of women's writing. Lynn Keller and Cristanne Miller summarize this critical tradition and consider "indirection" in the work of Bishop and her precursor in their "Emily Dickinson, Elizabeth Bishop, and the Rewards of Indirection," *New England Quarterly* 57 (December 1984): 533–53.

9   Elizabeth Bishop, *The Complete Poems 1927–79* (New York: Farrar, Straus & Giroux, 1983), 185. All further quotations of Bishop's poems are from this volume, hereafter abbreviated *CP* and cited in the text.

10 Kenneth Burke, *A Grammar of Motives* (New York: Meridian, 1945), 337. Hereafter cited in the text.

11   Cooper, "Nothing Has Been Used," 63.

12   Ibid., 44.

13   Robert Lowell, "Thomas, Bishop, and Williams," *Sewanee Review* 55 (Summer 1947); rpt. Schwartz and Estess, eds., *Elizabeth Bishop*, 188.

14   Randall Jarrell, "The Poet and His Public," *Partisan Review* 13.4 (September–October 1946); rpt. Schwartz and Estess, eds., *Elizabeth Bishop*, 180.

15   Chad Walsh, "Never Underestimate the Power of a Lady's Voice," *Washington Post Book World*, 27 April, 1969, 8.

16   Gilbert and Gubar, "The Man on the Dump vs. the United Dames of America," 406.

17   Moore's objection to "Roosters"' coarseness – a response which marked the end of her role as intensive tutor for Bishop's unpublished work – is well detailed in Keller's "Words Worth a Thousand Postcards." Bishop herself describes the mild altercation briefly in her "Efforts of Affection: A Memoir of Marianne Moore," *The Collected Prose*, ed. Robert Giroux (New York: Farrar, Straus & Giroux), 130: "I was scolded for having used 'water closet' in a poem, but by then I had turned obstinate" (130).

18   "Roosters" was first printed in the *New Republic* (21 April 1941): 547–48.

19   Ostriker, *Stealing the Language*, 54.

20   Rosamund Tuve, *Elizabethan and Metaphysical Imagery* (1947; rpt. Chicago: Univ. of Chicago Press, 1968), 203. Grace Schulman cites these lines in her discussion of Moore's "Evolution of an Inner Dialectic from Argumentation to Reverie," an analysis which suggests that Moore provided one model for Bishop's work with dialectic; see Schulman, *Marianne Moore*, 51.

21   Elizabeth Bishop to Marianne Moore, 17 October 1940. Papers of Marianne C. Moore, V. 05:02. The Rosenbach Museum and Library, Philadelphia.

22   For feminist theories of the relation between militarism, fascism, misogyny, and patriarchy, see for instance Enloe, "Feminists Thinking about War;" Betty Reardon, *Sexism and the War System* (New York: Columbia Univ. Teacher's College Press, 1985); Birgit Brock-Utne, *Educating for Peace: A Feminist Perspective* (Oxford: Pergamon, 1985); and Klaus Theweleit, who in his *Male Fantasies* offers his own version of a footnote playing the function this one does: "I am not about to use literature to make this point. Anyone who is interested can discuss it at length with actual women." Theweleit, *Male Fantasies*, trans. Stephen Conway (Minneapolis: Univ. of Minnesota Press, 1987) 1:444. Susan Gubar's "This is My Rifle" elucidates ways in which a feminist critique of fascism was current at the time of the war.
     As Lynn Keller points out, "Roosters"' militance here is partly blunted by the often "formal diction" of this section of the poem, and by the use of quotation marks, though, Keller writes, Bishop's "academic manner may intend, too, a mockery of such stereotypically male pretension." Keller, *Re-Making It New: Contemporary American Poetry and the Modernist Tradition* (New York: Cambridge Univ. Press, 1987), 91.

23   Elizabeth Bishop to Marianne Moore, 17 October 1940. Rosenbach Museum Collection.

24   George Starbuck, "'The Work!': A Conversation with Elizabeth Bishop," in Schwartz and Estess, eds., *Elizabeth Bishop*, 320. Starbuck's interview is hereafter cited in the text.

25   Elizabeth Spires, "The Art of Poetry XXVII," *Paris Review* 80 (Summer 1981): 80.

26 Bishop and Starbuck at one point begin to talk about Woolf's letters. "When she wrote *Three Guineas*," Bishop says, "Her first 'feminist' book, she was rather badly treated . . . Have you ever read *Three Guineas*? A wonderful little book" (324).

27 "Roosters" seems obviously connected to *Three Guineas* in its critique of masculine pretension and military hierarchy and in its link between "the tyrannies and servilities" of the private world and those of the public world (142). *Three Guineas* makes a strong case against male aggression in statements like "to fight has always been the man's habit, not the woman's," (6) but avoids pushing this argument to its limit; rather, elliptically, Woolf publically refuses the word "feminist," and in other passages links men and women in shared peril and as sharing the potential for violence and fascism (101–2, 142–44). In this set of moves, too, "Roosters" resembles Woolf's treatise.

28 Bishop, "Efforts of Affection," 144.

29 Ashley Brown, "An Interview with Elizabeth Bishop," in Schwartz and Estess, eds., *Elizabeth Bishop*, 296–97.

30 See chapter 9 for an extended discussion of the uses of New Testament imagery and narrative in modern war poetry.

31 Ostriker, *Stealing the Language*, 54.

32 Willard Spiegelman, "Elizabeth Bishop's 'Natural Heroism,'" in Schwartz and Estess, eds., *Elizabeth Bishop*, 157. I am indebted throughout this chapter to Spiegelman's insightful discussion of Bishop's negation or undercutting of traditional "heroic situations or devices" and her corresponding demonstration of a different "natural heroism."

33 Burke is quoted in William Rueckert, "Some of the Many Kenneth Burkes," *Representing Kenneth Burke: Selected Papers from the English Institute* (Baltimore: Johns Hopkins Univ. Press, 1982), 14. I owe to Barbara Bowen my first introduction both to Burke and to what Jameson calls "dialectical thinking," in a paper on Milton's displacements of perspective she wrote at Yale some years ago which led me also to consider seventeenth-century dialectical models.

34 In the Spires interview, for instance, Bishop said of the Depression years, "All the intellectuals were Communists except me. I'm always very perverse so I went in for T. S. Eliot and Anglo-Catholicism." Spires, "Art of Poetry," 78. In the Brown interview she gives a modified account, in which "socialism" functions much as "feminism" does for her elsewhere: "I was always opposed to political thinking as such for writers . . . Politically I considered myself a socialist, but I disliked 'social conscious' writing. I stood up for T. S. Eliot when everybody else was talking about James T. Farrell. The atmosphere in Vassar was left-wing; it was the popular thing. . . . I felt that most of the college girls didn't know much about social conditions. Then I tried anarchism, briefly. I'm much more interested in social problems and politics now than I was in the 30's." Brown, "Interview with Elizabeth Bishop," 293–94.

35 Fredric Jameson, *Marxism and Form: Twentieth-Century Dialectical Theories of Literature* (Princeton: Princeton Univ. Press, 1972), 307.

36 Jeredith Merrin, "An Enabling Humility: Marianne Moore, Elizabeth Bishop, and the Uses of Tradition" (Ph.D. diss., University of California-Berkeley, 1987). Helen Vendler discusses Bishop's indebtedness to Herbert in her "The Poems of Elizabeth Bishop," *Critical Inquiry* 13 (Summer 1987): 825–38.

37 Stanley Fish, *Self-Consuming Artifacts: The Experience of Seventeenth-Century Literature* (Berkeley: Univ. of California Press, 1972), 155. Hereafter cited in the text.

38   The punctuation here might be compared to that at the end of "Love Lies Sleep-
      ing," which concludes, as David Bromwich nicely puts it, "with a doubt exactly
      the size of the comma." Bromwich, "Elizabeth Bishop's Dream-Houses," in *Con-
      temporary Poets*, ed. Harold Bloom (New York: Chelsea House, 1986), 42.
39   Keller, *Re-Making It New*, 91. As Keller emphasizes, the end of "Roosters" brings
      "uncertainty . . . to the fore."
40   Although "Roosters" draws, then, in the most obvious ways upon the Western
      fund of Christian imagery, its relation to Christian faith remains skittish, and
      it flirts with irreverence to the end. Compared with other Second World War–period
      lyrics with which it shares some central distinctive features, "Roosters" seems rela-
      tively distanced from the Christian masterplot it so openly invokes. Bishop's poem
      belongs to a peculiar forties subgenre of war poetry we might call the "meteorologi-
      cal crucifixion"; other striking examples of this type are Edith Sitwell's famous "Still
      Falls the Rain" (whose full title adds "The Raids, 1940. Night and Dawn"), Kath-
      leen Raine's "See, see Christ's blood streams in the firmament" (which takes its title
      from the line from Marlowe's *The Tragical History of Doctor Faustus* used in Sit-
      well's poem), and F. T. Prince's "Soldiers Bathing." Each of these poems renders
      a Passion which is also a meditation on war making which is also an emphatic
      or encoded "naturalistic" representation of sunset or sunrise. In Sitwell's, Raine's,
      and Prince's versions, the suffering of Christ dominates the scene itself, and the
      possibility of redemption from violence is categorically and dramatically, even
      operatically, linked to the grace of a Christian God. In contrast, "Roosters'" turn
      to the Catholic Lateran cock seems a deflected, elusive version of oratory, and the
      poem's further "protestant inquests," as David Bromwich has called them ("Dream-
      Houses," 34), remain in slant relation to its almost comically rendered scene of
      the old holy sculpture of Rome. Readers familiar with Bishop's later work might
      remember that in her next book the poem "Brazil, January 1, 1502" develops an
      explicit critique of Christianity. There, rather than holding out the promise of
      transformation of (masculine) aggression, the Christian exemplifies it; armored
      male Christian colonizers rip into the tapestried Brazilian landscape and, "hum-
      ming perhaps / *L'Homme armé*," set out to conquer it by raping Indian women,
      "directly after Mass."
41   "Reality is a cliché from which we escape by metaphor. It is only *au pays de la
      métaphore qu'on est poete.*" Stevens, "Adagia," *Opus Posthumous*, 179.
42   The fine line which the third part of "Roosters" has to tread is clarified, for in-
      stance, by John Crowe Ransom's proclamation to Allen Tate that art demands
      "our rejection of Third Terms; our denial of Hegel's right to resolve a pair of con-
      tradictions with a Triad. . . . Give us a Dualism or we'll give you no art." "Roosters'"
      own slippery "third term" may be usefully read, as well, in the light of Ransom's
      later claim that contradictions may be brought to harmony or synthesis through
      art alone. See Albert Gelpi's summary of Ransom's "development from a dualistic
      to a triadic ontology of the poem": *A Coherent Splendor: The American Poetic
      Renaissance, 1910–1950* (New York: Cambridge Univ. Press, 1987), 47.
43   On Burke's personal relation to Moore, and on the relation of their work, see
      Costello, *Marianne Moore*, 112–14.
44   Passages from the *Grammar* which are illuminating and illuminated when read
      next to "Roosters" include Burke's discussion of the uses of the concepts "war" and
      "peace" as "constitutive anecdotes" (330–37); more generally, his section on "Dialec-

tic in General"; and his treatment of irony in "Four Master Tropes." Also of interest here is the motto of the book: "Toward the Purification of War." Two essays in *Representing Kenneth Burke*, Fredric Jameson's "The Symbolic Inference, or, Kenneth Burke and Ideological Analysis" and Frank Lentricchia's "Reading History with Kenneth Burke" analyze what Lentricchia calls Burke's "anti-Hegelian impulse[s]" (121).

45 Jameson, "Symbolic Inference," 86.

46 Ibid., 88. Christine Oravec disagrees with this characterization in her "Kenneth Burke's Concept of Association," in *The Legacy of Kenneth Burke*, ed. Herbert W. Simons and Trevor Melia (Madison: Univ. of Wisconsin Press, 1989), 174-95. See Burke's response to Jameson, arguing against this sense of his work. Kenneth Burke, "Methodological Repression and/or Strategies of Containment," *Critical Inquiry* 5 (1978): 401-16.

47 Kenneth Burke, "Motives and Motifs in the Poetry of Marianne Moore," *Accent* (Spring 1942): 162.

48 In her "Feminists Thinking about War," Cynthia Enloe provides a cogent summary of various inquiries along these lines, raising questions about "the causal links between . . . [domestic] abusive behavior and the wider militaristic culture that legitimates all forms of violence," and about militarization as "a surface symptom of more basic assumptions in the culture about marriage, property, reproduction, and heterosexuality — all of which are essential to the maintenance of male privilege and the permission for interpersonal violence on which such domination often rests" (389).

49 Enloe, *Does Khaki Become You?*, 210.

50 Ibid., 210. See also Enloe's discussion of "Masculinity militarized, militarism masculinized" in "Feminists Thinking about War," 382-84.

51 "Bishop's own poems are active displacements of perspective," David Bromwich writes in his "Dream-Houses" (27). Much writing on Bishop's work is pertinent here. Jane Shore considers how Bishop generally "seems to call into question the accuracy of her images as she writes them," in "Elizabeth Bishop: The Art of Changing Your Mind," *Ploughshares* 5 (1978): 182. Barbara Page emphasizes "the adjustments of judgment or understanding or feeling that arise in the course" of Bishop's poems; see Page, "Shifting Islands: Elizabeth Bishop's Manuscripts," *Shenandoah* 33.1 (1981-82): 59. Joanne Feit Diehl, "At Home with Loss: Elizabeth Bishop and the American Sublime," in Middlebrook and Yalom, eds., *Coming to Light* 123-37, focuses on Bishop's subversion of dualist opposition and hierarchy. Lynn Keller discusses Bishop's demonstration "that the proper psychic or moral response to otherness arises only in the process of careful observation." Keller, *Re-Making It New*, 89.

52 The tension between choice and factors that inhibit or prevent choosing is one of Bishop's most characteristic topics, enacted most overtly when, in the course of composing "Questions of Travel," she runs through several versions of one line — "The choice perhaps is not great . . . but fairly free," "My choice was never too wide and never too free" — and settles finally on the metrically constrained "the choice is never wide and never free." Barbara Page discusses this revision in "Shifting Islands," 55-56.

53 Bishop turned repeatedly to the aubade, as Lloyd Schwartz has noted; Schwartz, "One Art: The Poetry of Elizabeth Bishop, 1971-1976," in Schwartz and Estess, eds., *Elizabeth Bishop*, 147-48.

54 On the "themes of outsiderhood and marginality" in Bishop's work as they con-
    nect, in their "encodings and obscurities, with a lesbian identity," see Adrienne
    Rich's tribute, "The Eye of the Outsider: The Poetry of Elizabeth Bishop," *Boston
    Review* 8 (April 1983): 15–17. Ian Hamilton's *Robert Lowell: A Biography* (New
    York: Random, 1982) suggests that before Bishop's move to Brazil in 1950 she
    was involved in relationships with men as well as women (135). I am not arguing
    that "Roosters" is conclusively a "lesbian" poem; I *am* arguing that nothing but
    heterosexist bias excludes that possible reading. It seems likely that one of Bishop's
    objections to wartime's "terrible *generalizing* of every emotion" lay in the heterosex-
    ism of that generalizing.

55 See Bromwich, "Dream-Houses," 34, for a sharp exploration of the disturbing
    implicit love poem here. Keller and Miller, in their essay on "the rewards of in-
    direction," discuss Bishop's common use of "subtle manipulations of language"
    to create a subtext revealing "a more daring and more intensely personal involve-
    ment of the poet with her subject than the surface of the poem suggests" ("Rewards
    of Indirection," 534). Alan Williamson describes this device as "the trick of turn-
    ing the poem to an overwhelming personal sorrow in the last line — and then turn-
    ing it off" in his "A Cold Spring: The Poet of Feeling," in Schwartz and Estess,
    eds., *Elizabeth Bishop,* 99.

56 Julia Kristeva, "Women's Time," trans. Alice Jardine and Harry Blake, *Feminist
    Theory: A Critique of Ideology,* ed. Nannerl O. Keohane, Michelle Z. Rosaldo,
    and Barbara C. Gelpi (Chicago: Univ. of Chicago Press, 1982), 52. Hereafter cited
    in the text. Klaus Theweleit puts this another way: "The pathway to knowledge
    might just be that of . . . allowing history (Fascism) to be 'lived through' by it,
    in such a way that our understanding of history is *through the experience of our
    own unconscious* . . . It will not do to conceive of fascism — or any historical
    object — as something alien and opposed to the individual self." Theweleit, *Male
    Fantasies,* 225–26. I am grateful to Jacqueline Rose for her reference to both these
    passages in a talk given at the University of Sussex in January, 1988, which sent
    me back to reread "Women's Time" and clarified my own reading of Theweleit.
    I thank her, too, for showing me some of her recent work on Sylvia Plath, which
    considers "violence . . . in the very place where it operates with the maximum
    intransigence" more extensively than I have done here, and to which I am indebted.

57 The work of one contemporary, the British poet Kathleen Raine, closely resembles
    Bishop's in this regard. Raine's war aubade "Good Friday," for instance, represents
    a "death-cold dawn" ushered in by the crow of the cock, heralding a day in which
    lovers must part, "each entering his dimension like a tomb," and men, later specifi-
    cally identified as soldiers, must "clock in again" to "do wrong." Her "Far-darting
    Apollo" develops a critique of masculine aggression as pointed as that in "Roost-
    ers'" early stanzas; in Raine's poem the male sun, "like a young M.P. risen to the
    occasion," both imperiously conducts and callously exposes world war. Both
    poems end with inward turns toward a barely revealed world of private and
    presumably erotic impulse. But Raine's projection in "Apollo" of wrongdoing onto
    the male figure is less mitigated than that in Bishop's poem, where, after all, the
    sun invites identification; and Raine's evil day in "Good Friday" is countered by
    a wholehearted longing for the innocent night. Both Raine's poems, that is,
    develop more extreme positions than the self-checking dialectic of "Roosters."

58 Bishop's poem might, then, be said to be part of the "conversation" David Cratis

Williams has described in an essay on Burke and Derrida: "a conversation which is engaged in dialectically but which concerns the very process of dialectic, one which seeks not the clarification and rigidification of difference but rather the murky margins between, those margins of overlap which inaugurate and which limit the very functioning of dialectic." Williams, "Under the Sign of Annihilation," in Simons and Melia, eds., *Legacy of Kenneth Burke*, 218.

59 Compare Bishop's discussion of the relationship between irrationality and the solid case of argument in her famous "Darwin letter" to Anne Stevenson, reprinted in part in Schwartz and Estess, eds., *Elizabeth Bishop*, 288. On "the thought of a difference that is not a dialectical difference, one that cannot be subsumed within the self-developing identity of dialectical reason," see William Desmond, *Desire, Dialectic, and Otherness: An Essay on Origins* (New Haven: Yale Univ. Press, 1987), 3. Desmond's initial summary of philosophical critiques of dialectic provides a useful framework within which to place Bishop's more elusive negotiations with dialectical traditions:

Existentialist concern with concrete existence as resistant to categorical abstraction, psychoanalytic probing of desire and the elusive recesses beyond the threshold of self-possessed consciousness . . . and the pervasive repudiation of the clarity and distinctness of the Cartesian *cogito* are all indications of movement into realms of otherness, seemingly resistant to philosophical dialectics." (2)

Whether Bishop might dismiss the modifying "seemingly" in that last clause is a question "Roosters" leaves open.

60 On the "troping of what is schematic" in poetry, see John Hollander, "Breaking into Song," 88, and his further extensions of this point in *Melodious Guile: Fictive Pattern in Poetic Language* (New Haven: Yale Univ. Press, 1985).

61 Charles Sanders has pointed out the connection between "Roosters" and the Crashaw poem, in "Elizabeth Bishop's 'Roosters,'" *Explicator* 40.4 (Summer 1982): 55–57. Hereafter cited in the text. I was pointed to the Sanders essay by Heather Weidemann (see note 63 below).

62 Richard Crashaw, "Wishes. To his (supposed) Mistresse," *Crashaw's Poetical Muses*, ed. L. C. Martin (Oxford: Clarendon, 1957), 195. All further quotations are from this edition, hereafter cited in the text.

63 Heather Weidemann, "'Griefe Brought to Numbers': Gender, War and Poetic Tradition in Elizabeth Bishop's 'Roosters'" (Unpublished paper, University of California-Berkeley, 1989). Weidemann focuses on Bishop's allusions in "Roosters" and elsewhere to the "eyes and tears" poems of the seventeenth century, a body of poetry she notes was "specifically produced in the shadow of war."

64 Cooper, "Nothing Has Been Used," 47.

65 Cooper characteristically acknowledges her debts and gratitude not only to Bishop but to Berryman. Ibid., 124.

66 See, for instance, Plath's famous use in "Daddy" and "Lady Lazarus" of governing "historical" reference to fascism in connection with contemporary and "personalized" familial and erotic situations; Cooper's early, long-unpublished poems in *Maps and Windows*; and Dickinson's many open or slant explorations of the use of war as metaphor. Shira Wolosky's *Emily Dickinson: A Voice of War* (New Haven: Yale Univ. Press, 1984) is an important guide to Dickinson's indirected war poems, though Wolosky's book conspicuously avoids consideration of gender as a significant factor, or as a factor at all, in Dickinson's war work.

67 The relation of Bishop's work to her childhood losses is discussed quietly and elegantly in Helen Vendler's "Domestication, Domesticity and the Otherworldly" in Schwartz and Estess, eds., *Elizabeth Bishop*, 32–60, and in David Kalstone, "Elizabeth Bishop: Questions of Memory, Questions of Travel," in Schwartz and Estess, eds., *Elizabeth Bishop*, 3–31. Bishop recorded the experiences in question quietly and elegantly herself, in her "In the Village" and "The Country Mouse," both in her *Collected Prose*.

68 Joseph Cornell, quoted in *Art Since Mid-Century: The New Internationalism* II (Greenwich, Conn.: New York Graphic Society, 1971), 154.

69 "Objects & Apparitions," in Bishop, *Complete Poems*, 275–76.

70 Spiegelman, "Bishop's 'Natural Heroism,'" 159.

71 On the Byron poem's probable reference to Buonaparte, see *Lord Byron: The Complete Poetical Works*, ed. Jerome J. McGann (New York: Oxford Univ. Press, 1981), 3: 472.

72 Lord Byron, "The Destruction of Semnacherib," *Poetical Works of Lord Byron*, ed. Ernest Hartley Coleridge (London: John Murray, 1905), 347.

73 Bishop thus does here obviously what Penelope Laurens has shown she does implicitly throughout her work: she uses formal and metrical modulations to keep "the poetry from sentimental excess and give . . . it its elegantly muted, modernist quality." Laurens, "'Old Correspondences': Prosodic Transformations in Elizabeth Bishop," in Schwartz and Estess, eds., *Elizabeth Bishop*, 75–95.

74 George Herbert, "Affliction IV," *The Works of George Herbert*, ed. F. E. Hutchinson (Oxford: Clarendon, 1941), 89–90.

75 Unlike some other restless modern poems in which unabated wars and seas collide in open metaphor — Stevens's "Dry Loaf," for instance, where "the waves, the waves were soldiers moving," or Joyce's "I hear an army charging upon the land," or, earlier, Arnold's "darkling plain" — "Wading" places gentle emphasis on the possibilities of respite.

76 Gloria Bowles's discussion of "The Female Heritage: Ambivalence and Revision" in *Louise Bogan's Aesthetic of Limitation* provides a useful context here. See also the disparaging discussion of Mrs. Hemans as war poet in Lilian Rowland Brown's "War Poetry of Women," 442.

77 John Hollander well describes "Casabianca" as a "wrenching early epigram" which "makes figures of figures." Hollander, "Elizabeth Bishop's Mappings of Life," in Schwartz and Estess, eds., *Elizabeth Bishop*, 247.

78 On Dickinson's subversive play with the conventions of definition, see Robert Weisbuch, *Emily Dickinson's Poetry* (Chicago: Univ. of Chicago Press, 1972), 63–76.

79 Kaplan, *Salt and Bitter and Good*, 95.

80 Spiegelman overtly relates "Wading at Wellfleet" to dialectic. "Bishops 'Natural Heroism,'" 159.

81 Mrs. Felicia Hemans, *The Poetical Works* (Boston: Crosby and Nichols, 1864), p. 160.

82 In Bishop's autobiographical "The Country Mouse," she recounts being made as a child during the Great War to recite patriotic verse to her grandmother: "Most of the words made no sense at all. *Between his loved home and the war's desolation* made me think of my dead father, and conjured up strange pictures in my mind" (*Collected Prose*, 27). In the light of this overt association of poetic/martial inculcation with the dead father, it is tempting to read remote hints of autobiographical implication in Bishop's "Casabianca"'s strange scenes of abandonment.

83 Robert Southwell, "The burning Babe," *English Seventeenth-Century Verse*, ed. Louis L. Martz (New York: Norton, 1969), 11–12.

84 Riffaterre, *Semiotics of Poetry*, 19.

85 See Lee Edelman's fine discussion of Bishop's common appeal to the literal, and at the same time her consistent realignment of truth with trope: Edelman, "The Geography of Gender: Elizabeth Bishop's 'In the Waiting Room,'" *Contemporary Literature* 26.2 (1985): 179–96.

86 Theweleit, *Male Fantasies*, 1: 292.

87 Carol Cohn, in conversation with me. See Cohn's "Sex and Death in the Rational World of Defense Intellectuals."

88 Elizabeth Bishop, "Gerard Manley Hopkins: Notes on Timing in his Poetry," *Vassar Review* (February 1934); the relevant passage is part of the excerpt of this piece reprinted in Schwartz and Estess, eds., *Elizabeth Bishop*, 275. Compare the late, and not entirely tongue-in-cheek, treatment of the media and scene of writing as violent and militarized in "12 O'Clock News."

Chapter 9. Myrrh to Myrrh: H.D., War, and Biblical Narrative

1 Alexander Blok, "The Vulture," trans. Jon Stallworthy and Peter France, in *War and the Creative Arts*, ed. J. Ferguson (London: Macmillan, 1972), 151.

2 H.D., "The Flowering of the Rod," *Trilogy*, in H.D., *Collected Poems 1912–1944*, ed. Louis L. Martz (New York: New Directions, 1983), 583. Further references to *Trilogy* are cited in the text; hereafter the initials W, T, and F designate the three sequential parts of the poem, and section numbers within those parts are cited rather than the page numbers. Further references to other poems from this edition are cited in the text with the abbreviation *CP* and the appropriate page number.

3 Norman Holmes Pearson, foreword, in *Trilogy*, by H.D., ed. Norman Holmes Pearson (New York: New Directions, 1973), xii.

4 Stephen Spender, introduction, *War Pictures by British Artists (Second Series: Air Raids)* (New York: Oxford Univ. Press, 1943), 6.

5 The three poems which comprise *What Do I Love?* are published in the "Uncollected and Unpublished Poems" section of *CP* (485–504), with no overarching title and in the apparent order in which they were written, or at any rate the calendar order in which they are dated: "R.A.F." (dated "17 September, 1941") first, then "May 1943," then "Christmas 1944." The original 1950 printing of the Christmas card pamphlet reversed the order of the first two poems; it is worth noting that this sequence places initial emphasis on civilian experience rather than on the male combatant of "R.A.F." For an account of the origins of the Christmas 1950 edition, see Martz's notes, *CP*, 621. H.D. discusses these poems at some length, both linking them loosely to and distinguishing them firmly from *Trilogy*, in the informal, long-unpublished work usually referred to as "Notes on Recent Writing" but recently printed under H.D.'s original title "H.D. by Delia Alton," *Iowa Review* 16.3 (Fall 1986), 199–200, 203.

6 Catherine Reilly's collection *Chaos of the Night* does not, for instance, include any reference to H.D.; neither, even more surprisingly, does Reilly's monumental *English Poetry of the Second World War: A Bibliography*, which includes a massive survey of poets published in anthologies as well as individual volumes. This neglect was coupled in the war years with an often open hostility to H.D.'s work,

particularly in the United States where reviews by critics such as Bogan and Jarrell scathingly dismissed *Trilogy*. See Jarrell, "PWP," 130, and "H.D." in *Kipling, Auden and Co.* 135; Bogan, "Verses," 94; Bogan's review of "Tribute to the Angels," *New Yorker*, 29 December 1945, 68; and her review of "Flowering of the Rod," *New Yorker*, 14 December 1946, 147. A notable exception to this general pattern was the wartime "Reading of Famous Poets" before the royal family, organized by the Sitwells, in which H.D. took part in April 1943; for a description of that event see Guest, *Herself Defined*, 263. Osbert Sitwell provides, in addition, an exceptionally sympathetic contemporary review of the second part of *Trilogy*, "Tribute to the Angels," *Life and Letters Today* 46 (July/September 1945): 58.

7   Robert Duncan, "From the *H.D. Book*, Part II, Chapter 5," *Stony Brook*, 3/4 (Fall 1969): 165. The British civilian experience of aerial bombardment rendered the distinction between combatants and noncombatants much less pertinent than it had been before (it had been intensely pertinent in H.D.'s earlier work); general surveys of the war years in England, with emphasis on the literary scene and on women's experience, respectively, may be found in Hewison, *Under Seige*, and in Reilly, *Chaos of the Night*, xxi–xxvi. For accounts of the period by those close to H.D. during the war, see her daughter Perdita Schaffner's "Running," *Iowa Review* 16.3 (1986): 10–11; Perdita Schaffner, "Unless a Bomb Falls . . . ," in H.D., *The Gift* (New York: New Directions, 1982); her close friend Sylvia Dobson's "'Shock Knit Within Terror': Living Through World War II," *Iowa Review* 16.3 (1986): 232–45; Sylvia Dobson, "Remembering H.D.," *Agenda* 25.3–4 (Autumn/ Winter 1987–88): 139, 143–45; and the war memoir of Winifred Bryher, the woman with whom H.D. lived for many years, including the Second War years, *The Days of Mars: A Memoir 1940–1946* (London: Calder & Boyars, 1972). Guest's biography gives a helpful overview (*Herself Defined*, 253–79). The statement that H.D. moved at this time "as a poet to the battlefront" should not obscure her life-long concern as a writer, across five decades, with war and with the gendering of war roles. Rachel Blau DuPlessis provides a useful summary of the prose works which take up these issues in *H.D.: The Career of That Struggle* (Bloomington: Indiana Univ. Press, 1986), 106–7. And Gary Burnett's "A Poetics Out Of War: H.D.'s Responses to the First World War" is an excellent analysis of the writer's movement toward and away from "battlefronts" in the Great War years. Burnett, *Agenda* 25.3–4: 54–63. Note that Bryher, describing her first reading of H.D.'s earliest published poems, the pastoral *Sea Garden* (1916), wrote that they satisfied her need for a kind of war poetry: "But now — (now one had breathed war) — one needed something fierce and authentic. . . ." Winifred Bryher, *Two Selves* (Paris: Contact, n.d.).

8   I use the words "dangerous symptom" with a deliberate and ambivalent nod toward Freud's application of that phrase to H.D.'s famous visions of "the writing on the wall" in the immediate aftermath of the Great War. "The only dangerous 'symptom,'" H.D. records him saying, and then responds by adding to his diagnosis her own word, "inspiration." H.D., *Tribute to Freud* (New York: McGraw-Hill, 1974), 41, 51; hereafter abbreviated *TF* and cited in the text. On the symptom/inspiration conflict, see Susan Stanford Friedman, *Psyche Reborn: The Emergence of H.D.* (Bloomington: Indiana Univ. Press, 1981), 101 and throughout the first five chapters of that book, which focus on H.D. and psychoanalytic tradition. H.D. herself links the two visions related to the two World Wars in "H.D. by *Delia Alton*," 190, 192.

 9 Rachel Blau DuPlessis, "Romantic Thralldom in H.D.," *Contemporary Literature*
    20.2 (1979): 196. See Friedman, *Psyche Reborn*, 27–30 and Guest, *Herself Defined*,
    278–79 for accounts of H.D.'s 1946 breakdown.
10 Susan Stanford Friedman, in her "H.D. Chronology: Composition and Publica-
    tion of Volumes," states that "Christmas 1944" was composed in 1944 (presumably
    accepting the poem's own account of its timing), and we know from the notebooks
    that "Flowering of the Rod" was written between December 18 and 31 in 1944.
    Friedman warns, however, that H.D. "may have fictionalized some dates to give
    the work a favorable 'natal horoscope.'" Friedman, *H.D. Newsletter* 1.1 (Spring
    1987): 12–16. Adalaide Morris eloquently describes this creative burst in her "The
    Concept of Projection: H.D.'s Visionary Powers," *Contemporary Literature* 25.4
    (1984): 429–30.
11 One might also add to this list the "Advent" section of *Tribute to Freud*, completed
    in December 1948, another text in which both Christmas and war figure as sub-
    jects of analysis, and the later "Sagesse" (1957), which develops a retrospective
    narrative of London during the bombing around the figure of a psychic child com-
    pared to the "Christkind." H.D., "Sagesse," in *Hermetic Definition* (New York:
    New Directions, 1972), 77–81. "Sagesse" is hereafter cited in the text. These Christ-
    mas references were intensely personal. H.D. was born in Bethlehem — Bethlehem,
    Pennsylvania — into a family culture laden with Christmas associations. *The Gift*
    describes the Christmas ceremonies and folk customs of the town's prominent
    Moravian community, of which H.D.'s mother was a part, and elaborates on
    H.D.'s theories of the meaning of Christmas; see, in addition to the text printed
    by New Directions (especially 27–33), the unedited version ("The Gift") in the
    Beinecke Library, as yet unpublished, especially Box 40, Folder 1036, Part IV,
    6, 21–23. See also the "Two Poems for Christmas, 1937," *CP*, 469–70. At several
    points in H.D.'s accounts of her analysis with Freud a constellation of meanings
    around Christmas emerges, as in the dramatic passage from "Advent" in which
    Freud interprets the significance for H.D. of her birth in "the town of Mary" (*TF*,
    123–24). At the same time as it retains its personal meanings, Christmas in H.D.'s
    autobiographical prose takes on broad collective, and specifically political, asso-
    ciations as well. Her autobiographical First World War novel *Bid Me To Live*,
    for instance, draws on Christmas associations in ways which seem to me to be
    connected to the mythology surrounding the famous, temporary Christmas truce
    of 1914, in which soldiers on both sides of the trenches briefly laid down their
    weapons. I would argue that the Christmas images throughout *Bid Me To Live*
    (hereafter abbreviated *BML* and cited in the text) depend for part of their reso-
    nance on this cultural association of the 1914 Christmas with both the possibility
    and the impossibility of ending the war.
12 Cora Kaplan, "Red Christmases," *Sea Changes: Culture and Feminism* (London:
    Verso, 1986), 217.
13 Susan Stanford Friedman traces H.D.'s politics and argues persuasively against
    charges that her writing is naive and apolitical in "Modernism of the 'Scattered
    Remnant': Race and Politics in the Development of H.D.'s Modernist Vision,"
    in *H.D.: Woman and Poet*, ed. Michael King (Orono: National Poetry Founda-
    tion, 1986), 92–116.
14 H.D., quoted without further reference in Guest, *Herself Defined*, 10.
15 Important feminist work on *Trilogy* began with Robert Duncan's extraordinary

H.D. Book, published in various parts; see, for instance, "The *H.D. Book*, Part 2: *Nights and Days*, Ch. 2," *Caterpillar* 6 (January 1969): 29–34; "Part 2, Chapter 3," *Io* 6 (Summer 1969): 117–40; "Part 2, Chapter 4," *Caterpillar* 7 (April 1969): 42–60; "Part 2, Chapter 5," *Stony Brook* 3/4 (Fall 1969): 336–47. The classic, comprehensive overview of *Trilogy*, as of all H.D.'s work, is Friedman's *Psyche Reborn*. See also her "'I go where I love': An Intertextual Study of H.D. and Adrienne Rich," *Signs* 9.2 (Winter 1983): 228–45. Other landmark analyses of *Trilogy* include Susan Gubar's "Echoing Spell of H.D.'s *Trilogy*"; Alicia Ostriker, "The Poet as Heroine: Learning to Read H.D." *Writing Like a Woman* (Ann Arbor: Univ. of Michigan Press, 1983), 29–35, and her "No Rule of Procedure: The Open Poetics of H.D.," *Agenda* 25.3–4 (Autumn/Winter 1987–88): 145–54; Rachel Blau DuPlessis's discussions of the poem in her *Writing Beyond the Ending*, 116–21, and her *H.D.*, 86–100; Adalaide Morris's "The Concept of Projection"; Albert Gelpi's "Re-Membering the Mother: A Reading of H.D.'s *Trilogy*," in King, ed., *H.D.*, 173–90, and Gelpi's chapter on H.D. in his *Coherent Splendor*; Deborah Kelly Kloepfer's "Mother as Muse and Desire: The Sexual Poetics of H.D.'s *Trilogy*," in King, ed., *H.D.*, 191–206; and Paul Smith's chapter on H.D. in *Pound Revised* (London: Croon Helm, 1983). I am indebted throughout this chapter to all of these works and to the essays cited in note 16 below.

16 I take the word "horizon" from two places: Hans Robert Jauss's idea of the "horizon of expectations" in his *Toward an Aesthetic of Reception*, trans. Timothy Bahti (Minneapolis: Univ. of Minnesota Press, 1982), and the title of Cyril Connolly's influential British literary magazine of the early forties. Several essays have placed *Trilogy* specifically in the context of one famous wartime poem or another. Jennifer Clarvoe's "The Diamond and the Shell: Small Models for the Self in Ezra Pound's *Pisan Cantos* and H.D.'s *Trilogy*" (Unpublished essay, University of California-Berkeley, 1985) and Cyrena N. Pondrom's "*Trilogy* and *Four Quartets*," *Agenda* 25.3–4 (Autumn/Winter 1987–88): 155–65 thoroughly analyze two of *Trilogy*'s most significant and subtle wartime intertexts.

17 *Christmas Under Fire*, film produced by British Ministry of Information, with commentary by Quentin Reynolds of Colliers (London, Archives of the Imperial War Museum). The Second World War established Christmas as never before as a "national" holiday uniting the "United Kingdom"; in Scotland, for instance, Christmas had been before the war celebrated only minimally, but during the Second World War Scottish troops enjoyed the festivities and brought them home to their local populations. See also, in the IWM's archives, the Second War newsreels "Santa Claus in Wartime," "The World at Christmas Time," and "Christmas 1943."

18 Jane Waller and Michael Vaughan-Rees, *Women in Wartime: The Role of Women's Magazines 1939–1945* (London: Macdonald Optima, 1987), 55.

19 Nancy Cunard exploits this use of "Christmassing" in her representation of an air raid in the poem *Man Ship TANK Gun Plane* (London: New Books, 1944). On references to nuclear weapons as Christmas trees, see Carol Cohn, "Sex and Death in the Rational World of Defense Intellectuals," 698.

20 Denise Levertov, "Christmas 1944," *Collected Earlier Poems 1940–1960* (New York: New Directions, 1979), 24–25; Dylan Thomas, "Ceremony After a Fire Raid," *Deaths and Entrances* (London: J. M. Dent, 1946), 39. Poems in circulation in London during the Second World War which relate a Christmas scene explicitly or implicitly to the war include: Henry Treece, "Carol," *Life and Letters Today*

(December 1942): 171; Maurice Lindsay, "Poem at Christmas," *Life and Letters To-day* (December 1944): 125-27; Alex Comfort, "France," *Poems for France Written by British Poets on France Since the War*, ed. Nancy Cunard (London: La France Libre, 1944); Wrey Gardiner, "From the Gates of Silence," *New Road 1944: New Directions in European Art and Letters*, ed. Alex Comfort and John Bayliss (London: Grey Walls Press, 1944); and see also the many Christmas/war poems — they are his specialty — in Robert Lowell's *Lord Weary's Castle* (London: Faber & Faber, 1950): "the Holy Innocents" (14), "Christmas in Black Rock," (16) and "Christmas Eve Under Hooker's Statue" (27). Stephen Spender's 1944 meditation on the uses of religious symbolism in poetry focuses, though obliquely, on Christmas images, not surprisingly in the context of recurrent Christmas imagery in this period. Spender, "The Crisis of Symbols," *Penguin New Writing* 19 (1944): 129-35.

21 H.D., "The Gift," Beinecke Library, Box 40, Folder 1039, 19.

22 Foregrounding biblical narrative here means giving short shrift to other equally striking mythic systems invoked in and underlying the poem — to classical and Egyptian mythologies, for instance — though, as I shall show and as any reader of *Trilogy* knows, none of these myths is separable here from the others. Even in my consideration of the New Testament plots alone, I will be offering a drasti-cally foreshortened and flattening view of the poem's intertextual field.

   Imagine, for a moment, that T. S. Eliot sits down to illustrate one of his prin-ciples in "Tradition and the Individual Talent" with H.D.'s *Trilogy*, showing that the poem is part of an ideal (sometimes for H.D., we might add, very much less than ideal) order of existing past monuments which direct it and are altered by it. He will need to include the following in an only very partial list of the modern texts which might comprise these monuments: Pound's early, slight book of love poems to H.D., *Hilda's Book*, and his later, weightier "I gather the limbs of Osiris," "The Alchemist," *Spirit of Romance*, and prewar *Cantos*; Rilke's *Duino Elegies*, in wide circulation in London during the Second World War; Yeats's *A Vision*, "The Magi," *Calvary*, and notes to that play; Eliot's own *The Waste Land*, his "The Journey of the Magi," and other "Ariel" poems; Lawrence's *The Man Who Died* and *Apocalypse*. Other texts emerging at around the same time of *Trilogy's* composition further expand this field, particularly Eliot's *Four Quartets* and Edith Sitwell's war poems, Auden's *For the Time Being: A Christmas Oratorio*, Pound's *Pisan Cantos*, Stevens's late poems, and Williams's *Paterson*. And still other less canonical texts of the same period also bear a clear relation to *Trilogy*. Between Lawrence's *Apocalypse* and *Trilogy's* version of Revelation, for instance, the well-publicized theoretical statements of the forties Apocalypse movement might in-tervene; between Eliot's magi and H.D.'s, might come Dorothy Sayers's biblical radio plays of the early forties; or between Rilke's angels and H.D.'s, the lesser known "Nocturne" and "Azrael" by Kathleen Raine (and other documents in a fad-dish forties "angel culture" as well, including, not least, the odd celebrations of angelic familiars with names like Astriel and Zabdiel in Lord Dowding's spiritua-list books of the war years).

23 George Barker, "Funeral Eulogy on García Lorca," *Life and Letters Today* 23 (1939): 63.

24 Paul Fussell discusses "the sacrificial theme" in which the soldier becomes Christ crucified "at the heart of countless Great War poems" in *Great War and Modern Memory*, 117-20, emphasizing such factors as the atrocity story of the Canadian

crucified by Germans and the "Field Punishment No. 1" in which an offender was spread-eagled in a way that called crucifixion imagery to mind. Judith Rosen, in a brilliant unpublished paper, "'The Truth Untold': Religious Imagery in the War Poems of Wilfred Owen" (Harvard University, 1983), analyzes the similarity between Owen's oppositional figures of the soldier/Christ and identical imagery used in patriotic Great War discourses. See also Nosheen Khan's account of the female-authored Great War crucifixion/war poem in her *Women's Poetry of the First World War*, 49-53, and Reilly, ed., *Scars Upon My Heart*, xix. On D. H. Lawrence's identification with Christ "because he found in the Passion an image of individual participation in the war's immeasurable suffering," see Paul Delany, *D. H. Lawrence's Nightmare: The Writer and His Circle in the Years of the Great War* (Brighton: Harvester, 1979), 27-29.

25   Richard Aldington, "Vicarious Atonement," *Images of War* (London: Beaumont Press, 1919), 1. This volume was published with illustrations by the famous war artist Paul Nash. John Cournos, *Miranda Masters* (New York: Knopf, 1926), 141.

26   *Wilfred Owen: Collected Letters*, ed. Harold Owen and John Bell (London: Oxford Univ. Press, 1967), 562.

27   David Gascoyne, "Ecce Homo," *Poems 1937-1942* (London: Nicholson & Watson, 1943), 6. Second World War poems which employ the figure of the crucified Christ include some very famous ones (the "The wounded surgeon plies the steel" section of Eliot's "East Coker," Sitwell's "Still Falls the Rain," and Pound's *Pisan Cantos*, cantos 74 and 80, for instance). Other examples — here again the image is at the heart of countless Second War poems — include F. T. Prince, "Soldiers Bathing," in *Collected Poems* (London: Anvil, 1979), 55-57; Lowell, "The Soldier," *Lord Weary's Castle*, 45; Edward Thompson, "Was It Nothing To You?," in Cunard, ed., *Poems for France*, 16-17; Nicholas Moore, "The Double Yew" and "The Star," in Cunard, ed., *Poems for France*, 42-44; Pamela Holmes, "Missing, Presumed Killed," in Reilly, *Chaos of the Night*, 61; Kathleen Raine, "See, see Christ's blood streams in the firmament," *Stone and Flower: Poems 1935-43* (London: Nicholson & Watson, 1943); Roy Campbell, "Talking Bronco," in Ferguson, ed., *War and the Creative Arts*, 262-63; Dorothy Sayers, "For Albert: Late King of the Belgians," *Life and Letters Today* (July 1940): 36. On David Jones's uses of the crucifixion scene in his *In Parenthesis* and *The Anathemata*, see J. A. W. Bennett, *Poetry of the Passion* (Oxford: Clarendon, 1982); Bennett also more generally discusses the Passion in modern war poetry, 196-206. H.D.'s own unpublished or uncollected poems from the Second War years frequently make ambivalent use of the crucifixion image; see "Ecce Sponsus" (*CP*, 480-81) and "Erige Cor Tuum Ad Me In Caelum" (*CP*, 479-80), and compare the refusal to mourn for an unspecified "slain" one in "Body and Soul" (*CP*, 478).

28   Gilbert, "Soldier's Heart," in Higgonet et al., *Behind the Lines*, 198.

29   H.D., *Pilate's Wife* (1924; unpublished, Beinecke Library, Yale University). Quoted in Janice S. Robinson, *H.D. The Life and Work of an American Poet* (Boston: Houghton Mifflin, 1982), 202. Friedman provides a useful account of the novel in *Psyche Reborn*, 180-83.

30   H.D. "H.D., By *Delia Alton*," 207.

31   This passage might be read as not only representing but also, in its implicit equation of the abject and inhuman "worm" with Jewish victims, as itself exemplifying anti-Semitism; but see the positive image of the worm as self in "Walls Do Not Fall," sections 6 and 7.

32 For more strenuous resistance to anti-Semitic uses of crucifixion imagery in the
    discourse of war, see the work of Isaac Rosenberg. In Rosenberg's Great War poem
    "Chagrin," for instance, Christ is the torturer, not the tortured. Rosenberg, *Collected Works of Isaac Rosenberg*, ed. Ian Parsons (New York: Oxford Univ. Press,
    1979), 95.
33 Jacqueline Rose, *Sexuality in the Field of Vision* (London: Verso, 1986).
34 H.D., "Joan of Arc," *Close Up* 3.1 (July 1928): 20. Hereafter abbreviated J and
    cited in the text. See Gary Burnett's important work, clearly pertinent here, on
    how the "angular abstractions of the Futurists and Vorticists provide [H.D.] with
    an aesthetic she can identify as an equivalent to the war," in his "Poetics Out
    of War" (56).
35 Compare H.D.'s rejection of the masterwork "Saint Matthew's Passion" for the
    folk song of the four Maries in her unpublished note to *The Gift*, discussed by
    Rachel Blau DuPlessis in her *H.D.*, 98.
36 H.D., "An Appreciation," *Close Up* 4.21 (February 1929): 59–60. Hereafter abbreviated A and cited in the text. Pabst's Great War memories involved a group
    of interned Austrians who killed themselves after the armistice — hence they are
    awarded "no name on tablets."
37 Alicia Ostriker analyzes *Trilogy*'s "formal correlatives" — inconspicuous off-rhymes,
    for instance — "of the poem's premise that order, beauty and meaning remain permanently present in our shattered world but not permanently obvious," in her
    "No Rule of Procedure" (150).
38 See H.D.'s *Notes on Thought and Vision* (written in 1919; San Francisco: City
    Lights, 1982), "Magician" (1933; *CP*, 434) and *Pilate's Wife*. In *Bid Me To Live*,
    the intensely masculine war trauma of the Aldington soldier-as-Christ figure eclipses
    the traumas of his wife: "My agony in the Garden," Julia says, "had no words"
    (*BML*, 46). The first part of *Trilogy*, part of a long line of H.D.'s work, recovers
    an image of Christ for war literature which is not circumscribed within a solely
    male homosocial circle, one whose outstretched limbs neither obscure the presence and participation of women in scenarios of violence and redemption nor
    suppress the words needed to describe women's experience of those scenes.
39 Here we can usefully compare Yeats's *Calvary*, which, as Yeats explained in his
    notes to the play, divides between Christ, on the one hand, and some birds in
    flight, on the other, the opposing, hierarchically ranked attributes of "objectivity"
    and "subjectivity." Christ is (negatively and admonitively) "objective," because
    he conceives of himself and arranges himself always *as* an object, like a good
    soldier, and always *for* a collective object; he puts himself into the service of a
    pity system, thinks only of the welfare of "some cause or institution." The "subjective" birds, in contrast, seek always only "that which is unique or personal,"
    are "sufficient" unto themselves, and "have served neither God nor Caesar, and
    await for none or for a different savior" (57). These birds don't even need to resist
    a draft; they just catch their own crosscurrents. The desire for an alternative to
    the objectifications of Golgotha motivates "Flowering"'s migration imagery in much
    the same way as Yeats's. But H.D. is milder than Yeats with her Christ. In her
    version he acquires wings, and himself embodies the fantasy of absolute freedom
    from controlling institutional structures. W. B. Yeats, "Notes" to *Calvary* (1920);
    rpt. Yeats, *The Variorum Edition of the Plays* (Toronto: Macmillan, 1966), 789–90.
40 Julia Kristeva, "Holbein's Dead Christ," *Fragments for a History of the Human*

Body, ed. Michel Feher, with Ramona Naddaff and Nadia Tazi (New York: Urzone, 1989), 263; Andrew Ross, *The Failure of Modernism: Symptoms of American Poetry* (New York: Columbia Univ. Press, 1986), 72. Ross is discussing Eliot's "The Love Song of Saint Sebastian"; he aptly, following Eliot's own comments on this poem, links the passive masochism of the martyr to a "feminine position." At the same time, however, in the aftermath of men's "supreme sacrifices" in the Great War, martyrdom must have seemed a form of "femininity" peculiarly men's own. In differing ways, a number of male authors, some whose work I discuss in this chapter—Yeats, George Moore (see note 103 below), Lawrence, Aldington, and Owen—used the Christ sacrifice plot to critique the *masculine* ("feminine") object-position in which the "hero" places himself or finds himself placed. H.D., watching men who volunteered or were drafted into the specific military structures of "supreme sacrifice" through two wars, wrote from a different "feminine position."

41 See Yeats on the "negligible sect" responsive to Christ in early Christian culture, surrounded by "an antithetical" civilization in which "all is rigid and stationary, men fight for centuries with sword and spear." *A Vision* (1925; rpt. London: Macmillan, 1962), 263. H.D.'s Mary and Kaspar after his conversion seem to represent the possibility of a kind of spiritual life Yeats calls "primary": "levelling, unifying, feminine, humane, peace its means and end" (263).

42 These sections are reprinted in *CP,* 622–24 and are hereafter cited in the text with page numbers to distinguish them from the authoritative text cited by section number.

43 In a sense here, then, I am in agreement with Paul Smith, who argues in his *Pound Revised* that "an all-powerful godfather" provides a "ratificatory signature" to *Trilogy,* unfortunately simplifying and quelling the text's "multiple heiroglyphs" (125). But H.D.'s excision of the most dramatic moment of this "ratification" suggests a more dissident relation to it than Smith allows. See DuPlessis's argument with Smith in *H.D.,* 147–48.

44 Dorothy L. Sayers, *The Man Born To Be King: A Play-Cycle on the Life of Our Lord and Saviour Jesus Christ, Written for Broadcasting* (Suffolk, England: Richard Clay, 1943). See the foreword by J. W. Welch and the introduction by Sayers for accounts of the loud controversy surrounding the production of the plays. They were condemned in the House of Commons, and some detractors went so far as to assert that Singapore fell because they were broadcast. H.D.'s "O, there are Marys a-plenty" (F 16) may echo these lines from Sayers, but for opposed and far less orthodox ends: "For Jesus Christ is unique—unique among gods and men. There have been incarnate gods a-plenty, and slain-and-resurrected gods not a few; but He is the only God who has a date in history" (21).

45 Think of Yeats's pale, unsatisfied Magi with their eyes impassively, even catatonically, fixed, like their desire, on the "uncontrollable mystery on the bestial floor"; or his terrible, triumphant "staring virgin" standing, in the first song from *Calvary,* "where holy Dionysus died"; or Eliot's worn-out, impotent, ambivalent Mage for whom the catastrophic import of Christ's birth, however necessary, feels like death: a panoply of exhausted, depleted, dead and buried figures of the barbaric past, all masculine, all done in once and for all by the Nativity long before its consequent triumphant Passion. And compare, for a another kind of difference from *Trilogy,* modernity's dislocated gaze at the "manger" in Williams's "Burning

the Christmas Greens," *The Collected Later Poems* (New York: New Directions, 1963), 16–18, or in Elizabeth Bishop's "Over 2,000 Illustrations and a Complete Concordance," *Complete Poems*, 59 — views situated *beyond* any religious belief system, on the other edge of Christianity.

46   Nancy Huston, "Tales of War and Tears of Women," *Women's Studies Int. Forum* 5 (3/4[1982]), 271–82. Hereafter cited in the text.

47   D. H. Lawrence, unpublished draft of part 2 of *The Man who Died* (which Lawrence called *The Escaped Cock*), in Gerald M. Lacy, ed., *The Escaped Cock* (Los Angeles: Black Sparrow, 1973), 125; hereafter cited in the text. I will continue to refer to its title as *The Man Who Died*, for convenience's sake, since this was the title H.D. used.

48   Robinson, *H.D.*, 252.

49   Ezra Pound to H.D., 31 May 1954 (Unpublished letter, Beinecke Library, Yale University).

50   D. H. Lawrence, "The Risen Lord," in Lacy, ed., *Escaped Cock*, 127.

51   Ostriker, "Poet as Heroine," 40.

52   Laura Riding, "Christmas 1937," *The Poems of Laura Riding* (Manchester: Carcanet New Press, 1980), 320.

53   I am indebted here to Cora Kaplan, who phrased a similar question in a lecture at the University of Sussex, Spring 1988.

54   Adrienne Rich, *Of Woman Born: Motherhood as Experience and Institution* (New York: Norton, 1976), 192.

55   Julia Kristeva, "Stabat Mater," in Suleiman, ed., *Female Body in Western Culture*, 116. Kristeva's article is hereafter cited in the text.

56   D. H. Lawrence, *Apocalypse and the Writings on Revelation*, ed. Mara Kalnins (Cambridge: Cambridge Univ. Press, 1980), 127.

57   Henry Reed, "The Poetry of Edith Sitwell," *Penguin New Writing* 19 (1944), 109–22.

58   Edith Sitwell, "Lullaby," *The Canticle of the Rose* (London: Macmillan, 1949), 166. Robert Duncan's Vietnam-era "My Mother Would Be A Falconress," *Bending the Bow* (New York: New Directions, 1968), 52–54, might also be read as a son's exploration of maternal *pere-version*; Duncan pays homage to Sitwell as well as H.D. in "The *H.D. Book*, "Part 2, Chapter 3," *Io* 6 (Summer 1969): 129.

59   Raine, "Christmas Poem," *Stone and Flower*, 21.

60   Sylvia Plath, in later years, made particularly fierce and expert use of the Pietà/ war formula, in her "holocaust" poem "Mary's Song," for instance, with its lines "O golden child the world will kill and eat"; see also her "Nick and the Candlestick." Both are in Plath, *Ariel* (New York: Harper & Row, 1961).

61   DuPlessis, *H.D.*, 31–69.

62   Sitwell, "Still Falls the Rain," *Canticle of the Rose*, 165.

63   Anne Ridler, *The Shadow Factory* (London: Faber & Faber, 1945). Hereafter cited in the text.

64   See T. S. Eliot, *The Idea of a Christian Society* (London: Faber & Faber, 1939).

65   For a recent meditation on "trends toward sexual indifferentiation of child-bearing and war-making activities," see the conclusion of Huston's "Matrix of War," 135. Huston's discussion of the maternal relation to the military in Western culture and Suleiman's "Writing and Motherhood" in Shirley Nelson Garner et al, eds., *The (M)other Tongue: Essays in Feminist Psychoanalytic Interpretation* (Ithaca: Cornell Univ. Press, 1985), 352–77 are usefully read alongside Kristeva's "Stabat Mater"

in thinking about the maternal and the martial. See also, in a related context, Homans's discussions of the Madonna in *Bearing the Word*. Fussell analyzes the representation of the mother in modern war literature in "The Fate of Chivalry and the Assault Upon Mother," *Thank God for the Atomic Bomb*, 221–48.

66 Note that in Ridler's version, and in most traditional interpretations of the Magi, Caspar or Kaspar brings frankincense; Balthazar is the giver of myrrh. Caspar is, however, traditionally marked as the special bearer of "inherited wisdom," the oldest and most learned "Wise Man," and since in H.D.'s text the Mage is in part a version of Freud she gives him Kaspar's name.

67 Compare Auden's wartime Christmas oratorio *For The Time Being* — along with Eliot's "The Journey of the Magi," another likely model for Ridler (and a text H.D., too, was likely to have known well). Auden's Magi are rationalist scientists who learn at the manger "how to be truthful now," "living now" and "loving now." In one extraordinary passage, the Nativity is represented as Joseph's crisis of masculinity, and his marginal role in the manger scene is defined explicitly as atonement for the violent psychic structures of patriarchy. At the same time, Auden's Mary is, however, a stereotypical Madonna, treated without irony or complexity.

68 Denise Riley, "Some Peculiarities of Social Policy concerning Women in Wartime and Postwar Britain," in Higgonet et al., eds., *Behind the Lines*, 269. Riley's analysis of pronatalism in this period provides a rich context in which Ridler's play could be read in much more depth; I am indebted to Riley's essay for my application of the term "pronatalism."

69 Bethlehem sometimes functions in H.D.'s work as the locus of freedom from rigid gender (and other) norms. There is an exuberantly dramatized moment in *TF* for instance, when Freud, bowled over by H.D.'s account of a Moravian Christmas ceremony in which "The girls as well as the boys had candles," leaps up, as H.D. tells it, to say reverently to his analysand, "If every child had a lighted candle given, as you say they were given at your grandfather's Christmas Eve service, by the grace of God, we would have no more problems" (124). More often, however, in texts written by H.D., as early as *Asphodel* (1921–22) and as late as *Sagesse* (1957), Christmas narratives and customs function as stringent forms of social control exerted particularly over children and women, and most particularly over adolescent girls coming of age. In the Blitz narrative of *Sagesse*, a London child compared by a German refugee to the "Christkind" is told by her mother: "that's German for a good girl, / are you a good girl, duckie?" (80). In *Asphodel*, the heroine, trying to decide whether to have a child, thinks: "What did the Virgin Mary do on this occasion? Of course, God, her lover, would look after her . . . and the beauty of the moment and the joy of her own realization of her acceptability to God, entrapped her" (quoted in Robinson, *H.D.*, 252). What here is pleasurable entrapment in the role of the mother is phrased, in *Hedylus*, in even harsher terms: "Weren't women, so importunate as to let God love them, always later tacitly abandoned?" H.D., *Hedylus* (Stratford: Basil Blackwell and Houghton Mifflin, 1928), 175. In the nightmare confusion of the girl child in *The Gift*, out of a terrifying picture of a witch threatening "to stick the little girl right through with her long pointed stick and that was what would happen in the night if you went to sleep and had a bad dream," a connected fear emerges: "It is terrible to be a virgin because a virgin has a baby with God" (59–60). In this regard it is worth noting that the oppressive Biblical pageant the Rico/D. H. Lawrence character

oversees in *Bid Me To Live* has its roots in an event Lawrence staged at a Christmas party.

70   Plath, "Nick and the Candlestick," 40–41.

71   Ross, *Failure of Modernism*, 32.

72   Riffaterre, *Semiotics of Poetry*, 12.

73   As a metaphor for Mary with child, the flowering rod resembles that in Arnaut Daniel's sestina, in which the end word "verga" (rod) is used in one stanza to indicate the birth of Christ. Here is the pertinent stanza, taken from Peter Makin's *Provence and Pound* (Berkeley: Univ. of California Press, 1978), 178, with Makin's editorial interjection:

> Since the dry rod [*verga*, i.e. the Virgin] flowered,
> or nephew or uncle descended from Adam,
> I do not believe that such a fine love as the one that is
> entering my heart was ever in body, or even in soul. . . .

I have no indication that H.D. knew this poem, but Pound, of course, knew Daniel's work well, and H.D.'s negotiations with what Pound called "Mariolatry, its Pagan lineage, the romance of it" (Makin, *Provence and Pound*, 171) are always also, in part, negotiations with Pound as self-appointed guardian of that tradition. See also H.D.'s meditations on the Mariolatry behind courtly love in her *By Avon River* (New York: Macmillan, 1949), 23, 92.

74   Yeats, *A Vision*, 156.

75   In "Flowering," section 2, the self is compared to "rain that has lain long / in the furrow," giving or being willing to give "life to the grain"; but that position — we might read it as the position of the (earth) mother — is then provisionally rejected, as long as the conditions are not appropriate for that nurturing role, for another image of a self as rain evaporating away from the field of destruction. Like the "field-furrow" full of rain water in "Tribute," section 10 which offers only in its splintered, broken form a reflection of the star of the mother-goddess, this furrow invokes and celebrates images of female fertility, but also refracts and disperses them. Compare Bogan's use of furrow imagery, described in the introduction to this book.

76   Duncan, "The *H.D. Book*, Part 2, Chapter 4" *Caterpillar* 7 (April 1969): 60.

77   Rose, *Sexuality in the Field of Vision*, 159. For Kristeva on "herethics" and on negativity, see "Stabat Mater," 117–18, and "La femme, ce n'est jamais ça," trans. Marilyn August, *New French Feminisms*, ed. Elaine Marks and Isabelle de Courtivron (Brighton: Harvester, 1981). For another important treatise on an ethics which includes and values maternity, see Ruddick, *Maternal Thinking*.

78   Pertinent here are Jan Montefiore's comments on H.D.'s elusive, visionary ironies in her "What Words Say: Three Women Poets Reading H.D.," *Agenda* 25.3–4 (Autumn/Winter 1987–88): 178.

79   Schreiner, *Women and Labour*, 178.

80   "Flowering," section 14 hints, however, that myrrh may have originated in *women's* hands — in the hands of the princesses of the Egyptian Hyksos kings. Here, as elsewhere, an origin in the female, strongly tied to the female body, may be inferred but is not univocally asserted.

81   Marcel Detienne, *The Gardens of Adonis: Spices in Greek Mythology*, trans. Janet Lloyd (Brighton: Harvester, 1977), 6. Hereafter cited in the text.

82 Hence the need, frequently remarked upon by critics, for the radical purifica-
tions enacted in *Trilogy*'s alchemical etymologies, in which the word "Venus," for
instance, recovers its meaning "venerate" in convergence with other roots and
offspring — "venery," "venereal" — traditionally degraded in misogynist readings.

83 Pound's and Eliot's very different revisions of economic exchange would be use-
fully contrasted here; see, for instance, Eliot's uses of Christmas as an alternative
to commodified exchange in his *The Cultivation of Christmas Trees* (New York:
Farrar, Straus & Cudahy, 1956). In formulating this point I have benefited from
conversations with JoEllen Green at the University of California at Berkeley. Ada-
laide Morris, "A Relay of Power and of Peace: H.D. and the Spirit of the Gift,"
Contemporary Literature 27.4 (Winter 1986): 493–524, is an important study of
"the spirit of the gift" as opposed to "the ethos of an individualistic market economy"
in H.D.'s life and thought.

84 H.D., *End to Torment: A Memoir of Ezra Pound* (New York: New Directions, 1979),
30. Hereafter abbreviated *ET* and cited in the text.

85 Charles Olson to Ezra Pound, 14 June 1947, in Helen Gardner, *The Composition
of the Four Quartets* (London: Faber & Faber, 1978), 34. Duncan links *Four Quar-
tets* to "The Shrine" in "The *H.D. Book*, Part 2, Chapter 3," *Io* 6 (Summer 1969): 120.

86 Susan Stanford Friedman analyzes H.D.'s early, complex, revisionary responses
to Pound's "Hilda's Book" in her *Hermione*; see Friedman, "Palimpsest of Origins
in H.D.'s Career," *Poesis* 6.3/4 (1985): 56–73.

87 Richard Aldington, "An Old Song," *Images of Desire* (London: Elkin Matthews,
1919), 9.

88 Richard Aldington, "The Blood of The Young Men," *Collected Poems* (London:
George Allen & Unwin, 1929), 106–109. Poems in this collection (abbreviated *C*)
are hereafter cited in the text. Compare the functions of the whore in war which
Kristeva has analyzed in Celine's work: "An unbridled woman then arises, eager
for sex and power, nevertheless a grotesque and sorry victim in her raw
violence. . . . it is especially with prostitutes and nymphomaniacs. . . . Even
though demoniacal, such femininity is nonetheless in the position of a fallen demon
who finds being only with reference to man." Julia Kristeva, *Powers of Horror: An
Essay on Abjection*, trans. Leon S. Roudiez (New York: Columbia Univ. Press, 1982),
167. "War! War! War!," Kristeva quotes Celine: "It had to keep going, the whole
shebang . . . a whore without men is a flabby thing" (167). Aldington's "Blood
of The Young Men" imagines a similar "whole shebang"; H.D.'s Kaspar's explosive
vision triggered by the Magdalene's hair might be read as offering an alternative
shebang, one which recuperates the prostitute and the demons and loosens their
relation to the heroic and/or sacrificed male hero.

89 Susan Gubar, "Sapphistries," *The Lesbian Issue*, ed. Estelle B. Freedman et al.
(Chicago: Univ. of Chicago Press, 1985), 100.

90 Ibid., 104. The extensive intertextual links between Aldington's early poems and
H.D.'s have not yet been sufficiently examined. Each one's poems resemble the
other's in the early years enough to make it sometimes difficult to tell them apart,
as when a manuscript at the H.D. collection in the Beinecke Library turned out
upon careful investigation to be part of Aldington's *Myrrhine*. See Dale Davis,
"The Matter of Myrrhine for Louis," *Iowa Review* 16.3 (Fall 1986): 165–73.

91 Richard Aldington, *The Love of Myrrhine and Konallis and Other Prose Poems*
(Chicago: Pascal Covici, 1926): 87–88.

92 Owen, "Greater Love," *Collected Poems*, 41.
93 Marguerite Waller, "Academic Tootsie: The Denial of Difference and the Difference it Makes," *Diacritics* (Spring 1987): 8.
94 Interestingly, in the preliminary rough draft of this poem the titles "To Physical Beauty" and "To any beautiful one" raise the possibility that the addressee might be male. Later drafts, however, insist upon the female identity of the "you." One late fair copy ends most explicitly: "Weep, woman, weep." See Stallworthy, ed., *Complete Poems and Fragments*, 337–41.
95 Wilfred Owen, "Whereas most women live this difficult life," in Stallworthy, ed., *Complete Poems and Fragments*, 68.
96 Robinson, *H.D.*, 189.
97 H.D., "Compassionate Friendship," quoted in Robinson, *H.D.*, 155.
98 Ibid.
99 Robinson, *H.D.* 444.
100 Quoted in Robinson, *H.D.*, 107–8.
101 H.D.'s name was deleted from the letter in this edition, as Janice Robinson recounts (*H.D.*, 108), but a letter to Bryher, quoted in Robinson (*H.D.*, 282), shows that she clearly recognized where her name belonged: "These letters . . . put a whole lot on the map for me, and it is as well anyhow, I think to have this printed record (though not explicit/ no mention of my name or anything to give it away, of course). . . . "
102 The Lawrence-centered biographical reduction which his relation to H.D. sometimes summons in H.D. criticism needs to be strongly warded off here. I am not interested in any of the texts considered in this chapter as autobiographies per se, and it seems to me that in order to read them merely as such — as Janice Robinson, for instance, reads *The Man Who Died* and *Pilate's Wife* — one has to ignore significant broader intertextual connections; the political debate conducted through biblical narrative in the war literature I have been tracing is, in my opinion, a far more pertinent and pressing source and ground for these works than the personal relations of Lawrence and H.D. Even when H.D. writes in open biographical terms of Lawrence, as in *Bid Me To Live*, mythic configurations shape the narrative; I would argue that Rico's gesture of repulsion, his "Noli me tangere," (*BML*, 82) has as much to do with the need for just such a moment in a novel riddled with crucifixion imagery as with some actual autobiographical scene.
103 See *TF*, 141–42: "I had told friends of a book that I wanted to write, actually did write. I called it *Pilate's Wife*. It is the story of the wounded but living Christ, waking up in the rock-tomb. I was certain that my friends had told Lawrence that I was at work on this theme. My first sudden reaction was, 'Now he has taken my story.' It was not my story. George Moore, among others, had already written it." The text by George Moore referred to here is his *The Brook Kerith: A Syrian Story* (London: William Heinemann, 1927). In Moore's version of the "Greater Love" plot, Joseph of Arimathea rescues the still-living Christ from the tomb (leaving the grieving, gossippy Marys to spread the false rumor of Christ's resurrection); Christ lives to exempt himself from the ideological systems he had heretofore embraced, and is healed by an old nurse, a different kind of "Myrrhine" figure, who applies "her own famous balsam, the secret of which was imparted to her by her mother, who had it from her mother; and her great-grandmother learned it from an Arabian" (246). In another, even more strongly ironic version,

Moore's *The Apostle* (Dublin: Maunsel, 1911), the healed Christ is killed by the Apostle Paul, who doesn't believe that he didn't die and sees him as a threat to the establishment of Christianity. Oscar Wilde also staked a claim to this story; see Richard Ellmann, *Oscar Wilde* (New York: Knopf, 1987), 358. Dominic Hibbard has suggested that Owen's "Greater Love" is "in a form and style taken from Swinburne and Wilde," and is influenced in particular by Wilde's *De Profundis*. Here the Owen/H.D. link through Wilde and Swinburne is suggestive. See Hibbard, *Owen the Poet*, 157–60. On H.D.'s relation to the Decadents, see Cassandra Laity, "H.D.'s Romantic Landscapes: The Sexual Politics of the Garden," *Sagetrieb* 6.2 (Fall 1987): 57–75. The frequency of modern plots which defy and undo the crucifixion on grounds like Wilde's, Moore's, and Lawrence's suggests that when Alice Walker's Meridian says "the only new thing now . . . would be the refusal of Christ to accept crucifixion," she is imagining a very old only new thing. Walker, *Meridian* (New York: Pocket Books, 1977), 151.

104 On Sappho's origination of the name "myrrh," see Detienne, *Gardens of Adonis*, 142. H.D. associates Sappho with myrrh in her "The Wise Sappho," *Notes on Thought and Vision & The Wise Sappho* (San Francisco: City Lights, 1982), 63. On the importance of Sappho to H.D. as lyric model, see Gubar's "Sapphistries" and Eileen Gregory's illuminating "Rose Cut in Rock: Sappho and H.D.'s *Sea Garden*," *Contemporary Literature* 27.4 (Winter 1986): 525–52.

105 Duncan, "The *H.D. Book*, Part 2, Chapter 3," *Io* 6 (Summer 1969): 137.

106 Sayers, *Man Born To Be King*, 59.

107 Detienne, *Gardens of Adonis*, 4.

108 Sayers, like H.D., develops the figure of a returning or twinned Mage who bears myrrh both to the birth and to the crucifixion of Christ. Her Balthazar shows up at the foot of the cross, in a scene Sayers described as her one deliberately "stylized . . . lyrical and fantastical note," invented in order to link Christ's end back to beginnings which in turn prefigure his rebirth. *Trilogy*, in its own phantasmic, lyric, stylized scenarios — perhaps directly informed by Sayers's play, perhaps simply working along similar lines in a long tradition of such loops — devises its own circle of myrrh: "It had happened before, / it would happen again" (F 37).

109 Edmund Leach, "Why Did Moses Have a Sister?" in *Structuralist Interpretations of Biblical Myth*, ed. Leach and D. Alan Aycock (New York: Cambridge Univ. Press, 1983), 48.

110 Readers of *Tribute to Freud* will be familiar with the special resonance that the figure of Moses' sister Miriam had for H.D.; Leach's analysis of Miriam's function, too complex to sum up here, adds new depth to interpretations of H.D.'s famous Miriam dream. See especially 42–46 in "Why Did Moses Have a Sister?" which also dwells in detail on the blurred identities of the various New Testament Marys.

111 Compare the functions of the hyphen in the name of "Mary-myrrh" with that of the "of" or "in" in Helen's various names in H.D.'s *Helen in Egypt*. "Helen of Troy," "Helen in Egypt," "Helen of Sparta," "Helen in Leuke": each encodes Helen's relation, at once separate and inseparable, to differing and even opposing aspects and locations of the self in the world.

112 Ovid, *Metamorphoses*, tr. Frank Justus Miller (The Loeb Classical Library, New York: Putnam, 1926), 10: 85–99.

113 Quoted in Burnett, "Poetics Out of War," 54.

114 Compare the Ovidian story of the origins of that other Mage's gift, frankincense.

Leucothoe, born "in a land where perfume fills the air," falls in love with the sun; her father punishes her by burying her alive. The sun sprinkles nectar over her dead body, and she turns into frankincense. See Ovid, *Metamorphoses* 4:11.240ff. I am grateful to Jennifer Clarvoe for pointing me to the Leucothoe myth.

115   Gregory, "Rose Cut in Rock," 550.

116   DuPlessis, *Writing Beyond the Ending*, 121.

117   The act of the Magdalene's anointment, Adalaide Morris writes, "in H.D.'s astonishing rewriting . . . seeds the resurrection. When Mary washes the feet of Christ, she anoints him with the elixir of life and insures that his crucifixion will be the first step in triumphant regeneration." Morris, "Concept of Projection," 435. I would argue that this is one side of the story of Mary's ointment, certainly the desirable side; but I do not think the deathly, tearful, embalming aspects of the anointing can be so completely overcome or entirely suppressed. Myrrh is, as Paul Smith puts it, "doubly inscribed . . . and so registers . . . the tensions of H.D.'s entire output." Smith's analysis of that double inscription puts it in terms different from but related to my own; he emphasizes the contradiction between myrrh as sign of the mother-goddess and myrrh as tribute to Christ. Smith, *Pound Revised*, 128.

118   Claude Lévi-Strauss, *The Elementary Structures of Kinship* (Boston: Beacon Press, 1969), 496.

119   Gayle Rubin, "The Traffic in Women: Notes Toward a Political Economy of Sex," *Toward an Anthropology of Women*, ed. Rayna Reiter (New York: Monthly Review, 1975), 201.

120   Aristophanes, *Lysistrata*, trans. Doros Alastos (London: Reynard, 1953), 91.

121   Davis, "Matter of Myrrhine," 169.

122   Freud is quoted in a letter from Bryher to Kenneth Macpherson; see Friedman, *Psyche Reborn*, 134. In her poetic tribute to Bryher "Let Zeus Record," however, H.D. distinguishes Bryher's "star" from "the stained and brilliant one of War" (*CP*, 283).

123   Primo Levi, *If This Is A Man*, trans. Stuart Woolf (1960; rpt. New York: Penguin, 1979), 72.

124   Wallace Stevens, *The Collected Poems* (New York: Knopf, 1954), 349–50.

125   Quoted in Robinson, *H.D.*, 354.

126   H.D., "The Gift," Beinecke Library, Box 40, Folder 1036, 2–3.

127   John Brenkman's analysis of the ways in which Blake's "A Poison Tree" "announces the necessity of an ethical consciousness that cannot yet be lived in society or represented," enacting a struggle "between the social conditions of the poet's speech and the latent possibilities of speech," is pertinent here: Brenkman, "The Concrete Utopia of Poetry," *Culture and Domination* (Ithaca: Cornell Univ. Press, 1987), 117. It's worth noting that Norman Holmes Pearson, to whom "The Flowering of the Rod" was dedicated, was employed at the time in X-2, the top secret counterintelligence branch of the OSS in London, very actively involved in the war effort. For an account of Pearson's activities see Robin Winks, *Cloak and Gown: Scholars in America's Secret War* (London: Collins Harvill, 1988).

128   Christa Wolf, *Cassandra: A Novel and Four Essays*, trans. Jan Van Heurck (London: Virago, 1984), 178.

129   Jennifer Clarvoe makes a related point in "Diamond and the Shell": "It is the context of the war itself that allows H.D. such a hopeful, peaceful, unproblematic

vision" (27). She contrasts the violence against women represented more directly in *Helen in Egypt*.

Conclusion

1   Lorine Niedecker to Louis Zukofsky, 19 May 1946, in "'Knee Deck Her Daisies': Selections from Her Letters to Louis Zukovsky," ed. Jenny Penberthy, *Sulfur* 18 (Winter 1987), 114.
2   Niedecker links Christmas and the bomb also in "O Tannenbaum," in which one child sings "atomic bomb" to the tune of that carol. See *From This Condensery: The Complete Writing of Lorine Niedecker*, ed. Robert J. Bertholf (Highlands, N.C.: Jargon Society, 1985), 52. My thanks to Glenna Breslin for pointing "O Tannenbaum" out to me. On the problems with the Bertholf edition, see Eliot Weinberger, "The New Niedeckers," *Sulfur* 16 (1986): 145–54. An especially useful general essay on Niedecker is Marjorie Perloff's "Recharging the Canon: Some Reflections on Feminist Poetics and the Avant-Garde," *American Poetry Review* 15.14 (July/ August 1986).
3   This poem was probably written in 1950; it was part of the manuscript of "Group Two" in the sequence "For Paul" which Niedecker sent to Zukofsky on December 14, 1950. The poem was published as part of a sequence in *New Mexico Quarterly Review* 21.2 (Summer 1951): 205–11. *From this Condensery* prints it twice, on 54 and 108; all subsequent quotations of the poem are from these pages. The notes on 319 record an alternative to the second and third lines of the first stanza: "the glow of contemplation / in our time / along this road." I am grateful to Glenna Breslin for her suggestion that the "snowfall" might recall fallout; she suggests, too, that Niedecker may be collapsing time in her use of December rather than August 1945, invoking the December of Pearl Harbor.
4   Niedecker, *From This Condensery*, 281.
5   Niedecker's consciousness of social class informs many of her war poems. One of the first poems in her first volume *New Goose*, for instance, contrasts the sheltered sleep of the wealthy "in apartments deep in the ground" and the "safe vaults of the Bank of England" with the only shelter available to London's poor during the air raids, the Underground. Niedecker, "Bombings," *New Goose* (Prairie City, Ill.: James A. Decker, 1946), 10.
6   On the question of the text's "distanciation," see John Brenkman, following Ricoeur: Brenkman, *Culture and Domination*, 234–35.
7   Fussell, *Thank God for the Atom Bomb*, 137.
8   Nancy K. Miller, "Emphasis Added: Plots and Plausibilities in Women's Fiction," *The New Feminist Criticism: Essays on Women, Literature and Theory*, ed. Elaine Showalter (New York: Pantheon, 1985), 340.

Acknowledgments

Grateful acknowledgment is made to the following for permission to reprint material: Richard Aldington, lines from "Blood of the Young Men," and "Prayer," in *Collected Poems* (George Allen & Unwin, 1929), reprinted by permission of the author's literary estate, copyright © 1961 by Richard Aldington; W. H. Auden, lines from "Spain," in *Selected Poems*, ed. Edward Mendelson (Random House, 1979), reprinted by permission of Random House Inc., copyright © 1979 by Edward Mendelson, William Meredith and Monroe K. Spears; Elizabeth Bishop, lines from "Brazil, January 1, 1502," "Casabianca," "The Map," "Roosters," "Santarem," "Sleeping Standing Up," and "Wading at Wellfleet," in *The Complete Poems 1927–1979* (Farrar, Straus and Giroux, 1983), reprinted by permission of Farrar, Straus and Giroux, Inc., copyright © 1979, 1983 by Alice Helen Methfessel; Elizabeth Bishop, excerpt from a letter to Marianne Moore (Oct. 17, 1940), in the Papers of Marianne C. Moore, V:05:02, The Rosenbach Museum and Library, Philadelphia, reprinted by permission of the Rosenbach Museum and Library and by Alice Helen Methfessel; Louise Bogan, lines from "To My Brother Killed, Haumont Wood, Oct., 1918" "Chanson Un Peu Naive," and "Cassandra," in *The Blue Estuaries: Poems 1923–1968* (Farrar, Straus and Giroux, 1968), reprinted by permission of Farrar, Straus and Giroux, Inc., copyright © 1968 by Louise Bogan; Louise Bogan, excerpts from "Verses," in *The New Yorker* (Oct. 21, 1944), reprinted by permission of the *New Yorker* and Ruth Limmer; Gwendolyn Brooks, lines from "Gay Chaps at the Bar," "Negro Hero," and "The Mother," in *Blacks* (The David Company, 1987), reprinted by permission of the author, copyright © 1987 by Gwendolyn Brooks; Jane Cooper, excerpts from "Nothing Has Been Used in the Manufacture of This Poetry That Could Have Been Used in the Manufacture of Bread," in *Scaffolding: New and Selected Poems* (Anvil Press, 1984), reprinted by permission of Anvil Press, copyright © 1984 by Jane Cooper; H.D., excerpts from the unpublished manuscript of "The Gift," reprinted by permission of the Collection of American Literature, Beinecke Rare Book and Manuscript Library, Yale University, copyright © 1991 by the Estate of Hilda Doolittle.; H.D., lines from "The Walls Do Not Fall," "Tribute to the Angels," "Flowering of the Rod," "Magician," "Christmas 1944," and "Let Zeus Record," from *Collected Poems: 1912–1944*, ed. Louis L. Martz (New Directions, 1983), reprinted by permission of New Directions Publishing Corporation, Agents for the Estate of Hilda Doolittle, copyright © 1982 by the Estate of Hilda Doolittle; H.D., excerpts from *Sagesse* (New Directions, 1957), reprinted by permission of New Directions Publishing Corporation, copyright © by the

Estate of Hilda Doolittle; Owen Dodson, lines from "Black Mother Praying in the Summer 1943," in *Powerful Long Ladder* (Farrar, Straus and Giroux, 1946), reprinted by permission of Farrar, Straus and Giroux, Inc., copyright © 1946 and renewal copyright © 1974 by Owen Dodson; Louise Driscoll, lines from "The Metal Checks," in *Poetry* 5.11 (November 1914), reprinted by permission of the Editor of *Poetry*, copyright © 1914 by the Modern Poetry Association; Ada Jackson, excerpts from *Behold the Jew* (Macmillan, 1944), reprinted by permission of the author's literary estate; Randall Jarrell, lines from "Eighth Air Force," in *The Complete Poems* (Farrar, Straus and Giroux, 1969), reprinted by permission of Farrar, Straus and Giroux, Inc., copyright © 1947, 1969 by Mrs. Randall Jarrell; Taro Katayama, "Agronomy," in *Trek* (Feb. 1943), reprinted by permission of Mrs. Taro Katayama; Daniel Marlin, excerpts from his translations of Jacob Glatshteyn's "Ada Jackson," and "Kadia Molodowsky," printed by permission of Daniel Marlin, copyright © 1991 by Daniel Marlin (Berkeley, California); Archibald MacLeish, excerpts from "The Fall of the City," and "Air Raid," in *Six Plays* (Houghton Mifflin, 1980), reprinted by permission of Houghton Mifflin Co., copyright © 1980 by Archibald MacLeish; Edna St. Vincent Millay, excerpts from *The Murder of Lidice* (Harper and Row, 1942), reprinted by permission of Elizabeth Barnett, Literary Executor, copyright © 1942, 1969 by Edna St. Vincent Millay and Norma Millay Ellis; Edna St. Vincent Millay, excerpt from Letter 228 in *The Letters of Edna St. Vincent Millay* (Harper and Brothers, 1952), reprinted by permission of Elizabeth Barnett, Literary Executor, copyright © 1952, 1980 by Norma Millay Ellis; Janice Mirikitani, lines from "Slaying Dragon Ladies," in *Shedding Silence* (Celestial Arts, 1987), reprinted by permission of Celestial Arts (Berkeley, California), copyright © 1987 by Janice Mirikitani; Marianne Moore, lines from "In Distrust of Merits," in *Complete Poems* (Macmillan, 1964), reprinted by permission of Macmillan Publishing Company, copyright © 1941 and renewed 1969 by Marianne Moore; Marianne Moore, lines from "The Labours of Hercules," "Nevertheless," and "Keeping Their World Large," in *Complete Poems* (Macmillan, 1969), reprinted by permission of Macmillan Publishing Company, copyright © 1935 by Marianne Moore, renewed 1963 by Marianne Moore and T.S. Eliot. Copyright © 1944, and renewed 1972, by Marianne Moore. Copyright © 1951 by Marianne Moore, renewed 1979 by Lawrence E. Brinn and Louise Crane; excerpts from unpublished material by Marianne Moore, reprinted by permission of the Rosenbach Museum & Library, Philadelphia and by Marianne Craig Moore, Literary Executor for the Estate of Marianne Moore. All rights reserved. Chiye Mori, lines from "Vain," in *Reimei* 1.1, and "Japanese American," in *Reimei* 1.2, reprinted by permission of Chiye Mori Oshima; Lorine Niedecker, lines from "In the Great Snowfall," in *From This Condensery: The Complete Writings of Lorine Niedecker*, ed. Robert J. Bertholf (Jargon Society, 1985), reprinted by permission of Cid Corman, Literary Executor; Wilfred Owen, lines from "Greater Love," "The Send-Off," "S.I.W.," "The Letter" and "Whereas Most Women Lead This Difficult Life," in *The Poems of Wilfred Owen*, ed. Jon Stallworthy (Hogarth Press, 1985), reprinted by permission of The Hogarth Press and the estate of Wilfred Owen; Sylvia Plath, lines from "Nick and the Candlestick," in *Ariel* (Harper and Row, 1961), reprinted by permission of Harper Collins Publishers, copyright © 1966 by Sylvia Plath; Ezra Pound, excerpt from letter to H.D. (May 31, 1954), reprinted by permission of the Collection of American Literature, Beinecke Rare Book and Manuscript Library, Yale University; Anne Ridler, excerpts from *The Shadow Factory* (Faber and Faber, 1945), reprinted by permission of Faber and Faber Limited, Publishers; Muriel Rukeyser, lines from "Orpheus," "Correspondences," "Letter, Unposted," "Nine Poems for an Unborn Child," and "Mediterranean," in *Collected Poems* (McGraw-Hill, 1982), reprinted by permission of William L. Rukeyser, copyright © 1982 by Muriel Rukeyser; Muriel Rukeyser, lines from "Gift-Poem," "Who in One Lifetime," "Sixth Elegy. River Elegy," "The Meeting," "Long Past Moncada," and "Letter to the Front," in *Beast in View* (Doubleday, 1944), reprinted by permission of William L. Rukeyser, copyright © 1944 by Muriel Rukeyser; Muriel Rukeyser, lines from "Over the Cradle/ The Only Child," reprinted by permission of William L. Rukeyser, copyright © by Muriel Rukeyser; Muriel Rukeyser, "Many Keys," reprinted by permission of William L. Rukeyser, copyright © 1991 by William L. Rukeyser; Karl Shapiro, lines from "V-Letter," in Oscar Williams, ed., *The War Poets* (John Day, 1945), reprinted by permission of the author, copyright © Karl Shapiro by arrangement with Weiser and Weiser, Inc.; Edith Sitwell, lines from "Lullaby," and "Still Falls the Rain," in *The Canticle of the Rose* (Macmillan, 1949), reprinted by permission of Macmillan Publishers and the author's literary estate; Wallace Stevens, lines from "Late Hymn from Myrrh Mountain," in *The Collected Poems* (Knopf, 1954), reprinted by permission of Alfred A. Knopf Inc., copyright © 1954 by Wallace Stevens; Wallace Stevens, lines from "Life on a Battleship," in *Opus Posthumous* (Knopf, 1957), reprinted by permission of Alfred A. Knopf, Inc., copyright © 1942 by Wallace Stevens and renewed 1970 by Holly Stevens; Toyo Suyemoto, lines from "Gain," in *Trek* (Dec. 1942), "Hokku," and "Tanka," in *All Aboard* (Spring 1944), "In Topaz," in *Trek* (Feb. 1943), and "Japonica," in *Current Life* (March 1941), reprinted by permission of Toyo Suyemoto Kawakami; Toyo Suyemoto, lines from "Retrospect," and "Gift of Quince," in *The Yale Review* (Winter 1946), reprinted by permission of *The Yale Review,* copyright © 1946 by Yale University; Dylan Thomas, lines from "Ceremony After a Fire Raid," in *Deaths and Entrances* (J.M. Dent, 1946), reprinted by permission of Dent/New Directions Publishers and the author's literary estate; Mitsuye Yamada, lines from *Camp Notes* (Shameless Hussy Press, 1976), reprinted by permission of Mitsuye Yamada, copyright © 1976 by Mitsuye Yamada; Mitsuye Yamada, lines from "Lethe," and "My Cousin," in *Desert Run* (Kitchen Table Press, 1988), reprinted by permission of Kitchen Table: Women of Color Press (P.O. Box 908, Latham, N.Y. 12110) and Mitsuye Yamada.

Every effort has been made to locate and obtain permission from the estates of Louise Driscoll and Jacob Glatshteyn.

A version of chapter 6 appeared in *American Literary History;* portions of chapter 7, in *Arms and the Woman: War, Gender and Literary Representation,* Helen Cooper, Adrienne Auslander Munich and Susan Merrill Squier, eds. (Chapel Hill: University of North Carolina Press, 1989); portions of chapter 1, in *Critical Inquiry.* I am grateful to these periodicals and publishers for permission to reprint all or some of these essays.

Index

371